T0211732

Lecture Notes in Computer Science   **9102**

Commenced Publication in 1973
Founding and Former Series Editors:
Gerhard Goos, Juris Hartmanis, and Jan van Leeuwen

More information about this series at http://www.springer.com/series/7409

Antoine Geissbühler · Jacques Demongeot
Mounir Mokhtari · Bessam Abdulrazak
Hamdi Aloulou (Eds.)

Inclusive Smart Cities and e-Health

13th International Conference on Smart Homes
and Health Telematics, ICOST 2015
Geneva, Switzerland, June 10–12, 2015
Proceedings

 Springer

Editors
Antoine Geissbühler
University of Geneva
Geneva
Switzerland

Jacques Demongeot
Université Joseph Fourier
Grenoble
France

Mounir Mokhtari
Institut Mines Télécom Paris, CNRS IPAL
  (UMI 2955 Singapore)
Paris
France

Bessam Abdulrazak
Université de Sherbrooke
Sherbrooke
Québec
Canada

Hamdi Aloulou
Institut Mines Télécom, CNRS LIRMM
Paris
France

ISSN 0302-9743   ISSN 1611-3349   (electronic)
Lecture Notes in Computer Science
ISBN 978-3-319-19311-3   ISBN 978-3-319-19312-0   (eBook)
DOI 10.1007/978-3-319-19312-0

Library of Congress Control Number: 2015939434

LNCS Sublibrary: SL3 – Information Systems and Applications, incl. Internet/Web and HCI

Springer Cham Heidelberg New York Dordrecht London

Printed on acid-free paper

Springer International Publishing AG Switzerland is part of Springer Science+Business Media
(www.springer.com)

Preface

During the last decade, Ambient Assisted Living (AAL) initiatives focused on diverse domains in order to ensure end-users' safety and quality of life at home. New paradigms on personal health management, health prevention, and therapeutic education have emerged in the scientific community with an increasing interest of clinicians. Today, with the large-scale development of social media and mobile data, we are able to unobtrusively collect large data volume at high frequency; hence, e-Inclusion and e-Health could benefit to promote new concepts of healthy lifestyle for frail and dependent aging people.

After twelve very successful ICOST conferences held in France (2003), Singapore (2004), Canada (2005), Northern Ireland (2006), Japan (2007), USA (2008), France (2009), Korea (2010), Canada (2011), Italy (2012), Singapore (2013), and USA (2014), the 13th International Conference on Smart homes, Assistive Technologies, Robotics and Health Telematics was held in Geneva, from 10th to 12th June 2015.

ICOST 2015 hosted by the University of Geneva and the associated partners, provides a premier venue for presentation and discussion on research related to design, development, deployment, and evaluation of Smart Environments, Assistive Technologies, Robotics and Health Telematics systems. ICOST brings together stakeholders from clinical, academic, and industrial perspectives along with end-user representatives and family caregivers. The goal is to explore how to utilize technologies to foster independent living and offer an enhanced quality of life. ICOST 2015 invites participants to present and discuss their experience in design, development, deployment, and evaluation of assistive and telehealth solutions, as well as ethical and policy issues. The conference features a dynamic program incorporating a range of technical, clinical, and industrial related keynote speakers, oral and poster presentations along with demonstrations and technical exhibits.

With the rise of smart cities in the field of digital health, it is the responsibility of the scientific community to provide novel answers to the inclusion of frail people in communities and modern societies. The aim should be to strengthen frail people social link and promote their healthy lifestyle. This year, ICOST conference is organized under the theme "Inclusive smart cities and e-health."

We are pleased to present, gathered in these proceedings, the papers presented at this year's edition of ICOST conference. We received 47 submissions, whose 20 papers were accepted as full papers to be presented during oral sessions. Each paper was reviewed by at least three international reviewers and scored accordingly. We have also accepted 16 short papers to be presented during poster regular sessions. We greatly appreciate all the Program Committee members who devoted their time for reviewing the papers. We would like to thank the Organizing Committee for their hard work in preparing and supporting this edition of ICOST conference. We also would like to thank the keynote speakers and panelists who accepted our invitation, all the authors for their valuable contributions, and all the contributors to this ICOST conference. We hope that we have succeeded in disseminating new ideas and results, motivated new collaborations, and shaped new approaches to improve the quality of life of aging population worldwide.

We hope you enjoy and benefit from the papers in this volume and we wish you a memorable and rich experience in ICOST 2015 Geneva.

June 2015

Antoine Geissbühler
Jacques Demongeot
Mounir Mokhtari
Bessam Abdulrazak
Hamdi Aloulou

Organization

General Chair

Antoine Geissbühler   University of Geneva, Switzerland
Jacques Demongeot   Université Joseph Fourier, Grenoble, France

Co-chairs

Mounir Mokhtari   Institut Mines Télécom, CNRS LIRMM,
                             France/CNRS IPAL, Singapore

Scientific Committee

Christian Roux   Institut Mines Télécom, Ecole des Mines de
                             St Etienne, France
Jean-Louis Coatrieux   Université de Rennes 1, France
Bessam Abdulrazak   Université de Sherbrooke, Canada
Z. Zenn Bien   Korea Advanced Institute of Science and
                             Technology, Korea
Carl K. Chang   Iowa State University, USA
Sylvain Giroux   Université de Sherbrooke, Canada
SumiHelal   University of Florida, USA
Nick Hine   University of Dundee, UK
Ismail Khalil   Johannes Kepler University, Austria
Yeunsook Lee   Yonsei University/The Korean Gerontological
                             Society, Korea
Mounir Mokhtari   Institut Mines Télécom, CNRS LIRMM,
                             France/CNRS IPAL, Singapore
Chris Nugent   University of Ulster, UK
Tatsuya Yamazaki   National Institute of Information and
                             Communications Technology, Japan
Daqing Zhang   Institut Mines Télécom/TELECOM SudParis,
                             France
Cristiano Paggetti   I+ S.r.l, Italy
William Cheng-Chung Chu   Tunghai University, Taiwan OB

Program Committee

Chairs

Bessam Abdulrazak   Université de Sherbrooke, Canada

Members

Hamdi Aloulou   Institut Mines Télécom, CNRS LIRMM, France
Rami Yared   Université de Sherbrooke, Canada
Romain Endelin   Institut Mines Télécom, CNRS LIRMM, France
Thibaut Tiberghien   Institut Mines Télécom, CNRS IPAL Singapore,
                                     France
Patrice C. Roy   Université de Sherbrooke, Canada
Belkacem Chikaoui   Université de Sherbrooke, Canada
Iyad Ayoub Abuhadrous   Palestine Technical College, Palestine
Mark Donnelly   University of Ulster, UK
GuohuaBai   Blekinge Institute of Technology, Sweden
Ji-Hyun Lee   KAIST University, Republic of Korea
Liming Chen   École Centrale de Lyon, France
AbdallahM'Hamed   Institut Mines-Télécom SudParis - Evry, France
Carl K. Chang   Iowa State University, USA
Jeffrey King   University of Florida, USA
Yves Demazeau   CNRS - Laboratoire LIG, France
Victor Foo   Institute for Infocomm Research, Singapore
Ye-Qiong Song   LORIA - University of Lorraine, France
Stephane Renouard   Handco, France
Salim Hima   ESME Sudria, France
Daby Sow   IBM, USA
Ramiro Velazquez   Universidad Panamericana, Mexico
Mi-Jeong Kim   Kyung Hee University Republic of Korea
Nadine Vigouroux   IRIT Université Paul Sabatier, France
Manfred Wojciechowski   University of Applied Sciences Duesseldorf,
                                     Germany
Laurent Billonnet   University of Limoges, France
Kaori Fujinami   Tokyo University of Agriculture and Technology,
                                     Japan
Kasper Hallenborg   University of Southern Denmark, Denmark
Lyes Khoukhi   University of Technology of Troyes, France
Jean Meunier   Université de Montréal, Canada
Jeffrey Soar   University of Southern Queensland, Australia
Hongbo Ni   Northwestern Polytechnical University, China
Fulvio Mastrogiovanni   University of Genoa, Italy
David Menga   EDF R&D, France
Chris Nugent   University of Ulster, UK

Bin Guo	Institut Mines-Télécom SudParis, France
Janet Light	University of New Brunswick, Canada
Diane Cook	EECS, USA
Weimin Huang	Institute For Infocomm Research, Singapore
Philip Yap-Lin-Kiat	KhooTeckPuat Hospital, Singapore
Jérémy Bauchet	Université Joseph Fourier, Grenoble, France
Hisato Kobayashi	Hosei University, Japan
Farah Arab	Université de Sherbrooke, Canada
Lu Shijian	Institute for Infocomm Research, Singapore
Pierre Senellart	National University of Singapore, Singapore
Liu Yan	National University of Singapore, Singapore
Etienne André	Université Paris 13, Sorbonne Paris Cité, LIPN, CNRS, France
Victor Kaptelinin	University of Bergen, Norway
Jihad M. Alja'am	Qatar University, Qatar
Stephane Bressan	National University of Singapore

Organizing Committee

Members

Antoine Geissbühler	University of Geneva, Switzerland
Hamdi Aloulou	Institut Mines Télécom, CNRS LIRMM, France
Rami Yared	Université de Sherbrooke, Canada
Randriambelonoro Mirana Michelle	École polytechnique fédérale de Lausanne, Switzerland
Romain Endelin	Institut Mines Télécom, CNRS LIRMM, France
Caroline Perrin	Geneva University Hospitals, Switzerland
Rafael Ruiz	University of Geneva, Switzerland
Nicolas Vuillerme	Université Joseph Fourier, Grenoble, France
Christophe Villemazet	IRT, Université Joseph Fourier & CEA, Grenoble, France

Local Organizing Committee

Antoine Geissbühler	University of Geneva, Switzerland
Caroline Perrin	Geneva University Hospitals, Switzerland
Randriambelonoro Mirana Michelle	École polytechnique fédérale de Lausanne, Switzerland
Rafael Ruiz	University of Geneva, Switzerland

Media and Webmaster

Hamdi Aloulou   Institut Mines Télécom, CNRS LIRMM, France
Romain Endelin   Institut Mines Télécom, CNRS LIRMM, France

Sponsors

University of Geneva, Geneva, Switzerland
Image and Pervasive Access Lab, CNRS UMI 2955, Singapore
Joseph Fourier University, Grenoble, France
Institut Mines Télécom, Paris, France
Geneva University Hospitals, Geneva, Switzerland
National Center for Scientific Research, France
Campus Biotech, Geneva, Switzerland

Invited Talks

Smart Cities and Big Data: Opportunities and Challenges

See-Kiong Ng

Programme Director of the Urban Systems Initiative by the Science and
Engineering Research Council of the Agency of Science, Technology and Research

Abstract. Since the industrial revolution in 19th century, technology has always
been a key driver in the development of the society. The recent arrival of the
Big Data era brings an unprecedented opportunity for us to understand the city
better. Technologies brought about by the Big Data revolution can potentially
transform how cities monitor, manage, and enhance the liveability of their communities in new ways. In fact, many cities aiming to become smart are turning
to data analytics and ICT innovations, developing state-of-the-art urban solutions
for transportation, environment, energy, etc., that use big data analytics and machine learning to extract patterns and rules from historical data to manage the
future better. However, big data is both a challenge and an opportunity for cities
and states. While large amounts of city data are routinely collected by the public
and private sectors, the data are usually kept isolated in proprietary information
systems with no one having cross-domain access to these datasets, as well as
the right analytics tools to generate the insights needed. The internet revolution
has also generated high expectations and response from the citizenry that need
to be addressed. Smart cities will have to leverage on big data to provide an efficient and sustainable transportation system, a liveable and well-planned built
environment, and reliable security in the city as well as in cyber space. In order
to effectively turn the big data in the city into actionable insights, it is useful for a
smart city to develop a data exchange platform designed specifically for data analytics, with the capability to bring together data of diverse natures to be managed,
retrieved, integrated and analyzed. In this way, the massive volumes and variety
of data generated by the city can then be turned fully into useful insights that lead
to new urban solutions for the city. We will present our initial efforts to create
inclusive smart cities through intelligent and scalable data sensing and analytics.

Futuring Cities

Francis Jutand

Scientific Director, Institut Mines-Télécom

Abstract. Based on the digital convergence data, knowledge and content, and more and more powerful infrastructures of communication, computing, storage, and monitoring of the physical world, the Digital metamorphosis has launched a deep transformation of the whole human society. The way we live, work, socialize, and even the human cognitive structure. In the field of health, autonomy and quality of life, the smart cities is going to provide a fluent frame for disabled people to better live with more security, more access to services, more social links, and at the final a better global social inclusion and efficiency. These are core research topics to ensure a more easy to live city for people.

How Patient Engagement Is Transforming Chronic Disease Management Through e-Health

Bettina Experton

Adjunct Professor, UC San Diego School of Medicine

Abstract. Across the developed world, highly specialized and fragmented care rendered to large aged and chronic disease populations have led to inefficient and uncoordinated care plaguing our economies and causing unnecessary harm. In the U.S., the Institute of Medicine has estimated that one third of healthcare costs are wasted due to medical errors, redundant and unnecessary care. This is particularly illustrated by the 65+ years old individuals covered by the U.S. Medicare program who on average sees seven different physicians in a given year. A lack of complete information at the point of care often leads to costly and dangerous diagnostic and therapeutic errors. Care coordination models on both the clinical (Medical Homes) and financial sides (Accountable Care Organizations) have relied on provider-centric communication, through various forms of provider-to-provider health information exchange (HIEs). However, these HIEs have mostly failed because of usability issues and business barriers to the exchange of information between competitive health care organizations. However, provider to patient HIE is not barred by competitive business issues. As a result, patients are becoming the de facto e-communicators of their medical histories when given the rights and tools to access and share their medical records across multiple providers. This session will explore the adoption in the U.S. of new regulatory policies and new e-Health tools, especially mobile ones that is transforming health care through engaging patients to become more active participants in the management of their own care.

Supporting the Information Needs of Frail Elders and Their Families

Charles Safran

Associate Professor of Medicine, Harvard Medical School

Abstract. Little is known about the information needs frail elders and their families, partly because the definition of old is frequently assume to be 65 years old and also because we have no systematic way of collecting data about family interactions around care. We have undertaken a five-year study to build a living laboratory seniors over the age of 75 and their families to explore their information needs. We call the technology to support this living laboratory InfoSAGE. This talk will describe our progress to date and lessons learned so far.

Contents

Assistive and Sentient Environments

Human Behavior and Activities Monitoring

Health IT and Supportive Technology

Invited Papers

Short Contributions

Design and Usability

Technical Challenges Towards an AAL Large Scale Deployment

Joaquim Bellmunt[1,2]($\boxtimes$), Thibaut Tiberghien[1,2], Mounir Mokhtari[1,2,3],
Hamdi Aloulou[1,3], and Romain Endelin[1,3]

[1] Institut Mines-Télécom, Paris, France
[2] Image and Pervasive Acces Lab (IPAL), CNRS, Singapore, Singapore
[3] Laboratoire D'Informatique, Robotique Et Microélectronique de Montpellier
(LIRMM), Montpellier, France
{bellmunt,thibaut.tiberghien,mounir.mokhtari,
hamdi.aloulou,romain.endelin}@mines-telecom.fr

Abstract. Nowadays, 13% of world's population aged 60 years and over
are dependent. AAL systems have to make the step forward and be
deployed in large scale in order to respond to the needs of this population.
In this paper, we present our feedback about our real deployments and
the challenges we have faced during the path in order to be ready for
our objective of a large scale deployment of 200 private houses. We hope
this paper may help research teams to find solutions to similar problems
and encourage them to externalize their solutions.

Keywords: AAL · Technical challenges · Real deployment

1 Introduction

Taking care of dependent people is becoming a major societal issue. The world's
population is aging rapidly with an estimation of 1 in 5 people over 65 years old
by 2030 compared to 1 in 10 today. According to world Alzheimer report, [1],
13% of the world's population aged 60 years and over are dependent; by 2050,
the number of people with dementia will nearly triple from 101 million to 277
million. Mokhtari et al., [2], have recently conducted an elder care survey with
127 aging people and their caregivers. They have noticed that 50% of surveyed
people are worried about unsafe houses, cognitive problems, decreased autonomy
and risks of accident. To manage this situation, health care actors are investing
many resources in Ambient Assisted Living (AAL, http://www.aal-europe.eu)
research since it responds to the necessity of increasing the quality of life and the
social integration for dependent people. There are a lot of AAL studies conducted
on this topic embedding the required devices for powering the context-aware
and the anticipatory services. However, many of them have been developed as
research projects, within laboratories facilities or only as prototypes [3]. For this
reason, we find it extremely important to export this research to the real world,
To be able to improve the performance and integration. Satisfactory results in

© Springer International Publishing Switzerland 2015
A. Geissbühler et al. (Eds.): ICOST 2015, LNCS 9102, pp. 3–14, 2015.
DOI: 10.1007/978-3-319-19312-0_1

this research domain would impact positively on the health of the patients, on the management of human resources and, of course, in the costs. Nevertheless, a real deployment raises many challenges may not be expected. In this paper, we present our real deployment feedback and the challenges that we had to overcome to bring an efficient solution and facing a large-scale deployment.

2   Related Work

Ambient Assisted Living, AAL, is nowadays a widespread topic with a large research community behind. In 2012, Mokhtari et al. presented a review of the new trends to support people with dementia [4]. They summarize the trends through 4 main requirements: remembering simple daily living task, maintain their social links, feeling motivated to participate in everyday life and boosting their feeling of safety. Back in 2005, Helal et al. presented an AAL prototype for houses [5]. They divided the system into 6 layers: physical or hardware, sensor, service, knowledge, context-aware and application.

More recently, in 2011, Marinc et al. [6] presented an overview of the general requirements that have to be fulfilled by an AAL platform to allow an efficient personalization by the user. They differentiate the basic requirements from the user-kind requirements. On the one hand, for basic requirements they highlight: the hardware abstraction layer as the user should be able to interact with all devices; the interaction with framework; the rule-based system; the service based on infrastructure; the context reasoning and, finally, the semantic description. On the other hand, they also take into account the user-kind requirements. They differentiate the expert users who are able to implement, see the details and receive a direct feedback; a regular user who is interested in a simple interaction with the system (help-files, simple interfaces and an attractive system front-end); and, finally, the impaired users who are usually skeptical with the system and his environment. The system, so, needs to be non-invasive, invisible and stoppable.

However, even though real AAL deployments are very recent, their use is lately increasing. Tapia et al. [7] in 2004 did one of the first implementations. They deployed in different residential environments with simple sensors looking for current activities. They obtained a wide accuracy percentage depending on the activity. The more frequent activities were easier to detect than the least frequent ones. More recently, in 2011, Morales et al. [8], presented the architectural part and the deployment of their systems. They expose the challenges of implementing a system in a medical environment, such as personal tracking in order to localize person with issues, humans' willingness, skepticism and interaction. Also, they highlight their lessons learned, such as that the tuning part for a system implementation takes usually more than expected and it is a continuous work; that basic simple services is one of the best advantages for AAL environments; and, finally, they encourage to use wireless communication with data flow control (Zigbee). Later, Falco et al. [9] in 2013 presented the MonAMI European project provisioning a deployment in Zaragoza, Spain. They ran a trial during four months with 15 patients obtaining a satisfactory feedback. Nevertheless, they also exposed the next steps to do in their solution, as including wireless reliability, context understanding services, and sensor detection. In 2014 Cubo et al. [10], presented a complete AAL system hosted in the cloud. Their work proposes a platform to manage the integration and behavior-aware orchestration of heterogeneous devices. They design a framework based on cloud computing technology. They implement and generate a novel cloud-based IoT platform of behavior-aware devices as services for ambient intelligence system. This paper inspired our work in the sensor integration. However, we focus differently in the service orientation as we prioritize the implementation services oriented to the final user. We also present how the sensors gateway connects to our cloud server and how the server treats this information. Finally, in 2014 Palumbo et al. [11] developed a sensor network infrastructure for home care. The system has been developed for a European project, GiraffPlus, and deployed in real homes across Europe. They identify the crucial features of the system in the easy and reliable integration of all the hardware and software components.

3   Context

Our research is focusing on the AAL for people with dementia [12]. For the past years, we have focused our work on developing an efficient rule-based reasoning based on semantic web [13]. At the same time, we introduced in this reasoning a physical uncertainty due to the sensors [14]. This research has been used during the last years in two main projects. From 2010 to 2012 we have deployed our solution in an Asian Nursing Home in three rooms with eight patients suffering mild dementia [15]. Then, in 2014, we have started a new deployment in a French elderly house [16]. It is expected that future research lines will include the validation of our reasoning including the logic uncertainty and a new reasoning layer in charge of the user plasticity.

Our ambition is to be able to bring an efficient large scale and deployable indoor system. Nowadays, we are running eight distant deployments. We have deployed in three private homes and five rooms in a nursing house with patients suffering from different chronic diseases. We are, also, collecting a ground truth that will be extremely useful for the reasoning validation and the logic uncertainty. Furthermore, we are preparing to make a step forward towards a large-scale deployment of 200 private houses.

A real deployment highlights some issues that might not be expected. These issues may arise system lacks that should be counterbalanced by making decisions in order to build a scalable and adaptable system. In this paper, we present the challenges that we have faced to achieve these projects. As well as the platform architecture and the technical choices we have made for shortcoming the issues.

4   Platform Architecture

Our platform is structured as a web app on a cloud server connected to many assisted houses, as presented in Fig.1. The platform is composed of two essential parts. The first part, **Sensing part**, is located in the patient residence and is composed of multiple sensors, a gateway, and communications devices. It is in charge of pre-processing the raw data from the sensors, converting it into events that are sent to the server via Internet. The second part is **Web platform**, which handles the communication with the Sensing part through the MQTT communication protocol (see section 5.3). It also manages the platform storage, reasoning and the service provisioning that will be explained later.

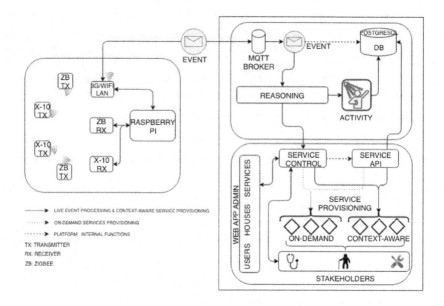

Fig. 1. Platform architecture

The reasoning part determines the activity and acts as a trigger for the service provisioning. The reasoning part, detailed in Tiberghien et al. [13]. is based on Semantic Web technologies, which provides "a common framework that allows data to be shared and reused across application, enterprises, and community boundaries" [17]. The web version of our framework uses Jos de Roo's Eye reasoning engine [18] but in its server-side it uses a wrapper made available by Ruben Verborgh [19]. We also use Ruben Verborgh's TripleStore for N3 in JavaScript, N3.js. Furthermore, advanced features that were needed (Tripleremoval [13]) but were not available in N3.js have been implemented and submitted by our team, and then integrated by Ruben Verborgh.

Once the reasoning has determined the current activity of a patient, it will be stored in the database. At the same time, this information will be available and accessible to the users through the platform services on the web front-end. The same information can be displayed by several services at the same time, but they will be treated differently depending on the services kind (see section 5.3).

In the next section, we will expose the three main challenges that we have faced when deploying our solution. They have driven the evolution of our system in order to reach our ambition of a large scale deployment.

5 Challenges in a Large Scale Deployment

Our previous real deployment brought to us some precious inputs on what to improve or even change in our system in order to make a significant step forward towards a large-scale real deployment. We have observed three main challenges and we have made technical choices to achieve them. First, our platform needs to handle Multiple-Users and Multiple-Houses natively and efficiently. Secondly, it has to be easy to deploy, upgrade and maintain, allowing adaptability to different needs and conditions. Finally, the user interaction must be natural, intuitive, adaptable and versatile.

5.1 Cater to Multiple-User and Multiple-House

The first challenge has been how to manage many houses and many users with a many-to-many correspondence network. We want to scale to a central server for many houses while maintaining a satisfying response time to events coming from each house. E.g. making sure that a faulty house flooding the framework with events would not cause a drop in performance for others houses. We have decided to run a unique server instance managing all houses at the same time, and simultaneously handling the users' actions and specifications (login, roles, profiles, ...). For that, we have opted to build our solution as a web app with an event-driven based on Node.js (JavaScript[19]).

As a cloud server addressed to many users we have also faced the challenge to provide a secure access for them. For that, we have integrated Sails.js framework [20] which is based on Ruby on Rails. This tool handles easily the boilerplate code. It allows us to provide to our users several services associated with their profile, role or houses, both for personal and professional users. Sails.js is organized on Model-View-Controller (MVC) structure [21], a software architectural pattern for implementing user interfaces. It, as well, includes an admin API with an interface since its installation. The scalability and the data managing have also been solved by using Sails.js, as it provides an Object-Relational-Mapping tool (ORM [22]) capable of interacting and bringing the database as flexible as required.

The last issue related to this challenge has been the reproduction of the sensing part for each house. We have chosen to use a generic sensor as PIR and read switch because they are, nowadays, industrially available, or X10 sensor, which is widely used amongst security systems. We have used a cheap and readily available gateway as is Raspberry Pi. It provides a large range of network adaptors both for the WSN and Internet and it has a low footprint in the user environment. As Raspberry Pi boots from a sd-card, we can easily duplicate, configure and replace ours even if it has a large number of gateways. Finally, we have opted for using MQTT [23], as a simple and scalable way to communicate with the server, since it is very efficient, lightweight, widely employed and specially dedicated for IoT and Node.js with a large community behind.

5.2   Ease of Deployment

The second challenge we have faced has been to build a solution of easy installation. That means the system needs to be simple and adaptable to the space. In the same way, it has to be easily maintained both on-site and remotely.

Adaptability and Setup: In order to build an adaptable solution, we have chosen to use simple sensors, such as a passive infrared sensor (PIR) and read switch. As detailed in the previous section, the aim is to adopt the industrial sensors as much as possible to our needs. Nevertheless, industrial solutions do not, always, cover all the needs, e.g. we could not find a commercially available bed sensor detecting whether the patient is lying on the bed and reporting this information in real time. For this kind of custom sensors, we have opted for building our own prototype embedding the detection processing and the communication. The prototype is composed of a simple sensor (force sensing resistor, FSR, in the bed case) connected to an Arduino board, which embarks a Zigbee transmitter connecting to the Gateway. Within the Arduino board, we are able to implement the specific code for each prototype and adapt his duty to the context.

Within the Sensing part, we have made the choice to build a custom gateway with a Raspberry Pi. It is a credit-card sized Linux machine which is able to embark different communication devices that connect the sensors with the cloud and vice-versa. In fact, the gateway receives the raw data from the sensors through X10 or Zigbee protocols. It treats this data to extract the events and send them to the cloud through Internet. The Internet connection can be established through most available networks. Specifically, we use LAN or WiFi in the spaces where these connections are available, otherwise the connection was provided through a 3G key. These previous choices have been made with the aim of building a simple and quick installable sensing part. Aloulou et al. [24] provided in 2012 a semantic plug-and-play solution allowing to easily integrate new sensors to the platform. Our objective is to be able to assume a serial provisioning that needs few installation steps and where including sensors is practically automatic.

Maintenance: The maintenance is a key point for a real deployment and becomes crucial for a large-scale deployment. From the moment that it is not possible to do it in situ when the system is located away, the maintenance becomes another strong argument for using industrial sensors since they are easy to connect and, overall, replace. Furthermore, these sensors usually have an efficient battery lifetime. For example, X10 battery holds one year. Moreover, our gateway software needs to be failure-proof and capable of restoring the different

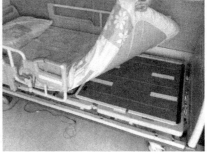

Fig. 2. Door sensor   **Fig. 3.** Bed sensor

Fig. 4. Position sensor   **Fig. 5.** Raspberry Pi

modules on the gateway. We, therefore, have leveraged Linux services systemD ensuring that our programs are running in any situation.

Here, we have explained our choices to achieve an efficient maintenance. However, it will be interesting to set a remote access to the deployed gateway in order to update or maintain the device software. Sometimes the gateway is hidden behind a proxy server and then it is not possible to reach it easily by a remote session. In order to handle this issue, we have used the Reverse Proxy mechanism establishing a point-to-point connection through a particular port on the proxy server.

5.3 Usage

The third challenge we have faced is how users, both, end-users or professional users, will interact with the services proposed by the system. We have divided this issue into two points. First, the end-user interaction with the services types and the users roles. Secondly, the admin and technician interaction, taking into account the access to data, maintenance of services and services management.

End-Users Interaction: The end-user interaction with the web app is done through the available services. We have provided the users with real-time activities visualization, tracking service with location maps, statistical visualization, and alert services. There are two ways of classifying the services. On the one hand by its nature as On-Demand or Context-Aware service. On the other hand, by their scope as Single House service or Multiple Houses service.

The On-Demand services, which are typically a 24h service, show charts of all the house activities in real time. E.g., one of the services shows the patient activity within his home, Fig.6, other provides statistical behavior or shows the current location and activity in multiple houses on real-time Fig.7.

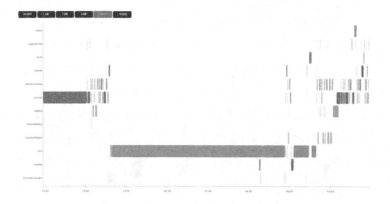

Fig. 6. User activity service

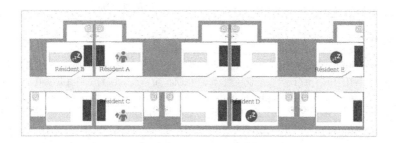

Fig. 7. Multiple activity service

On the other hand, the Context-Aware services stand-by waiting to be activated through the reasoning. E.g. based on the statistical behavior of the patient, is he does not wake up in the normal interval of time, the Context-Aware service charged to manage this situation will be triggered.

Complementarily, there are services dedicated only to one space, which are named single house services (**SHS**), and other services covering several houses, named multiple houses services (**MHS**). This type of classification leads to the creation of user roles. In the platform, we put at disposal 4 user profiles. The Personal profile is intended for patients, family or friends. A user can only have one personal account per house but may be present in different houses. This profile only provides access to SHS services. Secondly, there exists the Caregiver profile intended for health personal. They have access to the MHS in order to track several spaces at the same time. One user may have a Caregiver and Personal profile simultaneously but never in the same houses. Furthermore, there exist two more user profiles such as Tech and Admin. They are oriented to the platform maintenance and users administration. They will be explained in the Admin and Tech interaction.

Admin and Technician Interaction. This part is focused on the inner working of the platform. As we have introduced in the previous lines there are two main profiles charged to interact with the platform in a technical way. Firstly, the Technician profile, Tech, is allowed to visualize the sensor status service (Fig.8) determining if any maintenance action is required. This service shows the event flow reception from the gateway, if the Sensing part is having an abnormal behavior (e.g. it does not send data or sends large amounts of inconsistent data) the technician will note this situation and may act consequently.

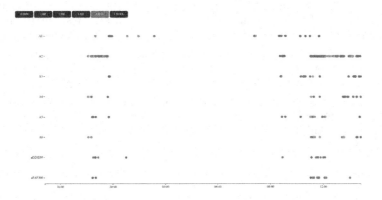

Fig. 8. Technician service

The Admin profile is in charge of the management, update and maintain of the platform. This profile is addressed to developers who will fix or improve the platform. As we have presented, the platform is finally a service provisioning for the stakeholders. In this way, we have built the system as a participative and collaborative web app. For this, we have conceived the service structure is a prototype extension that allows the access to the data through a limited API. The service prototype is available, providing a homogenous structure and interaction with the system.

Finally, we have implemented an easy service inclusion done through a Git repository. The platform verifies the structure submitted and if it meets the requirements the service is instantaneously available for the whole platform. Complementarily, the service deletion must be done by an Admin profile who will be able to erase completely the services from the platform.

6   Validation

As mentioned earlier, we have deployed our system in 8 living spaces. This deployment has been extremely useful to drive a validation phase. Concerning the challenge described in section 5.2 about the ease of deployment, the work described here has allowed an improvement in the installation time (setting up the sensors, the gateway and the server communication) from 1 day in 2011 to 20 minutes nowadays. Switching to the MQTT protocol has also made the communication more robust; indeed, during the last 5 months we have not detected any communication problem.

To validate our work related to the scalability of the framework (see section 5.1), we have conducted a server load test in order to determine how robust is our system and if it is ready to face a large-scale deployment. We have simulated the creation of 200 houses sending an average of 10 events per minute to determine the platform's response time when facing a high load. The results are provided in Fig.9.

We observe a relatively linear behavior of the response time under increasing load. However, we could not reach 200 homes as the system went out of memory around 170 homes. This is probably due to the fact that all the simulated houses were sending their events simultaneously. In a real use-case, events would be spread out over time and we expect the maximum charge to be slightly higher. The presented response time has been calculated by averaging over one minute of simulated events for each data point. The results are given for a cloud-based single core virtual machine running Ubuntu 14.04 x64 with 1GB of RAM. For a real deployment, the machine would definitely be upgraded, which leaves us satisfy with the results.

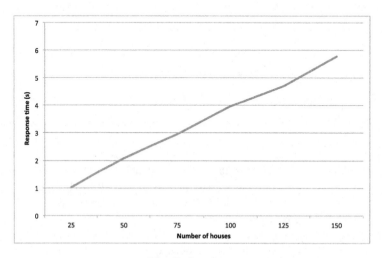

Fig. 9. Load test

7   Conclusions

In this paper, we have presented our research work in order to step forward towards a large scale deployment. We have focused this paper on explaining the main challenges that should be overcome. We have explained how each challenge affects the platform and what technical choices have been implemented to tackle them. We have used our current deployment in eight living spaces to validate our approach.

The system still presents some limitations, e.g. the sensor prototyping is not yet robust. It presents some hardware limitations and the data collected is not always reliable. The system has experienced a performance slow down after several weeks of continuous service due a lack of database optimization, thus inducing a reduced query performance with a growing database. There is still an interesting work to do in the area of notification services.

The next steps of our work will be to improve our platform, in line with the limitations exposed. We will use the reasoning and the ground truth collected for implementing, testing and integrating context-aware services. We will try to reduce the server load for a quicker response. And, we will keep working on implicating stakeholders to further design and adapt the framework and services to real world requirements.

References

1. Prince, M., Guerchet, M., Prina, M., B. U. P. Association, et al.: World Alzheimer Report 2013: Journey of Caring: An Analysis of Long-Term Care for Dementia. Alzheimer's Disease International (2013)
2. Mokhtari, M., Endelin, R., Aloulou, H., Tiberghien, T.: Measuring the impact of ICTs on the quality of life of ageing people with mild dementia. In: Bodine, C., Helal, S., Gu, T., Mokhtari, M. (eds.) ICOST 2014. LNCS, vol. 8456, pp. 103–109. Springer, Heidelberg (2015)
3. Blasco, R., Marco, Á., Casas, R., Cirujano, D., Picking, R.: A smart kitchen for ambient assisted living. Sensors **14**(1), 1629–1653 (2014)
4. Mokhtari, M., Aloulou, H., Tiberghien, T., Biswas, J., Racoceanu, D., Yap, P.: New trends to support independence in persons with mild dementia-a mini-review. Gerontology **58**(6), 554–563 (2012)
5. Helal, S., Mann, W., El-Zabadani, H., King, J., Kaddoura, Y., Jansen, E.: The gator tech smart house: A programmable pervasive space. Computer **38**(3), 50–60 (2005)
6. Marinc, A., Stocklöw, C., Braun, A., Limberger, C., Hofmann, C., Kuijper, A.: Interactive personalization of ambient assisted living environments. In: Smith, M.J., Salvendy, G. (eds.) HCII 2011, Part I. LNCS, vol. 6771, pp. 567–576. Springer, Heidelberg (2011)
7. Tapia, E.M., Intille, S.S., Larson, K.: Activity recognition in the home using simple and ubiquitous sensors. In: Ferscha, A., Mattern, F. (eds.) PERVASIVE 2004. LNCS, vol. 3001, pp. 158–175. Springer, Heidelberg (2004)

8. Morales, A., Robles, T., Alcarria, R., Alonso, D.: Communication architecture for tracking and interoperable services at hospitals: a real deployment experience. In: Bravo, J., Hervás, R., Villarreal, V. (eds.) IWAAL 2011. LNCS, vol. 6693, pp. 84–91. Springer, Heidelberg (2011)
9. Falcó, J.L., Vaquerizo, E., Lain, L., Artigas, J.I., Ibarz, A.: Ami and deployment considerations in aal services provision for elderly independent living: The monami project. Sensors **13**(7), 8950–8976 (2013)
10. Cubo, J., Nieto, A., Pimentel, E.: A cloud-based internet of things platform for ambient assisted living. Sensors **14**(8), 14070–14105 (2014)
11. Palumbo, F., Ullberg, J., Štimec, A., Furfari, F., Karlsson, L., Coradeschi, S.: Sensor network infrastructure for a home care monitoring system. Sensors **14**(3), 3833–3860 (2014)
12. Biswas, J., Mokhtari, M., Dong, J.S., Yap, P.: Mild dementia care at home – integrating activity monitoring, user interface plasticity and scenario verification. In: Lee, Y., Bien, Z.Z., Mokhtari, M., Kim, J.T., Park, M., Kim, J., Lee, H., Khalil, I. (eds.) ICOST 2010. LNCS, vol. 6159, pp. 160–170. Springer, Heidelberg (2010)
13. Tiberghien, T., Mokhtari, M., Aloulou, H., Biswas, J.: Semantic reasoning in context-aware assistive environments to support ageing with dementia. In: Cudré-Mauroux, P., Heflin, J., Sirin, E., Tudorache, T., Euzenat, J., Hauswirth, M., Parreira, J.X., Hendler, J., Schreiber, G., Bernstein, A., Blomqvist, E. (eds.) ISWC 2012, Part II. LNCS, vol. 7650, pp. 212–227. Springer, Heidelberg (2012)
14. Aloulou, H., Mokhtari, M., Tiberghien, T., Endelin, R., Biswas, J.: Uncertainty handling in semantic reasoning for accurate context understanding. Knowledge-Based Systems (2015)
15. Aloulou, H., Mokhtari, M., Tiberghien, T., Biswas, J., Phua, C., Lin, J.H.K., Yap, P.: Deployment of assistive living technology in a nursing home environment: methods and lessons learned. BMC medical informatics and decision making **13**(1), 42 (2013)
16. Tiberghien, T.: Strategies for context reasoning in assistive livings for the elderly. Ph.D. thesis, Institut National des Télécommunications (2013)
17. Berners-Lee, T.: Design issues: Linked data (2006). http://www.w3.org/DesignIssues/LinkedData.html
18. De Roo, J.: Euler proof mechanism - eye, pp. 1999-2013. http://eulersharp.sourceforge.net/
19. Verborgh, R.: Node-n3: Lightning fast, asynchronous, streaming of turtle/n3/rdf. GitHub (2012). https://github.com/RubenVerborgh/node-n3
20. Andreeva, J., Dzhunov, I., Karavakis, E., Kokoszkiewicz, L., Nowotka, M., Saiz, P., Tuckett, D.: Designing and developing portable large-scale javascript web applications within the experiment dashboard framework. Journal of Physics: Conference Series **396**, 052069 (2012)
21. Balderdash: Realtime mvc framework for node.js. http://sailsjs.org
22. Balderdash: An adapter-based orm for node.js with support for mysql, mongo, postgres, redis, and more. GitHub. https://github.com/balderdashy/waterline
23. Locke, D.: Mq telemetry transport (mqtt) v3. 1 protocol specification. IBM developerWorks Technical Library (2010). http://www.ibm.com/developerworks/webservices/library/ws-mqtt/index.html
24. Aloulou, H., Mokhtari, M., Tiberghien, T., Biswas, J., Lin, J.H.K.: A semantic plug&play based framework for ambient assisted living. In: Donnelly, M., Paggetti, C., Nugent, C., Mokhtari, M. (eds.) ICOST 2012. LNCS, vol. 7251, pp. 165–172. Springer, Heidelberg (2012)

Design Considerations for Adaptive Lighting to Improve Seniors' Mood

Alina Huldtgren[1(✉)], Christina Katsimerou[2], Andre Kuijsters[1],
Judith A. Redi[2], and Ingrid E.J. Heynderickx[1]

[1] Human-Technology Interaction Group Industrial Engineering and Innovation Science,
Eindhoven University of Technology, P.O. Box 513 5600MB, Eindhoven, The Netherlands
{a.huldtgren,a.kuijsters,i.e.j.heynderickx}@tue.nl
[2] Multimedia Computing Group Intelligent Systems, Delft University of Technology,
Mekelweg 4 2628CD, Delft, The Netherlands
{c.katsimerou,j.a.redi}@tudelft.nl

Abstract. The advance of LED technologies allows for new design opportunities in the area of lighting for psychological health. Research has shown that lighting in various colors and intensities can be used to improve people's moods, e.g. through its effects on melatonin levels. This is especially interesting in the context of ambient assisted living and care environments where people are less mobile and spend long hours indoors. The presented work aims at creating a technical system that can detect an older resident's mood and consequently adapt the lighting in the room to either calm or activate the person. As part of the system's design process we conducted interviews with caregivers in different care settings (day care, stationary care and home care) to gather requirements for the system. The study provides insights into moods of seniors and their detection, which is formulated in a preliminary mood model, as well as design considerations for different living- and care-settings.

Keywords: Mood · Ambience · LED-lighting · Seniors · Requirements

1   Introduction

Lighting can impact (psychological) health and wellbeing positively [4,9,12,14]. With the advance of LED technologies the design space of lighting for health and wellbeing has been broadened significantly. The large range of intensities and color variations that can be achieved with LEDs today offers vast possibilities to create lighting atmospheres tailored to specific settings. This has already been utilized in urban settings, public institutions and office buildings. Although the low costs of LEDs allow for use in the home context as well, application of LEDs for ambient lighting atmospheres and lighting for wellbeing is not widespread yet in this context. Some commercial products such as the Philips Livingcolors[1] or Hue[2] exist, and although the Hue system comes with a smartphone app allowing people to adapt the lighting settings,

---

[1] www.livingcolors.philips.com
[2] www2.meethue.com/

© Springer International Publishing Switzerland 2015
A. Geissbühler et al. (Eds.): ICOST 2015, LNCS 9102, pp. 15–26, 2015.
DOI: 10.1007/978-3-319-19312-0_2

human computer interfaces have to be developed more specifically to support people in making use of the health benefits and easy creation of relaxing or activating atmospheres in their homes. Especially for older people, who are less mobile, spend long hours indoors and are prone to negative moods, intelligent lighting systems could provide health benefits. With the advance of ambient assisted living (AAL) and smart homes, it becomes feasible to install lighting systems that react to users and automatically adapt to their needs. Research in this area is still rare.

We aim at designing a system that can detect seniors' negative moods and create pleasant affective atmospheres through lighting (and possibly sound and smell). The light settings, e.g. activating lights counteracting depression, are based on the psychological effects of lighting found in earlier research (see related work) and the effects of different lighting scenarios have been tested extensively in experimental studies in this project [11]. Besides finding light settings that positively impact a senior's mood, another important aspect of the project is the recognition of negative mood states. Also overall requirements of the system with regard to user perceptions, needs and wishes need to be taken into account to design the system to maximize user acceptance. The latter two aspects (moods in seniors, user requirements) were the focus of a set of interviews we conducted with caregivers in different care settings. We present data from these interviews and provide requirements and design considerations for an ambient lighting system for seniors.

2   Related Work

2.1   Impact of Lighting on Mood

Lighting of different intensities and colors has been found to influence biological and psychological processes in humans that impact people's moods. We will focus on major findings that are relevant for the project at hand.

Disruptions to circadian rhythms can cause mood disorders [1]. Biological effects of bright light on melatonin levels, which influence people's circadian rhythm, are well documented [4,9,13,15]. Research has shown that bright blue light "increases alertness during the night, improves sleep quality, may significantly reduce the symptoms of depression for seasonal mood disorders, and even for people with non-seasonal affective disorders, and may positively impact the treatment of patients with dementia" [10].

As we are interested in the improvement of seniors' moods, psychological effects of lighting are in the focus. Illuminance and correlated color temperature play an important role in influencing emotional wellbeing. However, results from previous research with younger target groups have been controversial. In separate studies in the work context Knez and colleagues [7,8] found different effects of warm (3000K) and cool lighting (4000K) on males and females. Other studies have focused on psychological effects of color on mood and found positive effects. Office workers, for instance, who judged their offices as colorful, experienced better moods than workers who judged their offices as neutral or colorless [12]. Furthermore, blue color is more often perceived as calming [2], while red as arousing [5]. The effects of illuminance and color on mood have so far mostly been studied disjoint. However, advanced LED technologies now allow combining these two aspects and creating lighting atmospheres that combine functional lights with ambient colored lighting. In our studies [10] we focused in particular on how to create lighting atmospheres that would be perceived by seniors as cosy or activating and whether such atmospheres have indeed the desired effect of improving the seniors' mood. We found that seniors preferred functional, reddish white lighting in combination with orange colored accent lighting for cosy ambiences and bluish white light with cyan colored accents for activation. More than one colored accent light should be avoided.

2.2   Lighting in Ambient Assisted Living

AAL[3] is a vibrant research field aiming to improve health, wellbeing and quality of life for seniors living independently. AAL comprises many technologies. "Among AAL/telecare solutions and service offerings, there is huge diversity in the different configurations of technologies and in the degree of involvement of health care professionals. However they all tend to encompass some or all of the following features: monitoring of safety and security, e.g., to detect water left running, via sensors that operate in isolation and generate alerts when events are detected; monitoring of activities of daily living (ADL) and lifestyle monitoring via a network of sensors in the home, again with some alerting function, e.g., for falls detection; and physiological monitoring, which usually involves some direct participation of the users e.g., in taking blood pressure measurements" [3].

Ambient lighting is rarely considered in AAL research. In [6] lighting was utilized for temporal and spatial orientation, which differs from our focus. We could only find one similar project, i.e. the ALADIN project [14], in which researchers focused specifically on developing an adaptive lighting system for seniors. However, several aspects differ from our work: (1) only white lighting was used and no accent lights, (2) lighting was focused stronger on supporting activities in the household and (3) the system was developed as an app for a television, that comprised not only lighting, but also recommendations for wellbeing and exercise. The latter makes it difficult to assess the impact of the lighting to the reported beneficial effects of the system.

3   Project Context

Researchers with expertise in psychology, human-computer interaction and artificial intelligence collaborate in this project with Philips to develop an intelligent lighting system that can automatically recognize the mood of a senior user and adapt several lamps in the room to provide an atmosphere with positive impact on the mood. When the project was initiated, we focused on care homes as the setting for the system because seniors often experience negative moods in the phase of relocation from home to a care home. However, in light of the current demographic developments and changes in the care system, we expanded our focus to also take into account the possibility of installing the system in private flats.

---

[3] www.aal-europe.eu

The system will be designed to classify moods either as negative with low arousal (e.g. depression), in which case an activating light will be chosen or as negative with high arousal (e.g. unrest), in which case a calming light will be chosen. To detect the mood of the resident the system uses input from cameras. While research on emotion recognition has focused on younger populations, and short affective states rather than longer mood states, we aimed to understand: (1) the difference between mood and emotion, (2) the recognition of seniors' moods, and (3) factors influencing the mood. Furthermore, we asked about the general attitude towards the envisioned system and its application to different care contexts. To get answers, we conducted interviews with caregivers in different senior care settings, who have extensive experience in recognizing and dealing with moods of the residents.

4   Interviews

We conducted two initial rounds of exploratory interviews with (1) six caregivers working for a senior daycare center in Delft, The Netherlands, where some seniors have been diagnosed with dementia, and a focus group of (2) three caregivers in a care home for people with dementia in The Hague, The Netherlands. Based on a qualitative content analysis of these initial interviews we learned about different features that help detecting a senior's mood and were able to categorize these into physical (facial expression and posture) and behavioral aspects (interactional and non-interactional, verbal and non-verbal). We realized, however, that in the context of daycare or care homes, a lot of interaction between residents can be observed and that physical features are also closely tied to this context. Considering our expanded project focus on independent living, we decided to run an additional interview study with caregivers from an organization offering independent living units as well as a care home to study how the requirements for the system would differ in these settings.

4.1   Study Set-Up

We interviewed caregivers of an extra-mural care unit of a large apartment building that is administered by a care organization in Eindhoven, The Netherlands. Senior residents live independently in bought or rented flats. The average age of people receiving care is 92 and the care levels range from household help to daily physical care. Some residents suffer from first to third stage dementia. Interviews were conducted on two days in a meeting room inside the apartment building, where caregivers worked, and took between 40 and 60 minutes.

4.2   Participants

We recruited eight participants through a manager at the Vitalis WoonZorg Groep. We specifically recruited participants with a range of ages (24-59), work experiences (2-37 years) and work times (15-32 h/week). All participants were Dutch and female, as there is only one male caregiver in the institution, who was not fluent in Dutch.

4.3   Materials

During the interviews we showed participants example photographs of cosy and activating lighting settings (Fig1). We used a smartphone for audio recordings.

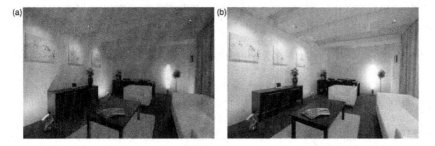

Fig. 1. Examples of lighting in the room used in the interviews: (a) cosy, (b) activating

4.4   Data Analysis and Results

The interview data was transcribed verbatim and coded (according to a coding manual derived from the first interviews). We looked for recurring ideas, which were then categorized into the higher level themes elaborated in the following.

Mood and Emotion

We found that both moods and emotions were seen as generally related. *"If someone is in a bad mood, then the emotions are, of course, also negative. (P1)"* Mood is long-term, and emotions are reactions to events and therefore short-term. *"Emotion is often a snapshot, for example, something funny happens and I laugh. That's an emotion. Moods are something longer, a longer period. (P3)"* Depending on the event, however, it is possible that people experience emotions with different valence from the mood. *"I think they are different, because you can be in a gloomy mood, but I think you can still laugh about a joke every now and then... So, I think that mood is something longer term and that different emotions can play a role in there. (P5)"* As spontaneous reactions, emotions can sometimes also be irrational. *"An emotional reaction, that is often when something intense happens,... or something they cannot accept...[Emotions] are not thought through, not rational. (P4)"* Considering mood duration, we were told that moods range between single days and weeks. When people are depressed or in a gloomy mood it usually takes longer. However, when it exceeds several weeks, caregivers would consult a doctor. *"I think if something holds on for several weeks, an alarm has to ring. (P5)"* Overall, the duration of mood is strongly influenced by external events and circumstances. *"There are people, who are sad the whole day... the mood stays. Also depends on what has happened (P1)"*.

Mood in Seniors with and Without Dementia

Caregivers also referred to differences in mood duration related to dementia. Closely linked to the progression of the disease people either experience negative moods more often (mild dementia), or moods change more quickly (severe dementia). *"Sometimes it goes by fast, when the forgetfulness begins to work. When you are in the beginning phase then you don't forget it … but people in the last phase forget it immediately (P8)." "Most demented people are a bit gloomy, because they know [what happens to them] or it depends in what phase they are… another resident is so far… after half a minute he forgot it already (P5)"*

In old age emotions can appear milder that in younger people. According to one participant *"overall people are generally more conscious about emotions and moods … to some extent they are more relaxed … I have the impression that they are milder when they become older (P3)"* In people with dementia this can lead to apathy *"The emotions are less and then they are in a state where they have this emotionless expression on their face (P8)"*. While we have to consider such findings with great care, because the caregivers are talking about single cases, it is important to consider that an automatic mood recognition system may fail in these cases. Generally, individual differences have to be taken account by the system.

Mood Recognition

Mood recognition is a common caregiver task that is done when entering the room. It gives the caregiver room to adapt the interaction. A prevailing theme of the interviews was the familiarity with the resident to be able to judge the mood. All caregivers mentioned that when knowing the residents well, it is very easy to recognize the current mood state, whereas this is almost impossible with new residents. *"Well, you know the residents, so you know what behavior they show normally. If someone is usually very cheerful, while when you come in, he does not say anything or just mumbles something. Yes, I definitely notice that someone is not feeling well. (P5)" "I cannot see it on her, because I don't know her … because maybe it always like that. You have to be able to compare. (P6)"* Regular contact is important. *"Then you can keep track of their progress, how is someone, and that someone is not getting worse (P5)" "When you work a few nights, you know how it went earlier. (P4)"* Another aspect is that knowing a person's background could help to assess why a person is in a certain mood. *"If you know the life story of people, then you understand more (P4)." "Someone you know for a long time, you know the background. Then you also know why they are depressive (P3).*

To get a first impression of the mood state two features were mentioned by all interviewees: the facial expression, most dominantly the eyes, and the voice of the person. *"When I come inside, I see immediately whether I am welcome or not. I see it on her, how she looks at you, the corners of the mouth downwards … I often see it in her eyes or from the expression on her face. (P6)" "Usually yes, you see it immediately in their faces. … Actually even before you see them. Then it is often the way they say good morning (P3)"*

Recognizing negative moods is key in our application, since we would like to provide an intervention in such cases. Therefore, the interviews focused specifically on negative mood states, such as being depressed, aggressive or sad.

Gloomy/Depressive. We found that the prevailing negative mood in residents was being gloomy, which is to be distinguished from being depressed. When talking about depression, caregivers referred to a medical condition that could be diagnosed and treated. Being gloomy describes similar mood states, which are not connected to a medical condition. Features for the recognition are facial expression, posture and social behavior. *"You can see it in the facial expression. I think they would be staring. You can see it in the eyes, the way they are standing, no smile on the face. (P5)"* *"Most of the time you see it in their faces. Expressions, they don't look happy, not awake, gloomy, the corners of the mouth down, and then they sit like this [puts her shoulders forward.] (P8)"* *"You see it from their posture. Yes, that is a bit collapsed. Contacts with other people they don't want then. (P2)"* Similar facial expressions were described for depression, but people were much more withdrawn. *"They are more focused on the inside, introverted. (P3)""Depressed, 'crawling' away and this withdrawal and not wanting anything (P4)"*

Scared/Nervous. Being nervous or scared is mainly observed with people suffering from mild dementia due to memory loss or disorientation. Features signaling nervousness are mainly behavioral, either non-interactional, such as wanting to move, or in interactional, such as not being able to focus on a conversation with another person. *"There are different types of unrest. For example, people want to get up from the chair ... they want to do certain things that they can't (P4)."* *"They want to begin an activity, but cannot finish it. (P3)"* *"I think that they want to walk a lot or they don't dare to (P5)."* *"When someone is very nervous, I think they cannot have a relaxed conversation or listen or they loose the red thread. (P5)"*

Caregivers reported that residents are rarely scared. Significant features are facial expression, in particular the look in people's eyes, a tense posture and vocal reactions like screaming. *"You often see it in the eyes, and the posture, that someone is very tense. (P2)""Yes, and in the look in their eyes... If someone is really scared, then you see it in their look, like looking fast, looking around, suspicious I would say (P3)."* *"Also, how someone lies in the bed, clinging, cringing, and tensing up. That is then pure fear, and then screaming. (P2)"*

Other Moods. Other negative moods are rarely observed on a regular basis. Two caregivers reported about a resident who suffered from Korsakoff syndrome, a neurological disorder linked to alcoholism and showing symptoms of dementia. This resident became aggressive when being drunk. He forgot that he had drunk and asked for more. Features were an angry look on the face, being loud and being physically aggressive to others. Sadness was another mood that was mentioned but did not occur regularly. Shedding tears was the most obvious sign. Otherwise the body language is similar to being gloomy.

Influences on Mood

Internal and external influences impacting a resident's mood are important for the context modeling of the system to make the mood recognition more accurate or help predicting the mood. In the interviews many external factors surfaced, including loneliness, weather, time of day, sound, light and smell and two internal factors, i.e. illnesses and memories of events (e.g. death day of relative).

External Factors. Loneliness was reported as a crucial factor leading to gloomy moods. *"Yes, there are people here, that sit alone the rest of the day [after caregiving] four days a week (P4)" "Surely because they live there alone, ... the family is busy, then they become lonely and gloomy. (P5)" "They are alone a lot. They cannot walk, because they have no one ... children live far away. (P8)"* Also the time of day has an impact on the residents' mood. Caregivers observed that many people have problems with the start of the day. *"I realized with older people, in the morning, starting the day, having the day ahead, ... while in the evening they can retreat, that is important for people between 80 and 90. (P4)" "I noticed that most depressing feelings are experienced in the morning, when starting the day ... later, people are calmer. (P3)" "With that one person it was the care in the morning, He did not like it, and at lunchtime it was fine again (P2)"*

Weather has a mediating role in that it does not affect the mood directly, but the mobility of the person. If people cannot go outside for several days they experience negative moods. *"People cannot go outside, cannot go for a walk... you get gloomy from that. (P4)" "When the sun shines at nine in the morning then the day is very good. Then they can go outside. That makes a big difference (P2)."* Different types of weather can play a role, since they influence the mobility in different ways. *"They don't like it too cold, then they cannot go outside (P6)" "Many people walk with a walker or cane and it gets really windy around these buildings and then they cannot go outside. (P2)"*

We specifically asked about light, sound and smell as they are directly relevant to the system. Light was seen as a positive factor by all caregivers. Sounds and smells were seen as playing a smaller role. Music is very personal, depends on the individual's preferences. Generally, residents like sounds that give the impression of 'life in the house', but too much noise can impact the mood negatively.

5   Discussion and Design Considerations

5.1   Mood Model Derived from the Data

Figure 2 presents an initial model derived from the interviews. On the left side, influencing factors impacting the mood are shown, divided into internal and external ones. On the right side the features for detected the mood are listed. It should be noted that behavioral factors are strongly influenced by a person's habits, which should be taken into account to accurately detect the mood.

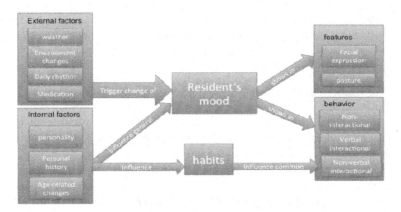

Fig. 2. Senior Mood Model

5.2   Considerations Based on Insights about Mood

Gloominess is the most observed mood in seniors living independently. It occurs due to few social contacts and resulting loneliness as well as compromised mobility, especially in bad weather conditions. Anxiety and connected nervous behaviors are mainly observed in people with mild dementia, who feel lost. People with extreme dementia, can experience rapid mood changes due to forgetfulness. Depression and aggression were moods that were rarely experienced and linked to medical conditions. Consequently, an AAL system intending to improve seniors' moods should be optimized to recognize gloomy moods and provide activating ambiences. In case of mild dementia, nervous behaviors should be detected and a cozy atmosphere used to counteract. To recognize moods the mood model above can provide guidance. Our system is trained on a few subjects and tested on new unseen ones. This makes it able to deal with unseen data, in the same way as the nurse judges the mood of a new resident. In particular, the system requires a user model that contains information about the personality (introverted, outgoing), diseases (dementia, depression) and behavior patterns in order to notice deviations from the normal state. In addition, a context model providing information about the current situation (time of day, weather, etc.) supports the prediction of residents' mood. Combined with real-time input from sensors on facial expression, posture and movement, the mood can be analyzed.

5.3   Overall Attitude and Expected Effects

The reactions to the system were diverse. Overall, the caregivers were positive towards the use of lighting to improve moods. Some doubts, however, were apparent towards the automatic sensing and adaptation of the lamps. The most beneficial effects were seen for people suffering from depression or gloomy moods. *"I think it could work very well, because light works very positively on people that are depressed. (P3)"* For anxious people, caregivers were not sure about the effects. Generally for *"people who are scared, … if the light is cozy, it would probably give them a feeling of safety (P3)"*, but for people with dementia doubts were mentioned. *"So, the light changes, but how that would be experienced by someone with dementia ... I think that it can also bring feelings of anxiety to the surface (P3)"*

5.4   Use of Camera and Sensors

Three themes emerged in the interviews: keeping control, privacy and suspicion. A common statement of the caregivers towards the installation of the system as such and specifically the use of cameras to recognize and automatically adapt the lighting, was that people live independently in the apartments and therefore, wish to be in control. *"Well, I think with people with dementia you can place anything, but here it is explicitly about people that want to keep control themselves (P4)"* In any case the system would have to be agreed upon with the residents and the family. As expected, privacy was one of the factors, which could hinder the use of the system. *"I think that more than half the people would not agree ... Privacy, I think. (P2)"* *"No that is always so sensitive, such things, all the privacy is gone (P7)."* Privacy is a general concern in AAL systems that monitor the users. For our system it is crucial to store some data about the users' behavior and therefore, a solution with high data security needs to be implemented. In addition, we will explore in interviews with seniors what the exact privacy concerns are. An aspect we had not considered before, is that people with mild dementia could react with suspicion towards the cameras, unobtrusive sensors may be a better option in this case.

5.5   The Right Setting for the System

As hypothesized after the first rounds of interviews we found differences in how caregivers perceived the use of the system in different care contexts. Several interviewees immediately stated that the system should be used in a care home. Four reasons were named for this. Independence of the residents (also linked to stage of dementia) and rebuilding their flats to install the system was seen as obstacles. *"See, in a care home on a floor with dement people you can install it, but in people's homes would you not do it so easily. (P8)"* *"Here people live independently, would you do this whole refurbishment here (P7)."* In care homes two aspects were seen as beneficial circumstance, i.e. more extreme moods that need to be handled and more supervision by caregivers in care homes. *"I think it is better in a care home, because aggression is occurring more often there. I think that the moods are more extreme there. They are together with more people and have more stimuli and obstacles there. (P5)"* *"Look, in care homes it is different, the doors are open and in the corridor there are caregivers (P6)."* *"Because it is easier to handle. You can monitor people more (P2)."* Closely linked to the living setting for the system was the aspect of automatic adaptation of the lights, which was perceived as opposing the idea of keeping control in independent living. *"People live independent, so you have to strive for them having control (P3)."* *"[Controlling the system themselves] would be very good, I think, because then they have the feeling that they are involved (P7)."* Another comment showed the importance of knowing the intended effect of a certain light setting: *"Then it is a lamp with a remote control … if it also says from high to low it is activating or calming, then I think it is better (P6)."*

Despite the concerns about compromising the independence with an automatic system, several caregivers emphasized that residents may have difficulties being aware about their negative mood state or would not take initiative to change it. *"I will put on another light, because I don't feel so happy. People would not do that (P8)" "I think that if someone needs to get calmer, they often don't have it under control and would turn on [the system] (P2)." "If someone is gloomy or depressed, then they are often in denial (P5)."*

Given the above a good solution could be to detect the mood automatically and provide a choice to the user to change the light in order to improve the mood. In this case the user would be involved and be in control, but at the same time issues with not taking initiative may be overcome.

6   Conclusions and Future Work

Insights obtained in interviews with caregivers working in different care settings were presented in form of a mood model as well as design considerations for an adaptive lighting system for the care context. The presented model can be used by others as a starting point in designing systems affecting the mood of seniors and can be applied to other design contexts than lighting. Overall, we can conclude that in the independent living context, control by the users is an important factor for acceptance of the system, whereas the automatic features dependent on cameras and sensors are more relevant in the institutional context. We have to distinguish situations in the home context, in which residents experience affective disorders, for instance, depression. Caregivers highlighted that depressed individuals would rarely initiate a lighting change to improve their moods. A combination of automatic sensing to detect a negative mood and a notification of lighting change would be an option. Generally, in the home context gloomy and anxious moods occur, while aggression or extreme nervousness is rare. The latter are more common in day care and care home context where several people were together. Depending on the context the system could be targeted to detect certain moods.

Currently we are interviewing seniors to get a first person perspective on the attitudes towards our system, which will be integrated into the design as well.

Acknowledgements. We are grateful to the Vitalis WoonZorg Groep for supporting us in our research. Furthermore, we would like to thank Philips to enable this project, and, in particular, Boris De Ruyter for valuable discussions.

References

1. Boyce, P., Barriball, E.: Circadian rhythms and depression. Aust Fam Physician **39**, 307–310 (2010)
2. Elliot, A.J., Maier, M.A., Moller, A.C., Friedman, R., Meinhardt, J.: Color and psychological functioning: The effect of red on performance attainment. J. Exp. Psychology **136**(1), 154–168 (2007)
3. Fitzpatrick, G., Huldtgren, A., Malmborg, L., Harley, D., IJsselsteijn, W.A.: Design for agency, adaptivity and reciprocity: re-imagining AAL and telecare agendas. In: Randall, D., Schmidt, K. & Wulf, V. (Eds.) Designing Socially Embedded Technologies: A European Challenge. Springer (2015)
4. Golden, R.N., Gaynes, B.N., Ekstrom, R.D., Hamer, R.M., Jacobsen, F.M., Suppes, T., Wisner, K.L., Nemeroff, C.B.: The efficacy of light therapy in the treatment of mood disorders: A review andmetaanalysis of the evidence. Am. J. Psychiatry **162**, 656–662 (2005)
5. Kaya, N., Epps, H.H.: Relationship between color and emotion: A study of college students. College Student Journal **38**, 396–405 (2004)
6. Kempter, G., Ritter, W., Künz, A.: Guiding light for the mobility support of seniors. In: Ambient Assisted Living. Springer, Heidelberg (2014)
7. Knez, I.: Effect of indoor lighting on mood and cognition. J. Environ. Psychology **15**, 39–51 (1995)
8. Knez, I., Enmarker, I.: Effects of office lighting on mood and cognitive performance and a gender effect in work-related judgment. Environment and Behavior **30**, 553–567 (1998)
9. Kobayashi, R., Fukuda, N., Kohsaka, M., Sasamoto, Y., Sakakibara, S., Koyama, E., Nakamura, F., Koyama, T.: Effects of bright light at lunchtime on sleep of patients in a geriatric hospital. Psychiatry Clin Neurosci. **55**, 287–289 (2001)
10. Kuijsters, A., Redi, J., de Ruyter, B., Seuntiens, P., Heynderickx, I.: Affective ambiences created with lighting for older people. Lighting Res. Technol., 1-17 (2014)
11. Kuijsters, A., Redi, J., de Ruyter, B., Heynderickx, I.: Improving the mood of elderly with coloured lighting. In: Constructing Ambient Intelligence, pp. 49-56. Springer, Heidelberg (2012)
12. Küller, R., Ballal, S., Laike, T., Mikellides, B., Tonello, G.: The impact of light and colour on psychological mood: a cross-cultural study of indoor work environments. Ergonomics **49**, 1496–1507 (2006)
13. Lieverse, R., Van Someren, E.J., Nielen, M.M., Uitdehaag, B.M., Smit, J.H., Hoogendijk, W.J.: Bright light treatment in elderly patients with nonseasonal major depressive disorder: A randomized placebo-controlled trial. Archives of General Psychiatry **68**, 61–70 (2011)
14. Maier, E., & Kempter, G.: ALADIN-a magic lamp for the elderly? In: Handbook of Ambient Intelligence and Smart Environments. pp. 1201-1227. Springer US (2010)
15. Riemersma-van der Lek, R.F., Swaab, D.F., Twisk, J., Hol, E.M., Hoogendijk, W.J.G., Van Someren, E.J.W.: Effect of bright light and melatonin on cognitive and noncognitive function in elderly residents of group care facilities: A randomized controlled trial. JAMA **299**, 2642–2655 (2008)

Perspectives on Collaboration
in Technology Innovation for Ageing

Piper Jackson[1(✉)], Judith Sixsmith[2], Alex Mihailidis[3], and Andrew Sixsmith[1]

[1] Gerontology Research Centre, Simon Fraser University Vancouver,
2800 – 515 West Hastings Street, Vancouver, BC V6B 5K3, Canada
{piper_jackson,sixsmith}@sfu.ca
[2] University of Northampton, Boughton Green Road,
Northampton NN2 7AL, UK
judith.sixsmith@northampton.ac.uk
[3] Rehabilitation Sciences, University of Toronto,
160 - 500 University Avenue, Toronto, ON M5G 1V7, Canada
Alex.Mihailidis@utoronto.ca

Abstract. Seven gerontechnology innovation projects spanning nineteen years were considered in terms of project activities, collaboration and management. The projects we considered were: PLANEC, OTIS, Care in the Community, SAPHE, SOPRANO, Smart Distress Monitor and COACH. Three interviews with project partners identified the nature and goals of the project, the composition of the team members, and the challenges, solutions, successes, and failures. Thematic analysis revealed three common themes spanning the projects which are likely to be issues in other technology innovation and research projects. The themes are navigating boundaries, succeeding at "things you're not very good at", and managing disparate teams. In this article we discuss the factors contributing to these thematic concerns, and present solutions that were helpful for the projects in the expectation that the knowledge generated from those working experiences is transferable to other projects that involve the intersection of technology development and social concerns.

Keywords: Gerontechnology · Transdisciplinarity · Collaboration · Project management

1   Introduction

Advances in information and communications technology (ICT) have changed the way we live, and promise a bright future, where technology helps us to deal with many of challenges that now face us. One area of pressing concern is how to deal with an ageing population, as we see people across the globe living longer lives [1]. ICT does not only provide tools for directly addressing the physical ailments associated with ageing, it also can help us to improve quality of life, support independent living and social interaction, and assist in managing and providing care. We refer to this gerontology-informed technology development as *gerontechnology* [1].

© Springer International Publishing Switzerland 2015
A. Geissbühler et al. (Eds.): ICOST 2015, LNCS 9102, pp. 27–37, 2015.
DOI: 10.1007/978-3-319-19312-0_3

However, the promise of creating innovative technological solutions to social problems is not without its challenges. The issues being addressed can be fundamentally
complex, involving physical, mental, and social aspects, in addition to technological
complications. Thus they require experts from diverse disciplines to collaborate in
developing shared understanding, concepts, models and methods in order to produce
innovative solutions: in this sense they are *transdisciplinary* in nature. Stakeholders
from other groups can be included in this process, such as users, policy makers, and
clinicians. Further, in order to save costs and make widely applicable solutions, these
projects may involve participants from many regions, or even many countries. Finally, technology is still changing even as we try to implement solutions. The question
for people involved in such projects is "How do we work efficiently in this complex
and dynamic environment?"

The structure of this paper is as follows: Section 2 explains our methodology; Section 3 gives a general description of each of the projects we considered; Section 4
explores the themes identified from the interview, and provides specific examples
from to illustrate the points raised; finally, Section 5 concludes the paper with some
discussion.

2   Method

A case study approach was used to generate information from three experts in the
field of aging and technology research. Case studies are useful when exploring new
areas and are characterized by an emphasis on retaining information within the complex contexts which makes them meaningful [2]. In this instance, experts with considerable experience in working across multiple, large scale aging and technology projects were interviewed in order that tacit understandings of the complexity of under-
taking such research were revealed. A semi structured interview format was used in
order to encourage the expression of expert experiences while keeping the interviewee
on topic [3]. The interview revolved around the *Features, Challenges, Successes,* and
Failures of *Aging related technology projects,* the interviewees had participated in.
No further structuring of the interview (such as specific questions) was used, as the
interview was intended to be conversational in tone. The interviews lasted between 1
and 2 hours in duration and were conducted in an office on the Simon Fraser University site and in a cafe. Thematic analysis was used to analyze the data. This involved a
six step process (amended from Braun and Clarke, 2006) as follows: 1) the interviewer familiarized themselves with the audio interview data by listen to this several times
and reading through the interviewer field notes written during the interview and immediately afterwards; 2) the interviewer then captured categories of meaning perceived in the data; 3) these categories of meaning were then discussed between the
interviewer and the other researchers in an open reflective process whereby connections were drawn between categories and potential themes were identified; 4) potential themes were reviewed in relation to the data set; 5) the themes were iteratively
refined through discussions amongst the research team; 6) finally, the agreed themes
were written up and the analysis agreed upon between the research team members.

This team based, iterative analysis process was considered sufficiently robust as the themes were defined through lengthy discussions. Quoted statements presented in the analysis section of this article are taken from the interviews.

3   The Ageing and Technology Projects

In this section, we provide a short description of each of the projects discussed in this paper, focusing on the type of project, timeline, and collaborators involved. Specific experiences of interest are discussed in the Section 4 (Themes).

3.1   PLANEC (1996-1999)

Supporting IT development that aids in the monitoring, evaluation, and planning (MEP) of elder care was the goal of the PLANEC project [4]. Preceded by Cost15, PLANEC was a pan-European enterprise involving researchers, practitioners, and policy makers from Spain, the United Kingdom, Finland, Germany, and the Netherlands. The central idea was to adopt ideas from health economics (such as that developed at the University of Kent), and IT methods such as use cases and process modelling in order to better evaluate and plan elder care [5]. In terms of practical outcomes, PLANEC focused on establishing how telecare could fit into existing care processes.

3.2   OTIS (1999-2001)

The Occupational Therapy Internet School (OTIS) was a collaboration between four learning institutions to develop a virtual college [6]. The system allowed students at centres in Belgium, the Netherlands, Sweden, and the UK to study a common set of occupational therapy courses online, complete with virtual classrooms, chat rooms, and knowledge resources. This early example of remote learning was very successful during its lifetime, with dedicated effort provided by student developers, and an active user base of students. However, it did not sustain itself beyond the ending of the project time limits.

3.3   Care in the Community (2003-2006)

Care in the Community was a novel attempt to ascertain how sensor technology could improve the quality of life of older adults living independently [7]. Based in the UK, it was a joint project between several universities in the UK and British Telecom Research Labs. In particular, sensors focused on activity monitoring. While some of the methods tested were unorthodox (such as audio sensors on pipes to watch sink and toilet use), the project helped to establish guidelines for what kinds of activity monitoring is technically feasible and provides useful insight into quality of life.

3.4   SAPHE (2006-2009)

Smart and Aware Pervasive Healthcare Environments (SAPHE) sought to develop new methods for creating ambient sensor networks for monitoring health [8]. This included both wearable sensors, and those located in the regular living environment. It focused on health concerns experienced by older adults, such as chronic obstructive pulmonary disease (COPD). Continuing out of the previous project, Care in the Community, several industrial partners joined in this stage of the project, including Philips, Cardionetics, and Docobo. Although it preceded the ubiquity of wireless sensors due to the mass adoption of smartphones, SAPHE explored how ambient monitoring can be helpful in preventative health care.

3.5   SOPRANO (2007-2010)

Service-oriented Programmable Smart Environments for Older Europeans (SOPRANO) was a large-scale European project (budget of 15M Euro) with more than 20 partner organizations [9]. With a goal of supported independent living for older adults, a system to support exercise at home using a virtual character interface was developed. The design methodology was human-centric, and considered numerous dimensions such as cross-cultural validity [10].

3.6   Smart Distress Monitor (2008-2011)

This project involved the development of an infrared sensor for home (in)activity monitoring, with integrated logic to identify unusual behavior outside of an older adult's normal routines [11]. This would provide an opportunity for a family member or caregiver to look into the situation and intervene if necessary. The project team comprised an industry partner that focused on building the technology, university social scientists researching user needs and experiences, and an advisory group of older adult volunteers. While all partners were located in the same country, the industrial partners were geographically distant from the others.

3.7   COACH (1996-ongoing)

COACH (Cognitive Orthosis for Assisting with aCtivites in the Home) provides an intelligent supportive environment, such as in the home or at a care facility [12]. Most notably it has been implemented as an aid to help people with dementia to wash their hands correctly. COACH is capable of tracking the user's hands, understanding what those movements mean in relation to hand washing, and providing appropriate prompts when mistakes are made. Testing and development of coach involved cooperation between academic technology researchers and several community care organizations.

4   Themes

In this section we discuss the main themes that emerged from the interview when discussing the projects from Section 4.

4.1   Navigating Boundaries

The projects featured in this paper all involved multiple disciplines: they aimed to apply technology to aid with issues that have a strong social component. Accordingly, the individuals composing the project teams were comprised of a range of diverse disciplinary backgrounds: engineers and sociologists; clinicians, researchers, and administrators; people from Europe's north and south; speakers of English of varying levels of competency; men and women; and adults both young and old. These differences created a series of challenges which presented practical and ideational boundaries [13] to designing effective technologies which were 'fit for purpose' in the sense of improving older adults' everyday lives. Ideational boundaries, especially concerning power and authority structures which characterize the research world, were confronted when designing research and sharing conceptual and methodological ideas. On the one hand, difficulties arose when some disciplinary and paradigmatic perspectives were prioritized over others (e.g., technologists over social scientists) or when some voices were privileged over others (e.g., researchers over older people in advisory groups). Moreover, the development of shared understandings of key project ideas were elusive due to different disciplinary-based terminology and perspectives derived from the different disciplinary backgrounds. One example from the PLANEC project was the use of the terms "care of older people" vs. "service for older people". The subtle distinction between needs (in the former) and practice (in the latter) was lost upon non-native speakers of English, but crucial to the project since care needs would likely be similar across settings while service practices would vary depending upon context. Language issues were also problematic in the SDM project, especially when trying to convey important information between the different stakeholder groups:

> *"The other thing that we found incredibly difficult was the lack of a common language between ourselves as researchers and the technologists. So when we were trying to tell the advisory group what the project was about or how it would operate or what particular aspect of the algorithm that was developing, important or interesting, we didn't have the language to carry it out in a way that was interesting and informative."*

As the above quotation indicates, a common problem across these projects concerned the communication of project requirements between technical and non-technical experts. In the PLANEC project, a substantive challenge concerned identifying and defining the various categories of stakeholder for an aging-related technology project, such as client, family member, care provider, purchaser, and policy maker.

This was addressed by training all of the staff in the Unified Modelling Language (UML), which is often used in software development [5]. Contrary to expectations, the non-technical team members greatly appreciated the clarity of UML for communicating technical ideas and did not find it too difficult to apply within their domains of expertise. An example of a domain-based communication gap was experienced in the Care in the Community project, wherein the definition of *quality of life* used by the occupational therapists was tied directly to rehabilitation goals and did not match an understanding of *well-being* held by the sociologists that also includes physical, mental, social, and environmental considerations. This gap was overcome through the collaborative development of a conceptual model of quality of life that provides a holistic view of an individual's personal and contextual factors, activities, experience, and well-being [7].

Trust among team members can help productivity, since it can make people comfortable enough to speak their minds and ask questions during project discussions and decision making [14,15]. This helps to identify and solve problems before they have grown into unmanageable and intractable complications. Technology mediated communication is efficient and flexible, but it is not as rich as face-to-face contact in terms of the information transmitted, such as attitude and emotion seen in body language [16]. Socializing can also contribute to the level of comfort and sense of membership that collaborators feel towards each other. However, particularly in the European context, it is possible for enjoying social occasions together (e.g., drinking alcohol) to get out of hand, and be a hindrance to project success, especially if this progresses without regard to cultural or religious differences. Moreover, socializing events can reinforce gendered divisions and exacerbate differentials in power relations across the project if not well thought out, e.g., when such occasions are not jointly and democratically planned. Choosing appropriate forms of socializing is critical if the avoidance of social cliques is to be achieved. So, for example, meeting at a restaurant rather than a bar can help to set a more appropriate tone. Despite these concerns, the interviewees all found that making time for social activities can pay off well in terms of team unity, ease of interaction, and level of trust: *"We'd even do things like hold social events for their staff or residents to get to know the researchers and understand exactly what we were doing... whenever we went in and did one of those events, we always found that the buy-in from the staff and residents was a lot higher."* In general, navigating practical and ideational boundaries can be challenging, but intentionally allocating time and resources for improving communication and developing relationships was seen to be an effective mode of preventing boundary-related problems and addressing difficulties.

> *"We did do some transdisciplinary working, we had workshops to create use cases. So we took that seriously and I think that was very helpful for communicating to our IT people. Some of the IT people just didn't want to know. But that was helpful in terms of defining the problem in ways they could understand and also getting over some of these 'us and them' sort of barriers. So that was helpful. So the workshops, because there is a social dimension to them, helped with that."*

4.2   Succeeding at "Things you're not very good at"

With research and innovation: *"You're pushing the boundaries, so in a sense you're always trying to do things you're not very good at to push those boundaries."* This interview statement captures part of the reason why it is so difficult to organize research projects. By the nature of the doing something new, you are working on unfamiliar ground, never quite knowing whether or not a particular way of working would be effective: *"For me and my team... it was more not knowing what we weren't good at, until it didn't work, until we realized: Hang on! Nobody's getting what they want out of this. We've got to do it differently."*

For any project, poor decisions can have immense consequences, but with research, the high level of uncertainty makes decision making extremely challenging. In the SOPRANO project, voice recognition was recognized as a valuable feature, since it would make the end product much easier to use. However, at the time, voice recognition technology was in its infancy, so including it meant adding basic scientific development to the originally planned application. This was overly ambitious for a single project, even with a large budget. The SAPHE project took place before mass adoption of smart phones, and the state of technology at the time severely limited trials. For example, communication networks were limited, few users had mobile devices that could work with the system, and the battery lives of sensors were very short. In order to prevent problems like these, it is important for technical staff to maintain reasonable expectations about technology capabilities, since the other team members with less technical expertise may accept such 'over-promises' unquestioningly: *"The engineers would say they could do anything, and bizarrely enough, people like me believe them."*

Another consequence of working on projects with a substantial research component is that it can be difficult to know in advance how much each team member will be able to contribute. While personal factors and unknown future events can make this difficult to foresee in any project, transdisciplinary work involves numerous complex factors which need to be considered, further complicating project outcome predictions. For example, complex factors such as the value of a given domain of expertise to the project is difficult to ascertain at the outset; commitment of team members to multiple projects; differing goals and expectations (e.g., profit vs. career advancement vs. recognition vs. gratitude); the value of the contribution to a team member may change over time as the project goals evolve; and crucially, research collaboration is often poorly organized, with unclear roles, responsibilities and expectations. In the projects discussed here where outside management was not brought in, slow project advancement and unpredictable contributions were sometimes addressed by implementing an authoritarian management style. While this succeeded in bringing the projects back on track, it also tended to create great stress and a reduction in team cohesion, making it an undesirable method for managing teams of researchers.

Furthermore, such hierarchical managerial structures may also adversely affect direct communication across the research groups in order to prioritize efficiency or control. Communication imbalances tended to hamper the flexibility of development, for example in the Smart Distress Monitor project, in which it was initially assumed that user requirements would be gathered from the advisory group by the social scientists, and passed along to the technologists. In actuality, an ongoing dialogue between all three partner groups would have helped to establish (a) whether feedback was being acted upon, (b) how successful changes to the system were in addressing concerns, and (c) whether the changes resulted in subsequent issues to consider. When working on gerontechnological innovation, it is important to prioritize openness to different perspectives as a means of generating comprehensive understandings of the complex, dynamic, and uncertain problem space. Moreover, it aids in avoiding unexpected conceptual and methodological obstacles which can occur when disciplinary wisdom is challenged or transgressed.

4.3   Managing Disparate Teams

Since research and innovation by definition is concerned with new and/or difficult challenges, diversity is the rule rather than the exception in terms of team composition. Collaborators are selected due to their valuable skills, knowledge, and/or experience, and as such may have little in common with each other. Further, groundbreaking projects often require collaborators distributed across various institutions and locations, as new combinations of expertise are combined, and various stakeholder perspectives are considered. Managing such disparate teams is indeed challenging. Cockburn emphasizes the importance of physical proximity for encouraging incidental interaction between team members [16]. Further, the pace of activity varies greatly by sector. According to the interviewed experts, research projects usually advance over months and years, whereas policy and expectations may rapidly change within government organizations. This means that team interactions and expectations needs to be carefully planned and managed.

> "The research timetable is not the same as what an advisory group of older people in their instance thought. We had three (advisory group) meetings built into the year. It wasn't enough. They'd (advisory group members) lost interest in between...

> What we decided to do was a lot more frequent contact by telephone, by e-mails, and these social things. Once we started doing that, then it all fell out much, much better. So I think (it necessary) paying attention to the mechanisms of keeping people engaged throughout."

Kania & Kramer describe a mode of organizational collaboration that is effective in addressing social issues, which they call *Collective Impact* [17]. The conditions for collective success that they describe are likely transferable to research and innovation collaborations, since they address the management of a diverse and distributed team with unclear authority structures and motivations. The conditions are: (i) having a common agenda; (ii) sharing measurement systems; (iii) engaging in activities that are mutually reinforcing; (iv) maintaining continuous communication; and (v) having backbone organizational support. This last condition was apparent in two of the projects described here. Research on community coalitions has had similar results, citing a strong central leadership, and a healthy organizational climate as important qualities [18]. For both PLANEC and OTIS, an outside project manager was brought in to join the group. Budgets for academic projects rarely have space for externally contracted staff, so this was an unusual decision, but in both cases it was key in terms of making progress. This is contrasted to several of the other projects, such as SAPHE, where a lack of central organization lead to greatly different levels of contribution (in terms of effort) to the work.

5   Discussion and Conclusions

This paper begins a discussion about the characteristics of technology innovation projects that deal with ageing. Such projects are necessarily transdisciplinary in nature, requiring collaboration between researchers from various disciplines, as well as policy makers and other stakeholders. The three themes presented here focus on how to successfully work on a complex project. However, there are certainly other aspects worthy of discussion, such as: what about afterward? One question left unanswered here is how to best ensure that research and innovation is adopted successfully by organizations and/or the public. As one interviewee put it: *"There is this disconnect between the products that are out there and what we are doing in research. They're quite different in terms of their functionality and their level of sophistication and none of them, relatively speaking, are considered successful products."* For technology designed for older adults, there are a number of factors that complicate commercialization, such as a diverse and changing user base, complicated business models involving family and/or government, and the difficulty of successfully deploying complex solutions into unpredictable residential environments. Can the collaboration of team members or the organization of the project help with this? The AGE-WELL NCE is designed to provide researchers with support for this and other considerations [19]; we intend to share our findings from that initiative in the future.

Other innovative applications of technology to social issues, including those outside of ageing, share many characteristics with the projects discussed here. Considering the size of many of these projects, and the impact they can have on large user groups, it is important to ensure that they are pursued in an effective manner. While we are still in the early days of the ITC boom, we can already start to reflect upon our successes and obstacles. For this, we adopt one of the central goals of transdisciplinary working: to produce new knowledge from cross-disciplinary interactions [20]. In other words, once bridges are built and a complex project is successful, there is value in converting that understanding into a foundation for future innovation.

Acknowledgements. The authors would like to thank Dr. Sharon Koehn for sharing her comprehensive notes on organizing community participation: *Governance structures in community action/activated research, an annotated bibliography.*

References

1. Sixsmith, A.: Technology and the challenge of aging. In: Technologies for Active Aging, pp. 7-25. Springer US (2013)
2. Yin, R.K.: Case study research: Design and methods. Sage publications (2013)
3. Louise Barriball, K., While, A.: Collecting Data using a semi-structured interview: a discussion paper. Journal of advanced nursing **19**(2), 328–335 (1994)
4. Sixsmith, A., Lunn, K., Sharples, P.: Preliminary Results of the Specification of the Functional Requirements of the PLANEC System. Studies in Health Technology and Informatics, 269-272 (1998)
5. Lunn, K., Sixsmith, A., Lindsay, A., Vaarama, M.: Traceability in requirements through process modelling, applied to social care applications. Information and Software Technology **45**(15), 1045–1052 (2003)
6. Sixsmith, A., Beer, M., Green, S.: An occupational therapy Internet school. Journal of Telemedicine and Telecare **6**(suppl 1), 175–177 (2000)
7. Sixsmith, A., Hine, N., Neild, I., Clarke, N., Brown, S., Garner, P.: Monitoring the well-being of older people. Topics in Geriatric Rehabilitation **23**(1), 9–23 (2007)
8. Barnes, N.M., Reeves, A.A.: Holistic monitoring to support integrated care provision experiences from telecare trials and an introduction to SAPHE. In: Second International Conference on Pervasive Computing Technologies for Healthcare, Pervasive Health 2008, pp. 293-296. IEEE (January 2008)
9. Müller, S., Meyer, I., Bierhoff, I., Delaney, S., Sixsmith, A., Sproll, S.: Iterative user involvement in Ambient Assisted Living research and development processes-Does it really make a difference? Smart Healthcare Applications and Services: Developments and Practices. IGI, Niagara Falls (2010)
10. Rocker, C., Ziefle, M.: E-health, Assistive Technologies and Applications for Assisted Living: Challenges and Solutions. Medical Information Science Reference (2011)
11. Hollock, S., Johnson, N., Sixsmith, J.: A smart distress monitor for independent living. Gerontechnology **9**(2), 216 (2010)
12. Mihailidis, A., Boger, J.N., Craig, T., Hoey, J.: The COACH prompting system to assist older adults with dementia through handwashing: An efficacy study. BMC geriatrics **8**(1), 28 (2008)
13. Evans, J.: Ideational border crossings: rethinking the politics of knowledge within and across disciplines. Discourse: studies in the cultural politics of education **35**(1), 45–60 (2014)
14. Costigan, R.D., Iiter, S.S., Berman, J.J.: A multi-dimensional study of trust in organizations. Journal of Managerial Issues, 303-317 (1998)
15. Erdem, F., Ozen, J.: Cognitive and affective dimensions of trust in developing team performance. Team Performance Management: An International Journal **9**(5/6), 131–135 (2003)
16. Cockburn, A.: Agile Software Development. Addison-Wesley, Boston (2002)

17. Kania, J., Kramer, M.: Collective impact. Stanford Social Innovation Review **1**(9), 36–41 (2011)
18. Mansergh, G., Rohrbach, L.A., Montgomery, S.B., Pentz, M.A., Johnson, C.A.: Process evaluation of community coalitions for alcohol and other drug abuse prevention: A case study comparison of researcher-and community-initiated models. Journal of Community Psychology **24**(2), 118–135 (1996)
19. AGEWELL-NCE.ca. AGE-WELL I Canada's technology and aging network (2015). http://www.agewell-nce.ca/ (accessed March 26, 2015)
20. Stokols, D.: Toward a science of transdisciplinary action research. American journal of community psychology **38**(1–2), 63–77 (2006)

User Interaction Concepts in Smart Caring Homes for Elderly with Chronic Conditions

Cristian-Dan Bara[1,2(✉)], Miriam Cabrita[1,2], Harm op den Akker[1,3], and Hermie J. Hermens[1,2]

[1] Telemedicine Group, Roessingh Research and Development,
P.O. Box 310, 7500 AH Enschede, The Netherlands
{C.Bara,M.Cabrita,H.opdenAkker,H.Hermens}@rrd.nl
[2] Telemedicine Group, Faculty of Electrical Engineering, Mathematics and Computer Science, University of Twente, P.O. Box 217, 7500 AE Enschede, The Netherlands
[3] Centre for Monitoring and Coaching, University of Twente,
P.O. Box 217, 7500 AE Enschede, The Netherlands

Abstract. This article addresses the design and implementation of user interaction concepts for smart caring homes. Elderly suffering from age related frailty or chronic diseases, such as chronic obstructive pulmonary disease and mild dementia are the targeted primary users. Their informal and formal caregivers are regarded as secondary users. The current smart home approach to user interaction is either too intrusive or too unobtrusive. This article proposes an alternative that implements both concepts in complementary interaction paradigms, using multiple types of feedback devices.

Keywords: Ambient assisted living · Smart caring home · Elderly · Chronic disease · Human-Computer Interaction

1 Introduction

Healthy aging entails the need to cope with physical and cognitive changes that lead to an age-related functional decline. Common age-related physical impairments are audio and visual problems, muscle and bone weakness and balance difficulties. At a cognitive level, decline of memory function, perceptual reasoning and processing speed constitute the most common impairments [1]. Together with age-related factors, multimorbidity can aggravate functional decline [2-3].

Functional decline leads to disabilities in activities of daily living, negatively affecting independent living of the elderly. Formal caregivers (e.g. medical practitioners and visiting nurses), or informal caregivers (e.g. family and friends) play an important role in facilitating independent living for as long as possible. However, their availability can be limited, affecting the support to the elderly. In interviews conducted in eight European countries regarding the reasons for institutionalization of people with dementia, 15% of informal caregivers reported their heavy burden as one of the reasons [4]. At an economic level, e.g. in the Netherlands, it is expected that 50% of

© Springer International Publishing Switzerland 2015
A. Geissbühler et al. (Eds.): ICOST 2015, LNCS 9102, pp. 38–49, 2015.
DOI: 10.1007/978-3-319-19312-0_4

the increase in healthcare expenditure will be due to the increased number of people aged over 65 between 2010 and 2040 [5].

It is the objective of smart caring home installations to support independent living by offering specialized technology for self-management. By self-management, we mean strategies to cope with chronic diseases and/or age-related impairments, enabling the elderly to take a proactive role in managing health and well-being. Therefore, it is the aim of a smart caring home and self-management technology to enable prolongation of user's functional capacity, delay institutionalization, increase autonomy and prolong participation in society.

This paper describes ongoing research to develop a smart, caring home environment: the eWALL [6]. The eWALL is a modular software platform for the deployment of various care services to promote independent living and self-management of elderly users where a large central screen is used to provide rich, natural interaction. Specifically, the focus in this work is on the interaction between the user and the smart home. Our solution creates a smart home environment [7-9] oriented on elderly care, meaning an environment that senses and infers the wishes and needs of the person that lives in this house, providing unobtrusive daily support, notifying informal and formal caregivers when necessary and serving as a bridge to supportive services offered by the outside world.

Similar smart home technologies are discussed in Section 2, followed by a detailed motivation of our approach to self-management home care technology. Section 3 holds a detailed description of our approach and motivates the focus on *user-to-smart home* interaction. Section 4 describes the method undertaken for developing the eWALL system. It contains a description of requirements, system architecture and provided services within the scope of eWALL. In Section 5 we illustrate some examples of interaction with the eWALL system and we conclude by highlighting the importance of user-, and usability driven development of such caring home systems.

2   Background

Solaimani et al. conclude that the use of technology is considered a priority in a quantitative study regarding the process of developing Ambient Assisted Living (AAL) projects [10]. User studies and user-centric studies are becoming more frequently applied and integrated, often as part of developing technical requirements. A considerable effort is being put into adaptable technologies, which should fit the user's requirements in different life situations. Davidoff et al. developed principles of technology adaptation to daily family living, including: organic evaluation of routines and plans, coping with new or modified user behavior, understanding periodic changes, breakdowns, accounting for multiple coexisting and, sometimes, conflicting goals, and understanding the living space [11].

Human-Computer Interaction (HCI) was adopted, also in the case of AAL, by analyzing the intra-human thought processes, e.g. a seven stage model for deciding to take an action [11-12], and inter-human communication. Issuing commands with predictable outcome gives, to the user, the perception of control over the machine.

In contrast to this approach, Bellotti et al. [13] addresses interaction from the perspective of communication. Widely applicable in AAL systems, this approach is based on joint accomplishments from both the human user and the system. This implies that the system possesses capabilities to orient itself according to a sensed environment, inferred situation and classified pattern of causality, which allows it to compute possible outcomes of executing commands. In such case, a correct orientation may increase the user's trust in the system.

In both cases, user interaction plays an important role in AAL installations [14]. Primary user requirements vary and the level of technology intrusiveness is different in each implementation. We consider *intrusive*, hardware technology that requires frequent adaptation efforts from the users, whether worn on the user's body, or in very close proximity to the user. Intrusive technology requires the user to change her/his lifestyle in order to interact with it. This characteristic is influenced by various interfacing capabilities between modern technology and humans. Based on our survey, we distinguish two general approaches for offering feedback to the primary users: (1) the mobile follower, or robot approach, in which a technological personification follows its primary user within the home environment and (2) the fixed installation which consists, in most cases, of an enlarged control panel, allowing the user to choose whether he/she will interact or not with the caring technology.

An example of a lifestyle change in this case, is the user's need to accept and adapt to a robot [17-26] that follows her/him around the home. Good examples of this are the GIRAFFE robot, a telepresence application [20-21]; the Accompany robot that provides physical, cognitive and social support [22-23]; Mobiserv, a social companion robot [24-25]; and the Nao humanoid robot [26]. The robot provides the main feedback and system interfacing functionalities, but a more complex sensory infrastructure provides monitoring data. This implies a corresponding user adaptation to communicating with the technology and its intrusive behavior. Although providing helpful assistance [15], robots reduce the need for their user's mobility and create, in the long term, a greater dependency on the technology. Updates in robot functionality and, consequently, its form factors, will require a learning and adaptation process from the elderly user. Such limitations could hinder therapy and decrease long term acceptance [16]. One of the biggest limitations in today's state of the art robotic AAL systems is the reduced autonomous mobility outside the home environment. As such, these systems, as well as most other fixed installations, also provide a mobile device, such as Personal Digital Assistant (PDA), or smartphone, which can support similar interactions as most robots (speech recognition, touch gestures, GPS tracking) [8].

In an opposite approach, the AAL projects that adopt fixed feedback technologies such as projectors [8], all-in-one touchscreen PC's [27], custom home controllers like: the Gigaset home control [28], or DigiFlower [8]; or smart TVs [27, 29] are integrated tightly within the home environment. They have specific clear roles for offering feedback within a user initiated and control interaction episode, following more rigidly defined paradigms of use. They primarily implement the user issued command interaction type. Multimodal interactions are implemented with the constraint that they always occur in a fixed space within the household. Usually largely accessible rooms, like living rooms, support these installations. They mostly possess fixed forms and are not likely to dramatically change paradigms of use when updated. Opposed to the robot approach, the feedback mechanisms have tight integration with the home sensor network, giving the user a closely coupled sensory-feedback installation. The tight integration of these systems with the home environment is combined with a mobile device for outdoor use [8, 28-29], yet a complementary feedback mechanism (pairing mobile and home screens) is not a standard approach [8].

3   Approach

Smart caring homes are implemented in order to facilitate easy, reliable, and contextualized access to health care services. eWALL [33] is our approach to such a smart caring home which proposes a suite of self-empowering and self-management services, for elderly with age related frailty and multiple morbidities, and, in addition, care oriented services and healthy living assessment tools for informal and formal caregivers. As depicted in Fig.1, it consists of three main technological tiers: (1) the sensing installation for the primary end user (elderly), (2) the cloud infrastructure, for complex calculations and data storage, and (3) the front-end feedback consisting of: primary user main screen Graphical User Interface (GUI), primary user mobile GUI and secondary user (informal and formal care givers) portal GUI [7].

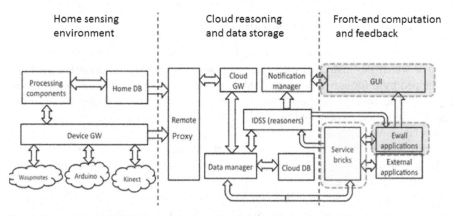

Fig. 1. Description of eWALL architecture divided in 3 technological tiers: the home sensing environment, the cloud reasoning and data storage and management and front-end computation (service bricks) and feedback (graphical user interfaces)

The eWALL installation for the primary user proposes a human-machine interaction paradigm which consists of two major components that complement each other in terms of functionality. The first component is the prefabricated wall containing a large screen (referred to as the main screen), installed in the primary user's home. It is immovable and allows complex interaction between the user and system. The second component is a smartphone that aims to provide relevant eWALL functionalities when the primary user is not within the home environment. Due to its nature, this system feedback component is highly mobile and can be considered as always reachable by the user, when eWALL functionality is needed outside the home environment. eWALL implements these two paradigms in a complementary way, by enabling the main screen to blend with the home environment, when no interaction is needed or being performed and keeping the smartphone widget set always reachable. Interface elements can be exchanged between devices through sliding gestures, or by button activated commands, e.g.: "send to phone", "expand on main screen".

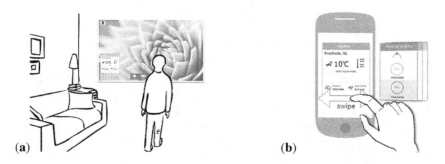

Fig. 2. a - Concept of the eWALL home screen displaying the active main screen interface; **b** - The eWALL mobile concept, reusing and adapting the main screen widget set

3.1   The "at Home" Interaction Paradigm

The home environment blending is done by implementing the "smart picture" metaphor, in which the main (large) screen will display a picture on its entire surface, overlapped by informative widgets displaying the current time and weather forecast (Fig. 2a). The widgets are positioned in a non-focal point area, giving value to the picture. Interaction is requested by eWALL, through a smart notification system. This system takes into account a complex set of parameters, some of which being: the therapy prescribed by the doctors, the person's state of health and a history of compliance to the notification messages. Interaction can also be initiated by the primary user, simply, by approaching the wall.

When the primary user is within reach of the main screen, eWALL switches to its active mode. In this mode, the user has access to a number of applications targeting several aspects of one's life. eWALL has initially three types of applications. First, eWALL targets independent chronic disease and frailty management through monitoring of physical and daily life activities. Maintaining and improving one's state of health is achieved through physical activity coaching, training the respiratory system through home exercises, or cognitive training through fun games. The third type is healthcare support, consisting of applications that enable the primary user to communicate with informal and formal caregivers.

3.2   The "Outside of Home" Interaction Paradigm

The system revolves around the primary user, which means that we target disease and frailty management during most life situations. A large number of such life situations happen outside the home environment, with different constraints and, therefore, different functional requirements. eWALL adapts to the outside environment situations by offering relevant functionalities to continue and complement self-health management. The primary feedback device is a smartphone (Fig. 2b) and the sensor network consists of the smartphone's GPS, microphone, camera and a wearable physical activity sensor for accurate detection and quantification of different physical activities.

4   Method

The development of eWALL started with a study of the targeted users. Our study produced personas – which encapsulate typical features and behavior of homogeneous sub segments of the target population. Based on these personas we identified a set of system requirements. The identified requirements led to a set of functionalities (services) that eWALL must support and a home/cloud based software architecture to support them.

In designing user experience, the most important trigger towards making good decisions is an in-depth knowledge of the users. In eWALL we target elderly suffering from Chronic Obstructive Pulmonary Disease (COPD), mild dementia and age related frailty, as our primary users, as well as informal caregivers (with limited relevant medical experience), and professional care practitioners as secondary users. Fig. 3 describes the communication needs of our users such as: frequency of visits and frequency of communication cumulating: in person and remote (telephone, sms, e-mail, video conferencing) communication.

The relationships between these types of users are centered on the primary user. They are the target of eWALL therapy, coaching and assisted living services. The secondary users are trying to offer help in various ways for sustaining, improving and reinforcing eWALL's aims.

Personas are stereotypical characters that allow the stakeholders to focus the development on specific user needs and disambiguate requirements [30-32]. Through the use of personas, the functionality development is directed towards an in-depth search for the best solution for a subset of users, rather than a generalized approach with less efficiency.

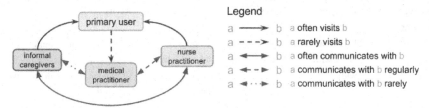

Fig. 3. A visual representation of the types of eWALL users and their complex communication needs

Our initial study resulted in the development of six primary user personas, described in Table 1. The secondary user personas consist of: a general practitioner, a visiting nurse and an informal caregiver, who is also the wife of one primary user with age related impairments.

eWALL targets three main service categories: *monitoring, coaching & training* and *healthcare support*. Monitoring allows the user to see all the tracked data relevant to her/his chronic condition, put into the context of daily life activities. The physical exercise monitoring is the main tool for tracking one's physical activity in a quantitative way. The daily activity monitoring shows daily life episodes interpreted from the user's home monitoring sensor network. Activities are chronologically ordered and separated by type. The sleep monitoring offers insights into the quality and quantity of the user's sleep (measures intervals of sleep and intervals of non-sleep during night, calculates patterns of sleep and searches for anomalous deviation from the sleeping patterns).

Coaching is essential for maintaining control over the state of the chronic condition. We approach coaching from two essential perspectives: training the body's robustness and expanding its adaptive capabilities (e.g. users with COPD will have periodic sessions of thoracic muscle training for a better ability to sustain the effort of breathing), and coaching the mind through fun games, in order to maintain a high level of cognitive stimulants.

The third service category refers to maintaining contact with other persons involved in the user's life, with the purpose of releasing the financial burden of both user, persons involved in the user's informal, or formal care and the health system itself. The *Healthcare Support* service category is designed to enable communication through various channels with informal and formal caregivers.

In order to allow these services to coexist in a coherent way, a distributed computing architecture was developed, which consists of two major components: the home, or local, component – handling sensor data capturing and low level metadata processing, as well as high level feedback and interaction with the user, and the cloud component – as well as an extremely powerful network of processing blocks and storage entities. A semantic model, called the user profile, represents all the data needed by the system.

Table 1. Overview of the six primary user persona's developed in the eWALL project [33], describing their specific domestic situation, issues and needs

Name, Age & Gender	Domestic situation	Issues	Needs
Michael 67 ♂	Living at home with wife	Hypertension, Forgetfulness, Social Anxiety, Lack of Motivation, Social Isolation, Experience with modern technology	Physical activity monitoring, Physical activity coaching, Communication with caregivers, Notifications for wellbe-
Simone 72 ♀	Lives alone, son lives far away	Reduced mobility, Social isolation, Hypertension, High cholesterol, No experience with modern technology	ing, System triggered alarms, User triggered alarms, Easy human-computer interaction

Table 1. (*Continued*)

Petra 49 ♀	Lives with husband and one daughter	COPD Stage 2, Overweight, Heavy smoker, Can't commit to physical rehabilitation programs, Experience with modern technology	Physical activity monitoring, Sleep monitoring, Physical activity coaching (breathing exercises), Communication with caregivers, Notifications for
Bob 65 ♂	Lives alone	COPD Stage 3, Ex-Smoker, Underweight, Hearing problems, Has trouble sleeping, No experience with modern technology.	wellbeing, System triggered alarms (including home air quality), User triggered alarms, Easy human-computer interaction
Jane 74 ♀	Lives alone	Cognitive decline, Memory deficits, Sleeping problems, Anxiety, Avoid social contact, No experience with modern technology	Daily functioning monitoring; Physical activity monitoring; Sleep monitoring; Cognitive training/games; Communication with caregivers; Notifications
Philip 66 ♂	Live with his younger sister	Suffered a stroke, Vision problems, Gaps in working memory, Social isolation, Low physical activity, Experience with modern technology	for wellbeing; System triggered alarms; User triggered alarms; Easy human-computer interaction

5   Scenarios and Use Cases

Within eWALL, applications are designed for different contexts of use. Context parameters are: user's geographical position, the type of task to be undertaken by the user, the type of possible interaction between user and system, the estimated time of interaction (long time interaction at home or short time interaction, when mobile). The user geographical positioning influences the feedback and input device that will provide it. We consider that interaction with the system at home allows for richer, prolonged periods of interaction, as opposed to outside interactions that are considered to be short and concise. These factors influence the type of tasks that are able to be undertaken by the primary user.

An example is contacting secondary users for additional support. Whether the primary user intends to communicate with informal, or formal caregivers, eWALL offers several ways of building messages: written messages can be typed, or handwritten, spoken messages can be exchanged through audio-visual communication applications.

Outside of the home, eWALL widgets will offer shortcuts to contacting caregivers in case of emergencies. The mobile smartphone communication functions are used in a conventional way.

COPD management involves daily physical activity as well as daily respiratory system training. eWALL supports these types of self-managing practices by offering a set of clinically validated applications including home training videos in a sequence configured by the primary user's physiotherapist [34]. During the exercise sessions, the primary user will wear a sensor that records movement and other relevant body measurements (heart rate, oxygen saturation), which will be recorded by eWALL and processed for extracting relevant information regarding the primary user's performance, within the context of therapy. The measurement data will be aggregated in easy to understand visualizations, presented by monitoring applications.

The primary user receives also messages stimulating outdoor activity [35]. In this case, the eWALL mobile device acts as a personal real-time quantifier of performance, recording the outdoor activity captured by the on-body sensor and putting it in context of the primary user's therapy and daily physical activity goals.

Mild dementia users have a number of cognitive stimulation games that engage multiple senses and train for better attention, hand-eye coordination, logical progression, etc. The games function in the home setup, using the main eWALL screen 10 finger touch recognition capabilities for a rich experience. The frequency and level of difficulty for the game therapy sessions are set up by specialized formal caregivers.

Sleep monitoring is another important factor in determining influences on the primary user's state of frailty. Bed sensors will detect and record sleeping patterns and anomalies. This data will be available for both primary end user and secondary eWALL users with proper access permissions. The eWALL home installation aggregates and interprets the information provided by the eWALL reasoners into meaningful, clear statements describing the quantity and quality of each night's sleep.

Formal caregivers will use relevant parts of the collected data for health state assessment and future therapy recommendations.

6   Conclusions

In this paper we identified the current interaction approaches in the field of smart homes as being intrusive, by following the primary user around the home [19, 21, 23], or too unobtrusive, by being placed in a fixed position inside the caring home and letting the user decide the type and time of interaction with the system. We describe our approach as a complementary mix of immovable unobtrusiveness and mobile intrusiveness according to the context of use and user's therapy needs. A distinction was made by orienting the paradigms of interaction between the user and the system towards episodes of use within the home environment and episodes of use outside.

At home, the caring systems should provide rich, longer lasting interaction possibilities between the user and the system. Feedback can be complex and with a higher degree of immersion, because the user can focus on operating with the system. This allows for complex therapy approaches and various gamification features to be implemented in the home installation application. A large surface for feedback (e.g. a large screen) can fulfill all these requirements. Complex system calculations and intelligent processing can be performed in a cloud infrastructure allowing a significant reduction of processing workload within the caring home technology and reducing infrastructure building and support efforts, as well as costs.

Outside the home, the primary user will need fast access to present context information, such as: the current status of physical activity compared to the daily goal and activity pattern, fast access to informal and formal caregivers in case of emergencies and the possibility of getting context relevant notifications. Interaction paradigms for the outside do not require an elevated degree of interaction possibilities, or immersive feedback; rather a reduced set of functionalities that allow the user to quickly react and interact briefly with the system through the smartphone.

Both outside and inside systems record and reason on sensor data and provide several types of feedback mechanisms. These systems will complement each other by generating knowledge commonly stored in the eWALL user profile. This allows devices to share information about their user seamlessly and performing a task, such as physical activity, will not be spread into home training episodes and outside training episodes, but continued by passing feedback from the home context, on the main screen to the outside context, on the smartphone and vice versa.

eWALL aims to give value and integrate commonly understood and adopted technologies (such as mobile smartphones, wearable activity sensors, positioning sensor networks, home exercise equipment, etc.) with innovative input and feedback mechanisms through novel interaction paradigms centered around the primary user needs, the context of use and the goal to be achieved. At the moment of writing, the home installation main screen, including the proxemics switch mechanism, physical activity, daily functioning, sleep monitoring applications, notifications and alarms, is in its initial prototype phase, undergoing usability tests, while the mobile software prototype is in a conceptual phase.

Acknowledgements. The work presented in this paper is being carried out in the eWALL project [33] and funded by the European Union's 7th Framework Programme. The authors would like to thank all consortium partners for their valuable contribution to this research.

References

1. Harada, C.N., Natelson Love, M.C., Triebel, K.L.: Normal cognitive aging. Clin. Geriatr. Med. **29**(4), 737–752 (2013)
2. Bianchi, L., Zuliani, G., Volpato, S.: Physical disability in the elderly with diabetes: epidemiology and mechanisms. Curr. Diab. Rep. **13**(6), 824–830 (2013)
3. Kalyani, R.R., Corriere, M., Ferrucci, L.: Age-related and disease-related muscle loss: the effect of diabetes, obesity, and other diseases. Lancet. Diabetes Endocrinol. **2**(10), 819–829 (2014)
4. Afram, B., Stephan, A., Verbeek, H., Bleijlevens, M.H.C., Suhonen, R., Sutcliffe, C., Raamat, K., Cabrera, E., Soto, M.E., Hallberg, I.R., Meyer, G., Hamers, J.P.H.: Reasons for institutionalization of people with dementia: informal caregiver reports from 8 European countries. J. Am. Med. Dir. Assoc. **15**(2), 108–116 (2014)

5. van Rooijen, M., Goedvolk, R., Houwert, T.: A vision for the Dutch health care system in 2040: towards a sustainable, high-quality health care system. World Economic Forum, McKinsey & Company (2013)
6. Mihovska, A., Kyriazakos, S.a., Prasad, R.: eWALL for active long living: Assistive ICT services for chronically ill and elderly citizens. In: IEEE Int. Conf. Syst. Man, Cybern., pp. 2204–2209 (2014)
7. King, N.: Smart home – a definition (2003). www.housingcare.org/downloads/kbase/2545.pdf
8. Jiang, L., Llu, D., Yang, B.: Smart home research. In: Third International Conference on Machine Learning and Cybernetics, Shanghai, pp. 659–663 (2004)
9. Lê, Q., Nguyen, H.B., Barnett, T.: Smart Homes for Older People: Positive Aging in a Digital World. Futur. Internet 4(4), 607–617 (2012)
10. Solaimani, S., Bouwman, H., Baken, N.: The smart home landscape: a qualitative meta-analysis. In: Abdulrazak, B., Giroux, S., Bouchard, B., Pigot, H., Mokhtari, M. (eds.) ICOST 2011. LNCS, vol. 6719, pp. 192–199. Springer, Heidelberg (2011)
11. Davidoff, S., Lee, M.K., Yiu, C., Zimmerman, J., Dey, A.K.: Principles of smart home control. In: Dourish, P., Friday, A. (eds.) UbiComp 2006. LNCS, vol. 4206, pp. 19–34. Springer, Heidelberg (2006)
12. Norman, D.A.: The Deasign of Everyday Things. First Doub. Doubleday/Curreny, New York (1990)
13. Bellotti, V., Back, M., Edwards, W.K., Grinter, R.E., Henderson, A., Lopes, C.: Making sense of sensing systems: five questions for designers and researchers. In: Proceedings of SIGCHI, vol. 1, no. 1, pp. 415–422 (2002)
14. Nehmer, J., Karshmer, A., Becker, M., Lamm, R.: Living assistance systems - an ambient intelligence approach. In: ICSE 2006, Shanghai, China (2006)
15. Rashidi, P., Mihailidis, A.: A Survey on Ambient-Assisted Living Tools for Older Adults. IEEE J. Biomed. Heal. Informatics 17(3), 579–590 (2013)
16. Bevilacqua, R., Cesta, A., Cortellessa, G., Orlandini, A., Tiberio, L.: Telepresence robot at home: a long-term case study, pp. 73–85 (2014)
17. Renteria, A., Pastor, C., Gaminde, G.: Intelligent homes to assist elderly people. In: Proceedings of International Workshop on Ambient Assisted Living, Valencia, Spain (2010)
18. Nadrag, P., Maseda, A., Grosdemouge, C., Delarue, S., Villanueva, M., Mìllàn, J.C., Hoppenot, P.: Remote control of a real robot taking into account transmission delays. In: 11th IFAC Workshop, Prague, June 7–9, 2010. doi:10.3182/20100831-4-FR-2021.00012
19. Companionable project. http://www.companionable.net/
20. Bevilacqua, R., Cesta, A., Cortellessa, G., Orlandini, A., Tiberio, L.: Telepresence Robot at Home: A Long-Term Case Study, pp. 73–85 (2014)
21. GiraffePLUS project. http://www.giraffplus.eu/
22. Pérez, J.G., Evers, V.: D6.1: Robot Roles, Personality and Interaction Behaviours. ACCOMPANY Del 6.1 Report (2013)
23. Accompany project. http://www.accompanyproject.eu/
24. Nani, M., Caleb-Solly, P., Dogramadgi, S., Fear, C., van den Heuvel, H.: MOBISERV: an integrated intelligent home environment for the provision of health, nutrition and mobility services to the elderly. In: Proc. of the 4th Companion Robotics Institute, Brussels (2010)
25. Mobiserv. http://www.mobiserv.info/

26. Panek, P., Edelmayer, G., Mayer, P., Beck, C., Rauhala, M.: User acceptance of a mobile LED projector on a socially assistive robot. In: Wichert, R., Klausing, H. (eds.) Ambient Assisted Living. 6. AAL-Kongress 2013, Berlin, Germany. Springer Science & Business Media, pp. 77–91 (2013). ISBN 3642379885
27. Long lasting memories. http://www.longlastingmemories.eu/
28. Gärtner, L.: Siemens smart home solutions agenda – siemens smart home. In: Totally Integrated Home Conference, Brussels (2006)
29. Kamel Boulos, M.N., Lou, R.C., Anastasiou, A., Nugent, C.D., Alexandersson, J., Zimmermann, G., Cortes, U., Casas, R.: Connectivity for healthcare and well-being management: examples from six European projects. Int. J. Environ. Res. Public Health 6(7), 1947–1971 (2009)
30. Van Velsen, L., Wentzel, J., Van Gemert-Pijnen, J.E.W.C.: Designing eHealth that matters via a multidisciplinary requirements development approach. JMIR Research Protocols 2(1), e21 (2013)
31. Cooper, A.: The origin of personas. Cooper Journal, May 15, 2008. http://www.cooper.com/journal/2003/08/the_origin_of_personas.html
32. Goodwin, K.: Getting from research to personas: harnessing the power of data. Cooper Journal, May 15, 2008. http://www.cooper.com/journal/2002/11/getting_from_research_to_perso.html
33. The eWALL project, funded by the European Union's Seventh Framework Programme under grant agreement no 610658 http://eWALLproject.eu/
34. Tabak, M., Brusse-keizer, M., Van Der Valk, P., Hermens, H., Vollenbroek-Hutten, M.: A telehealth program for self-management of COPD exacerbations and promotion of an active lifestyle: a pilot randomized controlled trial. Int. J. COPD, 935–944 (2014)
35. op den Akker, H., Tabak, M., Marin-Perianu, M., Huis in't Veld, M.H.A., Jones, V.M., Hofs, D.H.W., Tönis, T.M., van Schooten, B.W., Vollenbroek-Hutten, M.M.R., Hermens, H.J.: Development and evaluation of a sensor-based system for remote monitoring and treatment of chronic diseases - the continuous care & coaching platform. (Invited). In: Proceedings of the 6th International Symposium on eHealth Services and Technologies, EHST 2012, Geneva, Switzerland, pp. 19–27. SciTePress - Science and Technology Publications (2012). ISBN 978-989-8565-27-3

Assistive and Sentient Environments

Using Sensory Substitution of Median Sensory Deficits in the Traumatized Hand to Develop an Innovative Home-Based Hand Rehabilitation System

Alessandro Semere[1,2] (✉), Yohan Payan[3], Francis Cannard[4], Bruno Diot[2,5], and Nicolas Vuillerme[2,6]

[1] Plastic Hand and Burns Surgery, Grenoble University Hospital, Grenoble, France
a.semere@chu-grenoble.fr
[2] AGIM, Univ. Grenoble-Alpes, Grenoble, France
{alessandro.semere,nicolas.vuillerme}@agim.eu,
b.diot@ids-assistance.com
[3] Univ. Grenoble Alpes, CNRS, TIMC-IMAG, 38000, Grenoble, France
yohan.payan@imag.fr
[4] Texisense, Montceau-les-Mines, France
francis.cannard@texisense.com
[5] IDS, Montceau-les-Mines, France
b.diot@ids-assistance.com
[6] Institut Universitaire de France, Paris, France
nicolas.vuillerme@agim.eu

Abstract. Post-traumatic median nerve sensitive deficits are frequent. They are a source of permanent handicap that dramatically decreases the level of autonomy and the quality of life of persons suffering from these deficits. Surgical repair is possible, but the results are not always functionally useful. Therefore, prosthetic approaches do represent an alternative solution that needs to be explored. Along these lines, this paper describes an innovative home-basedhand rehabilitation systemdevice that exploits sensory substitution of median sensory deficits in the traumatized hand. It is composed of a glove bearing smart textile pressure sensors and a wristband providing vibratory biofeedback to the user. The goal of this sensory-substitution system is to provide for patients an effective method to compensate the lack of sensitivity of the finger pads and to recover a functional hand use. This innovative system is intended to be employed for assessment, training and rehabilitation exercises at home.

Keywords: Home rehabilitation · Sensory substitution · Hand trauma · Median nerve

1 Introduction

Hand traumas strike 1,400,000 patients every year in France; 620,000 of them lead to severe injuries. They are essentially caused by everyday life, occupational, and road accidents [1]. In the severe cases, sequelae are frequent. This has an important

© Springer International Publishing Switzerland 2015
A. Geissbühler et al. (Eds.): ICOST 2015, LNCS 9102, pp. 53–63, 2015.
DOI: 10.1007/978-3-319-19312-0_5

socio-economical impact: according to the FESUM (Fédération Européenne des Services d'Urgence de la Main –European Federation of Hand Emergency Services), 1/3 of the occupational accidents involve the hand, 1/4 of the lost days of work is because of these traumas, 1/10 of the accidents leads to a PPD (Permanent PartialDisability, which is an index rating the permanent handicap resulting of a trauma, after consolidation) and 1/3 of the PPD is the result of hand accidents. On average, a hand accident with a work stoppage costs from 1,000 to 2,000 euro: 80% of this amount is represented by indemnities (half by work stoppages, half by IPPs). This handicap is more important as the lesions impair fine hand use of manual workers. Hand motricity can be restored thanks to palliative interventions: nerve grafts, neurotizations and tendon transfers. Innervated digital flaps can locally restore sensitivity, but the donor site is then shorn of its function. Finally, in case of pluridigital deficit, there is no complete mean of substitution.Multi-daily sensory rehabilitation can help to recover useful (although uneven) sensitivity, but needs motivation, discipline, time and patience. Unfortunately, access to daily training with a specialist is not always possible. The lack of time of the patients or their living distance from the physiotherapy office are also obstacles to the rehabilitation. Finally, the cost of the care can quickly become exorbitant.

The work of Bach-y-Rita on sensory substitution for the blind [2] as well as the more recent scientific works on the Tongue Display Unit (TDU) for pressure ulcer prevention [3], balance problems [4] and the guiding of surgical gesture [5] have inspired the conception of an innovative device enabling to rehabilitate or to palliate these sensory deficits. Following this approach, this paper describes an innovative home-based hand rehabilitation systemdevice that exploits sensory substitution of median sensory deficits in the traumatized hand.

2   Materials and Methods

The device has been designed according to the organic facts and psychomotor theories on haptics. Its actual development was possible by the manufacture of smart textile pressure sensors [6].

2.1   Physiopathology of Hand Nervous Injuries

The hand is a complex organ. Its gripping functions are possible thanks to a perfect biomechanical structure made of bones, joints, ligaments and tendons. A two-way circuit controls these motor skills: the efferent nerve fibers command muscle contractions (motricity), the afferent nerve fibers give the central nervous system (CNS) a feedback of the force of these contractions and the actual localization of the fingers and joints in space (sensitivity), and the CNS synthesizes the inputs and outputs, coordinating the movements (integration).The three nerves carrying the efferent and afferent fibers are the median nerve, the ulnar nerve, and the radial nerve. Each of them has a different motor function and sensitive territory. The median nerve is functionally the most important to perform the bidigital grip: it innervates the flexor muscles of the fingers and the abductor muscles of the thumb, and its sensitive area covers the palmar side of the first, second, third, and radial side of the fourth finger. The sensitive and motor fibers circulate in mixed nerves. This implies that in case of complete section of a peripheral nerve, both efferent and afferent paths are interrupted. The treatment is nervesuture under optical magnifying, to restore the continuity of its channels and to guide the axonal regrowth. Nevertheless, the recovery is long and uneven. While motor skills often return to their previous level (or with a force limitationof 25% to 50%, but still functional), sensitivity is more problematic [7, 8]. Recent works specifically implicate sensitive deficits in the troubles of the function of the thumb-index grip [9]. They suggest that a loss of sensitivity leads to an alteration of the coordination of fine gestures. Actually, we can observe during prehension a degraded control of the values of the pad pressure because of the lack of feedback, which leads to an increase of the security margins [9–16], as well as an increase of the variations of these pressures of 11%-12% (vs 5%-6% for a healthy individual [10]). This implies that for light charges, objects are involuntarily dropped [10, 14]. Moreover, the displacement of the center of pressure of digital pads during fine pinch is multiplied by 5 in sensitivity troubles [10], leading to an increase of the tangential forces followed by a rotation of the object. The patient responds inappropriately by increasing his security margin, which more often can lead to the dropping of the object [10, 12].These troubles are independent of the maximal grip force of the patient, which is reduced by 25% to 35% [9, 10]. Indeed, the security margins are studied only during the manipulation of light objects (less than 500g), needing a force of 10N for a maximal force of 50N [10]. Finally, we can note that anticipation of the movement and visual control during its execution tend to normalize these results [14–15, 17], compensating the lack of touch.

2.2   Sensory Substitution

Sensory substitution is a concept introduced in the sixties by Professor Paul Bachy-Rita [18]. It consists of transforming the characteristics of one sensory modality into stimuli of another sensory modality. This has been used to restore the ability of people to perceive a certain defective sensory modality by using sensory information from a functioning sensory modality. In general, a sensory substitution device consists of one or several sensors, a coupling system and one or several stimulators. The sensor records stimuli and gives them to a coupling system that interprets these signals and transmits them to a stimulator. As stated above, the median nerve is the most important nerve implied in the fine grip, its injuries are fairly frequent, and its recovery is often poor. These facts and the literature [19, 20] led us to think that this concept of sensory substitution could be used to substitute the sensitivity of the median nerve by an artificial system, in order to improve the control of fine grip. The aim was to develop a device capable of transducing the sense of touch of this deficient area throughanother modality (true sensory substitution), or with the same modality (i.e. touch) but on another healthy localization. This needs a study of the sense of touch, together with a state of the art as concerns the existing artificial input and output systems.

There are 17 000 receptors in the glabrous hand, to sense the different types of stimuli: exteroceptive (pressure, stretching and vibrations), proprioceptive (positioning of joints in space), and thermoalgic (temperature and pain). Their stimulation is the first step of the afferent path. There are four basic types of exteroceptive receptors: Pacinian corpuscle, Meissner corpuscle, Ruffini endings and Merkel nerve endings. Each of them has a different response latency to stimuli (fast adaptive fibers FA or slow adaptive fibers SA), a variable pressure threshold, and various numbers of sensitive endings and depth under the skin [21]. This makes them more or less sensitive to pressure discrimination, spatial discrimination (two-point static detection), temporal discrimination (vibration), and stretching.The complexity of this system is high;it is therefore difficult to simulate precisely all of these criteria. Moreover, this is not necessarily suitable: indeed, an excessively exhaustive input information would proportionally complicate the output information. The result would be an increase of the cognitive load, hence a decrease of the accuracy and the speed of interpretation of the signal (which is exactly the opposite we aretrying to achieve). For the development of the device, we have decided that our sensors will detect only useful pressure changes with a useful spatial discrimination. This feedback is essential for grip control and shape recognition. We finally dropped the detection of stretching and vibration. The sensitivity of a hand to pressures is high. In clinical routine, it is measured with Semmes-Weinstein monofilaments (SWM), which are semi-rigid nylon threads, calibrated to bend at a precise force [22]. A normal hand has a minimal sensitivity of 0.008 gf to 0.07 gf (grams-force, 1 gf=9.80665 mN), with a spatial discrimination of 2 mm to 6 mm. Finally, the high sensitivity of the fingertips is not always needed. Indeed, some zones are functionally more important than others. The grips mostly used are the key grip (pad of the thumb and of the radial side of the index), the needle-thread grip (tip of the thumb and of the radial side of the index), the tridigital grip (thumb, index and radial side of the middle finger), the button push (index tip and pad) and the lighter (pad and tip of the thumb).

To supply a sensory feedback, all of the five senses are theoretically useful and usable. However, for our application, we needed something light and easily bearable all day long in everyday life.Sightis naturally complementary to touch, even in healthy people [23]. The evaluation of shape, volume and size of objects is done by eye control thanks to its wide receptive field, while textures are discriminated essentially by exploratory touch thanks to high vibrotactile accuracy. However, the only visual feedback about grip forces is given by the deformation or the slipping of the lifted objects, respectively translating the application of an excessive or an insufficient grip force, and leading to the breaking by fall or burst of non-deformable or fragile objects. We have decided not to implement a visual control, since it would overload this channel already sufficiently sought. Moreover, the permanent overlooking of a screen didn't seem appropriate for use in daily life. Hearingis a fast and precise modality of feedback, with great discriminatory amplitude, but we did not think that the permanent wearing of a headset would be comfortable for current use. Taste and smell are too slow, too imprecise and too variable according to physiological factors and seemed technically difficult to implement in our study.*Touch*was the first kind of feedback to be invented, and the simpler to implement. Moreover, simple and portable devices can be easily manufactured. We hence have decided to use this modality in our device.

Finally, touch can be stimulated by different kinds of devices [20].*Low frequency, low amplitude mechanical deformation*, raisingbumps against the skinand rendering a relief that can be explored by touch. One can distinguish between continuous contact with an object, and "make-and-break" contact, in which an object is brought in and out of contact with the body. The skin possesses an especially high sensitivity to the latter. For the same reason, *Vibrotactile stimulations* are also easily recognized, especially if frequencies are chosen to maximize Pacinian FA II receptor sensitivity (highest near 250Hz), and may be effectively transmitted through an air gap. *Electrotactile stimulation*excites the afferent nerves directly rather than the tactile receptors themselves, via electrodes of different types or by fine wires inserted into the skin. Variousafferent types can be excited differentially through the design of the drive signal and electrical contacts. *Force feedback* is by nature meant to access primarily the kinesthetic haptic channel. However, when force feedback devices interact with the cutaneous tactile sense, friction phenomena, vibration, or contact transients are inevitably generated. We found *thermal and air or liquid jets*displays too slow or complicated to be implemented in this project.

We decided to develop a vibrotactile device, acting as a low frequency mechanical stimulator. In other words, the variousforces sensed would be coded by variable bursts (in duration and/or in frequency) of constant high frequency vibrations.

3   Results

The device presented here is composed of three distinct elements:

(1) a glove (bearing smart textile pressure sensors),

(2) a software(receiving the data form the sensors, treating and recording the signal), and

(3) a wristband, providing vibrotactile feedback.

When the user grasps an object with his fingers, the wristband vibrates according to the pressure measured by the sensors. The sensory-impaired patient would have the possibility to use vibrotactile biofeedback to control his grip and to maintain an appropriate force to avoid the involuntary dropping of objects.

The glove(Texisense®) bears eight textile polyamide (nylon) sensors, thin-film coated with a piezo-resistive polymer (Fig. 1a). Each sensor is circular and has a 1 cm diameter. These sensors are fixed to the glove with glue and threads. They are placed on the three first fingers, four on the tip and pad on radial and ulnar sides of the thumb and two on the tip and pad on radial side of the index and middle finger. Each of them is connected to two conductive threads coated with silver. The threads run across the dorsal side of the glove, and are connected to metal buttons placed on the back of the wrist. Then, sixteen regular soft wires connect the glove to the acquisition circuit, powered by a 32 bit microcontroller unit (STM-32 Cortex from ST Microelectronics), which can be connected to a computer by a regular mini-USB to USB connection.

ST Microelectronics has provided the drivers for Microsoft Windows, which create and manage a virtual COM port between the glove and the computer. The signal acquisition and treatment software (Fig. 1b) has been written in C++ using .NET framework 3.5, with Microsoft Visual Studio 2008. It offers several basic functions to exploit the capabilities of the device. The acquisition circuit provides a 64-bit signal (8 bit from each sensor) that is recovered from a specific memory address, at a 10 Hz sampling rate. A simple mean 10-values filter has been implemented. The values of the sensors can be displayed in raw state or converted to Newtons (N) or to grams-force.The values for each sensor are displayed in real time in eight textboxes, as well as their minima and maxima. They are also visualized on dynamic .NET windows forms bars. Finally, a color graph (realized using the open source zedGraph library [24]) shows the curves of evolution of these values compared to the maxima. The values can be stored to a .txt file in realtime, raw or converted. Finally, to keep the useful values to control the feedbackonly, two operations are successively executed: (1) a threshold of 278 gf is applied to each value (each sensor exceeding the threshold being considered as "activated"), and (2) the mean value of the "activated" sensors is calculated.

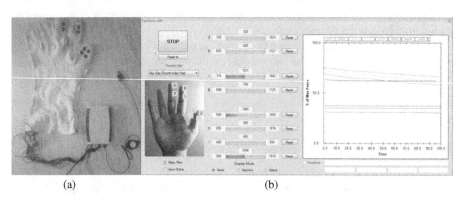

(a)   (b)

Fig. 1. The glove (a) and the signal acquisition and treatment software (b)

The feedback system is composed of a rubber and plastic wristband, containing an eccentric-mass brush motor and an USB motor controller. A Bluetooth vibrating wristband for mobile phones (MB20, Movon®) has been disassembled to keep only the motor (1.3 V, 70 mA, 9000-12000 rpm), and a serial resistor (100 Ohm, 1% tolerance) has been added. The power is provided by a 6V external stabilized transformer, via a modified USB cable.The control unit is an USB commercial motor controller (PhidgetMotorControl LV 1060, Phidgets®), powered by USB, and able to control the acceleration and velocity of the low-voltage brush motor thanks to the provided C++ librairies. Bursts of vibrating impulses are generated to provide vibrotactile feedback. The vibrotactile stimulation is absent if the mean value of the activated sensors is lower than 278 gf, becomes continuous if between 278 gf and 555 gf, then alternating gradually slower with the increase of the pressure. Over 1390 gf, the frequency of alternation is slow and constant.

We calibrated the sensors with an electronic precision scale (Mettler PE 1600, Max 1600g, Min 5g, e=0.1g, dd=0.01g),a laboratory articulated chassis, with an infra-millimetric manual movement control, anda metal cylindrical piece (diameter = 8mm), isolated at its tip by a rubber band. Each sensor has been put on the balance and under the cylindrical piece. A piece of wood has been put under and inside the glove. This avoids short-circuits between the sensors, the threads and the balance board. After putting the balance to zero, the cylindrical part was progressively lowered, until the desired force was obtained. These forces have been obtained by the conversion of the forces F (in gf) given by SWM in pressures P (Pa), by the formula P=F/S, where S is the surface of the section of the SWM given by the literature [25]. Then, each pressure value has been converted to a force value considering the section of the 8 mm diameter cylindrical metal piece. Finally, the raw value displayed by the software was then reported in a table. The raw curves have been drawn, and the equations of mean root square deviation lines have been calculated (Fig. 2). The latter are used by the software to convert the raw values to grams-force and to Newtons. The evolution after constant stimulation (278 gf) has been measured, to look for the implication of this mixed effect in time (Fig. 3). After one minute, the evolution is negligible (Maximum = 2.7%).

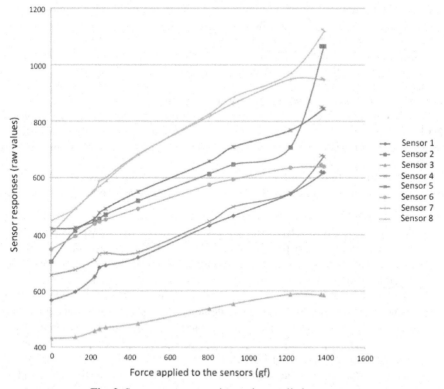

Fig. 2. Sensor responses to increasing applied pressures

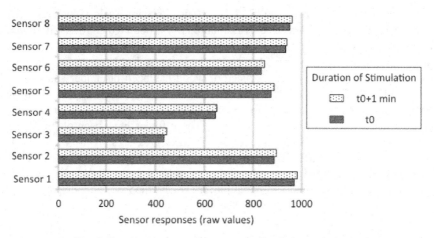

Fig. 3. Sensor responsesafter constant stimulation to 278 gf

4   Discussion

The presented work described an innovative home-based hand rehabilitation system device. It is composed of a glove bearing smart textile pressure sensors and a wristband providing vibratory biofeedback to the user that could be employed for training and rehabilitation exercises at home. This device exploits the concept of sensory substitution of median sensory deficits in the traumatized hand.It is designed to provide for patients an effective method to rehabilitate orto compensate the lack of sensitivity of the finger pads and to recover a functional hand use.

By showing that this device is actually able to sense a pressure and to send a vibrotactile feedback to the user, our results are encouraging and promising. However, because of several issues encountered during the development, several improvements still have to be introduced.

Indeed, while at first sight we could observe a linear relationship between forces and values returned, a more accurate analysis could have shownsome unwanted fluctuations.

- *Mixed piezo-resistive effect:* The sensors are made of fine knit polyamide fibers coated with a piezo-resistive polymer. Like any other piezo-resistive device, the resistance of the sensors decreases with the mechanical stress. This works on the principle of the tension divider bridge. However, these fibers have a far more complex behavior. The force applied on them is distributed considering their geometry, their type of knit, the tightening... The fibers being conductive and deformable, the squeezing increases the surface contact and decreases the resistance independently from the piezo-resistive effect. This mixture of effects implicates that the response of the sensors can only be approached by calibration. Another observation is that the raw value of the sensors, once stimulated and released, drops under the baseline level and progressively rises to return to its starting point. This is probably due to the hysteresis of the fibers, behaving like an elastic body.

- *Manufacture problems:* Each sensor is handmade so individual behavior is rather unpredictable. Moreover, the sensitivity seems to vary with the amount of glue used in the manufacturing. They are also fixed with a different amount of turns of conductive threads. This explains their variousprofiles of response, and the need for an individual calibration. Also, button connectors are loosely fixed to the glove and their movements and short-circuits cause variations and sudden drops of the sensed values. They tend to decrease the repeatability of the measurements. The measure of the varioussensors has been done several times with no load. The result was variable, and some sensors have a more reliable response than others (Fig. 4a). The best sensor has a standard deviation of 6.8 (M=871,6, less than 1%) and the worst 56.3 (M = 553,9, over 10%). This has been repeated with a charge of 278 gf with similar results (Fig 4b).

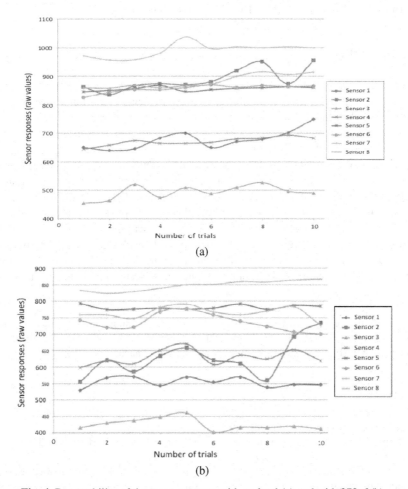

(a)

(b)

Fig. 4. Repeatability of the measurements with no load (a) and with 278gf (b)

- *Calibration method:* The precision of the setup for calibration could be questionable. While the pressure measured is digitally precise, the application of the force is not. With the above setup, the pressureapplied on the sensors is manually modified, and the observer reads and writes down the value. There is no digital synchronization between the device and the calibration system.

Finally, the feedback system has been manufactured with simple and low-cost materials for rapid proof-of-concept purposes. The stimulator needed a minimal discrimination level, to make the difference between "contact" and "no contact". The threshold level has been put to 278 gf, which corresponds to the lower precision of force detection of a normal hand (reported to a 8 mm diameter section). The decision has been taken to have the better compromise between noise and useful signal, but no systematic assessment has been done.Theevaluation of the most efficient vibrotactile pattern for discrimination is included in our immediate plans.

5   Conclusion

Home-based rehabilitation is increasingly used to improve compliance program and to reduce health-care costs. Along these, we have presented here innovative vibrotactile sensory substitution in hand sensitive deficits for hand home-based rehabilitation. Although some technical aspects (e.g., calibration of the sensors)still need to be further studied and developed, these preliminary results are very encouraging. The ultimate aim of this device is to empower the patients in their own rehabilitation, allowing them to become the major players of their healing. They could plan the training sessions at home according to their time schedule and adjust their exercises according to their pain and tiredness, without the need to physically move to the hospital or to the physiotherapy office. In the future, medical doctors and physiotherapist could also propose some rehabilitation programs and check the efficacy and treatment compliance of a home-based rehabilitation program, as well as the improvements made by their patients through a connected interface (so to quickly adapt the training protocol).

Acknowledgments. This work was supported in part by funding by IDS company, TIMC-IMAG Laboratory, the French national program "programme d'Investissements d'Avenir IRT Nanoelec" ANR-10-AIRT-05, and Institut Universitaire de France.

References

1. Livre Blanc de la FESUM (1998). http://www.gem-sfcm.org
2. Bach-y-Rita, P.: Sensory substitution and the human-machine interface. Trends Cogn. Sci. (Regul. Ed.) **7**(12), 541–546 (2003)
3. Chenu, O., Vuillerme, N., Demongeot, J., Payan, Y.: A wireless lingual feedback device to reduce overpressures in seated posture: a feasibility study. PLoS One **4**(10), e7550 (2009)
4. Vuillerme, N., et al.: Sensory supplementation system based on electrotactile tongue biofeedback of head position for balance control. Neurosci. Lett. **431**(3), 206–210 (2008)

5. Robineau, F., Boy, F., Orliaguet, J.P., Demongeot, J., Payan, Y.: Guiding the surgical gesture using an electro-tactile stimulus array on the tongue: a feasibility study. IEEE Trans. Biomed. Eng. **54**(4), 711–717 (2007)
6. Chenu, O., Vuillerme, N., Bucki, M., Diot, B., Cannard, F., Payan, Y.: TexiCare: An innovative embedded device for pressure ulcer prevention. Preliminary results with a paraplegic volunteer. J. Tissue Viability **22**, 83–90 (2013)
7. Najeb, Y., Trafeh, M.: Résultats de la réparation primaire des plaies du nerf médian et du nerf ulnaire au poignet. Chir Main (2009)
8. Lenoble, E., Vilain, R.: Résultats de la réparation primaire de vingt- huit plaies isolées du nerf médian au poignet. Ann Chir Main **8**(4), 347–351 (1989)
9. Witney, A., et al.: The cutaneous contribution to adaptive precision grip. Trends Neurosci. **27**(10), 637–643 (2004)
10. Dun, S., et al.: Lower median nerve block impairs precision grip. J. Electromyogr. Kinesiol. **17**(3), 348–354 (2007)
11. Schenker, M., et al.: Precision grip function after hand replantation and digital nerve injury. J. Plast. Reconstr. Aesthet. Surg. **59**(7), 706–716 (2006)
12. Li, Z.M., Nimbarte, A.D.: Peripheral median nerve block impairs precision pinch movement. Clin. Neurophysiol. **117**(9), 1941–1948 (2006)
13. Monzée, J., et al.: The effects of digital anesthesia on force control using a precision grip. J. Neurophysiol. **89**(2), 672–683 (2003)
14. Augurelle, A.S., et al.: Importance of cutaneous feedback in maintaining a secure grip during manipulation of hand-held objects. J. Neurophysiol. **89**(2), 665–671 (2003)
15. Hermsdörfer, D.A., et al.: Grip force control during object manipulation in cerebral stroke. Clin. Neurophysiol. **114**(5), 915–929 (2003)
16. Nowak, D.A., Hermsdörfer, D.A.: Selective deficits of grip force control during object manipulation in patients with reduced sensibility of the grasping digits. Neurosci. Res. **47**(1), 65–72 (2003)
17. Nowak, D.A., et al.: Moving objects with clumsy fingers: how predictive is grip force control in patients with impaired manual sensibility? Clin. Neurophysiol. **114**(3), 472–487 (2003)
18. Bach-y-Rita, P., et al.: Vision substitution by tactile image projection. Nature **221**, 963–964 (1969)
19. Massimino, M.J.: Improved force perception through sensory substitution. Control Eng. Pract. **3**(2), 215–222 (1995)
20. Visell, Y.: Tactile sensory substitution: Models for enaction in HCI. Interact. Comput. **21**(1–2), 38–53 (2009)
21. Lederman, S.J., Browse, R.A.: The physiology and psychophysics of touch. Sensors and sensory systems for advanced robots. NATO ASI Series **43**, 71–91 (1988)
22. Spicher, C.: Manuel de rééducation sensitive du corps humain. Médecine & Hygiène, Geneva (2003)
23. Whitaker, T.A., et al.: Vision and touch: Independent or integrated systems for the perception of texture? Brain Res. **1242**(C), 59–729 (2008)
24. Sourceforge. http://sourceforge.net/projects/zedgraph
25. Bell-Krotoski, J.: The repeatability of testing with Semmes-Weinstein monofilaments. J. Hand Surg. (1987)

QueFaire: Context-Aware in-Person Social Activity Recommendation System for Active Aging

Victor Ponce[✉], Jean-Pierre Deschamps, Louis-Philippe Giroux,
Farzad Salehi, and Bessam Abdulrazak

Université de Sherbrooke, 2500, boul. de l'Université, Sherbrooke, QC, Canada
{Victor.Ponce,Bessam.Abdulrazak}@USherbrooke.ca

Abstract. Active life style promotes healthy aging, and participation in social and physical activities improves aging people well-being. Nowadays, new media sources advertise large number of activities and for all age categories. These medias, however, are not adapted to the aging population. The paper presents a context-aware in-person social activity recommendation system for aging people named QueFaire. QueFaire interprets natural language descriptions of activities in social media and proposes suitable activities to aging people using fuzzy logic engine, taking in consideration user-profile and contextual information. Moreover, QueFaire provides support to help reach the location of a social activity.

Keywords: Social · Physical · Activity · Aging · Context-aware · Adaptation · Profile · Preferences · Recommendation · Assistance · Fuzzy logic · Natural language processing

1   Introduction

Aging is a process associated with cognitive and physiological decline, which causes activity limitations and participation restrictions [16]. While aging, people become less active and more prone to social isolation and loneliness, which complicates their health situation and causes premature mortality [5, 7, 21, 24, 25, 31, 35]. Participation in social and physical activities, however, results in lower risk of cognitive decline (e.g., dementia) [14, 34] and improves aging people well-being [22]. Physical activity slows down progression of diseases, and it is in general a promoter of health [26]. Increasing participation in social activities improves cognitive abilities for aging people [6, 7, 19, 36], and consequently leads to higher Quality of Life (QoL) [32]. Therefore, a key goal of active aging initiatives around the world is maintaining autonomy and independency of people as they age[1]. According to the lifestyle of Blue Zone people (people with the highest longevity in the world) physical and social activities are associated with a healthier and longer life [11].

---

[1] World Health Organisation, WHO | What is "Active Aging"?,
www.who.int/ageing/active_ageing/en/

© Springer International Publishing Switzerland 2015
A. Geissbühler et al. (Eds.): ICOST 2015, LNCS 9102, pp. 64–75, 2015.
DOI: 10.1007/978-3-319-19312-0_6

Active aging becomes more serious because the number of aging people is increasing constantly around the world. Due to the advantages of performing social and physical activities, communities and professionals are promoting non-technological solutions and services to increase activities among aging population and to promote healthy aging [9, 15, 29].

Social media has changed the way people interact with each other in the last decade. Web, Email, and social networks (like Facebook and Twitter) have changed the way younger people are communicating with each other. Moreover, many government services are now offered on Internet. Many people are taking advantage of these online services, which are faster and more accessible. Different communities are increasing their public participation using social media [18]. According to Buettner et al and Cohen-mansfield et al. [11, 12] there are many benefits for using technology for aging people including: psychological benefits (such as increasing of independence, self-respect, and acceptance in society) and fiscal benefits (relieving personal care cost). On the other hand, there are several ICT initiatives trying to promote healthier and more active lifestyle. Nevertheless, studies show that people over 65 years of age are excluded from this digital revolution [8]. Literature review also reveals that most of the ICT systems are designed for younger generations. Adapting solutions to aging people and their needs is a fact to be addressed [1]. We believe that, context-awareness tools can help building solutions to be more adaptive to aging people.

We present in this paper QueFaire, a context-aware in-person social activity recommendation system for aging people. QueFaire interprets natural language descriptions of activities in social media, and proposes suitable list of activities to aging people using fuzzy logic engine (based on user-profile and contextual information). In addition, QueFaire provides support to help reach the location of activities.

The rest of the paper is organized as follows. Section 2 reviews existing approaches promoting activities. Section 3 introduces the design and the concept of QueFaire. Section 4 discusses implementation of QueFaire. Section 5 presents results of preliminary evaluation of QueFaire. Finally, Section 6 concludes the paper and discusses future work.

2   Related Work

Numerous research efforts and Internet-based applications have been proposed for promoting people activities. We can classify existing related work into three categories: Gerontechnological, context-aware, and social media solutions.

2.1   Gerontechnological Systems for Promoting Activities

The gerontechnological category includes few solutions specifically designed for aging people, and well adapted to the aging people needs. *MELCO*[2] is an ICT system that targets aging people who are still able to have an independent life. Its main goal is to increase the social activity of aging people and monitor their health at the same time. The system enables to build a virtual social network among people, their families, and

---

[2]   MELCO project (Mobile Elderly Living Community): www.melco.cs.ucy.ac.cy

friends. Through a mobile phone application people are offered different prerecorded social activities in an outdoor environment [23, 33]. *Co-living³* aims to build an *"ICT-based Virtual Collaborative Social Living Community for aging People"* which promotes active living and independency. Its target group is aging people who are still active and live independently. The system is used in an extended care facility for aging people. It is composed of a virtual social network and a client application on tablet. Activities are promoted through this social network. *Playful* [30] is another existing activity promoting system that offers a solution to increase physical and social activities. The system is designed for aging people living in a care facility. Independently living aging people can use this system as well. Playful enables to register the most common activities performed and preferred by aging people, which help caregivers planning physical and social activities for a week. Each resident receives a list of planned activities via a weekly newspaper. The list is also displayed in different locations of the care facility. A light next to each display is switched on for a short time to remind aging people of a coming activity [30].

To conclude this subsection, the few existing gerontechnological solutions fit well for aging people's needs, however they are heavily depending on the activities entered in the system by administrators or caregivers. They do not support automated sources of activity, which limits the proposed activity list to the proposed environment (mainly care facilities).

2.2   Context-Aware Systems for Promoting Activities

Numerous solutions aim at increasing physical activities of regular users and reduce the risks of chronic diseases (e.g. Motivate, NEAT-o-Game, UbiFit). These solutions are not designed specifically for aging people, and use minimal and restricted contextual information. As an example, *Motivate* [20] is a context-aware system that provides advice for participation in physical activities. The contextual information is used in order to provide the right advice at the right time for user. The information includes user-profile, location, weather, environment (e.g. at home), time and agenda. The system includes 34 pieces of advice for physical activities. Each piece consists of a process and a template. Process is a set of if-then rules. These rules define which constraints must be met for the advice to be selected and presented to the user. Once a piece of advice is selected then a tailored message for the user is created based on the template. Rare are the systems designed for aging people. *Flowie* [4] is a system similar to Motivate. It is a virtual coach, in the shape of an animated flower, used to motivate aging people to walk more in order to reach a walking goal.

2.3   Promoting Activities on Social Media

Social media are among the most promising ICT that can promote activities in social networks and increase activity level of aging people. These media enable easy grouping of people and sharing information. Young people have been using these media (e.g. Facebook, Google+) in the last decade to boost their social life and increase ambient-awareness. The drawback of these media is that it promotes a sedentary life

---

³ Co-Living: http://project-coliving.eu

style, focusing mainly on activity in the virtual media [10, 17]. Such activities reduce in-person social participations and face-to-face interactions between people (i.e. not through virtual mediums like social networks). An example of in-person social activity could be going outdoor to meet a person face to face, while virtual social activity could be staying at home and communicate with a person by phone (over a medium). Generally speaking, social media can boost aging people's social activity, however their use by this population is still limited due to the non-adaptation of the proposed tools to the needs and abilities of aging people.

To conclude the related work, existing solutions related to promoting activities for aging people are limited, lack integration of the diverse of activities on social media/online communities and lack mechanisms to personalize the recommended activities according to user-profile. The personalization aspect is important for aging people because of decline associated with the aging process. In order to achieve active aging and consequently improve QoL of aging people, it is important to promote suitable in-person social activities.

3   QueFaire Approach

QueFaire is our attempt to promote personalized suitable activities for aging people. Our approach is based on analyzing user-profile and preferences to recommend the most appropriate activities among those advertised in social media and on the Web. QueFaire system operates via three phases: 1) Integrate and classify activities from social media; 2) Recommend activities based on user-profile; and 3) Support user to reach an activity.

QueFaire design includes a combination of models and software techniques focused on simplifying the decision-making for the end-user, as well as providing a support for attending activities. The two important aspects of our concept are: the representation of the profile of aging people (e.g., characteristics, needs, preferences) as context [3] and the hierarchical categorization of activities according to user-profile.

The diverse activity representations on social media/internet are always linked to the language of the person who models or uploads the data. Classifying these activities is challenging and requires and adequate tools that can deal with natural language descriptions. QueFaire user-profile modeling includes numerous context data related to users that may affect the activity choice (e.g. date of birth, sex, health conditions and additional characteristics of the person). When the user requires an activity recommendation, a fuzzy logic based reasoning engine infers the appropriate categories of activities for this user, and presents a list of recommended activities by predilection. The inference is based on a user-profile represented as soft constraints [13], correlating with available activities gathered from social media. When the user selects a recommended activity, the system presents selected detailed information gathered from the social media source provider. If the information contains accessible locations, QueFaire proposes a Maps area with the Geographic Information System (GIS) functionalities to assist the user to reach the desired activity (Fig. 1). The assistance is based on the context data (e.g., location) gathered from the platform.

Main Screen   **Activity**   **Map**

Fig. 1. Illustration of use case. Activity recommendations and support facilities

4 Software Architecture of QueFaire

QueFaire architecture (Fig. 2) includes three main components: (1) *Activity Integrator (AI)*, (2) *Activity Selector (AS)*, and (3) *End-user Client (EUC)*. AI used to collect activities from social media sources, process them and send them to AS for later use. AS processes the AI gathered activities, classifies them using NLP, infers the appropriate categories of activities based on user-profile using fuzzy logic engine. EUC is an interactive application enabling aging people to manage their user-profile, request activity, receive a list of recommended activities, choose an activity and receive assistance if needed.

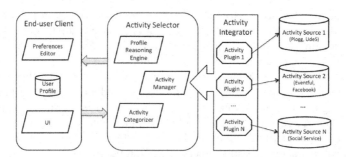

Fig. 2. QueFaire software architecture

The QueFaire prototype is implemented in a client-server architecture style with an Object-Oriented programming paradigm. AS, AI Plugins and related services are implemented as a Java server.

4.1 Activity Integrator (AI)

AI collects activities from social media sources, and integrates these activities through plugins (e.g. RSS, API, Web Service). Due to the various representation of activity on social media, each plugin is responsible for a specific source (e.g. Facebook, Eventful,

Plogg). The plugin parses activities from a source, integrating them into our QueFaire standard format for later use. Each plugin includes a mechanism to manage the frequency of collecting information, enabling the optimization of the load based on the updated frequency of a social media source.

4.2 End-User Client (EUC)

QueFaire is one application extension of our PhonAge mobile platform for aging people [2]. QueFaire prototype version runs on android mobile platform (A web version is under development). EUC enables aging people to be in control and manage their profile and contextual information. For privacy issue, user-profile (including characteristics, needs, preferences) is stored only on EUC. User data are exchanged with AS on request only. Each time the user requests an activity recommendation, EUC sends end-user-profile needed data and the contextual information (e.g. location) to AS. AS processes the request and sends the list of recommendations and the related data to the EUC. The most important part of the EUC is the friendly-designed interface (Fig. 1) that enables aging people to manage their profiles. From the main screen, the user can consult the list of recommended activities, access contextual location information, or request/receive assistance if needed. Once an activity is selected, EUC shows detailed information and a map API with the activity location. User can visualize the exact location on a map using GIS functionalities (e.g. zoom). Furthermore, EUC also assists user to reach the activity location. EUC utilizes the mobile GPS (if available on the device) to get the current geographical position of the device, and then contact the Maps API to calculate the best route for either driving or walking to reach the activity location (based on the profile). Then, the mobile application displays both location on an interactive map and navigation instructions on the same screen, allowing the user to reach the activity location by following the instructions.

4.3 Activity Selector (AS)

AS components process activities gathered by AI and classify them using NLP, as well as, infer the appropriate categories of activities using fuzzy logic. AS correlates the available activities with the selected categories, generating a classified recommendation for possible activities in which to participate. The main components of AS are: Activity Manager, Activity Categorizer and Profile Reasoning Engine.

Activity Manager (AM):
AM manages the integration and the classification of activities, as well as storage of the available activities gathered from social media sources.

Activity Categorizer (AC):
AC utilizes the Natural Language Processing (NLP) of Apache OpenNLP engine[4]. It classifies activities gathered from social media sources in correlation with user-profile. The NLP engine maximum entropy model [27, 28] determines the occur-

---

[4] Apache OpenNLP engine available on https://opennlp.apache.org

rence probability of each *activity category* (linguistic Classes) given the *attributes* of all activities (linguistic context). The result is a likelihood score per Class of activity. The score determines the optimal solution that satisfies linguistic constraints and maximizing the following conditional entropy H.

$$H(p) = -\sum_{x \in \mathcal{E}} p(x) \log p(x)$$

$$score = \underset{p \in P}{\mathrm{argmax}}\, H(p)$$

$$x = (c, a), c \in Classes, a \in Attributes\ of\ activity$$

Where:
- x is the individual assessment of the linguistic closeness of each category of activity c to the available attribute a gathered by the Activity Integrator (AI).
- $\mathcal{E} = C \times A$ is the space of all $(Classes, Attributes)$, and
- P is the assessed set of consistent probability models.

Social media web providers classify the activities in various sorts. An activity can belong to several sorts. We create an equivalence of categories between sorts, establishing standard categories. For example, the category "outdoors" (linguistic Class) corresponds to the sorts "attractions," "recreation," "outdoors," etc. Our NLP model defines the categories that correspond to the analyzed sources for the Activity Integrator (AI). We also used these sources as the training data set, querying the information of current activities. The prototype considers the title and description as information in the linguistic context as well as maintains the scores arranged by highest likelihood value (best categories for the activity).

Moreover, we developed a script to generate linguistic Classes of activities and train data set, in order to automate and speed up the process for the system re-training. The script enables the system to consider further details of activities in the linguistic context, such as time, location, and languages. The script also facilitates the adaptation of different linguistic Classes of activities defined in different social media sources.

Profile Reasoning Engine (PRE):
PRE utilizes jFuzzyLite fuzzy logic Engine [5]. The engine analyzes the recorded user-profile, and proposes the appropriate categories of activities. User-profile information consists of a fuzzy set of attributes of the Type $Profile = (attribute, value)$. The process starts pre-processing the attributes, and normalizing the values. Then, the fuzzy logic controller engine applies the rules for analyzing the data. Finally, the engine produces the fuzzy reasoning results, including threshold values. The threshold enables interpreting user's data in different ways, e.g. common activities, predilection or dislike of activities, as well as, advanced functionalities such as: learning from preferences. Our prototype proposes appropriate activities ordered by predilection,

---

[5] jFuzzyLite fuzzy logic engine available on www.fuzzylite.com/java/

based on the configuration of the fuzzy logic engine. Our configuration of the fuzzy logic engine includes the model of the inputs (attributes of the profile) and output (inferred categories of activities), in addition to the controller itself, with parameters and rules for the engine. The inputs are modeled for each attribute of the profile and preferences, using different linguistic term mathematical functions. The prototype utilizes basic terms such as triangular, s-shape, z-shape and ramp functions. The output is modeled as a linear function of the form:

Classification Function:

$$Output \ (category \ of \ activity) \ = a_1 x_1 \oplus a_2 x_2 \oplus ... \oplus a_n x_n + c$$

Where xi is an attribute of the Profile, c is a constant that represents the weight of each activity category, ai is a constant value 1 (means that this attribute has to be considered for this category) or 0 (otherwise). The controller includes the parameters of configuration and the definition of logic rules. The fundamental parameters are related to the activation and accumulation of rules, handling the conjunction and disjunction in rules, and processing the result (defuzzification). The prototype uses the algebraic product for conjunction and activation, the algebraic sum for disjunction and accumulation, and the weighted average to calculate the result.

5   Preliminary Evaluation Results

We evaluate QueFaire performance of the classifying process (on the server). We started by simulating a profile of an aging people. Followed by integration of activities from different three social media sources [[S1)] University of Sherbrooke Cultural Center[6], [S2)]Eventful[7], and [S3)]Plogg[8]]. After, the classification of activities and recommendation of suitable activities was assessed. The user is over 65 years old with basic mobility and no predilection (level = 0) for business activities, low predilection (level = 1) for activities that are related to dating and education; more predilection (level=2) for religion, more predilection (level = 3) for civic, volunteering and exercise; and the highest predilection (level = 4) is for leisure activities.

Three plugins linked to three social media sources were implemented: RSS based for S1-S3 and API based for S2. At the evaluation time, the three sources (S1, S2 and S3) have 395 possible activities to be considered (85, 300 and 10 activities respectively). The system assigns (in NLP) scores for each category of activities for all gathered activities. The training data set enables classifying of 28 categories.

An activity category collected form media sources may differ from QueFaire categories, e.g. when there is a new category in a social media source, or because of the precision of training data set. To overcome this problem (without re-training), QueFaire system considers the two categories of activities with the highest score.

---

[6] University of Sherbrooke Cultural Center website www.centreculureludes.ca
[7] Eventful website http://eventful.com
[8] Plogg website http://plogg.ca

We present in Fig. 3 a comparison of the performance of the classification process for the activities gathered from each source. The execution time for gathering activities from social media sources is disregarded for the evaluation because it depends on external variables such as the available resources to access to the repository, the protocol for accessing and the format of the data. The classification process depends on the number of activities to analyze and the description of each activity (where the NLP maximum entropy algorithm realizes the linguistic analysis).

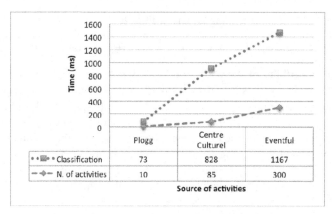

Fig. 3. Performance of activities classification process.

QueFaire recommends activities by proceeding as follows. The reasoning engine analyzes the profile and preferences and returns the selected categories of activities based on the Classification Function (4.3). The engine also assigns a degree of activation, representing the ranking of predilection for each category of activities, with a higher value for the categories that are more likeable by user. The results are 14 of 28 recommended categories of activities for this user (Table 1).

Table 1. Recommended categories of activities sorted by order of likeability

Order	Activity	Degree of likeability
1	Films	0.87200
2	Food	0.84000
3	Holiday	0.80000
4	Spirituality	0.40000
5	Technology	0.20000
6	Arts	0.20000
7	Education	0.20000
8	Science	0.20000
9	Literary	0.20000
10	Politics	0.11946
11	Fundraisers	0.09671
12	Health	0.08533
13	Galleries	0.02844
14	Museums	0.02844

Considering the 14 categories, the system recommends 100 possible activities to consider for participation (reducing from 395 without recommendation). In addition, QueFaire enables the user to configure the system such that it recommends only the top n suitable categories of activities, which decreases the total number of recommended activities. For example, the system returns 26 activities for the category Films (the most suitable according to the user-preferences/profile). The system recommends categories of activities that require mobility, for the user in this example according to his profile (basic mobility), such as visiting galleries or museums, but these activities have a lower degree of likeability (below top 4) and the number of recommended events are less than 15. The execution time of the recommendation process is not part of our evaluation section because it depends on the reasoning engine and the total number of available activities.

6   Conclusion and Future Directions

We present in this paper QueFaire, a context-aware in-person social activity recommendation system for aging people. QueFaire interprets natural language descriptions of activities in social media, and proposes suitable list of activities to aging people based on their profile and contextual information. QueFaire also provides support for aging people to reach the location of an in-person social activity.

Since social media advertises a large number of various activities, for all age categories, our goal is to use QueFaire system to encourage aging people to perform and increase their social activities, by recommending the most suitable activities that correspond to them. The architecture of QueFaire considers the dynamism of social media in several aspects, such as the integration of different sources for activities, the frequency of gathering activities and the natural language descriptions of activities. Furthermore, we are working on extending the system, including additional activity sources, and consolidating different types of activity linguistic details, e.g., time, language, cost. The aim is to create a comprehensive formal activity description (profile of activities) for aging people. We believe that processing more activity details in the selection process will enable to define more fine-grained rules, increase the precision of the recommendation, and consequently better meet aging people's needs.

We believe that QueFaire is an important and essential step to promote active aging, and consequently improves quality of life of aging people. Our team is working on the second version of QueFaire that is going to be ecologically evaluated in our city.

References

1. Abdulrazak, B., Malik, Y.: Review of challenges, requirements, and approaches of pervasive computing system evaluation. IETE Tech. Rev. **29**(6), 506 (2012)
2. Abdulrazak, B., Malik, Y., Arab, F., Reid, S.: PhonAge: adapted smartphone for aging population. In: Biswas, J., Kobayashi, H., Wong, L., Abdulrazak, B., Mokhtari, M. (eds.) ICOST 2013. LNCS, vol. 7910, pp. 27–35. Springer, Heidelberg (2013)

3. Abdulrazak, B., Roy, P., Gouin-Vallerand, C., Belala, Y., Giroux, S.: Micro Context-Awareness for Autonomic Pervasive Computing. International Journal of Business Data Communications and Networking 7(2), 48–68 (2011)
4. Albaina, I.M., Visser, T., van der Mast, C.A.P.G., Vastenburg, M.H.: Flowie: a persuasive virtual coach to motivate elderly individuals to walk. In: International ICST Conference on Pervasive Computing Technologies for Healthcare, ICST, pp. 1–7 (2009)
5. Alspach, J.G.: Loneliness and social isolation: risk factors long overdue for surveillance. Crit. Care Nurse 33(6), 8–13 (2013)
6. Barnes, L.L.: Mendes de Leon, C.F., Wilson, R.S., Bienias, J.L., Evans, D.A., Social resources and cognitive decline in a population of older African Americans and whites. Neurology 63(12), 2322–2326 (2004)
7. Bassuk, S.S., Glass, T.A., Berkman, L.F.: Social Disengagement and Incident Cognitive Decline in Community-Dwelling Elderly Persons. Ann. Intern. Med. 131(3), 165–173 (1999)
8. Bolton, M.: Older people, technology and community: the potential of technology to help older people renew or develop social contacts and to actively engage in their communities, Independent Age, London (2010)
9. Bouma, H.: Gerontechnology. IOS Press, Amsterdam (1992)
10. Brewer, J., Williams, A., Dourish, P.: Nimio: an ambient awareness device. In: Proc. of ECSCW 2005 (2005)
11. Buettner, D.: The blue zones: lessons for living longer from the people who've lived the longest. National Geographic Society, Washington, D.C. (2009)
12. Cohen-Mansfield, J., Biddison, J.: The Scope and Future Trends of Gerontechnology: Consumers' Opinions and Literature Survey. J. Technol. Hum. Serv. 25(3), 1–19 (2007)
13. Domshlak, C., Hüllermeier, E., Kaci, S., Prade, H.: Preferences in AI: An overview. Artif. Intell. 175(7), 1037–1052 (2011)
14. Fratiglioni, L., Wang, H.X., Ericsson, K., Maytan, M., Winblad, B.: Influence of social network on occurrence of dementia: a community-based longitudinal study. Lancet 355(9212), 1315–1319 (2000)
15. Hagan, R., Manktelow, R., Taylor, B.J., Mallett, J.: Reducing loneliness amongst older people: a systematic search and narrative review. Aging Ment. Health 18(6), 683–693 (2014)
16. Helal, A., Mokhtari, M., Abdulrazak, B.: The Engineering Handbook of Smart Technology for Aging, Disability, and Independence. Wiley, Hoboken (2008)
17. Kaplan, A.M.: If you love something, let it go mobile: Mobile marketing and mobile social media 4x4. Bus. Horiz. 55(2), 129–139 (2012)
18. Kaplan, A.M., Haenlein, M.: Users of the world, unite! The challenges and opportunities of Social Media. Bus. Horiz. 53(1), 59–68 (2010)
19. Krueger, K.R., Wilson, R.S., Kamenetsky, J.M., Barnes, L.L., Bienias, J.L., Bennett, D.A.: Social engagement and cognitive function in old age. Exp. Aging Res. 35(1), 45–60 (2009)
20. Lin, Y., Jessurun, J., de Vries, B., Timmermans, H.: Motivate: towards context-aware recommendation mobile system for healthy living. In: 2011 5th Int. Conf. Pervasive Comput. Technol. Healthc. Work, pp. 250–253 (2011)
21. Luo, Y., Hawkley, L.C., Waite, L.J., Cacioppo, J.T.: Loneliness, health, and mortality in old age: a national longitudinal study. Soc. Sci. Med. 74(6), 907–914 (2012)
22. Morrow-Howell, N., Putnam, M., Lee, Y.S., Greenfield, J.C., Inoue, M., Chen, H.: An Investigation of Activity Profiles of Older Adults. Journals Gerontol. Ser. B Psychol. Sci. Soc. Sci., 1–13 (2014)

23. Neocleous, G.: Ageing and Information Communication Technology: The Case of MELCO in Cyprus **9** (32), 13–32 (2013)
24. Patterson, A.C., Veenstra, G.: Loneliness and risk of mortality: a longitudinal investigation in Alameda County, California. Soc. Sci. Med. **71**(1), 181–186 (2010)
25. Perissinotto, C.M.: Stijacic Cenzer, I., Covinsky, K.E., Loneliness in older persons: a predictor of functional decline and death. Arch. Intern. Med. **172**(14), 1078–1083 (2012)
26. Phillips, E.M., Schneider, J.C., Mercer, G.R.: Motivating elders to initiate and maintain exercise. Arch. Phys. Med. Rehabil. **85**(Suppl. 3), 52–57 (2004)
27. Ratnaparkhi, A.: A simple introduction to maximum entropy models for natural language processing (1997)
28. Ratnaparkhi, A.: Maximum entropy models for natural language ambiguity resolution. University of Pennsylvania (1998)
29. Raymond, É., Sévigny, A., Tourigny, A., Vézina, A., Verreault, R., Guilbert, A.C.: On the track of evaluated programmes targeting the social participation of seniors: a typology proposal. Ageing Soc. **33**(02), 267–296 (2013)
30. Romero, N., Sturm, J., Bekker, T., de Valk, L., Kruitwagen, S.: Playful persuasion to support older adults' social and physical activities. Interact. Comput. **22**(6), 485–495 (2010)
31. The American Occupational Therapy Association, Occupational Therapy Practice Magazine. Am. Occup. Ther. Assoc. **19** (14) (2014)
32. Unger, J.B., McAvay, G., Bruce, M.L., Berkman, L., Seeman, T.: Variation in the Impact of Social Network Characteristics on Physical Functioning in Elderly Persons: MacArthur Studies of Successful Aging. Journals Gerontol. Ser. B Psychol. Sci. Soc. Sci. **54B**(5), S245–S251 (1999)
33. Univerisity of Cyprus - Computer Science Dept, MELCO (Mobile Elderly Living Community). http://www.melco.cs.ucy.ac.cy
34. Wang, H.-X., Karp, A., Winblad, B., Fratiglioni, L.: Late-life engagement in social and leisure activities is associated with a decreased risk of dementia: a longitudinal study from the Kungsholmen project. Am. J. Epidemiol. **155**(12), 1081–1087 (2002)
35. Yang, Y.C., McClintock, M.K., Kozloski, M., Li, T.: Social isolation and adult mortality: the role of chronic inflammation and sex differences. J. Health Soc. Behav. **54**(2), 183–203 (2013)
36. Zunzunegui, M.-V., Alvarado, B.E., Del Ser, T., Otero, A.: Social Networks, Social Integration, and Social Engagement Determine Cognitive Decline in Community-Dwelling Spanish Older Adults. Journals Gerontol. Ser. B Psychol. Sci. Soc. Sci. **58**(2), S93–S100 (2003)

Human Behavior
and Activities Monitoring

Recommendations for the Creation of Datasets in Support of Data Driven Activity Recognition Models

Fulvio Patara[1]([envelope]), Chris D. Nugent[2], and Enrico Vicario[1]

[1] Department of Information Engineering, University of Florence, Florence, Italy
{fulvio.patara,enrico.vicario}@unifi.it
[2] School of Computing and Mathematics, University of Ulster,
Coleraine, UK
cd.nugent@ulster.ac.uk

Abstract. In the last decades, datasets have emerged as an essential component in the process of generating automated Activity Recognition (AR) solutions. Nevertheless, some challenges still remain: the lack of recommendations about which kind of information should be represented inside a dataset has resulted in the implementation of a variety of different non-standardized formalisms. On the other hand, this information is usually not sufficient to fully characterize the dataset. To address these challenges, this paper introduces a series of recommendations in the form of a dataset model with a well-defined semantic definition, for supporting those who are responsible for the creation, documentation and management of datasets. In addition, in order to better characterize datasets from a statistical point-of-view, we describe eight statistical analyses which should be included as additional measures within the dataset itself. We have validated our concepts through retrospectively analyzing a well-known dataset.

Keywords: Activity Recognition (AR) · Dataset model · Statistical characterization · Recommendations

1 Introduction

Activities of Daily Living (ADLs) [5] refer to a set of daily self care activities, which people perform habitually and universally, within both indoor and outdoor environments. These activities assume a key role in the objective assessment of the status of chronically ill and aging populations, in relation to evaluating effectiveness of treatment over time, tracking dynamics of disabilities and preventing adverse outcomes (e.g. preventive medicine) [10].

In the last decades, many datasets [2,13] have been recorded for the purposes of generating automated solutions for Activity Recognition (AR) [1,11]. Each of these datasets have had different characteristics, depending on: the number of people involved in the monitoring process (i.e. single person, multiple actors);

© Springer International Publishing Switzerland 2015
A. Geissbühler et al. (Eds.): ICOST 2015, LNCS 9102, pp. 79–91, 2015.
DOI: 10.1007/978-3-319-19312-0_7

the number and type of performed activities (i.e. single, interleaved, concurrent, multi-user); the number and type of sensors deployed in the environment (e.g. motion, state-change, temperature sensors); the topology of the environment (e.g. single room, apartment, house); the duration of the monitoring process (i.e. weeks, months, years) and the presence/absence of activity annotations.

Datasets in general have to accommodate two challenges: on the one hand, the lack of recommendations about which kind of information should be represented inside a dataset has resulted in the implementation of a variety of different non-standardized formalisms [6]. On the other hand, this information (even when completely available) is not able to characterize the dataset in its entirety. In the majority of cases, the information available is only a small portion of what the underlying data represents: the most information is in the data itself and needs to be mined from the data. However, there is not a clear appreciation of what exactly should be mined. Characterizing datasets from a statistical point-of-view assists with the process of AR, not only in pure probabilistic reasoning techniques, such as Bayesian Networks [9], Hidden Markov Models [13], and Conditional Random Fields [12].

In this paper, we report on the implementation of a series of recommendations for helping and supporting the creation of datasets in AR. Firstly, we present a dataset model with the intent of: providing a well-defined semantic characterization; allowing agile tailoring for the needs of different contexts in which datasets might be recorded; promoting automated conformance-checking techniques, so as to evaluate the compliance of an existent dataset with the proposed model. Secondly, we enrich the dataset model with statistical information that can be extracted by analyzing the entire dataset, about: activity duration; inactivity and delay between activities; inactivity between tasks; task duration; overall tasks occurring inside an activity, highlighting the most distinctive ones as well as the starting/ending ones.

The remainder of the paper is organized in three sections: Section 2 describes the proposed dataset model for supporting the creation of well-defined datasets; Section 3 describes eight statistics that should be included in the dataset; Section 4 shows the feasibility of the proposed model applied to a well-known dataset [13]. Conclusions are drawn in Section 5.

2   The Proposed Dataset Model

The dataset model proposed in this Section has been motivated by the intention of providing a formal structure that those responsible for the creation and management of datasets can follow and extend. Fig. 1 shows the design of the dataset model. The Dataset represents the starting point of our schema, and provides: general information about the dataset under consideration (*name, description*); personal information about Authors that have created the dataset (*name, surname, contact information*, and *affiliation*); information about Actors that have been involved (described by an *identifier* to safeguard privacy, *gender* and *age*); specific knowledge about the Environment used in the case study, as *name*, *description, type of setting* (i.e. `EnvirontmentType` as, for example, single room or flat), and `Sensors` deployed within the monitored area, specifying for each device, its `Position` (i.e. X-Y-Z coordinates). Each `Sensor` is identified by a unique *identifier*, and a `SensorType` that provides specific information about the device, like *sensing technology* (e.g. contact-switch, RFID-based, motion), *manufacturer* and distinguishing between `EnvironmentalType` and `WearableType` sensors.

The dataset model supports the instantiation of two different kinds of `Dataset`: `AnnotatedDataset`, when annotations in relation to performed activities are provided; `Non-AnnotatedDataset`, the situation when no annotations are provided. In both cases, the `Dataset` contains a set of `Events`, collected over time by some `Sensors`. Each `Event` is characterized by a unique *identifier*, and a *temporal reference* detailing the time at which the `Event` occurred. Given that different kinds of representation can be adopted for modeling `Events` [13], we accommodate multiple options in our schema.

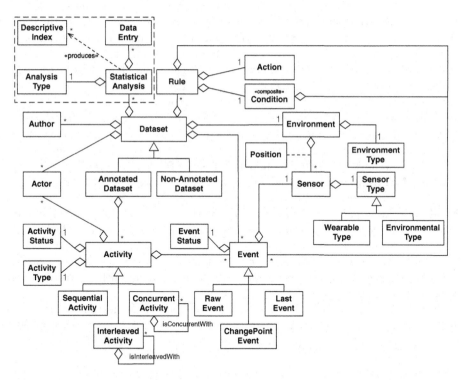

Fig. 1. The proposed dataset model provides a formal structure that those responsible for the creation and management of datasets can follow and extend. In addition, this model allows to characterize datasets from a statistical point-of-view (dashed box).

A `RawEvent` is an `Event` produced by a `Sensor` that generates a 1 when it is firing and a 0 otherwise; in this case, we need to represent the *start-time* and the *end-time* of each `Event`. A `ChangePointEvent` is seen as an instant `Event`, since the `Sensor` generates 1 only when it changes its status; for this reason, it is completely described by a single *timestamp*. Finally, a `LastEvent` continues to be 1 until a different `Sensor` changes state and so its time characterization is the same as that of a `RawEvent`. Note that, the `EventStatus` associated with each `Event` changes depending on the type of representation adopted: a `ChangePointEvent` can be in two different statuses (i.e. *started* and *completed*, for distinguishing between activation and de-activation events); a `RawEvent` (or `LastEvent`) can only be in one status (i.e. *completed*).

In the case of `AnnotatedDataset`, we need to provide information in relation to annotated activities performed during the monitoring period. Each `Activity` is univocally determined by an *identifier*, a *start-time* and an *end-time*, obtained through some form of annotation process, and is always performed by at least one `Actor`. In order to provide complete knowledge about the domain, each `Activity` is related with the set of `Events` occurring inside the `Activity`. The `ActivityStatus` allows the different statuses of an `Activity` (e.g. *suspended* or *completed*) to be distinguished. In addition, an `Activity` is associated with an `ActivityType`, to provide a definition (*name, description, references*) of the type of activity performed (e.g. basing on ADL or IADL classifications). However, the `ActivityType` is not able to provide a full characterization of all the `Activities` that can be represented into a `Dataset`. One of the main challenges in the AR process is to distinguish between `Sequential`, `Interleaved` and `Concurrent` `Activities`. To fulfill this important need, our model allows to specialize each `Activity` and to maintain cross-references between `Interleaved` (*isInterleaved-With* association) or `Concurrent` (*isConcurrentWith* association) `Activities`.

In order to provide a statistical characterization of the `Dataset` under consideration, we have enriched our model with some `StatisticalAnalyses`, each of them characterized by: an `AnalysisType`, i.e. the type of statistic taken into account (*name, description*) and that we have formalized in Section 3; a series of `DataEntry`, i.e. a pair of <*value, frequency*>, that represents the starting-point for extracting a set of `DescriptiveIndexes` (e.g. mean, standard deviation) generated as analysis outputs. Note that some of these `Indexes` can be generated only if values in the `DataEntries` are numerical quantities; in these cases, it is also required to specify the *unit* used to represent quantities, to produce consistent and interpretable results.

Finally, the proposed dataset model allows the representation of decision `Rules` based on the `Event-Condition-Action` approach [8], that enables mechanisms of decision support (e.g. alert messages) to be applied directly on the `Dataset` content.

3   A Statistical Characterization of the Dataset Model

We discuss here some statistical analyses (represented as `AnalysisTypes` in the proposed dataset model) that should be included as additional measures within the dataset, using a consistent format. Each statistic is divided into sections according to the following template (inspired by the structure of well-known design patterns [4]):

- *Intent.* What does the statistic do? What is its rationale and intent?
- *Applicability.* What are the situations in which the statistic can be applied?
- *Method.* How can the statistic be obtained? From which kind of data?
- *Healthcare relevance.* How does the statistic support its objectives? What are the results of applying this statistic in the healthcare context?

In each statistic, in order to better explain the healthcare relevance, the following example scenario is taken into account: we consider a subject that is performing a *hand-washing* activity, composed by five distinct ordered tasks (i.e. *wetting, soaping, washing, rinsing,* and *drying*).

Note that, in our dataset model, the concept of *task* is not directly represented. This is due to the fact that, especially in the case of binary sensors, tasks and events are implicitly related, and it is possible to derive a task from the related event, depending on the type of representation used for describing events in the dataset: *i)* in the *raw* case, a task T_k is the action performed for all of the event duration; *ii)* in the *change-point* case, a task T_k is the action performed between two events of the same type (i.e. activation and de-activation events). In so doing, Fig. 2 shows a stream of tasks $T_k, T_{k+1}, \ldots$ (e.g. *wetting, soaping*) inside some annotated activities $A_i, A_{i+1}, \ldots$ (e.g. *hand-washing*).

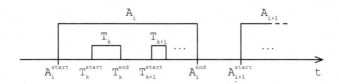

Fig. 2. A fragment of a tasks stream together with annotated activities

3.1 Activity Duration

Intent. This statistical analysis permits the evaluation of the activity duration in a set of activities of the same type.

Applicability. This statistic can be computed only for an annotated dataset. In fact, the presence of annotated activities is a prerequisite due to the nature of the data required.

Method. For each activity A_i of a given type, measuring the duration of A_i and plotting the frequency of each different value in the set of instances.

$$duration(A_i) = A_i^{end} - A_i^{start}. \tag{1}$$

Healthcare relevance. The duration of an activity is an important marker for classifying the health status of a subject. This statistic can be used as a support mechanism to evaluate: the capability of a subject to be able to conclude an activity (e.g. to accomplish a goal in a pre-defined range of time); the decay in activity performance over time; the variability in activity execution. In the scenario under consideration, the time to perform the *hand-washing* activity is important to establish if the subject is going to reach the target or may require a form of automated prompting as assistance.

3.2 Inactivity Between Activities

Intent. This statistical analysis permits the evaluation of periods of inactivity between consecutive activities.

Applicability. This analysis can be performed only on datasets in which it is possible to distinguish between periods of activity and inactivity.

Method. For each activity A_i, measuring the inactivity between consecutive activities as the idle-time between the end of an activity, A_i^{end}, and the start of the following activity, A_{i+1}^{start}; finally, plotting the frequency of each different value in the set of activities.

$$inactivity(A_i, A_{i+1}) = A_{i+1}^{start} - A_i^{end}. \tag{2}$$

Healthcare relevance. This statistic can be used to evaluate the status of inactivity of a subject. Increased time of inactivity, along with the duration of each activity, may be a good marker of risk of deterioration in health conditions (e.g. sedentary behavior).

3.3 Delay Between Activities

Intent. This statistic permits the evaluation of the delay between consecutive activities of the same type.

Applicability. Only on annotated datasets.

Method. For each activity A_i of a given type, measuring the delay as the inter-time between the end of an activity, A_i^{end}, and the start of the following activity of the same type, A_j^{start}; then, plotting the frequency of each different value in the set of activities.

$$delay(A_i, A_j) = A_j^{start} - A_i^{end}, \text{ with } j > i. \tag{3}$$

Healthcare relevance. This statistic permits the evaluation of the capability of a subject to perform a given activity in time. Consider, for example, a subject that has to perform a *taking medicine* activity three times a day (e.g. at 09.00, at 14.00, and at 19.00). The time between consecutive activities is important to establish if the subject has taken the medicines as prescribed by a doctor with temporal regularity (e.g. every 5 hours).

3.4   Inactivity Between Tasks

Intent. This statistical analysis permits the evaluation of the inactivity between consecutive tasks occurring in the same activity.

Applicability. This statistic can be computed only for an annotated dataset. In fact, the presence of activities is a prerequisite for this statistic, given that it is important to consider only tasks in the same activity.

Method. For each activity A_i of a given type, measuring the inactivity between consecutive tasks as the idle-time between the end of a task, T_k^{end}, and the start of the following task, T_{k+1}^{start}; finally, plotting the frequency of each different value in the set of activities.

$$inactivity(T_k, T_{k+1}) = T_{k+1}^{start} - T_k^{end}. \tag{4}$$

Healthcare relevance. This statistic can be used to evaluate the status of inactivity of a subject during the execution of an activity. In the scenario under consideration, the idle-time between all consecutive tasks inside an activity (e.g. *hand-washing*) is important to investigate if the subject faces some problems during the transition between one task to another one.

3.5   Task Duration

Intent. This statistic permits the evaluation of the evolution of the task duration in a set of task occurrences.

Applicability. This statistic can be computed in both annotated or non-annotated datasets. In the case of an annotated dataset, it is possible to correlate the statistic of each distinct task with the activity that contains the task, to improve the obtained results.

Method. For each activity A_i of a given type, for each distinct task T_k in A_i, measuring the task duration as: *i)* the difference between the *end-time* and the *start-time* of an event (i.e. *raw* case); the difference between timestamps of two consecutive events, that represent, respectively, the activation and the de-activation event of the task (i.e. *change-point* case); finally, plotting the frequency of each different value in the set of tasks.

$$duration(T_k) = T_k^{end} - T_k^{start}. \tag{5}$$

Healthcare relevance. This statistic can be used as a means of support to evaluate: the capability of a subject to be able to conclude a task (e.g. to accomplish a single-step in a pre-defined range of time); the decay in task performance; the variability in task execution. The duration of a task can be used to classify the health status of a subject at a more fine-grained level. In the *hand-washing* activity, the time to perform each task is important to establish if the subject is going to correctly conclude the activity.

3.6   Overall Tasks Inside an Activity

Intent. The aim of this statistic is to evaluate which are the tasks occurring inside an activity of a given type.

Applicability. Only for annotated datasets.

Method. For each activity A_i of a given type, computing the frequency of each distinct task T_k to occur in the set of activities.

Healthcare relevance. This statistic can be used to evaluate the capability of a subject to remind the sequence of tasks to perform during the execution of an activity. In the case of *hand-washing* activity, the presence of repeated tasks (e.g. <*wetting, soaping, soaping, soaping, ...*>) might be an indicator of difficulties to complete an activity in the correct order (e.g. forgotten steps).

3.7   Distinctive Tasks of an Activity

Intent. This statistic differs from the statistic of Section 3.6, considering which are the most distinctive tasks in each activity of a given type, and distinguishing characteristics tasks from noisy or incorrect tasks.

Applicability. Only for annotated datasets. Only for sequential activities, not interleaved or concurrent, except if the dataset provides details for each activity and for the set of related events, so as to distinguish events belonging to interleaved or concurrent activities. Note that, the proposed model is designed to allow this kind of annotations.

Method. For each activity A_i of a given type, computing the frequency of each distinct task T_k to occur *at-least-once* in the set of activities.

Healthcare relevance. This statistic can be used as a means to support the evaluation of the capability of the subject to focus his/her attention on the activity in progress, or to perform an activity in a rational manner, only going through tasks that permit the subject to move closer to the target. In the *hand-washing* activity, the presence of tasks totally unrelated to the activity (e.g. *brushing*) might be an indicator of difficulties during the activity in progress.

3.8   Starting/Ending Tasks of an Activity

Intent. The aim of this statistic is to evaluate which are the starting tasks (i.e. the first ones) and the ending tasks (i.e. the last ones) in each activity type.

Applicability. Only for annotated datasets.

Method. For each activity A_i of a given type, computing the frequency of each distinct task T_k to occur as the *starting/ending* task in the set of activities.

Healthcare relevance. This statistic can be used to evaluate the capability of a subject to correctly start (or end) an activity. In the case of the *hand-washing* activity, the presence of a starting task totally unrelated or that usually doesn't represent the first step of the activity (e.g. *drying*) might be an indicator of the difficulties of a subject to start the activity in the correct manner. In the same way, the presence of an incorrect ending task (e.g. *soaping*) might suggest the difficulties of a subject to remember the next steps to correctly conclude the activity in progress.

4   Results and Discussion

A number of open-source datasets are available online [2,13] from various institutes that have collected data generated from experiments conducted within Smart Environments [3,7]. To evaluate the feasibility of the proposed dataset model and in particular, the benefits of including statistical analyses into the dataset report, we have used a publicly available annotated dataset [13], containing 1 319 events collected by 14 binary sensors installed in a 3-room apartment, during a period of 28 days, when a 26-year-old subject was performing 7 distinct activities (i.e. *Prepare a beverage, Sleeping, Leave house, Preparing breakfast, Preparing dinner, Taking shower, Toileting*), by a total of 245 instances.

Based on the proposed approach, Table 1 presents the descriptive indexes that characterize the statistic about *activity duration*, computed for each distinct activity type in the dataset. The last column of Table 1, named *Idling*, presents the same indexes for the *inactivity between activities* statistic.

Due to the limited space, we are able to report here only some of the statistics described in Section 3, restricted to the case of *Sleeping* activity, whose indexes are shown in the second column of Table 1. As can be seen, this activity is composed by 24 instances, with a duration between 1 428 seconds (i.e. 24 minutes) and 39 367 seconds (i.e. about 11 hours).

Table 1. Descriptive indexes extracted from the statistics about *activity duration* and *inactivity between activities* (the unit for time is the second)

	Preparing a beverage	Sleeping	Leaving house	Preparing breakfast	Preparing dinner	Taking shower	Toileting	Idling
# of instances	20	24	34	20	10	23	114	220
Mean	53.25	29 141.63	39 823.09	202.75	2 054	573.39	104.62	1 442.5
Variance	4 497.79	1.14E+08	1.72E+09	22 417.59	1.26E+06	24 039.89	10 113.04	5.55E+06
SD	67.07	10 683.84	41 422.71	149.73	124.4	155.05	100.56	2 356.65
Min	9	1 428	2 446	74	721	156	16	2
Max	305	39 367	172 462	662	4 823	918	864	17 702
Range	296	37 939	170 016	588	4 102	762	848	17 700

Fig. 3 presents two different histograms. The first one, in Fig. 3(a), provides a more detailed view about the *distribution of the activity duration*, grouped in 4 distinct ranges of times. As can be viewed, in 75% of the instances, the duration of *Sleeping* is greater than 7 hours; only in 3 from 24 of the cases, the activity was lower than 3 hours: this may be an indicator of sleeping disorders; however, the percentage is very slow compared to the others that claim the opposite (e.g. more than 10 hours in the 25% of the cases), and combining this data with temporal information, we can exclude that these episodes are related to the night period. The second histogram, in Fig. 3(b), shows the *distribution of the delay* between *Sleeping* instances (whose indexes are presented in Table 2), grouped in 3 distinct range of times. There is no evidence of particular anomalies, except in 3 cases in which the delay is more than 24 hours: however, in all of these cases, the subject has left home for more than 1 day.

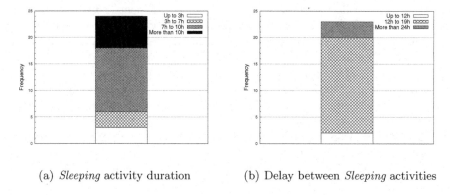

(a) *Sleeping* activity duration   (b) Delay between *Sleeping* activities

Fig. 3. Histograms of *activity duration* and *delay between activities* statistics

Table 2. Descriptive indexes about *delay between Sleeping activities*, in seconds

	# of instances	Mean	Variance	SD	Min	Max	Range
Delay between activities (s)	23	66 276.22	1.94E+09	44 048.32	6 114	214 984	208 870

In Fig. 4(a) we describe the statistic about *distinctive tasks* occurring inside the *Sleeping* activity. Four distinct tasks can be found in this activity: *hall-bedroom door* (23/24 instances); *toilet-flush* (14/24 instances); *hall-bathroom door* (14/24 instances); *hall-toilet door* (12/24 instances). On the one hand, due to its high frequency, the first task (i.e. the task associated to the event generated by a sensor located on the door of the bedroom) may represent a good marker for detecting this kind of activity. On the other hand, the other tasks, apparently unrelated to the activity under consideration, denote the presence of two distinct activities that, sometimes, occur in concurrency with the *Sleeping* activity (i.e. *Toileting* and *Showering*). Fig. 4(b) presents which of these tasks are the *starting/ending tasks* of the *Sleeping* activity: in 15/24 cases, as could have been expected, the *hall-bedroom door* task represents the start of the activity; the *hall-bathroom door*, otherwise (denoting the presence of a *Toileting* activity as starting activity inside). Vice versa, only the *hall-bedroom door* appears at the

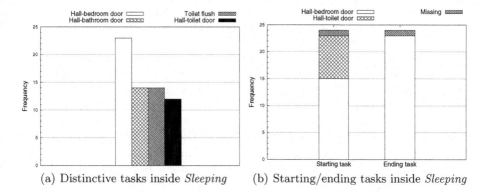

(a) Distinctive tasks inside *Sleeping*   (b) Starting/ending tasks inside *Sleeping*

Fig. 4. Histograms of *distinctive tasks* and *starting/ending tasks* statistics

end of each activity instances. Note that, in just one case (i.e. *missing* in Fig. 4), no starting/ending tasks were detected, given that any event was fired.

Table 3 describes the statistics about *overall tasks* occurring inside the *Sleeping* activity, and related *task duration*. For each task, we have reported the number of times the task has occurred in the entire *Sleeping* set (e.g. the *hall-bedroom door* occurred 118 times in 24 activity instances), and the descriptive indexes for the *task duration*. It is interesting to note that the statistics of the tasks in the first three columns are similar. In fact, they refer to events related with sensors located on doors. For this reason, the minimum value is equal to 1 for all of them (i.e. the minimum time to open and close a door), while the maximum value is between 25 793 seconds (around 7 hours) and 142 332 seconds (around 39 hours), highlighting the inattentiveness of the subject about closing the door after opening it. Finally, note that the indexes associated with the *toilet flush* task are very simple, due to the intrinsic limited interaction with the flush.

Table 3. Descriptive indexes about *task duration* in the *Sleeping* activity, in seconds

	Hall-bedroom door	Hall-bathroom door	Hall-toilet door	Toilet flush
# of instances	118	42	29	23
Mean	14 155.85	620.26	3 975.14	1
Variance	7.34E+08	1.55E+07	7.00E+07	0
SD	27 095.53	3 931.33	8 368.5	0
Min	1	1	1	1
Max	142 332	25 793	33 306	1
Range	142 331	25 792	33 305	0

5   Conclusion

The aim of this study was to introduce a series of recommendations for helping and supporting those who are responsible for the creation, documentation and management of datasets. In so doing, we have designed and implemented a dataset model with a high level of abstraction to facilitate its applicability in different contexts in which datasets might be recorded. We have enriched our model with statistical information that can be extracted analyzing the entire dataset, and can be used as additional information to provide a fuller characterization.

In this paper, we have described eight statistical analyses which should be included as additional measures within the dataset itself, providing for each of them, a formal definition about: its intent (i.e. the rationale of the statistic); its applicability (i.e. situations in which the statistic can be applied, and its utility), the method used to obtain the statistic from which kind of data; and its healthcare relevance (i.e. results of applying the statistic in a clinical context).

The feasibility of the proposed model applied to a well-known and publicly available annotated dataset [13] has been documented in this paper. The results demonstrate that the approach is capable to work with the diversity of an unseen dataset and has the ability to produce the necessary statistical measures.

Work will now continue to identify and describe additional statistical analyses that can be included in our dataset model, in order to improve the statistical characterization of datasets. Work is also planned to validate the proposed approach on datasets with different characteristics (e.g. number of instances, type of performed activities). Finally, the proposed model has the potential to be easily translated into an *XML* data schema, to better support its implementation.

Acknowledgments. Invest Northern Ireland is acknowledged for partially supporting this project under the Competence Centre Program Grant RD0513853 - Connected Health Innovation Centre.

References

1. Chen, L., Nugent, C.D., Biswas, J., Hoey, J.: Activity recognition in pervasive intelligent environments, vo. 4. Springer Science & Business Media (2011)
2. Cook, D., Schmitter-Edgecombe, M., Crandall, A., Sanders, C., Thomas, B.: Collecting and disseminating smart home sensor data in the CASAS project. In: Proc. of the CHI Workshop on Developing Shared Home Behavior Datasets to Advance HCI and Ubiquitous Computing Research (2009)
3. Cook, D.J., Das, S.K.: How smart are our environments? an updated look at the state of the art. Pervasive and Mobile Computing **3**(2), 53–73 (2007)
4. Gamma, E., Helm, R., Johnson, R., Vlissides, J.: Design patterns: elements of reusable object-oriented software. Pearson Education (1994)
5. Katz, S., Downs, T.D., Cash, H.R., Grotz, R.C.: Progress in development of the index of ADL. The Gerontologist **10**(1 Part 1), 20–30 (1970)
6. Nugent, C.D., Finlay, D.D., Davies, R.J., Wang, H.Y., Zheng, H., Hallberg, J., Synnes, K., Mulvenna, M.D.: homeML – An open standard for the exchange of data within smart environments. In: Okadome, T., Yamazaki, T., Makhtari, M. (eds.) ICOST. LNCS, vol. 4541, pp. 121–129. Springer, Heidelberg (2007)
7. Nugent, C.D., Mulvenna, M.D., Hong, X., Devlin, S.: Experiences in the development of a smart lab. International Journal of Biomedical Engineering and Technology **2**(4), 319–331 (2009)

8. Paton, N.W., Díaz, O.: Active database systems. ACM Computing Surveys (CSUR) **31**(1), 63–103 (1999)
9. Philipose, M., Fishkin, K.P., Perkowitz, M., Patterson, D.J., Fox, D., Kautz, H., Hahnel, D.: Inferring activities from interactions with objects. IEEE Pervasive Computing **3**(4), 50–57 (2004)
10. Serna, A., Pigot, H., Rialle, V.: Modeling the progression of Alzheimer's disease for cognitive assistance in smart homes. User Modeling and User-Adapted Interaction **17**(4), 415–438 (2007)
11. Turaga, P., Chellappa, R., Subrahmanian, V.S., Udrea, O.: Machine recognition of human activities: A survey. IEEE Transactions on Circuits and Systems for Video Technology **18**(11), 1473–1488 (2008)
12. Vail, D.L., Veloso, M.M., Lafferty, J.D.: Conditional random fields for activity recognition. In: Proceedings of the 6th International Joint Conference on Autonomous Agents and Multiagent Systems, pp. 235. ACM (2007)
13. Van Kasteren, T., Noulas, A., Englebienne, G., Kröse, B.: Accurate activity recognition in a home setting. In: Proceedings of the 10th International Conference on Ubiquitous Computing, pp. 1–9. ACM (2008)

Activity Playback Modeling for Smart Home Simulation

Sirui Liu, Sumi Helal[⊠], and Jae Woong Lee

Mobile and Pervasive Computing Laboratory, CISE Department,
University of Florida, 447 CSE Building, Gainesville, FL 32611, USA
{sirui,helal,jwlee}@cise.ufl.edu

Abstract. Simulation of human activities in smart spaces is becoming increasingly important due to the growing demands on datasets that captures user-technology interactions. Such datasets are critical to the success of human-centric research that relies on understanding user actions, activities and behavior in a given situation and space. But most existing activity models have been designed for the purpose of recognition and are not specifically optimized for visual simulation (playback) or for dataset generation. To address this limitation we propose an activity playback model and associated algorithms to facilitate activity simulation with high degree of realism and with inherent variability that mimics the human nature of performing the same activity variably. We present the activity playback model, algorithms, and a validation study to assess the realism of our approach.

Keywords: Human activity simulation · Smart homes · Modeling · Activity playback modeling

1 Introduction

For human-centered computing researchers, it is essential to have various sensory datasets to validate the fidelity of their systems, algorithms or models. Specifically, activity recognition and assisted living research, which build on the foundation of identifying the activities being performed or attempted by a resident, are in dire need of such datasets. However, it is prohibitively expensive and time-consuming to acquire adequately fitting and reliable datasets from real smart home deployments with human subjects. Consequently, effective smart home simulators that are capable of generating accurate human activity data are needed and have rapidly grown in importance to promote activity recognition and understanding research.

In order to support such simulations, powerful and scalable techniques to specifying activities to the simulator are needed. Also needed are methods to validate the realism of the simulated activities. To achieve realistic activity simulation, it is necessary to supply the simulator with an activity model that can explicitly define an activity and fine-tune its components and attributes to accurately mimic the variability of human activities [1]. Existing activity models, usually developed for the purpose of recognition [5][16], do not have these capabilities and therefore do not serve this purpose.

© Springer International Publishing Switzerland 2015
A. Geissbühler et al. (Eds.): ICOST 2015, LNCS 9102, pp. 92–102, 2015.
DOI: 10.1007/978-3-319-19312-0_8

This paper presents Activity Playback (APB), an activity modeling and simulation approach for human activities in smart spaces. It presents an explicit activity model that enables the user to design the components of activities and specify their attributes. The paper also presents an activity playback algorithm that plays the activity animation, which provides instant cognitive feedback to the simulation user with regards to the accuracy of the model and its attributes. Our approach is self-validating and self-evident in the sense that the user is able to visually assess the realism of the activity simulation. Even though APB is utilized within the Persim 3D context driven simulator for human activity [18][19], this paper focuses only on presenting the APB model and algorithm.

The paper is organized as follows. Section 2 presents an overview of our APB modeling approach and discusses the limitations of existing activity models and simulators of human activities in smart spaces. Section 3 provides detailed description of the APB modeling approach, including an overview of its framework, the components of the activity model, the methodology of activity model design, an example of the design process and the activity playback algorithm. Section 4 validates the APB modeling approach. Section 5 concludes the paper.

2   Overall Approach

2.1   Activity Playback Approach

Activity Playback is an approach to specifying and simulating human activities in a simulated pervasive environment. It enables smart home simulation users to design activity models under its framework and simulate the activities in the simulator. The goals of the activity playback approach are three fold. First, it produces realistic visualizations of the activity as it unfolds. Second, it reflects accurate effects of the activity on the virtual environment in which the activities are simulated. Third, it simulates an activity variably any number of times as the simulation user desires, creating slightly different activity instances every time which mimics typical human behavior in performing activities.

Preliminary studies from Helal et al. [15] on human activity simulation point to three major challenges to overcome in this area: simulation scalability, simulation realism and generated dataset accuracy. Simulation should be able to scale as it imitates extensive spaces and various and complicated activities. Also, the space and activities performed should have high realism so that their interaction is identical to that of the real world. Finally, the synthesized datasets should be similar to actual datasets collected from the real world in order to be effective as sample data for activity recognition.

Within the Persim 3D project [18][19], Lee [2][3][4] alleviated the simulation scalability issue by proposing a context-driven approach. Event-driven simulation, which has been used as a traditional simulation approach, is hardly scalable because it requires a huge amount of human efforts for specifying every single sensor event and lengthy combinations of these events that make up the activities. In addition to effort scalability, too many specifications may cause unconscious errors and make simulation vulnerable. In the context-driven approach, simulation entities such as state space and status of virtual characters are abstracted in a virtualized context structure. Context represents special state space of importance and significance, which enables the simulator to skip unimportant space states between two consecutive contexts in specification. It also automates scheduling of activities, and enriches possible sequences of activities without users' engagements. The experimental comparison to other simulations shows many enhancements in scalability.

However, to address simulation realism and consequently the accuracy of generated datasets, we introduce Activity Playback - a novel approach that allows Persim 3D users to exploit and leverage human knowledge cognition about activities as they specify the activities they wish to simulate. We present our Activity Playback model and algorithm, and show an example of creating realistic activity instances. We describe the APB approach in details in section 3.

2.2   Comparison to Other Approaches

There have been numerous attempts to model human activities. A widely used methodology is to model the action sequence of the activity based on a probabilistic model. In [5] and [6], activity models are based on Hidden Markov Model (HMM) and Conditional Random Fields (CRF). Duong [7][8] also used HMM based techniques to model activities, and took a step further using Coxian distribution to model the duration of the states. Similarly, it is an effective approach to augment HMM based activity models by modeling actions using a normal distribution [9]. Bose and Helal used probabilistic phenomena to model human walking behavior on a smart floor instrumented with sensors [10]. These probabilistic models are proven to be valid for activity recognition; however, they are not necessarily suitable for activity simulation, which requires an activity model that has accurate control over the number, order, duration and occurrence of actions comprising the activities, none of which could be fully supported using probabilistic models.

A number of smart home simulators have been developed aiming to simulate indoor human activities. SIMACT [11] is a 3D smart home simulator that allows the user to design and simulate activities. However, the user has to define activities in a scripting language, which creates a barrier for users who don't have programming skills. IE Sim [12] presents the simulation environment in a 2D user interface and provides a control panel for the user to set the properties of objects. DiaSim [13] and ISS [14] are simulators developed for a goal of providing pervasive services. DiaSim simulates pervasive applications such as indoor surveillance and fire situation detection, and generates notifications when needed. ISS is a context-aware simulation environment that is capable of detecting the location of the virtual character and the activity being attempted, and providing services (e.g., turns on TV automatically) accordingly. Although these simulators successfully achieve their goals of simulating activities or providing intelligent services, they lack an explicit activity model and thus the ability to simulate a variety of human activities with high degree of realism.

Persim 1.5 [15], an earlier event-driven incarnation of Persim 3D, is a powerful tool that enables the design and specification of various human activities. It provides a test environment for activity recognition research that simulates human activities and generates synthesis datasets in an event-driven manner. However, to generate an activity instance in Persim 1.5, the user has to configure an elaborate activity sequence in terms of the trace of sensor events that would be generated when the activity occurs. This requires too much user effort and suffers from the effort scalability issue, as more complex and longer period activities are attempted. The Activity Playback modeling approach, with which we are currently instrumenting Persim 3D, addresses these issue to enhance the fidelity of the simulation.

3   Activity Playback Modeling

In this section we describe the architecture of the Activity Playback approach. As shown in Fig. 1, it consists of two essential mainstays that work seamlessly together: an activity model and an activity playback algorithm. The former contains adequate activity knowledge that describes attributes of human activities, and the latter extracts its activity information and simulates activities under the rules imposed by the activity semantics, creating animated activity visualizations and sensory datasets through the Persim 3D simulation framework.

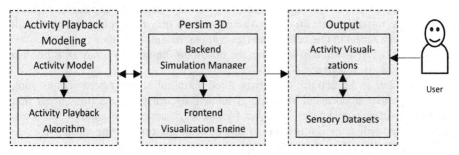

Fig. 1. Activity Playback approach within the Persim 3D simulator

3.1   Activity Model Components

To achieve realistic activity simulation, it is fundamentally important to have an activity model that accurately captures the characteristics of human activities. One major challenge is to deal with the inherent human activity variability. The same individual often performs the same activity differently at different times in essentially the same situation [1]. As discussed in the previous section, generic probability-based activity models are limited by the lack of capacity of action arrangement and are not suitable for activity simulation.

To overcome these limitations, we define the following nine elements for our activity model that enable it to capture the human behavior uncertainty. With these components, the activity model maintains control over the order, duration and occurrence of actions in the activity, sets attributes of the activity from different aspects, and defines rules that shape the process by which activities are simulated. These elements are concisely defined below.

Context Entities. A context entity is the combination of an object in the pervasive space and the attached or relevant sensor(s), or a property of the pervasive space (e.g., temperature) and the corresponding sensor(s).

Action Actuations. An action actuation is a binding between the context entity and the reading of its sensor(s), indicating how the sensors' values would change when the status of the context entity changes.

Actions. An action is a unit operation at which the virtual character interacts with a set of context entities and changes their status. An action contains four entities: a name, an animation, a duration and action actuations. When the character performs an action, it would trigger one or more sensor events through its actuations and play its animation over the specified duration. Hence, actions are visualized and affective. An activity consists of a set of actions.

Duration. The duration of the activity is the sum of the duration of all its actions.

Start Time. The start time of the activity is defined by a fuzzy membership function $s(t)$. The fuzzy value $s(t_0)$ is proportional to the probability of the start time being t_0. Implicitly, the end time of the activity is the start time plus its duration.

In order to better control the order and occurrence of actions in the activity and the activity duration, actions are modeled to have three more attributes with respect to a given activity, along with the modeling of action duration.

Action Importance. There are two importance levels for an action within a given activity: necessary and optional. A necessary action must occur at least once if the activity is performed, while an optional action may or may not occur. An action could be a necessary action in one activity and an optional action in another.

Action Max Occurrence. It specifies the maximum number of times an action can take place in a given activity.

Action Timing. An activity comprises three temporal stages where actions could take place: early, middle and late. In a given activity, early stage actions occur first, and then middle stage actions, followed by late stage actions. In addition, an action could belong to all-stage if it is likely to take place at any time during the activity.

Action Duration. An action has a minimum and a maximum value of its duration. When the action is to be performed, its duration is randomly determined from this range.

3.2   Activity Model Design

In order to apply the APB approach to build an effective smart space simulator, the user needs to utilize everyday knowledge to design activity models for the target activities in the bottom-up manner. In a given simulated environment, e.g., a smart home, the user first creates the context entities that will be involved in the simulation, then the actions that interact with them. With the action set ready, the user designs activities by organizing actions for them and setting the semantics of the actions with respect to the associated activities. The design process is described in detail as follows.

1. Define Context Entities $E = \{e_i\}$ in the pervasive space.
2. Create a global Action Set $C = \{c_i\}$. For each action c, set its name n, animation m, duration range $d(t)$ and action actuations u, where

$u = \{(e_k, v_k)\}$ can contain any number of actuations. Then, specify context entity e_k and its sensor reading v_k for each actuation in u.

3.   Create the activity set $A = \{A_i\}$. For each activity A_i:
   ▪   Set the activity name n
   ▪   Define the start time fuzzy function $s(t)$
   ▪   Select actions from Action Set C to build the action set $C_A = \{c_k\}$
   ▪   Determine the action importance p of every c_k in C_A
   ▪   Determine the max occurrence r of every c_k in C_A
   ▪   Specify temporal stage t of every c_k in C_A

Once the action and activity design process is completed, the activity models are ready to use for activity playback.

3.3   Activity Model Case Study

This section presents an example of activity playback model design process, which was used for Activity Playback in Persim 3D simulator to mimic the real activities performed by residents living in the Gator Tech Smart House (GTSH) [19][20]. Thus, the physical settings of GTSH were used as a reference in configuring the activity models. We choose the *Using Bathroom* activity as an example. It involves three context entities: bathroom door, toilet and bathroom tap. We selected three actions from a global action set for this activity: *Opening bathroom door*, *Using toilet*, and *Washing hands*, corresponding to the three context entities, respectively. For each action, from the animations currently supported by Persim 3D we chose the one(s) that are the most visually similar. The detailed attributes of these actions are shown in Table 1. Because this activity was usually the first activity the resident performed after getting up in the morning, and for the sake of simplicity, we set the activity start time to be randomly determined from the range of 6:30 – 7:30 AM.

Table 1. Attributes of Actions in Activity Using Bathroom

Actions	Associated Ani-mation	Actuations	Duration (seconds)	Importance	Max Occur	Stage
Opening bathroom door	- Stand - Right hand catch	Bathroom door sensor - on	1 – 2	Optional	1	Early
Using toilet	- Stand - Right hand catch	Toilet sensor - on	15 – 30	Necessary	2	Middle
Washing hands	- Stand	Bathroom tap sensor - on	2 – 20	Necessary	2	Late

3.4   Activity Playback Algorithm

Unlike the numerous activity modeling techniques developed for activity recognition [5][6][7][8][9], the activity model in the APB approach is specifically designed for activity playback and simulation, with a goal to enable the activity playback algorithm to not only effectively change the status of the simulation environment, but also produce realistic visualizations of the activity. As discussed earlier, actions are the building blocks of the activity. The activity playback algorithm extracts the information from the model of the target activity and constructs a sequence of actions. As the virtual character performs each action, it plays the animation over the action duration and changes the status of the objects in the simulated space through action actuations.

The activity playback algorithm exploits the flexibility created by the activity model to generate reasonably different instances of the same activity, achieving the goal of mimicking the intrinsic variability of human nature. The first step to simulate an activity is to construct its action sequence. For each action in the activity, the algorithm randomly determines the number of occurrence from its minimum and maximum occurrence range. It creates four bags of actions for the early, middle, late and all-stage respectively, and adds actions to the assigned stages for the same number of actions as the occurrence. It randomly shuffles the actions in the bag for early, middle, and late stages and appends them to one another, creating a longer action sequence E, to ensure that actions within a stage are randomly ordered but all early-stage actions precede middle-stage actions, which precede late-stage actions. The last step is to randomly insert all-stage actions into E. This process of action sequence construction is shown in Algorithm 1, where T_0, T_1, T_2 and T_3 are all-stage, early stage, middle stage and late stage respectively. Similarly, $B_0 - B_3$ are bags of actions in the four stage types.

Algorithm 1. Construct Action Sequence

```
action set S ← all actions of activity
for each action c in S
    number of occurrence of c ← random number from
    [c.min-occurrence, c.max-occurrence]
end for
for stage T₀ - T₃
    construct bag of actions B₀ - B₃
end for
randomly shuffle B1, B2 and B3
E ← B₁.append(B₂).append(B₃)
randomly insert actions of B₀ into E
```

Before the activity is played, the activity playback algorithm (shown in Algorithm 2) determines its start time using the activity start time semantic. At each action, it moves the virtual character to the location of the involved context entities and changes their status through action actuations. It randomly determines the action duration from the range of its minimum and maximum value and plays the action animation over the duration. It is possible that one action is associated with multiple context entities. In our experiment, we designed the actions in a way that all context entities of one action were in the same location from the perspective of the virtual character.

Algorithm 2. Play Activity

```
simulation_time ← activity start time
for i from 1 to E.length
  e ← context entities of c_i
  if character.location ≠ e.location
    character.moveTo(e.location)
  activate actuations of c_i
  c_i.duration ← random value from
    [c_i.min-duration, c_i.max-duration]
  play c_i's animation
  simulation_time = simulation_time + c_i.duration
end for
```

4   Validation

Activity Playback doesn't only generate synthetic datasets, but also produces animated human activity visualizations. With an appropriately designed activity model, the activity playback engine is able to generate numerous activity instances with perceivably reasonable variance, which makes it possible for the users to observe the activity playbacks and rate their realism.

We conducted a user study to have participating users visually assess the realism of activity playback. We recruited 6 subjects (3 males and 3 females) to participate in this study. Their ages ranged from 24 to 54 ($avg = 31$, $SD = 11.37$). Two had postgraduate degrees in engineering, one of which was Electrical and Computer Engineering, but none had experience in smart home research, computer simulation or related fields.

We used the activity playback algorithm to generate 3 activity instances for each of the 8 activities in Table 2 and screen-recorded the playback, yielding 24 video clips in total (screenshots shown in Fig. 2). For each activity, the 3 instances were annotated with the same activity name, but varied in the occurrence, order and duration of the actions. Following the well-known methodology in [17], we showed all 24 video clips to each subject in a random order, and asked the subject to rate the realism of the activity playbacks, namely how much they believed the videos could match their annotations, all on a scale of 1 to 7, with 1 being very poor realism and 7 being very high realism. On average, the participants gave activity playback a 5.17 with a standard deviation of 1.13. Table 2 summarizes subjects' overall ratings of the realism of activity playback broken down by activity.

After watching the videos, subjects were asked to give feedback and criticism on the realism of played activities. There was a consensus that the concept of activity playback was intuitive and easy to understand. Four subjects felt that it was a good approach to simulating general daily activities on a high level. Three stated they could understand the action sequences of the generated activity instances, but they were not highly realistic because of the lack of fine-grained granularity of animations of actions and transitions between them. Two subjects indicated the simulated activities were adequately realistic in general, but needed more low-level actions and human body movements to make them more natural.

Table 2. Subjects' Average Ratings of Realism of Activity Playback (Scale: 1 = Very Poor, 7 = Very High)

Activity	Mean	Std. dev.
Eating breakfast	5.28	1.18
Leaving home	4.78	1.31
Making breakfast	4.72	1.18
Going to bed	4.83	1.20
Taking medicine	5.28	1.02
Taking shower	5.67	1.14
Using bathroom	5.56	0.86
Watching TV	5.28	0.90

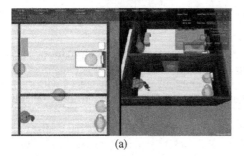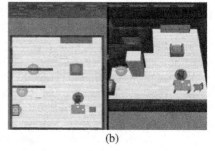

(a)   (b)

Fig. 2. Screenshots of activity playback. (a) The virtual character is performing *Eating breakfast* activity in the kitchen. (b) The virtual character is performing *Using bathroom* activity in the bathroom. Green circles represent sensors with their detection range. When a sensor is triggered by the virtual character, its color changes to purple.

The results of the user study suggest that the activity playback performance is, in general, acceptable with room for improvement. All subjects were able to easily understand the concept without too much explanation when they just started watching the activity playback videos. They all agreed that the action sequences made logical sense from their life experiences.

In the user study we found two participants constantly trying to make connections to their own ways of performing those activities while watching the playback. They both stated that the activity playbacks were fine, but somewhat far from their own particular ways of doing things, and therefore gave relatively low ratings. For example, one said before she went to take a shower, she would use the toilet first and then spend some time at the sink to remove the makeup and wash hands and face, none of which was demonstrated in the Taking Shower activity playback. Currently, the activity model and playback algorithm is designed to be able to reenact human activities in general, but not optimized for a specific character with certain personality and lifestyle. This disparity results from factors including personal lifestyle, culture, religion, age, gender, level of fitness, among other factors. We plan to improve the activity playback model so that it could be personalized to accommodate character profiles with different living habits to achieve a higher level of realism.

The common negative feedback the subjects gave was that the action animations needed to be better designed. Given the limited time and complexity of animation design, we only had 8 animations at the time of conducting the user study and some of the animations were reused for different actions. Most subjects expressed that a few actions were confusing because the animations didn't look very natural and it was necessary to design more low-level animations to better represent the human body movements, especially the ones that link two actions, to make the transitions smooth. After all, it was the animations, not the activity models or algorithms, that the users saw and rated the realism on. Therefore it is critical to use more realistic animations for the front end to more precisely visualize the actions and activities created from the back end. There is no end to improving accuracy and realism of the simulation, and it is a worthwhile pursuit.

5   Conclusion

Human centered research relies heavily on human activity data to verify the performance of the algorithms and modeling techniques. Unfortunately, it is very difficult to obtain sufficient datasets from real smart spaces due to the cost and labor. We presented the Activity Playback modeling – a simulation approach to producing realistic synthesis datasets as an alternative that reduces the cost significantly.

We described the framework of the APB approach and the components of the activity model, showing how they control the attributes of the activity from different aspects. We presented the methodology of activity model design and provided an example of the design process. We also presented the activity playback algorithm, and showed how it worked smoothly with the activity model to simulate activities. We conducted a user study to validate the realism of the APB approach. The study results verified its realism and efficacy for activity simulation, and pointed out to building personalized activity models as a future research direction.

References

1. Wray, R.E., Laird, J.E.: Variability in human behavior modeling for military simulations. In: Behavior Representation in Modeling and Simulation Conference (2003)
2. Lee, J.W., Helal, A., Sung, Y., Cho, K.: A context-driven approach to scalable human activity simulation. In: 2013 ACM SIGSIM Conference on Principles of Advanced Discrete Simulation, pp. 373–378. ACM, New York (2013)
3. Lee, J.W., Helal, A., Sung, Y., Cho, K.: Context-driven control algorithms for scalable simulation of human activities in smart homes. In: 2013 IEEE 10th International Conference on Ubiquitous Intelligence and Computing and 10th International Conference on Autonomic and Trusted Computing, pp. 285–292 (2013)
4. Lee, J.W., Helal, A., Sung, Y., Cho, K.: Context activity selection and scheduling in context-driven simulation. In: Symposium on Theory of Modeling & Simulation - DEVS Integrative. Society for Computer Simulation International, San Diego, CA, USA (2014)

5. Kasteren, T.V., Noulas, A., Englebienne, G., Kröse, B.: Accurate Activity Recognition in a Home Setting. In: 10th International Conference on Ubiquitous Computing. ACM, New York (2008)
6. Hasan, M.K., Rubaiyeat, H.A., Lee, Y.K., Lee, S.: A reconfigurable HMM for activity recognition. In: 10th International Conference on Advanced Communication Technology, vol. 1, pp. 843–846 (2008)
7. Duong, T.V., Bui, H.H., Phung, D.Q., Venkatesh, S.: Activity recognition and abnormality detection with the switching hidden semi-markov model. In: IEEE Computer Society Conference on Computer Vision and Pattern Recognition, vol. 1, pp. 838–845 (2005)
8. Duong, T., Phung, D., Bui, H., Venkatesh, S.: Efficient Duration and Hierarchical Modeling for Human Activity Recognition. Artificial Intelligence 173(7–8), 830–856 (2009)
9. Singla, G., Cook, D.J., Schmitter-Edgecombe, M.: Incorporating temporal reasoning into activity recognition for smart home residents. In: AAAI Workshop on Spatial and Temporal Reasoning, pp. 53–61 (2008)
10. Bose, R., Helal, A.: Observing walking behavior of humans using distributed phenomenon detection and tracking mechanisms. In: Proceedings of the IEEE/IPSJ International Symposium on Applications and the Internet, SAINT (2008)
11. Bouchard, K., Ajroud, A., Bouchard, B., Bouzouane, A.: SIMACT: a 3D open source smart home simulator for activity recognition. In: Kim, T.-h., Adeli, H. (eds.) AST/UCMA/ISA/ACN 2010. LNCS, vol. 6059, pp. 524–533. Springer, Heidelberg (2010)
12. Synnott, J., Chen, L., Nugent, C., Moore, G.: IE sim – a flexible tool for the simulation of data generated within intelligent environments. In: Paternò, F., de Ruyter, B., Markopoulos, P., Santoro, C., van Loenen, E., Luyten, K. (eds.) AmI 2012. LNCS, vol. 7683, pp. 373–378. Springer, Heidelberg (2012)
13. Bruneau, J., Jouve, W., Consel, C.: DiaSim: a parameterized simulator for pervasive computing applications. In: 6th Annual International of the Mobile and Ubiquitous Systems: Networking & Services, pp. 1–10. IEEE (2009)
14. Nguyen, T.V., Kim, J.G., Choi, D.: ISS: the interactive smart home simulator. In: 11th International Conference on Advanced Communication Technology, vol. 3, pp. 1828–1833. IEEE (2009)
15. Helal, S., Lee, J.W., Hossain, S., Kim, E., Hagras, H., Cook, D.: Persim - simulator for human activities in pervasive spaces. In: 7th International Conference on Intelligent Environments, pp. 192–199. IEEE (2011)
16. Chen, L., Nugent, C.D., Wang, H.: A Knowledge-Driven Approach to Activity Recognition in Smart Homes. IEEE Transactions on Knowledge and Data Engineering 24(6), 961–974 (2012)
17. Chin, J.P., Diehl, V.A., Norman, K.L.: Development of an instrument measuring user satisfaction of the human-computer interface. In: SIGCHI Conference on Human Factors in Computing Systems, pp. 213–218. ACM (1988)
18. Helal, A., Cho, K., Lee, W., Sung, Y., Lee, J.W., Kim, E.: 3D Modeling and Simulation of Human Activities in Smart spaces. In: 9th International Conference on Ubiquitous Intelligence & Computing and 9th International Conference on Autonomic & Trusted Computing, pp. 112–119. IEEE (2012)
19. Lee, J.W., Cho, S., Liu, S., Cho, K., Helal, S.: Persim 3D: context-driven simulation and modeling of human activities in smart spaces. In: Submission to IEEE Transactions on Automation Science and Engineering
20. Helal, S., Mann, W., El-Zabadani, H., King, J., Kaddoura, Y., Jansen, E.: The Gator Tech Smart House: A Programmable Pervasive Space. Computer 38(3), 50–60 (2005)

Activity Recognition in Assisted Living Facilities with Incremental, Approximate Ground Truth

Jit Biswas[1,2,3,4,5,6,7], Romain Endelin[8](✉), Clifton Phua[1],
Aung Aung Phyo Wai[1], Andrei Tolstikov[1],
Zhu Jiaqi[1], Thibaut Tiberghien[2,3,4,5,6,7], Hamdi Aloulou[8],
Philip Yap Lin Kiat[9], and Mounir Mokhtari[2,3,4,5,6,7,8]

[1] Institute for Infocomm Research (I2R), Singapore, Singapore
[2] IPAL joint Lab. CNRS France UMI 2955, Besançon, France
[3] Institut Mines-Telecom, Palaiseau, France
[4] Institute for Infocomm Research/A*STAR Singapore, Singapore, Singapore
[5] National University of Singapore, Singapore, Singapore
[6] UPMC Sorbonne University, Paris, France
[7] University Joseph Fourier, Saint-Martin-d'Héres, France
[8] CNRS LIRMM/Institut Mines-Télécom, Paris, France
`romain.endelin@lirmm.fr`
[9] Khoo Teck Puat Hospital, Singapore, Singapore

Abstract. In this paper we present the problems associated with acquisition of ground truth, which is a critical step in facilitating accurate and automated care in Assisted Living Facilities. The approach permits both bottom up and top down methods of reasoning about data. The trade-offs between granularity of ground truth acquisition and its impact on the detection rate are presented. It is suggested that the acquisition of ground truth should become a seamless operation incorporated transparently into the workflow of operations in these facilities. It is expected that with automation of collection, the increasing corpus of ground truth will lead to steady improvements in the detection rate and therefore the quality of automated monitoring and care provisioning. The methodology and models are substantiated with real data from two assisted living facilities, one in Singapore and the other in France. Although the results are preliminary they are quite promising.

Keywords: Ambient assisted living · Machine learning · Deployment and validation

1 Introduction and Rationale

It is important to automate the recognition of residents' activities in Assisted Living Facilities (ALFs). For quality and responsiveness of care, it is important that a resident's immediate needs be addressed as promptly and effectively as possible. Sometimes the needs are not voiced by the residents and sometimes the residents may not even know of their situations or their needs. Context aware

© Springer International Publishing Switzerland 2015
A. Geissbühler et al. (Eds.): ICOST 2015, LNCS 9102, pp. 103–115, 2015.
DOI: 10.1007/978-3-319-19312-0_9

assistance of the residents calls for automated recognition of the situations and contexts within the rooms in the ALFs. There is also the issue of paucity of staff. There is an ever-increasing shortage of manpower, and even with the existing manpower it is often not possible to observe the detailed behavioral patterns of the residents since this requires much time and careful observation.

It is being widely recognized that the way to automation of monitoring is through the use of wearable and ambient sensors. The field of smart nation is emerging rapidly and Internet of Things has become a reality. While the prospect of automated monitoring is greatly enhanced with these technologies, automation of monitoring is still dependent on obtaining of ground truth, which is a critical requirement. In many domains, especially in eldercare, ground truth must be collected at the site.

In this paper we discuss a multi-sensor system for monitoring modern assisted living facilities. Validation of the system was done over a one year period in Singapore when the system was deployed in a dementia hostel (located at Peacehaven nursing home in Singapore [1-3]). Many problems were resolved during the validation phase. The system has been deployed in a modern assisted living facility in France and has been in continuous operation for a number of weeks, in a pilot study that is expected to continue for several months. We present initial results of from both these exercises.

This paper also presents machine learning algorithms to recognize situations where residents are monitored at all times, especially during the off-peak hours. Bayesian Network based classifiers are developed for recognizing the activities of residents. The algorithms are based on the assumption that labeled ground truth is available. The ground truth may be obtained incrementally, and therefore the classifiers may be re-trained on the fly as new ground truth is made available through the data collection protocol. The quality of the recognition in terms of both sensitivity and specificity is expected to improve steadily, as more ground truth is made available. The methodology presented in this paper is designed to be aware of incomplete and potentially inconsistent labels and take suitable steps to correct errors and inconsistencies.

2   Problems with Collection of Ground Truth

In order to improve the quality of automated monitoring to an acceptable level it is advocated that the sensor data produced be analyzed through pattern recognition and machine learning, so that we can move beyond simply presenting the sensor data in a visual manner. One of the major challenges in this regard is the collection of accurate ground truth. With properly labeled and accurate ground truth, machine learning algorithms developed will have higher detection rates, while at the same time producing very few false alarms, so as to be acceptable to the end users.

The challenges with obtaining accurate ground truth are many. Since it involves diligent and painstaking recording and logging of events, ground truth taken by human observers always tends to be sparse, incomplete and often inaccurate. There are inaccuracies in labeling, timing and distinguishing between activities. In the field of monitoring elderly residents in ALFs, there could be personal habits and circadian shifts that make it difficult to generalize across the population. More data is needed in order to personalize the training of the classifiers. There is also a great need for validation with real data from modern assisted living facilities, without which the systems will not be reliable and dependable to the point of acceptance by the staff of the ALFs. However, there is a chicken and egg situation here, since without deployment in reasonable numbers, it is not possible to obtain the ground truth necessary for designing better classifiers for improved automation.

2.1   Use-Case: An ALF Room with Two Occupants

As an example, we consider a case that came out of a real life deployment during a trial conducted at the Peacehaven RLA (Resident Living Area) at Singapore. Although the deployment consisted of a number of sensors of different types along with a gateway (called a mini-server) that collected sensor data, this paper focuses on two sensing modalities, the Force Sensitive Resistor (FSR) sensor to detect bed occupancy and movement on the bed, and the Passive InfraRed (PIR) sensor to detect movements in the room or in the washroom. There are two FSR sensors for two beds in the twin-occupancy room and four PIR sensors, one in the bedroom and the other in the washroom. Fig 1 presents a schematic of the layout of these sensors.

Fig. 1. Two occupancy rooms in an ALF showing two types of sensors

In our deployment we prepared a simple manual form for data entry whereby the care-givers in charge of a particular ward are requested to fill in the form when it is convenient. Given their busy schedules and the fact that filling ground truth information is not an activity that the care-givers do as a part of their daily work, there was a significant amount of incompleteness in the forms. Forms were also sometimes filled out incorrectly or inaccurately, thereby introducing more uncertainty in the data. Wherever possible, simple strategies were used to deal with such anomalies. To deal with missing data in the ground truth, we used the most commonly occurring label in the corresponding six hour time segment. Manual review is still necessary to make sure that this did not introduce a semantic inconsistency. For example, if the label was missing for the time slot from 5am to 6am, and the label prior to that was 'showering', then it is highly unlikely that the label from 5am to 6am would be 'sleeping', even though that was the most commonly occurring label in the corresponding six hour time segment. Table 1 presents a snapshot of six hours of ground truth that were recorded by the nursing home staff.

Table 1. Manually collected Ground Truth for six hours

Hour	Midnight — 1am	1–2am	2–3am	3–4am	4–5am	5–6am
Resident 1	No GT	Sleep	Sleep	Toilet	Sleep	Sleep
Resident 2	No GT	Sleep	Toilet	Sleep	Toilet	Shower

This is an example of what we call partial labeled ground truth (GT). Notice that the GT is recorded only at certain times, and there are gaps when no data is recorded. Another problem is that the GT simply records an event, but does not state precisely when in the time window the event occurred. Also, care-givers sometimes record events en-block at the end of the shift (from their memory), and this may introduce errors and discrepancies into the GT.

Obs No.	1	2	3	4	5	6	7	8	9	10	11	12	13	14	15	16	17	18
Bed 1 FSR1 Sensor	181	124	170	191	234	239	272	188	233	247	286	189	178	273	252	213	139	185
Bed 2 FSR2 Sensor	167	75	79	99	139	127	138	93	117	122	143	115	83	139	123	116	71	93
Bedroom PIR1 Sensor	0	2	0	0	0	0	0	0	0	0	0	2	2	0	0	0	0	0
Shower PIR2 Sensor	0	0	0	0	0	0	0	0	0	0	0	0	0	0	0	0	0	0
Toilet PIR3 Sensor	0	2	0	0	0	0	0	0	0	0	0	1	0	0	0	0	0	0
Wash area PIR4 Sensor	0	8	0	0	0	0	0	0	0	0	1	6	2	0	0	1	0	0
Assigned Label	SS	SS	SS	SS	SS	SS	SS	SS	SS	SS	SS	SS	SS	ST	ST	ST	SS	SS

Obs No.	19	20	21	22	23	24	25	26	27	28	29	30	31	32	33	34	35	36
Bed 1 FSR1 Sensor	152	137	195	278	61	107	37	11	25	43	33	45	52	28	8	0	16	6
Bed 2 FSR2 Sensor	82	66	96	138	25	50	19	26	42	76	19	24	30	32	4	0	30	12
Bedroom PIR1 Sensor	0	0	0	0	1	1	0	2	1	0	1	4	0	1	1	0	0	0
Shower PIR2 Sensor	0	0	0	0	0	0	0	0	0	0	0	2	0	0	0	0	0	0
Toilet PIR3 Sensor	0	0	0	0	1	2	0	2	0	0	0	0	0	0	0	0	0	0
Wash area PIR4 Sensor	2	0	0	0	4	2	0	1	2	0	2	3	12	6	4	0	3	9
Assigned Label	SS	SS	TS	TS	SS	SS	SS	ST	SS	SS	SS	SS	SS	SS	SH	SH	SH	SH

Fig. 2. Consolidated labels derived from GT for six hours from 12 to 6 am

Our challenge is to take the ground truth of the type shown above and glean from it appropriate information with which to label each tuple of sensor data recorded by the sensors. There could be multiple ways of doing this annotation, depending on what assumptions we make about the relationship between the GT and the sensor data. Fig 2 presents a view of sensor data along with annotated ground truth. In the figure the sensor events have been aggregated into windows of time granularity 10 minutes each. The GT information from Table 1 has been used to (manually) assign two-person activity labels shown in the last row of the figure where S denotes Sleeping, T denotes Toileting and H denotes Shower.

With the labels in place, supervised learning algorithms may be used to automate the recognition of activities from the sensor data. Note that this is a case of two-person activity recognition, and is possible due to the fact that the number of possible labels are not that many given the fact that these are night-time hours (from midnight to six am), in a nursing home room. However, note that during the day time the possibilities are much more numerous. For example, there could be nurses, cleaners or visitors whose presence may cause sensor events. It may lead to error if we use night time derived GT to assign labels to daytime datasets.

3   Bayesian Networks and DBN Classifiers for Activity Recognition

The time interval over which features in the observation matrix are computed is of critical importance in the formulation of effective DBNs that enable the recognition of relevant situations and patterns. If the time interval is too small, the feature may not appear. On the other hand if the time interval is too large, gross features may take over, and the detail may be insufficient for us to recognize the activity being looked for. The key is to discover what is the appropriate time interval at which the features extracted are just right to permit recognition of activities.

Having collected data for motion sensors, vibration and FSR sensors, it is possible to experiment with range of time intervals, looking for temporal dependencies between abstract states at the higher level.

3.1   Labeling the Peacehaven Dataset

Records were available in the period of January and February 2012 from which information is gleaned as to the typical activities of the two residents on a daily basis. The day is divided into six segments, night, early morning, late morning, afternoon, early evening, late evening.

The care-giver provides ground truth of two types.

– Recollections after the fact. These are susceptible to errors since they may be wrongly remembered as to date and time of occurrence, person etc.
– On the spot recording. These may be incorrect as to value recorded, however the time is usually accurate since it is recorded by the system.

The value of inferences or classification based on this ground truth is only as good as the value or veracity of the ground truth itself. Thus it is important to ascertain the quality of the ground truth. Our task is to take partial and possibly erroneous labels at a high (human) level, as the only basis for ground truth, and then build machine learning algorithms based on assignment of labels to sensor data and features derived thereof.

A data driven approach towards the handling of uncertainty consists of building classifiers for activities of daily living such as sleeping, showering, toileting etc. These activities are represented in a partially ordered ADL graph. A conservative approach towards handling of uncertainty would assign a higher weight to the uncertain states, so that preventive action may be taken. Note that the states may be modeled arbitrarily to represent states of the human subject or the measurement apparatus. Thus this is quite a general approach. The classifiers for recognizing these activities are trained with incrementally appended ground truth as collected from independent observations by care-givers and operational staff. This allows for a system whereby, over a period of time, "unknown" sources of uncertainty are harnessed and incorporated into a data driven, or probabilistic framework. However, it is important to mention that, by now, there is no synergy of the learning between multiple patients. Therefore, in case a room's resident happens to change, the system must restart the learning process.

Applying the above formulation to the labeled dataset from Fig 2, the multiple person activities to be detected are SS, ST, TS and SH. Note that other labels such as HS are also possible, as also possibilities that include W (for the activity Wandering). A Bayesian classifier for the system was developed using MATLAB.

BN incorporates features that are extracted over time, however it does allow us to capture variation that take place over time. DBN brings in the time domain by introducing the previous activity into the evaluation process for determining the current activity based on the current observations. A DBN consists of many copies of the Bayesian Network, one for each time instance. In addition, there are conditional dependencies between past (parent nodes) and future (children nodes) which occur in the copies of the Bayesian Network. In Fig 3 an example of Dynamic Bayesian Network is shown.

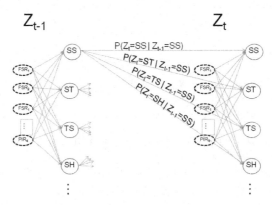

Fig. 3. Two steps of the DBN for the six hours dataset of Fig 2

An example of the DBN is shown in Figure 3, where SS, ST, TS, and SH respectively denote the activities identified previously. As pointed out in Murphy [5], the DBN is a special case of the HMM [4] with time incorporated. In the example above, the network is formulated with sensors at the base level, and hidden states as the activities of the residents. Since this is a two-person activity recognition situation, the hypothetical states were the combinations SS, ST, TS and SH. This is based on ground truth collected for that day. Other combinations are possible, but since they did not occur, they were not incorporated into the problem formulation. The objective was to determine if the methodology was appropriate and suitable. The intuition behind the choice of DBN [8] is indeed very compelling because of the fact that in nursing homes the time dimension is a key determinant of activities. Note that the above formulation of DBN is only an initial attempt. It needs to be investigated further in greater detail. Furthermore, although our reasoning performs in reasonable time, the scalability should be validated against more extensive tests, as DBN may be resource consuming.

The results of the application of these algorithms on the six hour dataset presented earlier is 61.9% sensitivity for BN and 61.7% sensitivity for DBN. The marginal difference is negligible. Thus there is no difference between DBN and BN for this case. This is not expected, since we expect that DBN will perform better than BN. The reason could be that the dataset is not large enough to provide enough instances of each type of event for statistical validity. For example there are only two instances of 'TS' and four instances each of 'ST' and 'SH'.

3.2   Dealing with Appropriate Time Granularities

The granularity time period used as lowest common denominator for all sensors, (system data rate) is 1 millisecond. For targeted activities this is expected to be adequate. The raw data as produced by the sensors is aggregated and stored at the system data rate. A passive infrared sensor detects when a person is moving in the room or in the washroom. This sensor can be calibrated to detect movements at levels of granularity ranging from very fine to very coarse, depending on the application. In this case the application dictated that the sensor detection threshold be kept moderately coarse so as not to get an avalanche of sensor events whenever someone moved in the room. However, it was important that the system was able to detect transition of the resident or occupant from one room to the other, or in this case from the bedroom to the washroom. The issue of sensor clocks was dealt with by recording time-stamps for each sensor event to be the time at which the event was recorded at the mini-server which also took on the role of gateway to all the wireless sensors and devices (such as iPAD) connected to the smart NH room.

Our system should achieve the dual purpose of monitoring of activities through the day as well as detecting potentially unsafe situations at certain times of the day. This calls for a mixed approach in terms of time granularities. Algorithms that monitor sleep / wake duration, showering / toileting frequency etc. typically operate on a time scale much higher than algorithms that detect potentially dangerous situations. Furthermore, depending on the nature of the activities that we would want to detect, we may not even be sure what is the appropriate time granularity at which to operate our algorithms and system.

4   Use-Case: Activity Recognition in Single Occupancy ALF Rooms

The second case examined is from single occupancy rooms at the Saint-Vincent-de-Paul Nursing Home in France. Here the data consists of sensor data recordings from multiple residents. Each resident occupies a single room with a non-shared toilet. High level reasoning using rules have been used to infer activities of each resident over arbitrary periods of time. Fig 4 depicts the output of such reasoning. The main problem with this output is that though it captures the reasoned effects of sensor observations, there is no validation of these reasoned activities (or activities derived from a purely logic based top-down approach). Specifically, there are instances of activities (or lack thereof) that are clearly questionable, such as the lack of toilet events over long periods of days. The latter took place because the toilet sensor was down. The point is that the validation and reconciliation of ground truth with sensor must be done in professional way, with proper validation. It is our thesis that this is possible when both top down and bottom up approaches are used in conjunction.

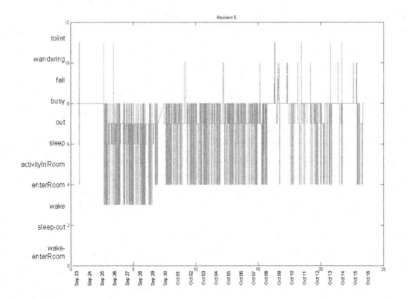

Fig. 4. Preliminary results of activity recognition through high level reasoning

4.1   Approach Using Habits and Summary Ground Truth

Five residents were selected for our initial study. The habits of each resident were obtained from the nurse in charge. For each of the five residents, two motion detection sensors were placed, one in the bedroom and one in the toilet. In addition a door sensor detecting whether the door is open or closed was also deployed. The sensors were deployed in the rooms of all five residents, and sensor data was gathered for a period of about seven and a half days from midnight 30th Jan to 10:30am on 6th Feb. The detailed plot of resident A is shown in Fig 5. There are 1511 events recorded for resident A in the entire period. The habits of resident A are shown in the top right hand corner of the figure.

4.2   Manual Collection of Ground Truth Data

For obtaining ground truth information, real life observation data had to be collected by an observer on site. A researcher observed the five selected residents for a period of ten hours from 7am to 5pm on one of the days. During the detailed study period, ground truth records were logged by the researcher, showing the time of occurrence of each entry, the resident involved, and the respective activity concerning that ground truth entry. Fig 5 shows a plot of sensor data for the entire 6 1/2 day period. In Fig 6 we present the events in a zoomed in segment of 10 hours for the same resident. A cursory examination of the ground truth collected showed that there were discrepancies between the real life observations and the sensor reported events. For instance, in figure 6, activities observed in the afternoon are due to a visit from the cleaning service, that was not included in the reasoning. This process of ground truth data acquisition requires a large human involvement. In order to reduce it, it could later be guided by the system. For instance, the system could seek for unusual data patterns, and ask the researcher to observe the ground truth accordingly, thus ignoring data pattern that are already known.

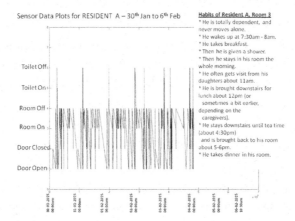

Fig. 5. Sensor data plots for a resident for six days. Note the connecting line simply denotes temporal ordering, and has no other meaning.

4.3   Eliciting Detailed Ground Truth from Summary Ground Truth

For machine learning we need to obtain detailed ground truth from the ground truth observed by the researcher. This is a challenging task, since no camera

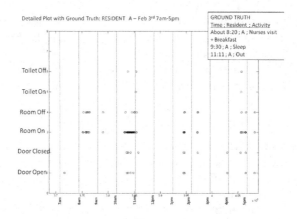

Fig. 6. Zoomed in segment of 10 hours duration from the plot of Fig 5

recording is available. All that we have is the summary ground truth and the habits. However with some reflection it is possible to make reasonably good guess of the detailed ground truth from these two snippets of information.

The procedure followed was roughly as follows:

- The activity labels were decided. There were two labeling schemes, simple and detailed. The simple labeling scheme assigns the labels Room Movement, Sleep, Toilet Movement, Out and the detailed labeling scheme assigns the labels Sleep, Breakfast, Resident Movement in room, Shower, Out, Housekeeping, Toilet activity.
- The sensor data was collected and plotted for observation period
- The daily habits were recorded for each resident
- For a segment of 10 hours on one of the days, ground truth was collected by manual observation.
- The period of observation was broken up into 10 minute intervals (optimal period)
- The recorded ground truth was transcribed into their appropriate 10 minute slots. The result of this exercise produced labeled datasets at 10 minute granularity level.
- The classifier was finally constructed by producing three-tuples of sensor values for the configuration Door, Bedroom, Toilet. Since this could be at arbitrary granularity limited only by the sampling rate, we obtained tuples at the level of one minute duration, obtaining 600 tuples for the entire period of ten hours.

The Peacehaven study in Singapore indicated that the ten minute interval was quite well suited for machine learning as discovered in our related work [3]. Thus we examined the France dataset at a level of granularity of 10 minutes. Thus for the example of Resident A presented above, given the ten hour period from 7am to 5pm we needed to label 600 tuples of aggregated sensor data from 178 sensor events. By examining each resident's habits, ground truth and sensor data, along with a list of explanations that were recorded by the observer (Fig 5-6), we were able to come up with a first cut detailed ground truth for each resident. The detailed ground truth for resident A is shown in Fig 6. 178 events are in the period selected for detailed study. At the top right hand corner of the figure are shown the ground truth that was collected for the resident.

4.4 Results

Using Bayesian classifiers we obtain a detection rate of 70% when using a simple labeling scheme, and 68% for a more detailed labeling scheme. These are preliminary results and for only one resident. The analysis is currently being repeated for the remaining residents and with more ground truth data. Also additional methods of automated ground truth collection are being investigated, that do not need the presence of the researcher. In other words GT collection mechanisms that fit in seamlessly into the workflow of the care-giver are being explored. An interesting dimension that remains to be explored is whether it is possible to carry out transfer learning [6]. Given that the patterns of behavior and the habits are similar between the residents, it could be possible to learn patterns from one resident and apply it to another.

5 Discussions

Motion detectors based on PIR sensors have been widely deployed for general use as well as for elder-care applications and has been commercialized successfully in at least one instance [9]. Though low-cost, robust and requiring minimal maintenance, their frame of discernment is restricted due to their lack of precision and range. In our work we have deployed a multi-modal sensor based activity monitoring system which augments the first generation PIR based systems in two fundamental ways: firstly, it improves the robustness of the system by having additional sources of information which have independent functioning and observation potential, and therefore bring in additional sources of evidence. Secondly, we enrich the set of activities that can be detected by diversifying the physical dimensions that can be explored by different types of sensors in the multi-modal sensing environment. Undoubtedly, bringing in additional sensors adds to the complexity of the system, however, if properly engineered, the system can, as we have seen, be made to operate with whatever set of sensor observations and ground truth is available in an incremental fashion, with the handling of partial failure also handled in an incremental fashion.

Incompleteness refers to the fact that ground truth is incrementally available. Thus the patterns of activity or behavior are actually 'emerging patterns' [7]. The manner in which we deal with this is to have the algorithm always update its classifier with fresh ground truth data and in this sense, adapt itself to the new information. This continuous learning approach is done by manual processes, but could be mechanized in future when volumes of data and numbers of deployment become large.

6   Conclusions

We report the result of our past and ongoing work in monitoring nursing home residents using ambient sensors. The system used has been revised over two trials and is capable of producing results for long periods without manual intervention, and over remote connection, via cloud services. We are getting about 62% correct detection with Bayesian classifiers using six hours of labeled Peacehaven data. With ten hours of data from a French nursing home we are getting about 70% correct detection using simplified labeling and 68% correct detection using more detailed and descriptive labeling. Of note is the fact that our approach uses no cameras for obtaining ground truth, and is targeted at simple mechanisms for continuous data collection on the fly, so that knowledge base for reasoning might increase and accuracy of correct detection improve over time. We have experimented with both Bayesian and dynamic Bayesian (HMM) approaches. Though there was no significant difference, this could be because of the limited amount of data used. Specificity (reduction of false alarms) is very important, especially in nursing home situations, and this aspect will be addressed once the classifier is improved to a level of accuracy (or sensitivity) which is higher. We are targeting an automated machine learning correct detection rate of 90% at which stage the system will go into operation to provide real time alerts, and we will have a better understanding of how to reduce false alarms.

Acknowledgments. We are grateful to the staff and residents of Peacehaven Nursing Home, Hope Resident Living Area, who participated in our trial in the AMUPADH project. We are also grateful to the participants and staff of the Saint-Vincent-de-Paul nursing home in France for their cooperation and assistance with data collection in the current deployment. This work was supported in part by the Home 2015 Program of A*STAR, Singapore.

References

1. Biswas, J., Mokhtari, M., Dong, J.S., Yap, P.: Mild Dementia Care at Home – Integrating Activity Monitoring, User Interface Plasticity and Scenario Verification. In: Lee, Y., Bien, Z.Z., Mokhtari, M., Kim, J.T., Park, M., Kim, J., Lee, H., Khalil, I. (eds.) ICOST 2010. LNCS, vol. 6159, pp. 160–170. Springer, Heidelberg (2010)
2. Mokhtari, M., Aloulou, H., Tiberghien, T., Biswas, J., Racoceanu, D., Yap, P.: New trends to support independence in persons with mild dementia - a mini-review. In: Gerontology, Karger (2012). doi:10.1159/000337827
3. Biswas, et al.: Monitoring of Elderly in Assisted Living Facilities: a multi-sensor approach (submitted for publication)
4. Rabiner, L.: A tutorial on hidden Markov models and selected applications in speech recognition. In: Proceedings of the IEEE, vol. 77, no. 2, pp. 257–286. IEEE

5. Murphy, K.: Dynamic Bayesian Networks: Representation, Inference and Learning, Ph.D thesis, the University of California at Berkeley (2002)
6. Pan, S.J., Yang, Q.: A survey on transfer learning. IEEE Transactions on Knowledge and Data Engineering **22**(10), October 2010. IEEE
7. Dong, G., Li, J.: Efficient mining of emerging patterns: discovering trends and differences. In: Proceedings of the Conference on Knowledge Discovery and Data Mining (KDD), pp. 43–52. ACM (1999)
8. Tolstikov, A., Hong, X., Biswas, J., Nugent, C., Chen, L., Parente, G.: Comparison of Fusion Methods Based on DST and DBN in Human Activity Recognition. Journal of Control Theory and Applications **9**(1), 18–27 (2011). Springer Verlag
9. http://www.careinnovations.com (last accessed February 26, 2015)

From User Requirements to Data: An XML Standard for Structuring Events in Monitored Environments

Rebekah Hunter[(✉)], Mark Donnelly, Dewar Finlay, and George Moore

Computer Science Research Institute, University of Ulster, Newtownabbey,
Northern Ireland
hunter-r9@email.ulster.ac.uk,
{mp.donnelly,d.finlay,g.moore}@ulster.ac.uk

Abstract. This paper describes the development and evaluation of a data model to store events that occur within monitored environments. The overall aim is to standardize the transfer of environment events, captured from heterogeneous sources. A case study is presented that focuses on behavioral events exhibited by children with autism. The paper focuses on describing the methodology adopted for acquiring user requirements, classifying the keywords common to a range of data sources, and consequently developing a suitable data model that has the flexibility to accommodate the addition of new data types. Also provided is a description of the resulting XML-based schema that defines the constraints on the data to ensure conformity to the data model.

Keywords: Data collection · Data modeling · xml · Monitored environments · Children with autism

1 Introduction

Continuous monitoring of human behavior is becoming more prevalent, as we live in an information age where the advances in pervasive computing support discreet data collection [1]. Remote support for people with chronic conditions including dementia, COPD and stroke can benefit from on-going data collection to help inform new treatment [2]. Similarly, continuous monitoring has been used to monitor the behavior of children with autism who often communicate by exhibiting challenging behaviors [3]. While a cure for autism does not yet exist, several approaches have been established to reduce challenging behaviors, such as Applied Behavior Analysis (ABA). ABA focuses on the science of analyzing behavior by gathering data surrounding behaviors to determine why they are occurring [4]. With this knowledge personalized interventions can be designed to adjust those behaviors, and through review of the intervention outcomes behavioral trends can be monitored.

Behavior monitoring has traditionally been conducted using pen-and-paper, where records are made during an intervention session and stored in a paper-based file [5]. Leveraging upon developments in touch screen technology and the portability of mobile devices offers the opportunity to conduct event annotation through digital means [6]. However, this only accounts for human observable events. Research began to emerge in the 1990's that explored the integration of physiological sensors to monitor an individual's

© Springer International Publishing Switzerland 2015
A. Geissbühler et al. (Eds.): ICOST 2015, LNCS 9102, pp. 116–126, 2015.
DOI: 10.1007/978-3-319-19312-0_10

heart rate, blood pressure, and respiration, for example [7]. Later studies considered the use of non-invasive sensors installed within an environment to monitor an individual's movements and their interactions with their environment [8].

In our previous work, we presented a framework for managing data within monitored environments in order to support home-based autism intervention [9]. Within this framework, a human observer would make annotations in real time using a tablet device, and data about behavioral event occurrences would be stored. This data would be augmented with sensor data, collected continuously during the session, to provide the behavior analyst with additional data to inform the causes of behavioral events.

This paper describes the set of steps taken to formally represent event data through XML, with the focus on meeting user requirements. It is envisaged that this approach could be used to represent event data in any domain. However, here we describe a case study on the collection of event data from multiple sources within the specific context of supporting children with autism in monitored environments. In section 2, related works and the opportunities for XML within monitored environments are identified before section 3 presents the steps taken towards developing a data model based on user requirements. Section 4 discusses the use of existing data to validate our model, and then section 5 describes the results and future work before the paper is concluded in section 6.

2   Background

Collecting data through paper-based records, sensor events and digital annotations result in the emergence of large heterogeneous datasets. Typically, the purpose for collecting these data is to present human understandable information about the events that have occurred over time. Indeed, data interrogation and visualization techniques would greatly assist the process of behavior analysis and so there exists a challenge in structuring such data in a way that they can be presented together. Nevertheless, before this can be achieved, challenges related to the storage, retrieval, and cataloguing of monitored environment data must be addressed [10].

In the realm of monitored environments, some research has been conducted in handling heterogeneous sensor data. One such study describes an XML-based model called homeML [11], which defines a structure for the transfer of heterogeneous sensor data within monitored environments. There are also other existing approaches to using XML for storing and transmitting sensor data such as SensorML [12] and EEML [13]. However there are no such XML-based approaches reported in the literature which hold data to complement sensor events, such as behavioral events and manual annotations which may provide further insight in to the understanding of sensor data. Another study has attempted to combining health and environment sensors into an ontology, and presenting an interface where the user can view these data in parallel [14]. Through a review of the literature, there does not appear to be a standard for structuring event data that includes both sensor and manually captured data. With both of these data being valuable in behavioral analysis, an opportunity has been identified to develop a model to combine these data.

There are several methods for structuring data, which include ontologies and schemas. An ontology provides a set of formal terms to describe data and the relationships between them. Database schemas define the structure of a database, and similarly XML schemas define the structure of XML documents, and specify constraints on the data it holds. XML presents an opportunity within monitored environments to describe data, and as such provides data modeling capability [15].

Despite advances in technology-based data collection and storage of events, paper-based methods are still preferred for observable, manually annotated events due to complex and unstandardized data needs of individual users [16]. Only through fully understanding the user requirements can a suitable model be developed to handle such data, and as such this is where the data modeling process begins.

3   Methods

A top-down approach towards data modeling was taken, as we began with the user requirements and worked towards developing the data model to meet those specific requirements. To bridge the gap between the end-users technical understanding and the engineers' clinical domain understanding, we identified a process to follow that would ensure the data model would be fit for purpose. The steps, as shown in Fig. 1., were: define the scope of the data, determine the users needs, identify data sources, classify common properties and finally to build the data model.

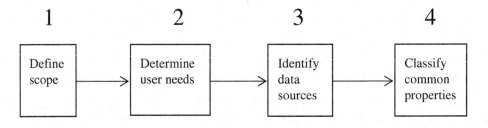

Fig. 1. The series of four steps taken to build a data model based on user requirements

Step 1 was to define the scope of the domain within which the data model was required. This would allow for conversion to a formal data model by identifying how it will be used, and by whom. In identifying the end-users we could determine the user requirements very specifically.

In the case study of children with autism, the scope specifically covered the recording and reviewing of events that occur in monitored environments. The end users are behavioral analysts who periodically review behavioral data to determine changes in behavior. Other stakeholders are parents observing day-to-day activities in the home setting, teachers leading educational lessons in a school setting, and healthcare professionals conducting behavioral interventions in a clinical setting.

Step 2 involved determining user requirements that would facilitate understanding of how the data would be used. An understanding of the potential uses of the data model would inform the data that it needed to hold, and as such the data model was built around the user requirements to ensure it could handle the necessary data. There are several ways to obtain user requirements such as a review of the literature, and through contact from both the user and domain experts through interviews, surveys, focus groups and field studies [17].

In the case of children with autism, behavior management initially involves parents or teachers recording baseline data to show typical behavior patterns. A behavior analyst will then review the baseline data and recommend interventions to reduce challenging behaviors. Interventions are conducted by a healthcare professional that records details of the interventions progress as a series of task events. The behavior analyst then compares baseline and intervention data to assess the effectiveness of the intervention. At that point they can provide recommendation to change the intervention [18]. Taking all of this in to consideration, the main user requirement is to have a standardized method of storing event data and any related influential factors. The behavior analyst needs to know which events are occurring, how often they occur, and how long they last for. In addition to this they need to know why behaviors are occurring through knowledge of the events prior to and immediately after an event has occurred. With that information in mind, they can make informed decisions on the course of therapy.

With knowledge of the user requirements, it was then possible to determine where the data would come from. In step 3 we identified the data sources, which informed us of the scope of data that needed to conform to the data model. The data model needed to represent the full scope of data to meet the user requirements, and so a list of all potential data sources would ensure that all data were supported. Data sources in monitored environments provide data through automatic or manual means, and these data contain details of events that occur. Manual annotations include: behavioral events, which describe specific information about a behavioral occurrence; and task events, which include data from interventions and school-based activities. A human observer traditionally records manual annotations on paper, but more recently research has been conducted into the introduction of handheld technology [19]. Annotations that are recorded based on sensor activity also play a vital role within monitored environments. Where physiological arousal is detected, such as a peak in heart rate, an annotation is recorded with details of the event [20]. Environmental events as identified by sensors such as contact sensors or video sensors both provide important information that may otherwise be missed by a human observer [9]. It may be possible that a data source is already represented in an existing XML-based standard that can be included. HomeML, as mention previously, is one such standard for the exchange and storage of sensor data in monitored environments [11].

Step 4 was to choose common keywords based on the data from the identified sources, which provide structure for the data model (Fig. 2.). The keyword that best describes the scope of the domain becomes the parent element, in this case 'Person' was chosen to allow the data model to cover a broader range of data – not just for children with autism. Within each person element, a profile is recorded that stores the personal details of the individual. As the focus of this paper is on the development of a structure to hold event data based on user requirements, a discussion of the profile element is outside of the scope of this paper.

Each of the three event types mentioned was considered, and the descriptions of the data each provided within an annotation were listed. By grouping together similar properties, the common keywords were identified. Table 1 illustrates the full breakdown of how the common keywords were identified through descriptions for the data for each event type.

Each time an annotation is made, the **location** and **context** are recorded. In the case of behavioral and task events, the location may refer to a room, and in the case of sensor events the location may refer to exact GPS co-ordinates. The context for a task event describes the intervention that is taking place, and for a behavioral event the context relates to any current setting or activity.

Within an annotation, a series of events can be recorded, and each of the events has a unique **id**. Each event also has a **type** – either behavioral, sensor, or task. In behavioral and task events, the name of the observer is of great importance as children with autism often form different attachments with caregivers [21], and as such they may behave differently depending on the observer. The name of the 'observer' in the case of a sensor event is the name of the device and so the **source** keyword best illustrates how the event was identified. Behavioral events are preceded by an antecedent [22], while task events are preceded by an instruction [5], and they are grouped together with the **cause** keyword to explain what provoked the behavior to occur. To define the specific details of an event, a behavioral event describes a behavior, a sensor event describes an extracted feature, and a task event describes the response to instruction. Each of these relate to the **event** keyword. Both behavioral and task events have consequences, so the common keyword of **consequence** was chosen for the data model.

Two properties of a behavioral event that are important in determining patterns and changes are intensity [23] and duration [24]. Combined, they will indicate to the behavior analysts the priority of behaviors to address through intervention. Intensity is best recorded on a scale so the observer can accurately describe the intensity with a number or keyword. In sensor events, as well as the description of the extracted feature, the actual sensor reading may be valuable. Task events in interventions are given a score to indicate if the instruction was carried out or not. Each of these figures is classified under the common keyword **value**. Duration is calculated through a simple deduction from the beginning to the end of an event, and as such **onset** and **offset** are the keywords used for each of the events [25].

Table 1. Descriptions for data surrounding behavioral, sensor and task events – leading to the identification of common keywords to use in the data model.

Behavior Event	Sensor Event	Task Event	Common Keyword
id	id	id	id
type	type	type	type
location	gps co-ordinates	location	location
setting	-	intervention	context
name	device name	name	source
antecedent	-	instruction	cause
behavior	extracted feature	response	event
onset	onset	onset	onset
offset	offset	offset	offset
intensity	sensor reading	score	value
consequence	-	consequence	consequence

Each element needs to be assigned with a data type that describes how the data must be presented to conform to the model. The location and setting elements would contain text only and therefore given the *string* data type as would the source, type, label, cause and consequence elements. Value would be numeric and therefore assigned the *integer* data type, and onset and offset would be given the *timeDate* data type that includes year, month, day, hours, minutes, and seconds.

Further restrictions can be added to the data in the XML schema to limit the number of characters, to define the maximum figure for numerical values, and to define the acceptable values for an element. Some elements may be required, and others optional. For example, a task event may occur instantaneously and a calculable duration is not necessary. Therefore, the offsetTime element should be *optional* to cater for such circumstances. Some elements, such as event, will appear multiple times as several events can occur during one annotation instance. The *maxOccurs* and *minOccurs* attributes can specify such constraints.

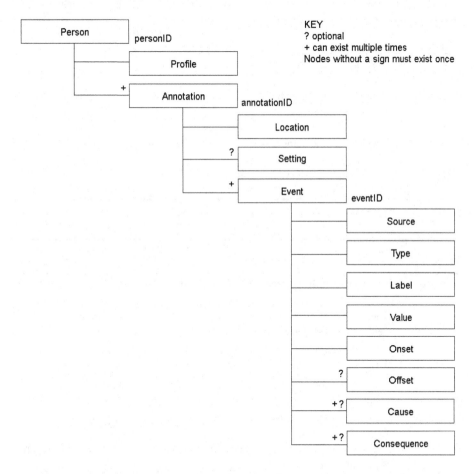

Fig. 2. The data model tree structure showing how parent and child elements are connected

Table 2. Description of elements and attributes of the person element in the data model

Element/ Attribute	Description	Required/ Optional	Data Type	Example
personID	A unique identifier for the person	Required	id	1
profile	The profile for the person	Required	-	-
annotation	The details of the annotations made	Required	-	-

Table 3. Description of elements and attributes of the annotation element in the data model

Element/ Attribute	Description	Re-quired/Optional	Data Type	Example
annotationID	A unique identifier for the action	Required	id	1
location	The location at which the annotation was made	Required	string	home
setting	The circumstances in which the annotation was made	Optional	string	before lunch
event	The details of the events that occurred	Required	-	-

Table 4. Description of elements and attributes of the event element in the data model

Element/ Attribute	Description	Required/ Optional	Data Type	Example
eventID	A unique identifier for the event	Required	id	1
source	The name of the person or device that made the ob-servation	Required	string	Susan Jones
type	The event type	Required	string	behavioral
label	A brief description of the event	Required	string	shouting
value	A numerical value relating to the event	Required	integer	4
onset	The date and time when the event started	Required	timeDate	2015-01-21T12:02:00
offset	The date and time when the event ceased	Optional	timeDate	2015-01-21T12:04:56
cause	The cause of the event	Optional	string	Activity denied
conse-quence	The consequence of the event	Optional	string	distracted

4   Evaluation

After completing the process of developing a data model based on user requirements, the XML schema has been produced. In order to evaluate the data model, we validated the XML schema by testing the structure using two dataset that were reported in the literature. The first selected dataset was collected through a smartphone application called BMAC (Behavior Monitoring for Autism in Children) [22], and consists of details of behavioral events that occur inside and outside of the home. As well as antecedent, behavior and consequence details, the application allows the user to input behavior intensity, duration and frequency. The BMAC application was used in a clinical trial to collect behavioral data for three children with autism, with their caregivers recording data using the application for five days. In order to translate the BMAC data into our data model structure, keywords were identified in the dataset that corresponded to the keywords used in our data model. For example, the data for co-ordinates were stored in the location element, and the data for recorded stored in the source element. An excerpt showing a complete annotation record is shown in figure 3.

```
<annotation annotationid="23">
    <location>54.68829812,-5.88069808</location>
    <setting>school</setting>
    <event>
        <source>teacher</source>
        <type>behavioural</type>
        <label>aggression towards others</label>
        <value>2</value>
        <onset>2014-04-09T11:25:32</onset>
        <offset>2015-01-19T11:26:32</offset>
        <cause>given task prompt/ instruction</cause>
        <cause>preferred activity denied</cause>
        <consequence>redirected to another response/activity</consequence>
    </event>
</annotation>
```

Fig. 3. BMAC data structured in XML, conforming to the XML schema

The data model was then also applied to the SSBD (self-stimulatory behavior dataset) [26], which consists of manual annotations of self-stimulatory behaviors in children as identified through videos available in the public domain. The dataset contains 75 videos under the three categories of arm flapping, head banging and spinning. The data provided in this dataset was translated in to our data model structure following the same principles as before – for example, the time in the dataset is stored as '0004-0012', and following out data model this is divided into an onset of '0004' and an offset of '0012'. Figure 4 shows an excerpt of this dataset following the structure of our data model.

Having validated the data model for storing events from monitored environments, there is now an opportunity to use the XML schema to retrieve new datasets for further analysis. With a common structure in place, the user is able to perform interrogation tasks to provide a meaningful insight into particular events. Future work will explore the implementation of a platform to perform abstracted visualizations, allowing interpretation of the data and identification of trends. In the case of children with autism this will enable a behavioral analyst to review different types of events that have occurred within the same context to provide a greater insight into the causes and maintainers of challenging behaviors. For example, a teacher could record that a child exhibited a certain challenging behavior in class, but only when sensor events could be viewed alongside it could it determined that the cause was due to elevated noise levels. By reviewing such data in parallel, behavior analysts can be better informed in providing interventions to continue an effective course of therapy.

```
<annotation annotationid="b_Set_01">
    <location>http://www.youtube.com/watch?v=oukupxRUA84</location>
    <event eventid="b_01">
        <source>annotator</source>
        <type>behavioural</type>
        <label>spinning</label>
        <value>high</value>
        <onset>0004</onset>
        <offset>0012</offset>
    </event>
    <event eventid="b_02">
        <source>annotator</source>
        <type>behavioural</type>
        <label>spinning</label>
        <value>high</value>
        <onset>0028</onset>
        <offset>0047</offset>
    </event>
    <event eventid="b_03">
        <source>annotator</source>
        <type>behavioural</type>
        <label>spinning</label>
        <value>high</value>
        <onset>0058</onset>
        <offset>0104</offset>
    </event>
</annotation>
```

Fig. 4. SSBD data structured in XML, conforming to the XML schema

5   Conclusion

With the ever-increasing utilization of technology within the healthcare domain, there is a vast amount of computer-based data being generated. As monitored environments become more prevalent, there is a need to standardize the way in which events occurring in such environments are structured. The work presented in this paper documents the steps taken to meet user requirements by generating a formal data structure for events, enforced through an XML-based schema. Through identifying data sources and classifying common properties, it was possible to create a model that handles all of the data, including sensor events, task events and behavioral events. The case study presented throughout the paper illustrated the creation of the data model for events occurring within monitored environments, particularly those that occur during autism interventions. By looking at the data from the data sources, the keywords were devised to ensure the scope of the structure covered each type of event that needs to be stored. The structure was validated through existing datasets as reported in the literature. With the data from various sources being stored in a common structure, the user is easily able to access a broad scope of data surrounding specific events – making the process of analyzing the data an easier task.

References

1. Krishnan, N.C., Cook, D.J.: Activity Recognition on Streaming Sensor Data. Journal of Pervasive and Mobile Computing. **10**, 138–153 (2014)
2. Varshney, U.: Pervasive Healthcare and Wireless Monitoring. Journal of Mobile Networks and Applications. **12**, 113–127 (2007)
3. Chiang, H., Lin, Y.: Expressive communication of children with autism: The use of challenging behavior. Journal of Intellectual Disability Research. **52**, 966–972 (2008)
4. Keenan, M., Dillenburger, K., Röttgers, H.R., Dounavi, K., Jónsdóttir, S.L., Moderato, P., Schenk, J.J.A.M., Virués, J., Roll-Petterson, L., Martin, N.: Autism and ABA: The Gulf Between North America and Europe. Review Journal of Autism and Developmental Disorders. **1**, 1–17 (2014)
5. Tarbox, J., Wilke, A.E., Findel-Pyles, R.S., Bergstrom, R.M., Granpeesheh, D.: A comparison of electronic to traditional pen-and-paper data collection in discrete trial training for children with autism. Journal of Research in Autism Spectrum Disorders. **4**, 65–75 (2010)
6. Cabral, D., Valente, J., Silva, J., Aragao, U., Fernandes C., Correia, N.: A Creation-tool for contemporary dance using multimodal video annotation. In: 19th ACM International Conference on Multimedia, pp. 905–908. ACM, New York (2011)
7. Togawa, T., Mizukami, H., Tamura, T.: Physiological Monitoring Techniques for Home Health. Journal of Biomedical Sciences and Instrumentation. **28**, 105–110 (1992)
8. Alyfuku, K., Hiruta, Y.: Networked Health Care and Monitoring System. Washington, DC, USA Patent #5,410,471, 25 April 1995
9. Hunter, R., Donnelly, M.P., Finlay, D., Moore, G.: Capture and access tools for event annotation and vis-à-vis. In: 7th International Conference on Mobile Ubiquitous Computing, Systems, Services and Technologies, pp. 134–139. IARIA (2013)
10. McDonald, H.A., Nugent, C.D., Moore, G., Finlay, D.D.: An XML based format for the storage of data generated both inside and outside of a smart home environments. In: 10th IEEE International Conference on Information Technology and Applications in Biomedicine, pp. 1–4. IEEE (2010)
11. Nugent, C.D., Finlay, D.D., Davies, R.J., Wang, H.Y., Zheng, H., Hallberg, J., Synnes, K., Mulvenna, M.D.: homeML – An Open Standard for the Exchange of Data Within Smart Environments. In: Okadome, Takeshi, Yamazaki, Tatsuya, Makhtari, Mounir (eds.) Pervasive Computing for Quality of Life Enhancement. LNCS, vol. 4541, pp. 121–129. Springer, Heidelberg (2007)
12. Botts, M.: OGC Implementation Specification 07-000: OpenGIS Sensor Model Language (SensorML). Open Geospatial Consortium. Wayland, MA, USA (2007)
13. Extended Environments Markup Language (EEML), http://www.eeml.org
14. Vergani, F., Bartolini, S., Spadini, F., D'Elia, A., Zamagni, G., Roffia, L., Cinotti, T.S.: A smart space application to dynamically relate medical and environmental information. In: Proceedings of Design, Automation and Test in Europe, pp. 1542–1547. Leuvan, Belguim (2002)
15. Mani, M., Lee, D., Muntz, R.R.: Semantic data modeling using XML schemas. In: Kunii, H.S., Jajodia, S., Sølvberg, A. (eds.) ER 2001. LNCS, vol. 2224, pp. 149–163. Springer, Heidelberg (2001)

16. Marcu, G., Tassini, K., Carlson, Q., Goodwyn, J., Rivkin, G., Schaefer, K.J., Day, A.K., Kiesler, S.: Why do they still use paper?: Understanding data collection and use in autism education. In: SIGCHI Conference on Human Factors in Computing Systems, pp. 3177–3186. ACM (2013)
17. Bahn, S., Corbett, B., Nam, C.S.: Scenario-Based Observation Approach for Eliciting User Requirements for Haptic User Interfaces. International Journal of Human-Computer Interaction. **30**, 842–854 (2014)
18. Foran, D., Hoerger, M., Philpott, H., Walker-Jones, E., Hughes, C.J., Morgan, J.: Using Applied Behavior Analysis As Standard Practise in a UK Special Needs School. British Journal of Special Education (2015)
19. Nazneen, N., Rozga, A., Romero, M., Findley, A.J., Call, N.A., Abowd, G.D., Arriaga, R.I.: Supporting parents for in-home capture of problem behaviours of children with developmental disabilities. Journal of Personal and Ubiquitous Computing. **16**, 193–207 (2012)
20. Goodwin, M.S., Groden, J., Velicer, W.F., Lipsitt, L.P., Baron, M.G., Hofmann, S.G., Groden, G.: Cardiovascular Arousal in Individuals with Autism. Focus Autism and Other Developmental Disabilities. **21**, 100–123 (2006)
21. Chandler, F., Dissanayake, C.: An investigation of the security of caregiver attachment during middle childhood in children with high-functioning autistic disorder. Journal of Autism. **18**, 485–492 (2013)
22. Burns, W., Donnelly, M., Booth, N.: Mining for Patterns of Behaviour in Children with Autism Through Smartphone Technology. In: Bodine, C., Helal, S., Gu, T., Mokhtari, M. (eds.) Smart Homes and Health Telematics. LNCS, vol. 8456, pp. 147–154. Springer, Switzerland (2014)
23. Qureshi, H.: The size of the problem. In: Emerson, E., McGill, P., Mansell, J. (eds.) Severe Learning Disabilities and Challenging Behaviours, pp. 23–36. Chapman and Hall, London (1994)
24. Hawkins, W., Kingsdorf, S., Charnock, J., Szabo, M., Middleton, E., Phillips, J., Gautreaux, G.: Using behavior contracts to decrease antisocial behavior in four boys with an autistic spectrum disorder at home and at school. British Journal of Special Education. **38**, 21–208 (2011)
25. Sano, A., Hernandex, J., Deprey, J., Eckhardt, M., Goodwin, M.S., Picard, R.: Multimodal annotation tool for challenging behaviours in people with autism. In: Proceedings of the 2012 ACM Conference on Ubiquitous Computing, pp. 737–740. ACM, New York (2012)
26. Rajagopalan, S.S., Dhall, A., Goecke, R.: Self-stimulatory behaviours in the wild for autism diagnosis. In: Proceedings of the 2013 IEEE international conference on Computer Vision Workshops (ICCVW), pp. 755–761. IEEE (2013)

Using Big Data for Emotionally Intelligent Mobile Services Through Multi-modal Emotion Recognition

Yerzhan Baimbetov, Ismail Khalil, Matthias Steinbauer$^{(\boxtimes)}$,
and Gabriele Anderst-Kotsis

Department of Telecooperation, Johannes Kepler University of Linz,
Altenbergerstraße 69, 4040 Linz, Austria
erzhanbai@tk.jku.at,
{ismail.khalil,matthias.steinbauer,gabriele.kotsis}@jku.at
http://www.tk.jku.at/

Abstract. Humans express and perceive emotional states in multi-modal fashion such as facial, acoustic expressions, gesture, and posture. Our task as AI researchers is to give computers the ability to communicate with users in consideration of their emotions. In recognition of a subject's emotions, it is significantly important to be aware of the emotional context. Thanks to the advancement of mobile technology, it is feasible to collect contextual data. In this paper, the authors descibe the first step to extract insightful emotional information using cloud-based Big Data infrastructure. Relevant aspects of emotion recognition and challenges that come with multi-modal emotion recognition are also discussed.

Keywords: Emotion recognition · Big data · Context awareness · Affective computing · Machine learning · Intelligent systems

1 Introduction

We, as human beings, are highly emotional and our emotional state is a fundamental component of our human-human communication. Communication between humans is based on their ability to reveal and to interpret signals from others. Some emotional states enrich the meaning of human communication, while others motivate human actions, therefore the emotion is a decision maker [2]. Consequently, emotion recognition is an important aspect to consider when implementing future information systems in order to provide human-centered computer interfaces that have the ability to reflect the users' emotional state.

With recent adavnces in machine learning, data analytics and big data processing, emotion recognition has become an emergent research topic. Humans express their emotional states through various channels such as facial expressions, vocal sounds, gestures and postures. As a result, emotional states of others are perceived from different available modalities. While a significant amount of current efforts are focusing on the development of single modal and bimodal

© Springer International Publishing Switzerland 2015
A. Geissbühler et al. (Eds.): ICOST 2015, LNCS 9102, pp. 127–138, 2015.
DOI: 10.1007/978-3-319-19312-0_11

emotion recognition systems [28], only a few studies have focused on near real time multi-modal emotion recognition.

Thanks to the advancement of pervasive computing and communication, it is easier than ever to study context. Context is a crucial factor for the interpretation of human emotional signals. For instance, a smile can be interpreted as a signal of politeness, irony, joy, or greeting depending on the context. Context that will influence the interpretation of emotional signals might be the expresser's location, the expresser's current task, the social context of the expresser, etc. [2]. An ideal automatic human affect analyser needs to have context sensitivity built-in [7].

A user's mobile phone is the perfect sensing device for a multi-modal emotion recognition system. However, a multi-modal emotion recognition system that potentially works with sensor data from thousands of mobile users will face three severe challenges. (1) The data received from mobile phones vary drastically in structure and content. Anything from structured data such as call and usage logs, to textual data such as the content of instant-, text-, and e-mail messages, to media data such as audio, pictures and video. (2) The data will arrive to the system at a relatively high velocity with varying load levels. There will be times of the day where many active users will need their sensor data to be processed, while other times of the day will experience almost no workload at all. Thus system scalability and adaptability is a critical factor. (3) Finally, the data itself will eventually grow very big in size, especially since the analysis of video and picture data comes with a critical size factor.

The challenges introduced here makes for a classical case of big data processing i.e. processing of data that is potentially unstructured, needs to be processed at high velocity, and is growing so big in size that it becomes impractical to handle by using traditional data processing systems. A topic now widely discussed in academia [9], [29] and industry [8].

In this paper we discuss how a cloud-based big data architecture can be of great help in the creation of a multi-modal emotion recognition system. The architecture is capable of handling sensory data from users' devices, annotate it with users' context, process it with well proven single-mode emotion recognizers, fuse the sensing results and interpret the results with respect to the users' context. To prove feasibility of this approach, a real world prototype implementation was created and first experiences with this architecture are discussed.

Currently, there are several emotional models which are used for building affective applications [2]. The relevant aspects concerning emotional models and emotion recognition will be presented in section 2. The Big Data architecture used in this work will be discussed in section 3 , while the real world prototype implementation will be introduced in section 4. Finally, section 5 concludes this paper with future work and research directions.

2   Related Work

As computer scientists who are planning, designing, and implementing software systems, we need to choose a model that is both easy to understand for humans and machines. This is why the two-factor theory of emotion [4], which is already described by ontologies [3], is used in this paper. As depicted in Fig. 1, an observer (human or computer) is able to observe the subject's stimuli, behaviours (outward expressions), and often the cognition (limited aspect of the personality). From these aspects and the context, emotion can be inferred.

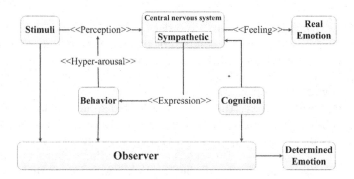

Fig. 1. The two-factor model of emotion in consideration of an observer [3]

Throughout different cultures, humans describe emotion in discrete categorical schemas to each other. This is deeply rooted in our languages [2] and a basic set of emotional states is understood across different cultures. A famous example are the six emotional states as proposed by Ekman [14]. Ekman describes happiness, sadness, fear, anger, disgust, and surprise as basic emotions that can be observed in facial expressions and are widely independent of the subject's cultural background. The model used in this work is an extension of Ekman's model, which uses three intensity states for each emotional category and adds an additional neutral state [3]. The model is displayed in greater detail in table 1.

Table 1. Basic Emotions and their intensity [3]

Distraction	Surprise	Amazement
Annoyance	Anger	Rage
Boredom	Disgust	Loathing
Pensiveness	Sadness	Grief
Serenity	Joy	Ecstasy
Apprehension	Fear	Terror
Neutral		

The idea of emotion recognition has been the subject of many publications and conferences in past years. The theoretical model of emotion recognition is a function ER that assigns a set of features F (stimuli, behavior, cognition) to an emotion label L [28].

$$L = ER(F_1, F_2, F_3, \ldots, F_n) \tag{1}$$

Emotions can be inferred from various observations such as facial expressions, speech, text and biometrics (electrocardiogram and electroencephalogram). There are plenty of scientific works on the different modalities of emotion recognition. However, integrating all possible modalities in one homogeneous system is still an open challenge. The next sections will discuss the different modalities of emotion recognition.

Acoustic Emotion Recognition. In order to fully understand human speech, it is increasingly important for computers to recognize the user's emotions. Acoustic information from speech is independent of culture and language, since speech emotion recognition applications can be applied in cross-language systems regardless of what language users are using [6].

There are various features that can be extracted from human speech. However, specifying features which are appropriate at distinguishing a certain emotion is difficult due to the large amount of features which could be considered [1], [6], [5]. The selected features should have information about emotions while also satisfying the requirements of classification [6]. In order to increase the recognition and reduce the computation time, it is recommended to divide various acoustic features into categories according to their dominant discrimination abilities in emotion classification [6].

Facial Emotion Recognition. Since facial expressions are tightly coupled with emotions, they are an extremely important part of determining others' emotions [3]. There are plenty of works on facial emotion recognition. A more detailed survey can be found in [2]. Ekman and Friesen [12] proposed the Facial Action Coding System (FACS), which was designed to measure all visually distinguishable facial movements. An action unit is a minimal unit that is automatically separate and visually clear enough to be recognized or identified as different. The facial expression is produced by action units in combination with other units or singly. The facial emotion recognition system extracts the facial action units as facial features using FACS, and then determines emotions from facial features using a rule-based algorithm [16] or a well-trained classifier such as the Bayesian Classifier [13], the Hidden Markov model [15] and others.

Textual Emotion Recognition. A significant amount of effort has been put into the development of emotion recognition from text. However, it is still a challenging task because textual emotion recognition is language dependent (emotional ambiguity of words and natural language is rich on emotional terminology). Textual emotion detection has several methods such as keyword-based detection, learning-based detection and hybrid detection [11]. None of these methods are perfect, each has advantages and drawbacks, because texts have inherent semantic ambiguity and imprecision [10].

Context Emotion Recognition. Emotion is tightly coupled with situation, which is experienced by the subject and his/her attitude toward it. The observers can misinterpret the subject's emotional expressions without context. Therefore, the context is a critical factor of the interpretation of human emotional signals. Maja Pantic et al. [7] described the characteristic of an ideal automatic human affective analyzer, which includes context-sensitiveness.

Thanks to the advancement of mobile technology, it is possible to study the subject's context where the observer is a mobile device with its sensors. In connection with popularization of mobile computing, there are several studies which explore the potential for adopting mobile technologies to the emotion recognition domain [18], [17], [28].

Using mobile phone sensors we can capture physical context, social context, content context, and behavioral context data. The physical context reflects the space around a user and how that influences on his/her emotional state, e.g. location, time, weather and surrounding people. The social context refers to the immediate social settings in which the user lives. The social context data can be retrieved from the social networking services, email, and phone contacts. Fischer et al. [20] demonstrated that our emotions are affected by what we perceive in the social environment. For instance, fear is caused by threat of social rejection or being alone, anger is caused by perceiving harm influenced by others. Obviously, the user's social context can be helpful to recognize user's emotional state.

Multimodal Emotion Recognition and Big Data. A multi-modal emotion recognition system is a system that, via multi-modal input retrieves emotional information from various types of sources and associates input data with a finite set of emotions. The concept of integration of all possible modalities in one system is still not matured, and continues to be a challenging issue. Facial expressions, voice, context and textual conversations together convey the information of emotional state. In general, there are several techniques of fusion such as feature-level fusion, decision-level fusion, and data-level fusion. More detailed information can be found in [23]. Choosing an optimal fusion type is a challenging issue. Several works [25], [23], [24] have discussed multi-modal fusion.

In our paper we discuss how we can extract the valuable and insightful information that best conveys the emotional states of mobile phone users from the huge amount of data they generate. With the respect to all related works above, most authors focus on multi-modal emotion recognition, skipping some details of the huge amount of data generated by users. It is the first step to see how insightful emotional information is extracted from huge data. We have researched both currently existing publications related to the emotion recognition [29], [30], and best practices documents [34], [35], [8] from Big Data domains that could contribute to the Big Data multi-modal emotion recognition architecture. Next section details the proposed system's architecture.

3   Big Data Architecture for MMER

A mobile phone is a personal device and people always carry their mobile phones with them. It has sensors that enable the capturing of a user's context continuously throughout the day [27]. While providing the ability to capture emotions in a continuous fashion, our approach should be unobtrusive, and not creating a feeling of being monitored. To capture a user's face expressions and voice we use the front-facing video camera of his/her mobile phone. The video is recorded by the front-facing camera when the user unlocks the screen of mobile phone. Voice of the user can be also captured by voice recorders, and calling applications. The GPS receiver and Bluetooth sensor of mobile phone play an important role to capture surrounding context. A contact list and a calendar of mobile phone can be helpful for the retrieving social context of the user. Also, instant messages can be captured in order to retrieve emotions from the text. To collect this data we designed a mobile application which runs as a background service and can be easily disabled by the user.

Mobile phones generate massive data, e.g. video, audio, text, GPS and Bluetooth logs. However, a mobile phone usually cannot provide a storage for a large amount of data. The second limitation of the mobile phone is its limited computation power. Since the multi-modal emotion recognition system requires high-performance computing and huge storage, in order to process audio, video files, all the computation and data need to move to the cloud, and the mobile phone can be seen as an array of sensors. The challenge is how to analyze data as soon as it arrives at the system and running complex machine learning on streams in a distributed environment.

After the capturing raw data in our model, every modality (facial, acoustic and textual) is processed independently. The following stage is a context-filtered block, where the system extracts information related to the user's current context and assesses the context influence on the user's emotional state.

At the relationship-aware stage in Fig. 2, information from different modalities and the context-filtered block is combined, relations between them are extracted, and finally emotion is determined using a rule-based approach and machine learning techniques.

We do not consider in our architecture pro-activity, however, the proactive emotion recognition system should infer the user's emotion in advance of a future situation based on patterns which it has learned before.

3.1 Data Collection and Pre-processing

When a connection is established between client and server, a collector, as shown in figure 2, collects mobile logs such as GPS coordinates, Bluetooth and device status logs. These logs are transmitted to the server at configurable time intervals using Internet protocols. The collected mobile logs are presented in table 2. All the data are logged with timestamps.

Since the interpretation of emotional signals is context dependent [2], we capture the physical context and social context of the user. The preprocessing module adds annotations for places and social relations in the data.

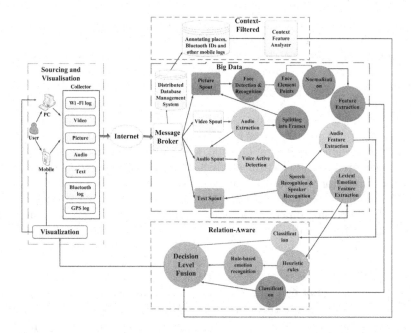

Fig. 2. Overall architecture

Table 2. Collected mobile data

Type	Attributes
Call	Phone number, type (send, receive, miss), start time, end time, audio
Messages	Type (send, receive), time, text message, message type (SMS, IM, etc.)
GPS	Time, latitude, longitude
Bluetooth	Time, is charging, power, nearby Bluetooth devices
Battery	Time, is charging, power
Video	Start time, end time, video
Audio	Start time, end time, audio

3.2 Feature Extraction and Emotion Recognition

The core abstraction in our architecture is a data stream which is an unordered sequence of tuples which can contain arbitrary data. A stream has a data source and can be processed by an arbitrary number of interconnected processing functions. In the figure 2 data sources are depicted as rectangles and processing functions as circles. The architecture has a data source for each modality such as picture, text, video and audio. When data in any modality (text, audio, video, etc.) are received the data tuple is recorded in a database management system to track metadata and is then processed by several processing steps depending on their modality.

For videos, audio data and still frames are extracted. The resulting data are forwarded to the input queues for audio and still images respectively. Still images are used for facial feature detection and run through several processing phases for face detection and recognition, face feature detection and feature extraction. This data can later be used by a classifier to detect emotion in the facial expressions. Similarly, audio data are processed. Audio data are sent to a processing function for speech-to-text extraction with the result being fed back into the text input queues. But an audio is also directly interpreted by an audio feature analysis function. Text, the last modality analyzed by the system is processed through lexical emotion feature extractors and a rule-based emotion recognition engine.

During the whole processing pipeline, the tuples which are passed on always carry unique input sample identifiers which allow the system to pick up metadata about the tuple from a database management system. The metadata contains the physical and social context of the input samples such that during the last phase of the processing pipeline, the emotion fusion function, physical and social context can be taken into account.

3.3   Fusion

We use a decision-level fusion method to combine information from metadata and modalities and classify them into discrete emotion categories. In real-world scenarios it is very likely that at any given point in time only a single modality is currently processed i.e. the mobile user just sent a text message. In this cases emotion fusion is a simple task as setting the current emotion label to the only single modality emotion label available.

In more complex scenarios, a rule-based approach based on the Confirmation Theory is used which also considers the social and physical context. In our case simple if-then rules are used where each if-then rule consists of two parts the antecedent (if) and the conclusion (then). Detailed information about the Certainty Factor (CF) can be found in [26]. CF have been assigned to each rule by the users during the study using questionnaires. The influence of social and physical context of emotional state can be described via questionnaires. If-then rules are represented in the form of *if A,B,C then D* with certainty factor X, where X is the confidence degree that this rule holds [16]. A CF of +1, means absolute belief, and -1 indicates absolute disbelief. For every contextual feature, emotions are assigned with a certain CF. For example, *if feature(weather) = sunny, then CF(happy) = 0.3 (high), CF(neutral) = 0.1 (low)*, so on. If the user does not assign a CF to certain emotions, then the system assigns $CF = 0$, e.g. *if feature(weather) = sunny, then CF(anger) = 0*. Less formally this means that the contextual feature does not influence the emergence of the certain emotions. The users use textual labels to assign certainty factors which are mapped according to the heuristics of P.Khanan et al. [16]. When several rules are triggered, the system will calculate the global CF by merging the rules the following way:

$$CF_{new} = CF_{old} + CF_{in} * (1 + CF_{old}), when CF_{old}, CF_{in} < 0 \qquad (2)$$

$$CF_{new} = CF_{old} + CF_{in} * (1 - CF_{old}), when CF_{old}, CF_{in} > 0 \qquad (3)$$

$$CF_{new} = (CF_{old} + CF_{in})/(1 - min(|CF_{old}|, |CF_{in}|)), otherwise \qquad (4)$$

CF_{old} is the CF of the conclusion of previous rules have been fired, CF_{in} is the CF of the new rule and the resulting conclusion of the merging rules is CF_{new}. When the contextual features are triggered, the system will merge triggered features and estimate their combined CF. Emotion with the biggest CF is a final decision of contextual emotion recognition. The same is done for textual, facial and acoustic modalities. CF is assigned for every modality. Using the Certainty Factor method the system determines the final emotion of the user.

4   Prototype

In order to show the feasibility of the approach described in this work a real world implementation of the architecture was created. The prototype implementation uses state of the art big data technology on its foundational layer. For the mobile sensing, we rely on the funf.org framework [21] and stream the recorded data to cloud storage. For this, the python data-storage service was adapted such that the data packets from the mobile devices are directly stored in a Hadoop distributed file system [31]. In our system, we considered the privacy issue. The mobile application requires an encrypted connection such as https before it uploads or downloads users data. All media files (audio, video and textual data) after processing in the cloud will be deleted. Contextual data and a users emotional are only accessible to the user and to the emotion recognition application in our cloud for the purpose of computation. At any point in time users can opt-out of the system and have their data deleted.

During the upload process for every data element stored, a new message is piped into our stream processing framework which is implemented as an Apache Storm topology [32]. Depending on the content type of the data element received, different pre-processing and recognition steps are performed as explained in section 3.

In the case of textual data, the input is split into sentences which are then fed into the Synesketch library [10] for emotion recognition. The emotional label is post-processed such that it fits into the six emotional categories described in section 2, and is then forwarded to the fusion component.

In the case of pictorial data, the Luxand FaceSDK framework [22] are used to perform face detection on the images. All found faces are cut out and are forwarded to the Luxand FaceSDK [22] library for facial feature extraction. The facial features are then in turn analyzed by the process described in section 3.2.

The analysis of audio data is a work in progress in the current state of the prototype. The analysis of audio data has two parallel phases (1) the extraction of text can be performed by speech recognition software, and (2) the audio signal can be used for direct emotion recognition. Text extracted in this step is fed back into the system through the distributed file-system and issuing a new text data message to the stream processor.

The case is similar to the analysis of video data. Video data is pre-processed through the Xuggler framework [33] such that audio information is extracted from video data and fed back into the system. Further, picture frames are extracted from the video data at a frame rate of $1fps$ (better heuristics needs to be found). This image data is then fed back into the system to perform facial analysis on top of it.

At the end of the processing topology, a fusion process is fusing the emotion labels that were output from different modalities. Currently, only a very simple rule-based fusion is in place. In the case of only a single modality outputs an emotion label, this label is used as the global state. If there are multiple emotion labels outputs, a rule is found with higher CF in conflicting cases.

5   Conclusions and Future Work

As highlighted in the previous section the current real world implementation of this architecture is still a work in progress. For some modalities (audio, facial) the classifiers are missing and are yet to be added to the system. In the future, the platform will be extended in a way that it is usable as a multi-modal emotion recognition system in real world scenarios. Future efforts will be centered on the improving the accuracy by collecting more data generated by mobile users. We will carry out experiments on the basis of the proposed architecture in order to show the efficiency of the proposed multimodal approach for emotion recognition. In general, using all the facial images, audio, video, textual messages and contextual data enables the system to sense a users emotional state continuously throughout the day.

From an architectural perspective the platform will be made available as a cloud-based service such that software vendors can tap into the system by submitting input data through a standardized service interface and can query the user's emotional state also through a standardized service interface.

In this work, the case for multi-modal emotion recognition is made and a cloud-based big data architecture for supporting multi-modal emotion recognition is described in detail. Relevant aspects of emotion recognition and challenges that come with multi-modal emotion recognition such as the large variety, the high volume, and the high velocity of the data are discussed.It is highlighted how the methodologies of big data can be used to create a highly scalable emotion recognition system that addresses the needs of real world applications.

A first insight into the feasibility of the approach is given by discussing a prototypical implementation of the architecture that already covers the most important steps of the recognition process.

References

1. El Ayadi, M., Kamel, M.S., Karray, F.: Survey on speech emotion recognition: Features, classification schemes, and databases. Pattern Recognition **44**(3), 572–587 (2011)
2. Zeng, Z., Pantic, M., Roisman, G.I., Huang, T.S.: A Survey of Affect Recognition Methods: Audio, Visual, and Spontaneous Expressions. IEEE Transactions on Pattern Analysis and Machine Intelligence **31**(1), 39–58 (2009)

3. Berthelon, F., Sander, P.: Emotion ontology for context awareness. In: Cognitive Infocommunications (CogInfoCom), 2013 IEEE 4th International Conference on Cognitive Infocommunications, pp. 59–64, 2–5 Dec. 2013
4. Schachter, S., Singer, J.: Cognitive, social and physiological determinants of emotional state. Psychological Review (1979)
5. Pavaloi, I., Musca, E., Rotaru, F.: Emotion recognition in audio records. Signals, Circuits and Systems (ISSCS), pp. 1–4, 11–12 July 2013
6. Asawa, K., Verma, V., Agrawal, A.: Recognition of vocal emotions from acoustic profile. In: Proceedings of the International Conference on Advances in Computing, Communications and Informatics (ICACCI 2012), pp. 710-716. ACM, New York, NY, USA
7. Pantic, M., Sebe, N., Cohn, J.F., Huang, T.: Affective multi-modal human-computer interaction. In: Proceedings of the 13th annual ACM international conference on Multimedia (MULTIMEDIA 2005), pp. 669–676. ACM, New York, NY, USA (2005)
8. An Oracle White Paper: Oracle Information Architecture: An Architect's Guide to Big Data. August 2012
9. O'Reilly Media: Big Data New, 2012th edn. O'Reilly Media Inc., Sebastopol, CA (2012)
10. Krcadinac, U., Pasquier, P., Jovanovic, J., Devedzic, V.: Synesketch: An Open Source Library for Sentence-Based Emotion Recognition. IEEE Transactions on Affective Computing 4(3), 312–325 (2013)
11. Kao, E.C.-C., Chun-Chieh, L., Yang, T.-H., Hsieh, C.-T., Soo, V.-W.: Towards Text-based Emotion Detection A Survey and Possible Improvements. In: Information Management and Engineering, 2009, ICIME 2009, International Conference on Information Management and Engineering, pp. 70–74, 3–5 April 2009
12. Ekman, P., Friesen, W.V., Ancoli, S.: Facial signs of emotional experience. Journal of Personality and Social Psychology 19(6), 1123–1134 (1980)
13. Metri, P., Ghorpade, J., Butalia, A.: Facial Emotion Recognition Using Context Based Multimodal Approach. International Journal of Artificial Intelligence and Interactive Multimedia 1(4) (2011)
14. Ekman, P.: Universals and cultural differences in facial expressions of emotions. Nebraska Symposium on Motivation 19, 207–283 (1972)
15. Zeng, Z., Tu, J., Pianfetti, B., Liu, M., Zhang, T., Zhang, Z., Huang, T.S., Levinson, S.: Audio-visual affect recognition through multi-stream fused HMM for HCI. In: IEEE Computer Society Conference on Computer Vision and Pattern Recognition, CVPR 2005, vol. 2, pp. 967–972, 20–25 June 2005
16. Khanna, P., Sasikumar, M.: Rule based system for recognizing emotions using multi-modal approach. (IJACSA) International Journal of Advanced Computer Science and Applications 4(7) (2013)
17. Niforatos, E., Karapanos, E.: EmoSnaps: A Mobile Application for Emotion Recall from Facial Expressions. CHI 2013, April 27 - May 2, 2013, Paris, France
18. Oh, K., Park, H.-S., Cho, S.-B.: A Mobile Context Sharing System Using Activity and Emotion Recognition with Bayesian Networks. In: 2010 7th International Conference Ubiquitous Intelligence and Computing and 7th International Conference on Autonomic and Trusted Computing (UIC/ATC), pp. 244–249, 26–29 Oct. 2010
19. Revelle, W., Scherer, K.R.: Personality and Emotion. In the Oxford Companion to the Affective Sciences, Oxford University Press (2010)
20. Fischer, A.H., Manstead, A.S.R., Zaalberg, R.: Socail influence on the emotion process. European Review of Social Psychology 14(1), 171–202 (2003)

21. Funf - Open Sensing Framework. http://www.funf.org
22. Luxand FaceSDK. https://www.luxand.com/facesdk
23. Wagner, J., Andre, E., Jung, F.: Smart sensor integration: A framework for multi-modal emotion recognition in real-time. In: ACII 2009, 3rd International Conference on Affective Computing and Intelligent Interaction and Workshops, pp. 1–8, 10–12 Sept. 2009
24. Lingenfelser, F., Wagner, J., André, E.: A systematic discussion of fusion techniques for multi-modal affect recognition tasks. In: Proceedings of the 13th international conference on multi-modal interfaces (ICMI 2011). ACM, New York, NY, USA, 19–26
25. Tang, K., Tie, Y., Yang, T., Guan, L.: Multimodal emotion recognition (MER) system. In: 2014 IEEE 27th Canadian Conference on Electrical and Computer Engineering (CCECE), pp. 1–6, 4–7 May 2014
26. Shortiffe, E.H., Buchanan, B.G.: A Multimodal of Inexact Reasoning in Medicine. Mathematical Bioscience **23**, 351–379 (1975)
27. Steinbauer, M., Kotsis, G.: Building an Information System for Reality Mining Based on Communication Traces. NBiS, 2012, pp. 306–310
28. Mousannif, H., Khalil, I.: The human face of mobile. In: Linawati, Mahendra, M.S., Neuhold, E.J., Tjoa, A.M., You, I. (eds.) ICT-EurAsia 2014. LNCS, vol. 8407, pp. 1–20. Springer, Heidelberg (2014)
29. Demchenko, Y., de Laat, C., Membrey, P.: Defining architecture components of the Big Data Ecosystem. In: 2014 International Conference on Collaboration Technologies and Systems (CTS), pp. 104–112, 19–23 May 2014
30. Demchenko, Y., Grosso, P., de Laat, C., Membrey, P.: Addressing big data issues in Scientific Data Infrastructure. In: 2013 International Conference on Collaboration Technologies and Systems (CTS), pp. 48–55, 20–24 May 2013
31. Welcome to Apache Hadoop! http://hadoop.apache.org/
32. Apache Storm. http://hortonworks.com/hadoop/storm/
33. Xuggler. http://www.xuggle.com/xuggler/
34. NIST Big Data Working Group (NBD-WG). http://bigdatawg.nist.gov/home.php
35. Big Data Reference Architecture. NBD-WG. NIST. http://bigdatawg.nist.gov/_uploadfiles/M0226_v10_1554566513.docx

Assistive and Sentient Environments

Smartphone-Based System for Sensorimotor Control Assessment, Monitoring, Improving and Training at Home

Quentin Mourcou[1,2]($\boxtimes$), Anthony Fleury[2], Céline Franco[1], Bruno Diot[1,3],
and Nicolas Vuillerme[1,4]

[1] Univ. Grenoble-Alpes, AGIM, La Tronche, France
{quentin.mourcou,celine.franco,nicolas.vuillerme}@agim.eu
[2] Univ. Lille Nord de France, EMDouai, IA, Lille F-59500, France
{quentin.mourcou,anthony.fleury}@mines-douai.fr
[3] IDS, Montceau-les-Mines, de France
b.diot@ids-assitance.com
[4] Institut Universitaire de France, Paris, France

Abstract. This article proposes an innovative Smartphone-based architecture designed to assess, monitor, improve and train sensorimotor abilities at home. This system comprises inertial sensors to measure orientations, calculation units to analyze sensorimotor control abilities, visual, auditory and somatosensory systems to provide biofeedback to the user, screen display and headphones to provide test and/or training exercises instructions, and wireless connection to transmit data. We present two mobile applications, namely "iBalance" and "iProprio", to illustrate concrete realization of such architecture in the case of at-home autonomous assessment and rehabilitation programs for balance and proprioceptive abilities. Our findings suggest that the present architecture system, which does not involve dedicated and specialized equipment, but which is entirely embedded on a Smartphone, could be a suitable solution for Ambient Assisted Living technologies.

Keywords: Smartphone · Inertial Motion Unit · Biofeedback · Home-based solution

1 Introduction

Smartphones has become a widely used device in developed countries. Its evolutions and innovations over time have turned it into one of the most outstanding device for pervasive computing [1]. Indeed, there are more than a billion of Smartphones sold worldwide in 2013, and the shipments has increased with 20.3% in the third quarter of 2014 [2]. The sharp decline in prices of mobile equipment now allows the growth of emerging markets. Although mobile phones are becoming more and more affordable, they remain powerful tools composed of a processor, a graphics chip, an advanced connectivity, and an inertial motion unit (IMU) featured with 3D-accelerometer,

© Springer International Publishing Switzerland 2015
A. Geissbühler et al. (Eds.): ICOST 2015, LNCS 9102, pp. 141–151, 2015.
DOI: 10.1007/978-3-319-19312-0_12

magnetometer, and gyroscope as standard. Albeit first used for game and user interfaces, built-in sensors can also be used for healthcare and activity monitoring.

With these features, Smartphones are quickly becoming an interesting tool for scientific research applied to medicine and, even more interesting for physical activity monitoring. First, they are embedded with telephony and short message services (SMS), which offers valuable opportunities to improve health by providing regular care and informational support [3]. Then, strategies were widely explored for tracking health interventions, for involving the healthcare team, for leveraging social influence, for increasing the accessibility of health information, and for entertainments [4]. Furthermore, new Smartphone models are now emerging to improve traditional healthcare with new services like health social networks, consumer personalized medicine and quantified self-tracking [5]. Additionally, Smartphones can be directly used to detect and classify daily physical activities such as walking, jogging, sitting, standing, walking upstairs and walking downstairs [6]. However, monitoring these free-living physical activities requires precise measurements that are generally provided by dedicated and specialized inertial motion unit(s) or external device(s). These measurements can be processed and interpreted on system board or on a more advanced computational system, for example, when processing more consistent data and calculations such as the use of Discrete Wavelet Transform and SVM-based approach for the classifications of sporting activities [7]. The use and interpretation of sensor data depend on different parameters, such as the reliability of the sensor, its positioning on the body, the algorithm used for interpretation, and possible data fusion with signals from other sensors. A typical health example is fall detection and prevention. Fall detection and prevention system can be designed in three phases which are 1) sense, to measure physical quantities 2) analysis, to use algorithms which can take decisions and 3) communication, to spread the interpretation of the results [8]. To measure human activity, the accelerometer is certainly the most used sensor nowadays. An accurate and reliable fall detection system will rely on the quality of the accelerometer signal and its range of measurement [8].

Other health applications use Smartphone to measure human body orientations and movements to assess balance and gait control [9] or proprioceptive abilities [10]. These health applications aim to provide clear and precise range of motion. They mainly use fusion algorithms provided by manufacturers, which use a combination measurement of the three sensors; the accelerometer, the gyroscope and the magnetometer. These sensors are used for measuring range of motion, and are already validated in several studies with dedicated IMU systems [11]. It is important to mention that such Smartphone-based solutions are only used to sense human movements and do not offer biofeedback. However, and very interestingly, Smartphones do also contain additional standard technologies such as a screen display, an audio system or a somatosensory feedback system that allows interaction with the user of the device. In this context, this more and more affordable, popular and powerful tool could be advantageously used independently (and/or complementarily) by citizen or patients to perform self-measurements/assessments and to execute improve their sensorimotor, cognitive and functional abilities thanks to home-based training or rehabilitation programs.

The aim of this paper is to propose an innovative "all-inclusive" architecture, only based on the Smartphone, with the following three main components: (i) the sensory input unit, (ii) the processing unit, and (iii) the sensory output unit (allowing biofeedback provision). This Smartphone-based solution is designed to be used for the objective and automatic measurement and monitoring of body or body segments orientations and movements with training / rehabilitation exercises using sensory biofeedback, performed in complete autonomy at home with the only usage of the Smartphone.

The remaining structure of this paper is as follows. Section 2 describes related previous works, since the arrival of IMU to Smartphone use, with their advantages and inconveniences. Section 3 presents the architecture and applications that could be used on Smartphone or wearable devices for motor control assessment, monitoring, improving and training at home. Conclusion and perspectives are finally drawn in Section 4.

2   Related Works

2.1   Dedicated Devices

Whether due to aging, accident, injury or trauma, loss of joint mobility can cause the increase of disability in daily life. There are already devices and methods supposed to help a user recover a body function at home. For example, Philips Research has developed solutions to increase the efficiency and effectiveness of rehabilitation with the Stroke Rehabilitation Exerciser [12]. Physiotherapist could prescribe neurological motor exercises with this device that can be done unaccompanied at home. Stroke patients are equipped with a motion sensor system that includes inertial sensors in a small matchbox. Each body segment could be tracked by this way during exercises. Feedback to the user is provided by a dedicated user interface on a computer. The screen provides instructions to put sensors, there are videos to explain exercises and, finally, feedback during exercises is provided by a 3D animated figure that mimics patient movements.

Another example is the MyHeart's Neurological Rehabilitation Concept [13] which proposes motion recognition based on strain sensors placed directly on the clothes. A motor therapy module, which is a touch-screen workstation, provides real-time feedback on the progress and accuracy of movements performed. This workstation is specifically made to provide real-time feedback to all patients, including wheelchair, blind or cognitive impaired users. It has speech recognition and touch screen to allow interaction from the user. Feedback provided by the screen is intended to avoid distraction for cognitive impaired users, it just contains a bar, and metaphor pedestrian lights to indicate exercises time and a simplified smiling (or frowning) face. During the test, a therapist is present to monitor the training session.

Taken together, the above-mentioned systems have provided proof-of-concept that home rehabilitation using sensors and feedback can be realized. The actual lack of those systems is that the installation of the devices is still laborious. In addition, they use dedicated equipment that can clutter the patient's home. This complexity of use of the system can prevent the patient to use the system. Moreover, users are generally not familiar with such specialized systems.

A more recent example is the Valedo system builds by Hocoma AG [14]. It is presented as a medical back therapy device with two motion devices. Each sensor is composed with a 3D gyroscope, a 3D accelerometer, a 3D magnetometer and Bluetooth connectivity. Motion devices should be placed in the lower back, at the level of L5 vertebra, and on the chest, at the high level of the sternum. Then, Valedo provides 45 therapeutic exercises including a set of 17 movements. Exercises and real-time feedback are provided by a tablet. However, this system is also too expensive to purchase for patients themselves, because they have to buy the dedicated system with its sensors network and a tablet or a Smartphone. Moreover, its exercises interface is not specifically adapted for elderly or people with disabilities.

2.2   Smartphone-Based Solution

Assessing body or body segment orientation and movement for postural and gait control or for joint goniometry could be done with the use of Smartphone. Due to the motion sensors (9D IMU), and the autonomous computation units, Smartphones can evaluate and measure angles, in quaternion or Euler space. Clinometer is one of these general applications that were used in clinical studies. It has been validated on healthy and traumatic populations for measuring shoulder and cervical ranges of motion [15-16]. The Angle application can calculate angles, using accelerometers, with respect to gravity, for all planes. It has been used in two surgery studies in which its reproducibility was evaluated against navigation surgery systems [17]. Even standard compass applications, provided by Smartphone manufacturer, were used for cervical range of motion [18]. Other applications such as Simple Goniometer [19] or Knee Goniometer [20] mimics goniometer to measure joint angulations during static range of motion. They were specifically designed for medical use and their validations were made compared to a standard goniometer. Scoligauge [21] or Hallux Valgus App [22] were specifically developed for, respectively, measure trunk angle while patient is performing the Adams forward bend test and measure hallux valgus angle. The only app validated for angle measurement with the Smartphone camera is DrGoniometer [23-24], applied to elbow and knee joint angle measurements.

In their recent review, Milani et al. describe all mobile Smartphone applications for body position measurement in rehabilitation [25]. Twelve mobile applications are presented, including those employing inertial sensors and/or camera to produce angle measurement. However, their conclusion underlines that these tools are validated for the moment within the framework of static protocol: "*A need exists, however, for validation studies on available or new apps focused on goniometric measurement in dynamic conditions, such as during gait or during performance of therapeutic exercises*" [Milani et al., 2014, page 1042].

Unlike the tools presented in the previous section, actual Smartphone application used for measuring joint angles simply imitates existing tools. Their use has been validated in the scientific and medical fields but only by the direct use of professionals in those fields, not by end users. Moreover, feedback was only provided to physiotherapist or clinicians and not to the patients themselves, preventing them from self training. In this context, the following section proposes an innovative architecture to build an all-in-one affordable tool for measurement of body and/or body segments orientations and movement, analysis, storage, and improvement thanks to biofeedback-based training and/or rehabilitation exercises designed to be performed in complete autonomy at home.

3   Rehabilitation at Home, an Actual Ideal Smartphone-Based Architecture

3.1   General Architecture

In order to keep all advantages from previous described solutions and without inconveniences, the present paper aims to describe an actual ideal architecture to objectively and automatically measure body and/or body segment's orientation and position and proposed adaptive training and/rehabilitation biofeedback-based exercises at home. The Smartphone application implements methods specifically developed for motor control assessment, monitoring, improving and training at home [26].

The principle of functioning of our Smartphone-based solution can be composed of the 6 following steps, illustrated in figure 1.

1. Measurement and processing to detect the current movement (or posture) achieved by the user,
2. Comparison of current movement (or position respectively) to a theoretical motion (respectively to a theoretical position),
3. Biological feedback that could allow the user to correct its current movement (respectively its current posture) so that it (respectively) to better match the theoretical movement (to the theoretical position, respectively),
4. Performing automatic or non-automatic update of a level of difficulty of the exercise or of the set of exercises.
5. Calculation of an index based on the result of this comparison, and store it,
6. Possible transmission of this index to a third party to enable it to monitor the user's performance.

Interestingly, following this architecture, Smartphone application is not only used for sensorimotor assessment and monitoring, but also for its improvement and training by the means of the provision of sensory biofeedback and the implementation of adapted training and/or rehabilitation exercises. This allows the patients to practice exercises at home without the help of any physiotherapists, medical doctor or trainer. The nature and the level of difficulty of these training exercises can further be automatically managed by the device, via a real-time analysis of the results during the tests, or managed remotely by the therapist. Biofeedback may consist of the issuance of a type of sensory stimuli (e.g., visual, auditory, tactile) and may vary depending on the sensitivity, capacity and / or user preferences accordingly. Different combinations of sensory outputs could be proposed. Likewise, the principle of the biofeedback provision can be either 'continuous' and/or 'intermittent'. For this last case, in for instance, the user receives real-time information about the difference (or error in direction and / or amplitude) between the current position of the joint and one that should be obtained in respect of the proposed exercise. In other words, in this case, if there is no error, there is no feedback. Two biological feedback variants, at least, could be proposed: 1) The attractive cuing, where user has to mobilize the joint in the direction of the feedback, and 2) the repulsive cuing, where the user has to mobilize the joint in the opposite direction of the feedback.

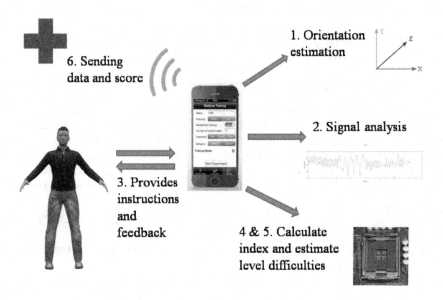

Fig. 1. Overall architecture of the Smartphone-based system

Ultimately, this application is intended to provide an all-in-one, gathering measurement functionality, analysis, storage, correction, feedback and adaptation. This device, by its communicative character, can be used to share information with a third party (e.g. a medical team) to check the results achieved for the exercises, and eventually adapt the sessions proposed to the user. Another feature of the solution resides in the secure transmission of the measured and analyzed data and their comparison to a database. Finally, the user interface must also take into account the user's profile and preferences in order to be easily usable (and effectively used!) by all.

3.2   Orientation Estimation

With the Smartphone built-in sensors, orientation measurement could be obtained from accelerometer, magnetometer and gyroscope 3D raw measurements. But none of these sensors bring noiseless information. In order to provide the most accurate angle estimation, orientation filters have to be used, such as the Kalman filter. Thus, the Earth gravitational and magnetic fields, respectively measured by accelerometer and magnetometer, will be merged with angular velocity from gyroscope to compute a single and complete estimate of orientation angles (Figure 2).

3.3   Use Cases

In this section, we will describe two Smartphone-based solutions developed with the goal to measure, assess, monitor, improve and train balance and proprioceptive abilities, called "iBalance" and "iProprio", respectively (Figure 3). Each application can provide visual, auditory and/or tactile biofeedback. Thereafter "iBalance" is illustrated in the case of its auditory biofeedback version and "iProprio" in the case of its vibrotactile biofeedback version.

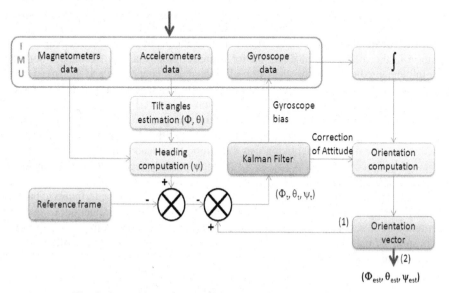

Fig. 2. Orientation estimation from the raw sensor measurement

Fig. 3. Screenshots of the iProprio (left) and iBalance (right) main screen

"iBalance" is a Smartphone application which monitors the trunk orientation and movement during different postural and locomotor tasks and helps the user to improve and train their balance capacities through the provision of adapted and adaptive exercises and a configurable visual, auditory and/ or tactile biofeedback [27-28]. The instructions can be automatically vocally supplied by the system. The Smartphone, placed at the level of L5 vertebra, records trunk orientations and movement. "iBalance" could provide multiple different combination of sensory feedback (e.g. tactile trough a number of vibrotactors placed on the used hips or shoulder, for instance , or auditory through a pair of earphones). This can be done continuously or in distinct situations, when user leaves the predetermined adjustable "dead zone" for example (Figure 4). The so-called "dead zone" can be set to 1° around the mean of the participant's trunk position in the medio-lateral direction for instance. Note that the "iBalance" software was implemented to allow the algorithm of biofeedback generation and the "dead zone" size to be easily and quickly modified according to the specific use of the "iBalance" system (e.g., user's balance ability, needs, and preferences). For instance, in the case of the generation of auditory biofeedback, when the user goes out of this "dead zone", the "iBalance" system provides a sound either to the left or the right earphone depending on whether the actual trunk orientation was exceeding the "dead zone" in either the left or right direction, respectively. A first proof-of-concept study recently has been conducted on young [27] and older [28] healthy populations. Results suggest that the "iBalance" application allows users to significantly decrease trunk sway (that is, to improve balance control) during standing exercises with real-time auditory biofeedback. Authors encourage more research to be done to confirm these data and to promote the use of this application for balance training and rehabilitation in targeted populations with impaired-balance capacities.

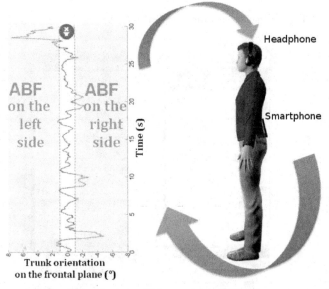

Fig. 4. iBalance principle of functioning which consists of (1) the measurements of trunk orientations and movements and (2) the provision of auditory biofeedback to the user during home rehabilitation exercises

"iProprio" is a Smartphone application developed to measure, monitor, improve and train proprioceptive function of different joints. This application uses inertial sensors included in a Smartphone to allow joint position sense measurement in an autonomous way and to provide a configurable visual, auditory and/or tactile biofeedback, with cheap external wireless devices for end-users at home (Figure 5). The instructions can be automatically vocally supplied by the system. For instance, in the case of knee joint proprioception management, the Smartphone is disposed distally of the tibia. Biofeedback is provided in the same way as described in Section 3.1: attractive cuing and/or repulsive cuing are provided when user leaves (or enters) the predetermined adjustable "dead zone". In the case of knee proprioception measurement and improvement, exercises used to assess knee joint position sense come from a standardized protocol named "active ipsilateral matching". This is commonly used and accepted in clinical routine [29-30]. Vocal instructions are provided by the Smartphone itself always with the aim of making the exercises in an autonomous way. It uses the same architecture as "iBalance" and the same assessment of its efficiency in improving knee joint position sense in young and older adults is in progress.

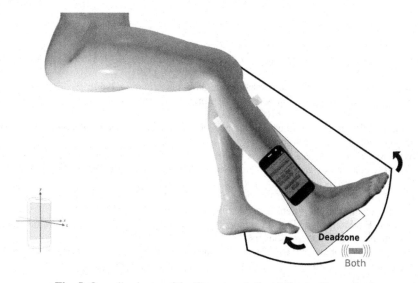

Fig. 5. Overall scheme of the iProprio solution (vibrotactile version)

4   Conclusion

This article proposes an innovative architecture designed to assess, monitor, improve and train motor control by means of exercises program using a sensory biofeedback system to perform at-home autonomous assessment and rehabilitation with an all-in-one tool: the Smartphone. Our solution keeps the advantages from previous proposed solutions, such as precise measurement of orientation with integrated 3D accelerometer, magnetometer and gyroscope and an adequate fusion algorithm.

Interestingly, this solution goes further than the current tools, which are only dedicated to angle and posture measurement, by further supplying biofeedback for rehabilitation purposes in an autonomous way. Smartphones have become a daily-used tool and are much more affordable and portable than dedicated devices. Presented use-cases, "iBalance" and "iProprio", illustrate the use of this architecture and the first results in the context of rehabilitation exercises and programs that are commonly used. In order to confirm the described architecture, clinical studies have to be performed with patients with balance and/or proprioceptive impairment, for other joints, other postural tasks and with others types of sensory biofeedback. Along these lines, "iBalance" and "iProprio" solutions are currently evaluated with targeted population in terms of effectiveness, efficiency, satisfaction, usability and acceptance with a specific designed model called TEMSED for "Technology, Ergonomics, Medicine, Society, Economics, Deontology" [31].

Acknowledgments. This work was supported in part by funding by IDS company, the French national program "programme d'Investissements d'Avenir IRT Nanoelec" ANR-10-AIRT-05, PhD scholarship of Mines Douai, and Institut Universitaire de France.

References

1. Islam, N., Want, R.: Smartphones: Past, Present, and Future. IEEE Pervasive Comput. **4**, 89–92 (2014)
2. Gartner, Inc. (NYSE: IT), http://www.gartner.com/newsroom/id/2944819
3. Krishna, S., Boren, S.A., Balas, E.A.: Healthcare via cell phones: a systematic review. Telemed. J. E-Health. **15**(3), 231–240 (2009)
4. Klasnja, P., Pratt, W.: Healthcare in the pocket: Mapping the space of mobile-phone health interventions. J. Biomed. Inform. **45**(1), 184–198 (2012)
5. Swan, M.: Emerging patient-driven health care models: an examination of health social networks, consumer personalized medicine and quantified self-tracking. Int. J. Environ. Res. Publ. Health. **6**(2), 492–525 (2009)
6. Arif, M., Bilal, M., Kattan, A., Ahamed, S.I.: Better Physical Activity Classification using Smartphone Acceleration Sensor. J. Med. Syst. **38**(9), 1–10 (2014)
7. Mitchell, E., Monaghan, D., O'Connor, N.E.: Classification of sporting activities using smartphone accelerometers. Sensors. **13**(4), 5317–5337 (2013)
8. Habib, M.A., Mohktar, M.S., Kamaruzzaman, S.B., Lim, K.S., Pin, T.M., Ibrahim, F.: Smartphone-based solutions for fall detection and prevention: challenges and open issues. Sensors. **14**(4), 7181–7208 (2014)
9. Lee, B.C., Kim, J., Chen, S., Sienko, K.H.: Cell phone based balance trainer. J.Neuroeng. Rehabil. **9**(10) (2012)
10. Algar, L., Valdes, K.: Using smartphone applications as hand therapy interventions. J. Hand. Ther. **27**, 254–257 (2014)
11. Zhu, R., Zhou, Z.: A real-time articulated human motion tracking using tri-axis inertial/magnetic sensors package. IEEE Trans. Neural Syst. Rehabil. Eng **12**(2), 295–302 (2004)
12. Timmermans, A., Saini, P., Willmann, R. D., Lanfermann, G., te Vrugt, J., Winter, S.: Home stroke rehabilitation for the upper limbs. In: Engineering in Medicine and Biology Society, EMBS 2007. 29th Annual International Conference of the IEEE, pp. 4015–4018. IEEE Press, Lyon (2007)

13. Giorgino, T., Tormene, P., Maggioni, G., Pistarini, C., Quaglini, S.: Wireless support to poststroke rehabilitation: myheart's neurological rehabilitation concept. IEEE. T. Inf. Technol. B. **13**(6), 1012–1018 (2009)
14. Valedo Therapy. (HOCOMA), http://www.valedotherapy.com/
15. Shin, S.H., du Ro, H., Lee, O.S., Oh, J.H., Kim, S.H.: Within-day reliability of shoulder range of motion measurement with a smartphone. Man. Ther. **17**, 298–304 (2012)
16. Tousignant-Laflamme, Y., Boutin, N., Dion, A.M., Vallée, C.A.: Reliability and criterion validity of two applications of the iPhone to measure cervical range of motion in healthy participants. J Neuroeng Rehabil. **10**, 69 (2013)
17. Jenny, J.Y.: Measurement of the knee flexion angle with a smartphone-application is precise and accurate. J Arthroplasty. **28**, 784–787 (2013)
18. Peters, F.M., Greeff, R., Goldstein, N., Frey, C.T.: Improving acetabular cup orientation in total hip arthroplasty by using smartphone technology. J. Arthroplasty. **27**(7), 1324–1330 (2012)
19. Jones, A., Sealey, R., Crowe, M., Gordon, S.: Concurrent validity and reliability of the Simple Goniometer iPhone app compared with the Universal Goniometer. Physiother. Theory. Pract. **0**, 1–5 (2014)
20. Ockendon, M., Gilbert, R.E.: Validation of a novel smartphone accelerometer-based knee goniometer. J Knee Surg. **25**, 341–345 (2012)
21. Franko, O.I., Bray, C., Newton, P.O.: Validation of a scoliometer smartphone app to assess scoliosis. J Pediatr Orthop. **32**, 72–75 (2012)
22. Ege, T., Kose, O., Koca, K., Demiralp, B., Basbozkurt, M.: Use of the iPhone for radiographic evaluation of hallux valgus. Skeletal Radiol. **42**, 269–273 (2013)
23. Ferriero, G., Sartorio, F., Foti, C., Primavera, D., Brigatti, E., Vercelli, S.: Reliability of a new application for smartphones (DrGoniometer) for elbow angle measurement. PM R. **3**, 1153–1154 (2011)
24. Mitchell, K., Gutierrez, S.B., Sutton, S., Morton, S., Morgenthaler, A.: Reliability and validity of goniometric iPhone applications for the assessment of active shoulder external rotation. Physiother. Theory. Pract. **0**, 1–5 (2014)
25. Milani, P., Coccetta, C.A., Rabini, A., Sciarra, T., Massazza, G., Ferriero, G.: A Review of Mobile Smartphone Applications for Body Position Measurement in Rehabilitation: A Focus on Goniometric Tools. PM&R. **6**(11), 1038–1104 (2014)
26. Vuillerme, M., Fleury, A., Franco, C., Mourcou, Q., Diot, B.: Procédé et système pour la mesure, le suivi, le contrôle et la correction d'un mouvement ou d'une posture d'un utilisateur, Patent FR-1461233, 20/11/2014
27. Franco, C., Fleury, A., Guméry, P.Y., Diot, B., Demongeot, J., Vuillerme, N.: iBalance-ABF: a smartphone-based audio-biofeedback balance system. IEEE T. Bio-Med. Eng. **60**(1), 211–215 (2013)
28. Mourcou, Q., Fleury, A., Dupuy, P., Diot, B., Franco, C., Vuillerme, N.: Wegoto: A Smartphone-based approach to assess and improve accessibility for wheelchair users. In: Engineering in Medicine and Biology Society (EMBC), 35th Annual International Conference of the IEEE, pp. 1194-1197. IEEE Press, Osaka (2013)
29. Lonn, J., Crenshaw, A.G., Djupsjobacka, M., Johansson, H.: Reliability of position sense testing assessed with a fully automated system. Clin. Physiol. **20**, 30–37 (2000)
30. Bennell, K., Wee, E., Crossley, K., Stillman, B., Hodges, P.: Effects of experimentally-induced anterior knee pain on knee joint position sense in healthy individuals. J. Orthop. Res. **23**, 46–53 (2005)
31. Rialle, V., Vuillerme, N., Franco, A.: Outline of a general framework for assessing e-health and gerontechnology applications: Axiological and diachronic dimensions. Gerontechnology **9**(2), 245 (2010)

"Get that Camera Out of My House!" Conjoint Measurement of Preferences for Video-Based Healthcare Monitoring Systems in Private and Public Places

Katrin Arning[(✉)] and Martina Ziefle

Human Computer Interaction Center (HCIC), RWTH Aachen University,
Campus Boulevard 57, 52074 Aachen, Germany
`{arning,ziefle}@comm.rwth-aachen.de`

Abstract. Facing the healthcare challenges of an aging society, the expansion of AAL system implementation in private and public environments is a promising way to improve healthcare in future smart homes and cities. The present study evaluated preferences for different video-based medical monitoring scenarios, which comprised the attributes medical safety (improved detection of medical emergencies), privacy (handling of video information), type and location of camera in a conjoint analysis. Medical safety was identified as key driver for preferences. Acceptance for video-based medical monitoring systems in public places was comparably high, given that privacy was protected. In contrast, acceptance for video-based monitoring in smart home environments was rather low due to privacy concerns. Based on the findings, recommendation for AAL system design and implementation were derived.

Keywords: Medical monitoring · Video cameras · Smart homes · Smart cities · Acceptance · Privacy · Medical safety · Conjoint analysis

1 Introduction

The demographic change in western societies puts enormous pressure on societies and healthcare systems. In 2010 the proportion of people aged 65 and older was 15% and it is predicted to raise to 25% by 2050, so it is the fastest-growing segment of the population [1]. Due to an increased life expectancy, improved medical healthcare in combination with a higher living standard as well as reduced fertility rates, a growing number of frail older persons will require long term care provided by health care systems [2]. Moreover, today's older adults have a more active and mobile lifestyle [3], therefore societies need to consider the special needs of older and frail people in the design of living environments, i.e. their homes but also of public spaces for future livable cities.

Ambient assisted living (AAL) systems provide a successful and promising way to meet this demographic challenge and to improve quality in healthcare. In AAL systems, the combination of ICT and health monitoring devices allows for an autonomous and unobtrusive recording and transfer of medical data from patients to remote healthcare providers [4].

© Springer International Publishing Switzerland 2015
A. Geissbühler et al. (Eds.): ICOST 2015, LNCS 9102, pp. 152–164, 2015.
DOI: 10.1007/978-3-319-19312-0_13

One major goal of AAL is the detection of emergencies, such as falls. Among seniors aged 65+ falls are one of the most serious health risks, which affect more people than stroke and heart attacks [5]. A fast detection of falls and immediate help reduce the risk of death by more than 80% [6]. Accordingly, most healthcare information collected and transferred by AAL systems is time- and life-critical [7], therefore the capturing and delivering of healthcare information in future smart homes and cities should be further expanded.

1.1 Video-Based Monitoring Systems in Healthcare

A huge variety of AAL solutions already exists (e.g. for an overview [8, 9]). Especially video-based monitoring systems are increasingly being developed. One advantage of video-based monitoring by stationary cameras is that they enable contactless observation without the need for additional equipment of patients, e.g. wearing a wireless help button or a tag. Leijedeckers et al. [10] developed a personalized smart homecare system, which mainly uses smart phones, wireless sensors, web servers and IP webcams. Fleck [11] proposed a SmartSurv 3D Surveillance System Prototype, a distributed and smart camera based approach, which covers geo-referenced person tracking and activity recognition for the detection of falls. To this day, many more video-based health monitoring systems for smart homes were developed, which primarily focus on fall detection (e.g. [12–14]).

Despite of the benefits provided by medical monitoring systems for healthcare and medical safety, most of the systems impose one problem: they ignore privacy of the person being monitored. Privacy is the right on protection of people's personal information [15], i.e., confidentiality, anonymity, self-determination, freedom of expression, and personal control of data. Especially in the context of video surveillance privacy is a highly important issue, since persons in the area covered by cameras have no possibilities to avoid being monitored. Some of the homecare approaches mentioned above proposed attempts to protect privacy, e.g. usage of video surveillance only at times of emergency or for scheduled meetings [10] or by not recording the camera feed if no accident was detected [14].

Privacy is one important determinant of AAL system acceptance (e.g. [16]). The understanding of these determinants that affect technology acceptance is essential for its successful adoption [17]. The most influential and best-established theoretical approach to explain and predict the adoption of technologies is the Technology Acceptance Model (TAM) [18], which was also adapted to the healthcare context [19]. However, these models cannot be easily transferred and applied to the design and implementation of video-based monitoring systems due to several reasons. First, technology acceptance models focus on an evaluation of complete technical systems or applications. They do not provide information about the evaluation of single technical characteristics of a system. Accordingly, practical design guidelines for AAL system design cannot be derived, e.g. "at which places video monitoring should be installed?", "which type of camera should be used?", or "for what purposes should video data be further used?". Second, in most user studies about AAL system acceptance, the design process of the product is usually finished and users are being confronted with technically mature prototypes, where only marginal changes can be made. In order to optimally support the acceptance of AAL systems, user needs and requirements should be assessed earlier in the system design life cycle [20]. Third, technology acceptance is highly context-specific. Depending on the usage context, identical technical systems or functions are perceived differently by users, e.g., users associated with a wireless mobile system in a job-related ICT-context mainly the fear of health damage caused by EMF radiation or data privacy concerns and, in contrast, in the AAL context the fear of technical unreliability [21]). Accordingly, existing knowledge about video-based crime surveillance systems cannot be applied to the design and implementation of video-based monitoring systems for healthcare purposes. Since most AAL applications and research activities focus on the private home environment, little is known about the acceptance and design requirements of video-based healthcare monitoring systems in public places.

To sum up, the design, implementation and acceptance of video-based monitoring systems in healthcare could be improved, if designers and planners knew about preferences of users. The goal of our study was, therefore, to capture preferences for video-based healthcare monitoring scenarios in the private and public environment under consideration of different camera types, locations of camera installation, benefits in terms of improved medical safety, and privacy concerns due to different data handling purposes.

2   Method

2.1   Conjoint Analyses

In the present study the conjoint measurement method was used to study respondents' preferences. Conjoint analysis (CA) methods, which combine a measurement model with a statistical estimation algorithm, were developed in the 1960ies by the psychologist Luce and the statistician Tukey [22]. Compared to survey-based acceptance studies, which are still the dominating research method in information systems and acceptance research, CA allow for a more holistic and ecologically more valid investigation of decision scenarios. They were predominantly used in market research, but nowadays they are widely used for evaluating the adoption of information system innovations or to understand acceptance patterns for existing technologies such as mobile communication network systems [23]. In CA, specific product profiles or scenarios are evaluated by respondents, which are composed of multiple attributes and differ from each other in the attribute levels. The analysis of conjoint data allows for the simulation of decision processes and the decomposition of preferences for a scenario as a combined set of attributes into separate part-worth utilities [24]. CA deliver information about which attribute influences respondents' choice the most and which level of an attribute is preferred. Preference judgments and resulting preference shares are interpreted as indicator of acceptance.

In the present study, a choice-based-conjoint (CBC) analysis approach was chosen, because it closely mimics complex decision processes, where more than one attribute affects the final decision [25].

2.2   Selection of Attributes

In the study we assume that respondents' preferences are influenced by a set of attributes that possess the highest utility. Based on literature analysis and expert interviews we selected relevant impact factors for video-based medical monitoring system acceptance:

Medical Safety, as major benefit of AAL system implementation, which was operationalized in terms of an improved detection of medical emergencies.

Privacy, as major concern or barrier of video-based AAL system acceptance, which was operationalized by different ways to process or use video data (e.g. archiving or face recognition).

Type of camera, which did not refer to specific technical solutions, but mainly to features of size, visibility and obtrusiveness of technology.

Location, where the private home environment as place of camera installation was contrasted to different public locations of camera installation.

2.3   The Questionnaire

The questionnaire was developed with SSI web Software [26]. The questionnaire consisted of four parts. First, demographic data was assessed (age, gender, education, type and area of residence, health status). Second, participants were introduced into the scenario. The scenario dealt with the installation of video cameras for medical monitoring purposes at different locations, i.e. own home (private), market place, shopping mall or train station (public). In the scenario, the cameras were able to record vital function data and – in case of a medical emergency – to send an emergency signal to a medical institution (e.g. hospital). In the fourth part, the CBC choice tasks with the following attributes (No. 1-4) and their respective levels (a-d) were presented:

1. Medical Safety - Improved detection of medical emergencies
   a. 0% (no improvement),
   b. +5%,
   c. +10%,
   d. +20%
2. Privacy - Handling of video information
   a. Face recognition (i.e. storage of video material which allows for face recognition)
   b. Determination of position (i.e. storage of video material which allows for determination of position),
   c. Archiving of video data by health insurance company,
   d. Archiving of video data in a patient data base (allows for faster medical therapies in case of emergencies)
3. Type of camera
   a. Conventional CCTV camera (big, obtrusive or visible camera)
   b. Dome camera (big, but more unobtrusive camera)
   c. Mini dome camera (small, unobtrusive camera)
   d. Integrated camera (integrated, invisible camera)

4. Locations
    a. Own house or apartment
    b. Shopping mall
    c. Market place
    d. Train station

Participants were asked to decide under which conditions and at which locations they would accept the installation of cameras. An example for a choice task is shown in Fig. 1.

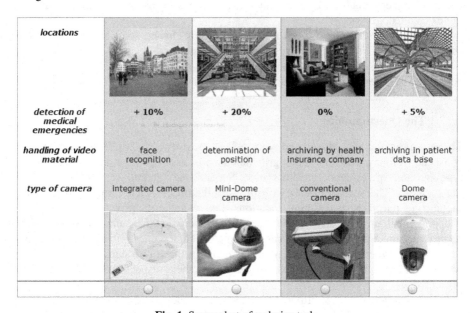

Fig. 1. Screenshot of a choice task

Since a combination of all corresponding levels would have led to 256 (4x4x4x4) possible combinations, the number of choice tasks was reduced, i.e., each respondent rated 10 random tasks and one fixed task. A test of design efficiency confirmed that the reduced test design was comparable to the hypothetical orthogonal design (median efficiency of 99%).

2.4   The Sample

Data was collected in an online survey conducted in Germany. Participants were invited to participate in the study via e-mail and were forwarded to the questionnaire. Completion of the questionnaire took approximately 30 minutes. In total, 194 participants took part in the study. As only complete questionnaires (no missing answers) were used for further statistical analyses, only 120 data sets were analyzed.

The mean age of the participants was M=28.68 years (SD = 11.78, range 18-75 years) with 47.5% females. Asked for their residence, 14.2% reported to live in a detached, 4.2% in a semi-detached and 15% in a terraced house. The majority of 67% reported to live in an apartment building. The participants were also asked for their housing conditions: 50.6% reported to be the house owner and 49.4% reported to rent. Regarding their area of residence, the majority (60%) reported to live in a city, and 29% in suburban area. Asked for their highest educational achievement 39.2% answered to have a university or a polytechnic degree, 45% answered to have a General Certificate of Secondary Education, and 5% reported to have a completed apprenticeship.

Regarding health status, a comparably healthy sample was under study: the majority reported to be in a very good (38.3%) or good (48.3%) health status, 13.3% reported health problems. Being asked for their experience with medical emergencies, 15.8% already experienced a medical emergency, and 48.3% witnessed a medical emergency in their family or in their closer circle of friends (34.2%). No experiences with medical emergencies at all reported 29.2%.

2.5 Data Analysis

Data analysis, i.e. the estimation of part-worth utilities, segmentation and preference simulations, was carried out by using Sawtooth Software (SSI Web, HB, SMRT). First, part-worth utilities were calculated on the basis of Hierarchical Bayes (HB) estimation and part-worth utilities importance scores were derived. They provide a measure of how important the attribute is relative to all other attributes. Part-worth utilities are interval-scaled data, which are scaled to an arbitrary additive constant within each attribute, i.e. it is not possible to compare utility values between different attributes [24]. By using zero-centered differentials part-worth utilities, which are scaled to sum to zero within each attribute, it is possible to compare differences between attribute levels. Finally, preference simulations were run by using the Sawtooth market simulator, which estimate the impact on preferences if certain attribute levels change within a specific scenario [27]. Preference simulations allow specific "what-if"-considerations, e.g. the effect of different camera locations within a public or private environment on respondents' preferences within a predefined scenario.

3 Results

In this section, the relative importance scores for the four attributes are presented, followed by part-worth utility estimation findings for respective attribute levels, and the simulation of preferences.

3.1 Relative Importance Scores

To evaluate the main impact factors on preferences for medical monitoring scenarios, the share of preference was calculated by applying Hierarchical Bayes Analyses. The relative importance scores of the attributes examined in the present study are presented in Fig. 2. The attribute "detection of medical emergencies" had the highest importance score (29.15%), followed by "handling of video material" (26.85%) and "locations" (26.65%). The least important criterion was "type of camera" (17.35%). The results indicate that improved medical care is the most dominant attribute to influence acceptance. The handling of data and the location where cameras are installed, were also important, but to a slightly lesser extent. Interestingly, the type of camera, especially the feature of its visibility, was the least important.

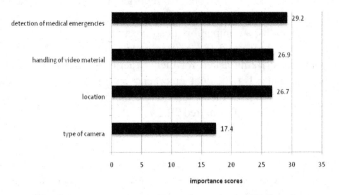

Fig. 2. Importance scores for attributes in the CBC study

3.2   Part-Worth Utility Estimation

The average zero-centered diff part-worth utilities for all attribute levels are shown in Fig. 3. The attribute "detection of medical emergencies" displayed the highest range between part-worth utilities, which caused the high importance scores (see 3.1). Focusing on absolute utility values, the attribute level "20% improved detection of medical emergencies" reached the highest utility value, whereas "camera location in the own house" received the lowest utility value.

Looking at the different attributes, an "improved detection of medical emergencies" by 20% reached the highest utility value, an improvement by 10% was also rated positively meanwhile 5% and 0% ("no improvement") reached the lowest utility values. Regarding "handling of video material", determination of position was preferred the most, followed by archiving in patient data base, archiving by health insurance companies and – to a much higher extent – face recognition was rejected. For "camera location" the own home was distinctly rejected, shopping mall, market place and train station were evaluated positively in ascending order. Looking at "type of camera", the dome camera (big, but unobtrusive) was preferred to the conventional camera (big, visible) and the mini dome-camera (small, unobtrusive). The only attribute level, which was rejected, was the integrated camera (invisible).

The most preferred scenario ("best case") – based on the highest utility ratings for each attribute – was a dome camera (big, but unobtrusive), installed at a train station, which allows for the determination of patients' position and leads to an increase in the detection of medical emergencies by 20%. The least preferred scenario ("worst case") was an integrated camera (small, invisible) with face recognition, installed at home, without improvements in detecting medical emergencies.

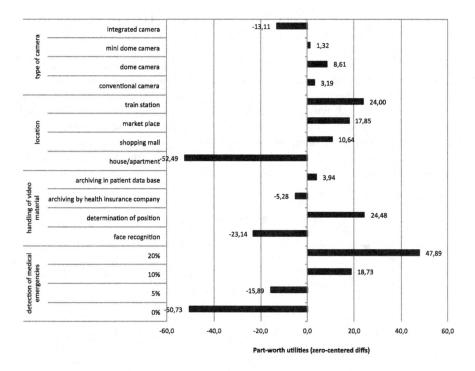

Fig. 3. Part-worth utilities (zero-centered diffs) for all attributes and levels in the CBC-study

3.3   Simulation of Preferences

In the next step, sensitivity simulations where carried out by using the Sawtooth market simulator [27]. In the simulation we investigated, to which extent the relative preferences of respondents change, when single levels of an attribute change while all other attribute levels are kept constant. Based on the identified preference patterns, a scenario was constructed, which focused on the installation of medical monitoring technologies at *public vs. private locations,* and sensitivity analyses were run.

The scenario investigated preference changes for three constant locations (public: train station, semi-public: shopping mall, private: home) for different levels of "improved detection of medical emergencies" (medical safety), handling with video material (privacy), and type of camera (Fig. 4).

The *public scenario,* i.e. the installation of cameras for medical monitoring purposes at a train station reached the highest relative preference (64.58%), compared to the semi-public (installation in shopping mall, 21.96%) and the private scenario (at home, 13.46%). For all single attribute levels, the preference for a public application of medical monitoring systems was higher than for the other two scenarios. The acceptance in the public scenario even increased, when video material was used for determination of position, i.e. privacy needs of respondents were considered (78.8%). The acceptance of the public scenario dropped to 57.64%, when the video data was used for face recognition, which indicates that face recognition is rejected in public areas since it apparently violates privacy needs. The type of camera did not play an important role in the public scenario, preferences decreased to 59.76% in case of integrated (invisible cameras), the most preferred camera type in public was the dome camera (big, more unobtrusive, but still visible, 64.58%). Regarding medical safety, i.e. the detection of medical emergencies, the highest improvement, (a detection rate +20%) was – not surprisingly – the most preferred (64.58%). The highest acceptance "leap" (+16.89%) was reached, when the detection rate of emergencies (medical safety) was raised from +5% (37.96%) to +10% (54.85%) by applying medical monitoring systems. But even if medical safety was not improved by installing medical monitoring systems (i.e. detection rate +0%), the acceptance of the public scenario was higher than in the semi-public or private scenario (26.45%).

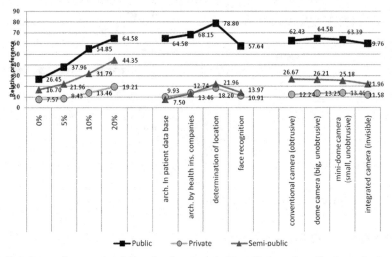

Fig. 4. Relative preference simulation for the scenario "installation of medical monitoring technologies at *public vs. private locations*"

In the *semi-public scenario*, in which cameras were installed in a shopping mall, the highest preference leap was reached by increasing medical safety, i.e. the higher the detection rate; the higher were preferences (up to 44.35% for +20% medical safety). Regarding the handling of video data, acceptance was the highest for determination of position (21.96%), but it decreased for face recognition to 13.97%, and – and even stronger – for archiving of video material by health insurance companies to 7.5%. Looking at the camera type, big and visible cameras were preferred, e.g. conventional cameras (26.67%) or dome-cameras (26.21%). However, more unobtrusive or invisible cameras did not lead to substantial preference drops (e.g. 21.96 for integrated cameras).

Looking at the *private scenario*, the total preference for camera-based medical monitoring was the lowest (13.46%). Only two attribute level changes slightly increased preferences: first, determination of position by using video material was perceived positively (18.2%) and second, very high levels of medical safety, i.e. a detection rate of +20% increased preferences in the private scenario to a maximum of 19.21%. Changes in other attribute levels further decreased preferences, e.g. to 8.43%

if medical safety was only increased by +5% or if video data was used for face recognition (10.91%) or for archiving purposes (9.93%). The type of camera did not strongly affect preferences; a mini-dome camera was preferred the most (13.46%), whereas integrated cameras were the least preferred (11.58%).

4   Discussion

Facing the healthcare challenges of an aging society, the expansion of AAL system implementation in private and public environments is a promising way to improve healthcare in future smart homes and cities. The present study evaluated preferences for different video-based medical monitoring scenarios, which comprised the attributes medical safety (improved detection of medical emergencies), privacy (handling of video information), type and location of camera in a conjoint analysis.

4.1   Perception and Acceptance of Video-Based Monitoring Technologies for Healthcare

In general, video-based medical monitoring technologies and scenarios were evaluated positively – under the condition that specific scenario criteria where met.

Medical safety was the most important factor in respondents' decisions for or against video-based medical monitoring scenarios. Acceptance increased linearly with improved medical safety. Accordingly, communication strategies should focus on this key benefit to support the adoption of AAL monitoring systems. The conjoint preference simulation findings also gave insights into expectations or benchmarks for healthcare improvements. Preferences shares were above 50% when the detection rate of medical emergencies in the public scenario was improved by 10%. In turn, in the private environment, even an improved detection rate by 20% was not sufficient to raise acceptance. Future studies will have to investigate if a higher detection rate in a smart home environment raises acceptance or if privacy, i.e. the way of data handling and processing, more strongly determines acceptance in the private context.

As indicated, respondents had well defined expectations regarding *privacy*, i.e. different ways of handling and processing captured video data. Privacy concerns were primarily related to the unwillingness of being visible or recognizable in health monitoring systems. In contrast, data privacy issues (e.g. due to archiving of medical monitoring data) caused less concerns. This shows that privacy is a multidimensional construct, and, that users' mental models about privacy in AAL systems need to be carefully uncovered and considered in system design. Determination of location, e.g. for fall protection systems, was accepted and preferred. In contrast, face recognition was clearly rejected, especially in the private scenario. This finding is especially important for AAL system design, where privacy protection should be taken on the agenda, when face recognition features are included. Moreover, a transparent communication of data usage and protection of privacy is highly important for the acceptance of video-based medical monitoring technologies.

The *location* of camera installation is also highly relevant: in *public* places video-based monitoring systems are comparably well-accepted – even in case of a rather low system effectiveness, i.e. low improvements of medical safety. However, preference differences for the public locations under study indicate, that respondents evaluate public locations differently, which should be addressed in further studies.

The more healthcare monitoring technologies invade into *private* spaces, the more they are perceived critically or even rejected. The most sensitive area is the own home, where our findings showed a comparably low acceptance of video-based medical monitoring. Especially privacy-related concerns reduced acceptance, i.e. face recognition and data archiving were "no-Go's" from the users' side. Since most AAL monitoring systems are developed for the private home care sector, future acceptance research is necessary to support long-term market success of AAL systems.

Technical features of *cameras* such as visibility or obtrusiveness were comparably unimportant. However, camera technology used for monitoring should be visible, but not too obtrusive or dominant. A seamless integration of monitoring systems into the home or public environment is therefore not desirable from the users' perspective.

4.2   Limitations and Future Research

In the present study a comparably young and healthy sample was under study. Since this might result in an underestimation of benefits, concerns and total preferences, future research should focus on older participants with health problems to include their specific demands and requirements into the design of AAL systems. A more detailed evaluation of private (e.g. sleeping vs. living room) and public locations (e.g. restaurants, transport hubs, parks, etc.) is necessary, since video-based monitoring system acceptance varied with respect to different public environments. A cartography of "acceptable" and "inacceptable" locations for camera installation and types of data processing would provide valuable planning support for AAL system designers and city planners. Moreover, cross-cultural analyses should be pursued to investigate if factors such as culture or literacy rate will have an impact on the outcomes. Finally, future conjoint analyses should focus on potential trade-offs between privacy and medical safety to optimally support AAL system design for future livable smart home environments and smart cities.

Acknowledgments. We owe gratitude to Julia van Heek and Valentina Kneip for research support.

References

1. World Health Organization (WHO): The European Health Report 2012: Charting the Way to Well-being. World Health Organization (2012)
2. Leonhardt, S.: Personal healthcare devices. In: AmIware Hardware Technology Drivers of Ambient Intelligence, pp. 349–370. Springer (2006)

3. Rosenbloom, S.: Sustainability and automobility among the elderly: An international assessment. Transportation. **28**, 375–408 (2001)
4. Denning, P.J.: The Invisible Future: The Seamless Integration of Technology into Everyday Life. McGraw-Hill, Inc (2001)
5. Rubenstein, L.Z.: Falls in older people: epidemiology, risk factors and strategies for prevention. Age Ageing. **35**, ii37–ii41 (2006)
6. Gurley, R.J., Lum, N., Sande, M., Lo, B., Katz, M.H.: Persons found in their homes helpless or dead. N. Engl. J. Med. **334**, 1710–1716 (1996)
7. Gururajan, R., Murugesan, S., Soar, J.: Introducing mobile technologies in support of healthcare. Cut. IT J. **18**, 12–18 (2005)
8. Memon, M., Wagner, S.R., Pedersen, C.F., Beevi, F.H.A., Hansen, F.O.: Ambient Assisted Living Healthcare Frameworks, Platforms, Standards, and Quality Attributes. Sensors. **14**, 4312–4341 (2014)
9. Cardinaux, F., Bhowmik, D., Abhayaratne, C., Hawley, M.S.: Video based technology for ambient assisted living: A review of the literature. J. Ambient Intell. Smart Environ. **3**, 253–269 (2011)
10. Leijdekkers, P., Gay, V., Lawrence, E.: Smart homecare system for health tele-monitoring. In: ICDS 2007. First International Conference on the Digital Society, 2007, pp. 3–3 (2007)
11. Fleck, S., Strasser, W.: Smart Camera Based Monitoring System and Its Application to Assisted Living. Proc. IEEE. **96**, 1698–1714 (2008)
12. Chen, B.-W., Chen, C.-Y., Wang, J.-F.: Smart Homecare Surveillance System: Behavior Identification Based on State-Transition Support Vector Machines and Sound Directivity Pattern Analysis. IEEE Trans. Syst. Man Cybern. Syst. **43**, 1279–1289 (2013)
13. Yu, M., Rhuma, A., Naqvi, S.M., Wang, L., Chambers, J.: A Posture Recognition-Based Fall Detection System for Monitoring an Elderly Person in a Smart Home Environment. IEEE Trans. Inf. Technol. Biomed. **16**, 1274–1286 (2012)
14. Aghajan, H., Augusto, J.C., Wu, C., McCullagh, P., Walkden, J.-A.: Distributed vision-based accident management for assisted living. In: Okadome, T., Yamazaki, T., Makhtari, M. (eds.) ICOST. LNCS, vol. 4541, pp. 196–205. Springer, Heidelberg (2007)
15. Patton, J.W.: Protecting privacy in public? Surveillance technologies and the value of public places. Ethics Inf. Technol. **2**, 181–187 (2000)
16. Wilkowska, W., Ziefle, M.: Privacy and data security in E-health: Requirements from the user's perspective. Health Informatics J. **18**, 191–201 (2012)
17. Rogers, E.: Diffusion of Innovations. NY Free Press, New York (2003)
18. Davis, F.D.: Perceived usefulness, perceived ease of use, and user acceptance of information technology. MIS Q. 319–340 (1989)
19. Yarbrough, A.K., Smith, T.B.: Technology Acceptance among Physicians A New Take on TAM. Med. Care Res. Rev. **64**, 650–672 (2007)
20. Kowalewski, S., Arning, K., Minwegen, A., Ziefle, M., Ascheid, G.: Extending the Engineering Trade-Off Analysis by Integrating User Preferences in Conjoint Analysis. Expert Syst. Appl. **40**, 2947–2955 (2013)
21. Arning, K., Gaul, S., Ziefle, M.: ``Same Same but Different'' how service contexts of mobile technologies shape usage motives and barriers. In: Leitner, G., Hitz, M., Holzinger, A. (eds.) USAB 2010. LNCS, vol. 6389, pp. 34–54. Springer, Heidelberg (2010)
22. Luce, R.D., Tukey, J.W.: Simultaneous conjoint measurement: A new type of fundamental measurement. J. Math. Psychol. **1**, 1–27 (1964)
23. Arning, K., Ziefle, M., Kowalewski, S.: Health concerns vs. mobile data needs: Conjoint measurement of preferences for mobile communication network scenarios. Int. J. Hum. Ecol. Risk Assess. (2013)

24. Orme, B.: Interpreting the Results of Conjoint Analysis, Getting Started with Conjoint Analysis: Strategies for Product Design and Pricing Research. Res. Publ. LLC Madison WI. 77–89 (2010)
25. Chrzan, K., Orme, B.: An overview and comparison of design strategies for choice-based conjoint analysis. Sawtooth Softw. Res. Pap. Ser. (2000)
26. Orme, B.K.: SSI Web v7. 0 Software for web interviewing and conjoint analysis. Sequim: Sawtooth Software. Inc (2011)
27. Orme, B.: Market simulators for conjoint analysis. Get. Started Conjoint Anal. Strateg. Prod. Des. Pricing Res. Second. Ed Madison Res. Publ. LLC (2010)

Privacy-Preserving Energy-Reading for Smart Meter

Gianpiero Costantino$^{(\boxtimes)}$ and Fabio Martinelli

Istituto di Informatica e Telematica, CNR, Pisa, Italy
{gianpiero.costantino,fabio.martinelli}@iit.cnr.it

Abstract. Smart Meters belong to the Advanced Metering Infrastructure (AMI) and allow customers to monitor locally and remotely the current usage of energy. Providers query Smart Meters for billing purpose or to establish the amount of energy needed by houses. However, reading details sent from smart meters to the energy provider can be used to violate customers' privacy. In this paper, our contribution is twofold: first, we present an architecture to turn traditional energy meters into Smart Meters, and then we illustrate a privacy-preserving solution, which uses Secure Two-party Computation, to preserve customers' privacy during energy-readings. In particular, we deployed a Smart Meter built upon an existing energy meter available in Italy. Then, we collected and analysed an energy trace of two months, and we tag customers hourly/daily/monthly habits by observing their consumes. Finally, we provide the feasibility of our solution to protect customers' privacy.

Keywords: Smart meter · Privacy · Secure Two-party computation · Energy trace · Raspberry pi

1 Introduction

The current energy infrastructure provides electric meters that run basic operations, e.g. showing the energy used in an embedded display. Over last ten years, Italy has maintained the electric meter leadership with ENEL and its "Telegestore", which is able to communicate with the energy provider through narrowband Power Line Communication (PLC).

The interest in developing and deploying new meters, called Smart Meters, is one of the next years goals. In 2007, the US Congress decided to modernise its electricity transmission distribution network via the Energy Independence and Security. In 2009, the European Union passed a directive asking all Member States to conduct an economic assessment of smart metering[1]. In *Energy: Commission paves the way for massive roll-out of smart metering systems*[2] published in 2012, the European Commission asserts that only 10% of houses have some

---

[1] European Parliament and Council, 'Directive 2009/72/EC concerning common rules for the internal market in electricity and repealing Directive 2003/54/EC

[2] http://tiny.cc/sfyzvx

© Springer International Publishing Switzerland 2015
A. Geissbühler et al. (Eds.): ICOST 2015, LNCS 9102, pp. 165–177, 2015.
DOI: 10.1007/978-3-319-19312-0_14

sort of smart meter installed, and that 80% of all electricity meters in the EU will be replaced by smart meters by 2020. As negative fact, in November 2014, the UK's Department of Energy and Climate Change announced that the UK's smart metering deployment is delayed for other twelve months[3] without giving a clear reason for that choice.

From the above situations, the installation of Smart Meters into every house appears to be a long process. Thus, in this paper we propose an architecture to turn current energy meters into Smart Meters to bridge the gap between the Smart Meters roll-out and the existing energy meters. In particular, we developed a meter in which customers are able to know in real time their energy consumption both locally and remotely by using any device connected to the Internet, plus the opportunity to record the energy consumptions for analytics.

Then, we show a privacy study of our energy trace[4] that illustrates how to identify some human behaviours analysing the energy consumption. In fact, the adoption of "smart" devices brings new privacy issues that attackers may exploit for different purposes. For instance, attackers could observe the energy consumes of a house to learn the daily activities of the landlord in order to discover the right period to burgle his house.

Not only privacy issues hit Smart Meter, but also security problems can create damages to Smart Meters and their owners. As an example, Spanish researchers[5] proved how to send to the energy provider fake values of energy reads to get a "lighter" bill. In this attack, the researchers were able to discover the keys adopted by the smart meters and the provider nodes to spoof exchanged messages.

Finally, we propose the use of Secure-Two-party Computation (STC) to preserve customers' privacy. STC is part of the cryptographic field, and it can be used for privacy-preserving computation in which the goal of the two parties is to jointly compute the outcome of a generic function $g(x, y)$ without disclosing to the other party the own input. Our solution allows customers to keep protected their values of energy, but at the same time providers have indication on how much energy customers need.

The structure of this paper is the following: in Section 2 we provide our architecture to turn traditional energy meters into Smart Meters. In Section 3, we plot energy consumes and we illustrate how it is possible to rebuild customer hourly/daily/monthly pattern by observing his energy consumption. In Section 4, we provide our solution to preserve customers' privacy using STC. Section 5 shows some work related to ours. Finally, Section 6 concludes the paper.

2   Smart Meter Architecture

In this section we show the architecture that we use to turn an energy meter into a smart one. Figure 1 shows the building blocks of our architecture. We use the

---

[3] http://tiny.cc/7gyzvx

[4] We recorded two months of energy consumption with our Smart Meter.

[5] http://www.bbc.com/news/technology-29643276

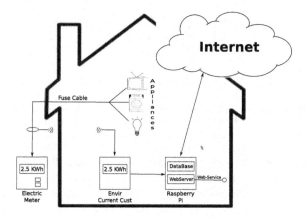

Fig. 1. Smart Meter Architecture

Envir Current Cost[6] to estimate the energy required by all capabilities attached at the house energy net, and the *Raspberry Pi*, which is programmed to store all energy consumes and to expose a web service able to communicate the current energy usage to remote entities connected to the Internet, such as Smartphones, Tablets and so on.

The Envir device is composed by two main components: the *transmitter* and the *receiver*. The transmitter is attached to the energy meter through a sensor jaw, instead the receiver is located into the house and displays the current energy usage plus other details, such as the indoor temperature, time and so on.

The Raspberry Pi is a tiny and low cost computer with 700 Mhz ARM processor, 512 Mbyte of RAM that runs a Unix Operating System. In our architecture the Raspberry Pi hosts a MySQL database plus an Apache TomCat WebServer, and the Raspberry Pi is connected to the Internet with an additional WiFi interface.

Figure 1 summarises our architecture. On the left side, the sensor jaw is hooked up the fuse cable of the energy meter of the building. The Envir receiver is located inside the building and shows the current energy use. The displayed values are updated every six seconds, and an outgoing serial cable connects the receiver to the Raspberry Pi.

2.1   Recording Energy Consumes

The data stream sent from the Envir device to the Raspberry Pi is evaluated using a Python script, see code listed in 1.1. The port variable expresses the mounting point of the serial port into the Raspberry Pi operating system, the baud rate specifies the number of symbols sent per second, while the timeout specifies the number of seconds to wait until the program stops with a connection

---

[6] Available here: http://www.currentcost.com/product-envir.html

error. We use the object "Serial" to read the stream from the cable, while the meter variable is a string containing all data read from the serial cable.

```
port = '/dev/ttyUSB0'
baud = 57600
timeout = 10
...
meter = serial.Serial(port, baud, timeout=timeout)
```

Listing 1.1. Python code to read from the serial port

From the data stream, we extrapolate two main values: i) last monitored energy consume, and ii) the current indoor temperature. These two values are saved into local variables and, then stored into a MySQL table. In the same SQL-insert tuple, we introduce two more variables, indicating time and date. For performance reasons, we decide to store data into the database roughly each minute although the data stream is read every six seconds.

2.2 Remote Reading

To make more powerful our Smart Meter, we installed a web-server into the Raspberry Pi. It aims at exposing one or more web services that can be remotely called to provide real time information. Web-services are called through a unique web address and the output is given as a "html" page.

The web-server we adopted is Apache Tomcat[7], and web-services implementation usually follows two approaches: *SOAP*[8] and *REST*[9]. The first one exposes a set of methods that can be invoked remotely by clients, while REST allows developers to define a set of resources that clients can request using the HTTP/HTTPs protocol.

In our implementation we prefer the REST technology since it is lightweight and fast, which are essential features for developing technologies on Smart Meters. For our purpose, we expose a single web-service in which users can visualise through a web browser last monitored energy consumption and internal temperature.

Figure 2 completes the architecture of our smart meter connected to the Internet. The traditional energy meter is linked to the home area network by means of the Envir device and the Raspberry Pi. This latter exploits the Internet connection to expose the web-server. At the same time, the web-service allows any authorised user to reach the Smart Meter information using her own device. Access control is managed using username and password authentication for users who want to access the web-service.

2.3 Pros and Cons

We acknowledge this architecture has some limitations. For instance, we admit that a customer has only the power to "read" data from his/her meter and not

---

[7] http://tomcat.apache.org
[8] http://www.w3.org/TR/soap/
[9] http://tiny.cc/esswhx

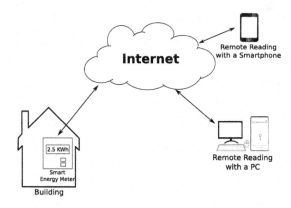

Fig. 2. Our Smart Meter connected to the Internet

to "write". In fact, a customer is not able to change any kind of data saved in the meter. However, this sort of limitation can be seen also as positive feature since a potential customer/attacker has not ability to corrupt smart meter data.

A strength of our architecture is its versatility. It is enough to plug the sensor jaw to the fuse cable of the meter to know the energy used, then the Raspberry Pi completes the architecture to turn a meter into a smart one. In this way, customers are able to manage their consumes, and can forecast the billing price as well as compare the energy used declared in the bill with that one estimated by the smart meter.

3   Privacy Study

The architecture introduced in the previous section found its application in a flat located in Italy. Currently, ENEL's customers have installed at home the *Telegestore*[10] meter. Advantage of the "Telegestore" is to be already connected with the Enel servers, through narrow-band Power Line Communication (PLC). This kind of communication avoids that Enel-employees pass house-by-house to collect the consume of energy of each meter. Nevertheless, customers at home do not have direct control of the meter as well as remote reading of the current energy consume. In fact, they can read the energy consumption through a display embedded into the meter. Generically, meters are located outside the building and in some cases they are not easily accessible.

For our experiments, we started collecting energy consumes at the end of April 2014, and we had collected data for two months, up to the end of June.

In Figure 3 we plot the consumes recorder in a single hour. Values collected are 54 since the measurements are saved into the database roughly every minute. Observing all consumes it is possible to extrapolate a particular detail. We found

---

[10] http://www.enel.com/en-GB/innovation/smart_grids/smart_metering/telegestore/

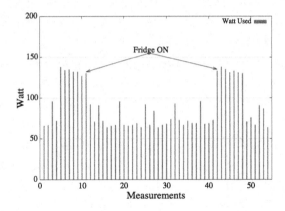

Fig. 3. One hour flat consumes

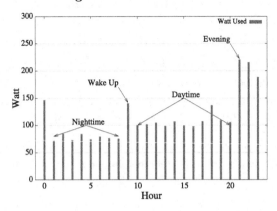

Fig. 4. 24 hours flat consumes

an energy peak every 30 minutes related to an appliance that we link to the fridge. In fact, it remains "on" for about seven minutes and then switches to "off". After half an hour it goes "on" again.

In Figure 4, we plot the energy consumes per hour in a single day. Values reported for each hour are obtained averaging all consumes. Results of this figure are very interesting since we identify different periods of the day. Starting from midnight, in which it is recorded a high consume of energy, then we observe a low consume of energy during the nighttime. Afterwards, around "09:00" in the morning a new peak of energy identifies the moment in which there was activity in the flat. During the daytime the consume of energy is low and pretty uniform saying that nobody was in the flat except an usage activity monitored around "18:00". Finally, after "20:00" new peaks of energy are registered representing again more request of energy.

In Figure 5 we show the energy consumes monitored during May 2014. Consumes of each days are plotted as the mean of the entire day consumes. During this month we identify three different intervals in which consumes are low. Those periods correspond to a holiday time, from first to fourth of May, and

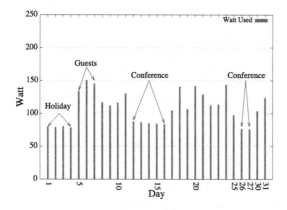

Fig. 5. Flat consumes in May

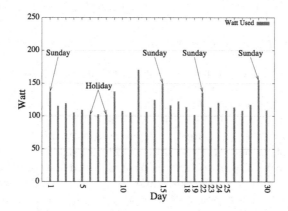

Fig. 6. Flat consumes in June

two conferences, from twelfth to sixteenth of May and at the end of the same month. Then, for three days, from fifth to eighth of May, we observe the highest consume of energy explained by the presence of additional people in the flat. In the same figure we do not have measurements for two days at the end of the month since our Smart Meter lost the connection with the database did not record any energy value.

In Figure 6 we plot the average-consumes per day in June. At first glimpse, we notice weekly high peaks of energy that correspond to those days in which the activity at home is higher than other days, e.g. "Sunday". Then, we tag another interval of days as "Holiday" in which we notice a low consume of energy that corresponds to a period in which nobody was at home. An empty space is present in the data trace during the 20th and 21st of June since we experienced again a network issue.

Energy Trace. Our values of energy may be useful for the community of researchers working in this field. For this reason, we share our consume trace giving the chance to others researchers to make their sturdies on real energy consumes.

In the file we share, there are energy consumes of the flat that we used as test-bed in May-June 2014 period. Each row in the file is composed by three fields separated by ";" that represent: *"Data"*, *"Time"* and *"Watt"*. Our trace file can be imported into a database or can be directly analysed using the text file. It is available here[11].

4   Privacy Solution

In this section, we propose a privacy solution apt to protect customers' real-time readings done by providers. In particular, our solution makes use of Secure Two-party Computation to indicate in a range the effective customers' energy consumption without revealing the exact smart meter reading to the provider.

4.1   Using STC Inside Smart Meters

We believe that the cryptographic field may help proposing methods that can reduce the privacy issue seen above. In Secure Two-party Computation two parties are involved, generically called Alice and Bob, each holding some private data x and y, respectively. The goal of STC functions computation is to allow Alice and Bob to jointly compute the outcome of a function $f(x,y)$, without disclosing to the other party their own input. The straightforward way to solve the above problem would be to have a Trusted Third Party (TTP) to which Alice and Bob securely send the data, and to have the TTP compute $f(x,y)$ and separately send the outcome to Alice and Bob. The business in secure two-party computation amounts to securely compute $f(x,y)$ without the need of a TTP.

The first implementation of Secure-Two party Computation was made by Yao in the 1980s [1], presenting a solution for the well-known "Millionaire Problem". In the Millionaire Problem, the two parties want to know whom of them is richer without revealing to the other party his/her own amount of money. The problem requires the evaluation of $x < y$ condition, where Alice knows only *"x"*, and Bob knows only *"y"*. At the end of the protocol execution, Alice knows only the outcome of the evaluation of condition $x < y$, without knowing y (similarly for Bob).

Over the last ten years, researchers have proposed different Secure Two-party Computation frameworks able to run secure functions. FairPlay [13] is a well-know framework that allows users to write functions using its high level language (SFDL), and to compile functions into garbled boolean circuits, which will mask the real inputs of both participants. FairPlay has strong security properties in the context of two-party computation. The framework is shown to be secure against a malicious party; in particular *i)* a malicious party cannot learn more

---

[11] http://tiny.cc/5v41vx

information about the other party's input than it can learn from a TTP that computes the function; and *ii*) a malicious party cannot change the output of the computed function. New versions of this framework are FairplayMP [2], which is the extension of Fairplay that works with more than two parties, and Mobile-Fairplay [5],[6], which is the version of Fairplay ported to Android Smartphones.

A more recent STC framework is MightBeEvil [11]. It allows people to easily write functions that can be run in a secure way, in a similar way done by Fairplay, however, MightBeEvil is faster and less memory-hungry than Fairplay.

The STC framework that we use in our smart meter is CBMC-GC [10]. It is composed by two main parts: one is the compiler that translates functions written in C into garbled circuits, while the other part is the interpreter able to execute compiled functions [12]. Compared with Fairplay, CBMC-GC offers a more flexible high language that allows developers to express more detailed and complicated functions. Moreover, thanks to its optimisation steps during the compilations phase, CBMC-GC runs STC function using less memory than framework like Fairplay.

STC attacker model. The aforementioned STC frameworks are secure against the *honest-but-curious* attacker model. In this model, an attacker follows all protocol steps as per specifications, but she can try to learn additional information about the other party, with the purpose of acquiring at least part of her private profile. Moreover, notice that, as customary in secure two-party computation, there is an asymmetry on the provided security guarantees: in particular, there is no way to prevent Alice from terminating the protocol prematurely, and not sending the outcome of the computation to Bob. This situation can be detected by Bob, but cannot be recovered from.

4.2   Our Solution

Here, we propose the use of STC to preserve customers' privacy when providers remotely read the energy value from the smart meter. We ported the CBMC-GC framework to our smart meter and we allow both provider and customer to run STC functions. To preserve customer's privacy, we wrote a function in which the customer's smart meter provides its current usage of energy as input, and the provider uses three intervals of energy as indication of energy usage. The output of our function indicates to the provider in which range the smart meter's input falls on, but the provider will never know its exact value. For instance, let suppose that the provider uses the following ranges in Watt (W): $[0, 1000]W$, $[1001, 2000]W$, $[2001, 3000]W$, and last meter reading is 547W. After running the STC function the provider knows that last monitored consume ranges in the interval $[0, 1000]W$, but it does not know the exact value, although it had been used to evaluate the energy consumption.

The listing in 1.2 shows the STC function that we wrote in C. The range function calculates the exact range of usage and it uses four variables: x is the reading done by the meter, y, t, and z are respectively the first, second, and third interval limit. In addition, each range is mapped as single progressive number, i.e. $[0, 1000]W \rightarrow 1$, $[1001, 2000]W \rightarrow 2$, $[2001, 3000]W \rightarrow 3$. To obtain a more fine-grained output, our program may consider more than three intervals.

```
int range(int x, int y, int z, int t)
{
   int output = 0;
   if ((x >= 0) && (x <= y))
      output = 1;
   else if ((x > y) && (x <= z))
      output = 2;
   else if ((x > z) && (x <= t))
      output = 3;
   return output;
}

void meterCheck(int INPUT_A_x, int INPUT_B_int1, int INPUT_B_int2, int
    INPUT_B_int3)
{
   int OUTPUT_meterCheck = range(INPUT_A_x, INPUT_B_int1, INPUT_B_int2,
       INPUT_B_int3);
}
```

Listing 1.2. STC function written in C

Implementation. The C-function listed in 1.2 is translated into garbled circuits by the CBMC-GC compiler, and the garbled circuits are distributed to the provider's computer and to customer's smart meter. The CBMC-GC running environment is also installed both on the smart meter and the provider's pc as it is depicted in Figure 7. In particular, the CBMC-GC instance installed in the meter waits for incoming queries from the provider, and once the connection is established they start the secure computation. Only at the end of the computation the provider is able to know in which range the smart meter reading falls on.

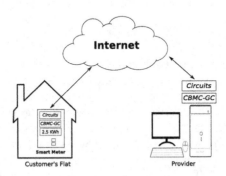

Fig. 7. Customer's smart meter and provider's PC with CBMC-GC

Empirical test conducted in our lab showed that using a Virtual Machine (VM) with Ubuntu OS and 16Gbyte of RAM to represent provider's PC, and the Raspberry Pi to represent smart meter, the time needed to run the function with CBMC-GC framework is about *40* seconds. The high computational time is due to the complexity of mathematical operations required by the STC framework and, particularly by the low computation power of our Raspberry Pi. We believe that in this context 40 seconds are a feasible time, and to support our belief, in this document[12], Enel claims that its Smart Meter saves every two minutes the KiloWatt taken. So, in practice Enel would have the time to run the STC function without losing any data precision.

5 Related Work

Privacy issues related to smart meters' reading have been studied in papers [8], [16], [17] and previously acknowledged in [4], [9]. The authors of [3] show how to apply homomorphic schemes for aggregation in smart metering data to protect customers' privacy, and in particular they discuss the applicability of the method presented by Mármol et al. [14]. A similar data aggregation is performed by Sankar et al. [19] in which data collected by multiple meters are aggregated before sending them to the utility. Rial and Danezis in [18] propose a protocol for privacy-preserving meter readings, and at the same time prove the reading correctness of the meter. Molina et al. in [15] shows how to apply Zero-Knowledge Proofs to low-cost microcontrollers to produce certified meter readings. In [7] the authors propose a solution to preserve customers' privacy providing encrypted meter reading with the adoption of secret-sharing-based secure multi-party computation techniques. Thoma and Cui in [20] make use of secure multi-party computation to know customers energy demand keeping hided the amount of energy needed by each consumer.

In the market there exist commercial tools to monitor energy consumption using indoor display or web-browser. TED pro-home[13] is a commercial for residential electricity monitoring and its price starts from 300$. The Egauge System company[14] sells its powerful product "EG3000" for energy monitoring starting from 500$. Openenergymonitor[15] is a project to develop open-source energy monitoring tools. This project proposes different hardware solutions and sensors that can be built together to create a monitoring system accessible by a web-application.

None of these contributions is totally related to ours, although we are not the first that apply cryptographic solutions to protect customers' privacy. To the best of our knowledge, our research paper is the only one that integrates an architecture to turn current meters into smart ones, with a cost of around 100€, and a mechanism to protect customers' privacy all in a single feasible solution.

---

[12] There exists only the italian version: https://www.enel.it/it-IT/doc/reti/ enel_distribuzione/Contatore_Monofase_v1.pdf
[13] http://www.theenergydetective.com/tedprohome.html
[14] https://www.egauge.net
[15] http://openenergymonitor.org/emon/

6   Conclusion

In this paper we have presented an architecture to turn traditional energy meters into new Smart Meters with a solution to preserve customers' privacy. In particular, our prototype of Smart Meter allowed us to record energy consumes for two months in a fine-grained fashion, i.e. roughly each minute. With the collected energy values, we illustrated how it is possible to identify human patterns, and for this issue, we implemented a solution that makes use of Secure-Two-party Computation to preserve customers' privacy during the real time monitoring. Finally, we showed the feasibility of our intuition by porting the CBMC-GC framework inside our smart meter prototype.

As further step, our intention is to use the new Raspberry Pi 2 —quad-core of 900Mhz and 1GByte of RAM— within our architecture. Benchmark tests claim that the Pi 2 is 6x faster that the previous model. This means that our STC computation will get a substantial speed up respect to the current implementation.

Acknowledgments. Work partially supported by project *Security Horizon* and by the EU project FP7-295354 *SESAMO*.

References

1. Andrew, C., Yao, C.: Protocols for secure computations. In: 23rd IEEE Symposium on FOCS, pp. 160–164 (1982)
2. Ben-David, A., Nisan, N., Pinkas,B.: Fairplaymp: a system for secure multi-party computation. In: Proceedings of the CCS Conference, pp. 257–266. ACM, New York, NY (2008)
3. Biselli, A., Franz, E., Coutinho, M.P.: Protection of consumer data in the smart grid compliant with the german smart metering guideline. In: Proceedings of the First ACM Workshop on Smart Energy Grid Security, SEGS 2013, pp. 41–52. ACM, New York, NY (2013)
4. C. P. U. Commission. The future of privacy forum and truste launch a smart grid privacy seal program, May 2011. http://tiny.cc/jlpwhx
5. Costantino, G., Martinelli, F., Santi, P.: Investigating the Privacy vs. Forwarding Accuracy Tradeoff in Opportunistic Interest-Casting. Transactions on mobile computing (2013)
6. Costantino, G., Martinelli, F., Santi, P., Amoruso, D.: An implementation of secure two-party computation for smartphones with application to privacy-preserving interest-cast. In: Proceedings of the 18th International Conference Mobicom, pp. 447–450. ACM (2012)
7. Danezis, G., Fournet, C., Kohlweiss, M., Béguelin, S.Z.: Smart meter aggregation via secret-sharing. In SEGS@CCS, pp. 75–80 (2013)
8. Greveler, U., Justus, B., Loehr, D.: Forensic content detection through power consumption. In: IEEE ICC, pp. 6759–6763, June
9. Heck, W.: Smart energy meter will not be compulsory, April 2009. http://tiny.cc/9vpwhx

10. Holzer, A., Franz, M., Katzenbeisser, S., Veith, H.: Secure two-party computations in ansi c. In: Proceedings of the CCS Conference, CCS 2012, pp. 772–783, NY, USA (2012)
11. Huang, Y., Chapman, P., Evans, D.: Privacy-preserving applications on smartphones. In: Proceedings of the 6th USENIX Conference on Hot Topics in Security, HotSec 2011, pp. 4–4. USENIX Association, Berkeley, CA (2011)
12. Kolesnikov, V., Schneider, T.: Improved garbled circuit: free XOR gates and applications. In: Aceto, L., Damgård, I., Goldberg, L.A., Halldórsson, M.M., Ingólfsdóttir, A., Walukiewicz, I. (eds.) ICALP 2008, Part II. LNCS, vol. 5126, pp. 486–498. Springer, Heidelberg (2008)
13. Malkhi, D., Nisan, N., Pinkas, B., Sella, Y.: Fairplay—a secure two-party computation system. In: Proceedings of the 13th Conference on USENIX Security Symposium - vol. 13, SSYM 2004, pp. 20–20. USENIX Association, Berkeley, CA (2004)
14. Mármol, F., Sorge, C., Ugus, O., Pérez, G.: Do not snoop my habits: preserving privacy in the smart grid. IEEE Communications Magazine 50(5), 166–172 (2012)
15. Molina-Markham, A., Danezis, G., Fu, K., Shenoy, P., Irwin, D.: Designing privacy-preserving smart meters with low-cost microcontrollers. In: Keromytis, A.D. (ed.) FC 2012. LNCS, vol. 7397, pp. 239–253. Springer, Heidelberg (2012)
16. Molina-Markham, A., Shenoy, P., Fu, K., Cecchet, E., Irwin, D.: Private memoirs of a smart meter. In: Proceedings of the SenSys Workshop (Builsys), BuildSys 2010, pp. 61–66. ACM, New York, NY (2010)
17. Quinn, E.L.: Privacy and the new energy infrastructure, p. 43, February 2009
18. Rial, A., Danezis, G.: Privacy-preserving smart metering. In: Proceedings of the 10th Annual ACM Workshop on Privacy in the Electronic Society, WPES 2011, pp. 49–60. ACM, New York, NY (2011)
19. Sankar, L., Kar, S., Tandon, R., Poor, H.V.: Competitive privacy in the smart grid: an information-theoretic approach. CoRR, abs/1108.2237 (2011)
20. Thoma, C., Cui, T., Franchetti, F.: Privacy preserving smart metering system based retail level electricity market. In: Power and Energy Society General Meeting (PES), 2013 IEEE, pp. 1–5, July 2013

Human Behavior
and Activities Monitoring

Anti-fall: A Non-intrusive and Real-Time Fall Detector Leveraging CSI from Commodity WiFi Devices

Daqing Zhang[1,2(✉)], Hao Wang[1,2], Yasha Wang[1,3], and Junyi Ma[1,2]

[1] Key Laboratory of High Confidence Software Technologies,
Ministry of Education, Beijing 100871, China
{dqzhang,wanghao13,wangys,majy}@sei.pku.edu.cn
[2] School of Electronics Engineering and Computer Science,
Peking University, Beijing, China
[3] National Engineering Research Center of Software Engineering,
Peking University, Beijing, China

Abstract. Fall is one of the major health threats and obstacles to independent living for elders, timely and reliable fall detection is crucial for mitigating the effects of falls. In this paper, leveraging the fine-grained Channel State Information (CSI) and multi-antenna setting in commodity WiFi devices, we design and implement a real-time, non-intrusive, and low-cost indoor fall detector, called Anti-Fall. For the first time, the CSI phase difference over two antennas is identified as the salient feature to reliably segment the fall and fall-like activities, both phase and amplitude information of CSI is then exploited to accurately separate the fall from other fall-like activities. Experimental results in two indoor scenarios demonstrate that Anti-Fall consistently outperforms the state-of-the-art approach WiFall, with 10% higher detection rate and 10% less false alarm rate on average.

Keywords: Fall detection · Activity recognition · CSI · Wifi

1 Introduction

Falls are the leading cause of fatal and nonfatal injuries to elders in the modern society [1]. In 2010 falls among older adults cost the U.S. health care system over $30 billion dollars [2]. According to the Centers for Disease Control and Prevention, one out of three adults aged 65 and over falls each year [2]. Most elderly people are unable to get up by themselves after a fall, studies have shown that the medical outcome of a fall is largely dependent on the response and rescue time [3], thus timely and automatic detection of falls has long been the research goal in the assistive living community.

Various techniques ranging from ambient device-based to wearable sensor-based solutions have been proposed and studied [3][4][5]. As the most popular ambient device-based solution, the vision-based fall detection systems require high-resolution

© Springer International Publishing Switzerland 2015
A. Geissbühler et al. (Eds.): ICOST 2015, LNCS 9102, pp. 181–193, 2015.
DOI: 10.1007/978-3-319-19312-0_15

cameras installed and a series of images recorded for scene recognition, the main problem is the privacy intrusion and inherent requirement for line of sight and lighting condition [5]. The other ambient device-based fall detection systems [3] [4] try to make use of ambient information, e.g., audio noise or floor vibration, caused by falls to detect the risky activity. The main problem with these systems is the high cost incurred and the false alarm caused by other sources leading to similar audio noise and floor vibration as human falls. Both wearable sensor-based [6] and smartphone based [7] fall detection systems employ sensors like accelerators to sense the acceleration or velocity on three axis. However, carrying wearable devices or smartphones are not always possible in home environment, especially for elders.

Due to the limitations of the above-mentioned fall detection solutions, very few fall detection systems have been widely deployed in real home settings so far [8]. In recent years, the rapid development in wireless techniques has stimulated the research in studying the relationship between the wireless signal and human activities. In particular, the recently exposed physical layer **Channel State Information (CSI)** on commercial WiFi devices reveals multipath channel features **at the granularity of OFDM subcarriers [9],** which is much finer-grained than the traditional MAC layer RSS. Significant progress has been made in applications in motion detection [10][16], gesture recognition and activity recognition [11] [12]. The rationale behind all these research efforts is that wireless signals are affected in a different way by different human activities, and human activities can be recognized in real-time by understanding the wireless signal patterns.

With this motivation, in this paper, we propose a real-time, non-intrusive and robust fall detection system, called Anti-Fall, leveraging cheap and widely deployed WiFi devices at home, without requiring the subjects to wear or carry any objects. The main contributions of this work are as follows:

1. To the best of our knowledge, we are the first to use **both the phase and amplitude features of CSI** in WiFi to detect falls in real-time in indoor environments. Anti-Fall proves to be the first effective and automatic **activity segmentation and fall detection system** using commodity WiFi devices.
2. Instead of collecting the fall and other activity RF signals manually for training and testing, we find a robust way to **segment the fall and fall-like activities** using the **phase difference of CSI over two antennas** as the salient feature. We further extract features from the amplitude and phase information of CSI, which harness both the space and frequency diversity, to differentiate the fall and fall-like activities.
3. We prototype Anti-Fall on commodity WiFi devices and validate its performance in different indoor environments. Experiment results demonstrate that Anti-Fall can segment the fall and fall-like activities reliably in the WiFi wireless signal streams and consistently outperform the state-of-the-art fall detector WiFall, with fall detection precision of 89% and false alarm rate of 13% on average.

The rest of the paper is organized as follows. We first review the related work in Section 2. Then we introduce some preliminaries about channel state information and fall activities targeted in Section 3. In Section 4, we present the detailed system design and algorithms of our proposed fall detector, Anti-Fall. Followed by the evaluation and comparison results in Section 5. Finally, we conclude the work in Section 6.

2   Related Work

In this section, we review the related work from two perspectives: *research on fall detection* and *research on WiFi CSI-based activity recognition*.

Related Work on Fall Detection. Fall detection has attracted a lot of attention in assistive living and healthcare community in the past two decades. Yu [5] and Natthapon et al. [8] reviewed the principles and approaches used in existing fall detection systems. Roughly, the fall detection systems can be classified into two broad categories: ambient device based systems and wearable sensor based systems. *The ambient device based fall detection systems* intend to detect falls in a non-intrusive way by exploiting the ambient information including visual [5], audio [4] and floor vibration [3] data produced by a fall. The earliest and most researched approach in this category is based on vision techniques. In these systems, high resolution cameras are equipped in the monitoring environment and a series of images are recorded. By using activity classification algorithm, the fall activity is distinguished from other events [5]. The major problem with vision-based methods is the privacy intrusion, especially in the bathroom setting. Besides, the vision-based fall detection systems fail to work in darkness or when the elders stay outside of the focus of the cameras. The other type of ambient device based fall detection systems are based on the principle that different human activities will cause different changes in acoustic noise or floor vibration. However, specific devices need to be installed in the dwelling environment. Moreover, false alarms are often incurred by other sources causing the same effect. For example, an object fall might also cause similar pattern changes in vibration or sound. *Wearable sensor based fall detection systems* attempt to detect falls leveraging sensors embedded in wearable objects such as coat, belt and watch. The widely used sensors include accelerators, gyroscopes and barometric pressure sensors [6]. These detection systems can only work on the premise that all the devices are worn or carried by the subject during fall. *Smartphone based fall detector* is one of the promising fall detection systems with great potential due to the popularity of sensor-rich smartphones [7]. While these solutions are appropriate for fall detection in outdoor environment, the "always-on-the-body" requirements make the subject difficult to comply with, especially for the elders at home.

Related Work on WiFi RF-Based Activity Recognition. The WiFi signal strength RSS has been exploited for indoor localization for more than a decade. However, only recently research attempts have been made to use WiFi RF signal for gesture and activity recognition [11][12]. While [11] first explores and uses WiFi RF signal to recognize different body or hand gestures, they use special instruments to collect special RF signals, which are not accessible with commodity WiFi devices. With the CSI tractable on commodity WiFi devices [9], Wi-Sleep [14] extracted the human respiration times in a controlled setting. And [10][16] employ RSS and CSI information respectively to detect the human motion in indoor environment.

The only work using WiFi commodity devices to detect fall is presented in [12], where it also exploits the WiFi CSI information at the granularity of OFDM subcarrier for fall detection. But the work only makes use of **the amplitude information of CSI** and differentiates the fall from few other specified activities. As all the human activities will cause variation in the amplitude of CSI across different sub-carriers, thus using the amplitude alone can only be used when a few human activities are specified. *When the elders live normally in the home environment with various activities, the solution will fail and produce huge number of false alarms.* In this paper, we intend to leverage both the amplitude and phase information of CSI from commodity WiFi devices to detect fall in real-time. Most importantly, we exploit **the phase difference over two antennas as the salient feature**, which was not explored before, to **robustly segment the fall and fall-like activities from the other activities**. Then with only the fall and few fall-like activities sifted out, we further employ both the amplitude and phase information to extract proper features to separate the real fall from other activities, which makes the real-time fall detection using the WiFi RF signal streams feasible in real home setting.

3   Preliminaries

In this section, we first introduce the Channel State Information (CSI) available on commodity WiFi devices, then define the fall activity types we aim to detect at home.

3.1   Channel State Information in 802.11n/ac

In frequency domain, the narrow-band flat-fading channel with multiple transmit and receive antennas (MIMO) can be modeled as

$$y = Hx + n$$

where y and x are the received and the transmitted signal vectors respectively, n denotes the channel noise vector and H is the channel matrix. Current WiFi standards (e.g., IEEE 802.11n/ac) use orthogonal frequency division modulation (OFDM) in their physical layer. OFDM splits its spectrum band (20MHz) into multiple (56) frequency sub-bands, called *subcarriers*, and sends the digital bits through these subcarriers in parallel. To estimate the channel matrix H, a known training sequence called the *pilot sequence* is also transmitted and the channel matrix H is measured at the receiver side in the format of Channel State Information (CSI), which reveals a set of channel measurements depicting the amplitude and phase of every OFDM subcarrier. CSI of a single subcarrier is in the following mathematical format:

$$h = |h|e^{j\sin\theta} \tag{1}$$

where $|h|$ and θ are the amplitude and phase, respectively.

In indoor environments, WiFi signals propagate through multiple paths such as roof, floor, wall and furniture. If a person presents in the room, additional signal paths are introduced by the scattering of human body. WiFi RF-based activity recognition leverages the fact that *human activities cause the channel distortion, involving both amplitude attenuation and phase shift in the CSI streams.*

3.2   Fall Activity Types Targeted

There are many ways in which an elder can fall, and in this work we aim to detect the fall occurred in situations with respect to two transition activities: 1) Stand-fall refers to the situation that the fall occurs when an elder transfers out of a bed or chair, e.g., the elder may just stand up from the chair and feel dizzy due to cerebral ischemia; 2) Walk-fall refers to situation that the fall occurs while an elder is walking. According to a study by SignalQuest on falls in the elderly, 24% of falls occurred in the first case and 39% occurred in the second [19]. Hence, we aim for 63% of the fall situations in this work and plan to address the other fall types which occur while ascending or descending stairs or engaging in outdoor activities, in future work.

4   The Anti-fall Fall Detection System

Our proposed real-time and non-invasive fall detector, Anti-Fall, consists of three functional modules: *the signal preprocessing module, the signal segmentation module and the fall detection module.* As shown in Figure 1, the system takes the CSI signal streams as input, which can be collected at the receiver side with commodity WiFi device (e.g., Intel 5300 NIC). The CSI signal streams are collected from each subcarrier (e.g., totally 30 subcarriers with Intel 5300 NIC) on a wireless link and totally two links are set up in the experiment between two antennas at the receiver side and one at the transmitter side. In order to obtain reasonably stable wireless signal for fall detection, each CSI signal stream is first preprocessed using a 1-D linear interpolation algorithm as suggested in [15], to ensure the received CSI evenly distributed in time domain. And the interpolated CSI signal stream is further processed by filtering out the temporal variations and long term changes, using a low-pass filter as suggested in [16]. After signal preprocessing, the CSI signal stream is fed into the core modules of Anti-Fall, which are *Activity Segmentation* and *Fall Detection* as shown in Figure 1.

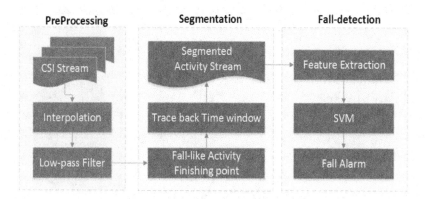

Fig. 1. Overview of the Fall Detection System Anti-Fall

4.1 Activity Segmentation

The main function of the activity segmentation module is to single out the fall and fall-like activities for further classification. It consists of two steps: in step 1 the ending point of the fall or fall-like activities is identified automatically by detecting the variance of CSI phase difference; then in step 2 the starting point of the fall or fall-like activities is determined by estimating the optimal window size of fall activities.

Identify the Ending Point of Fall or Fall-Like Activities. Through intensive experiments, we find that the variance of CSI phase difference over a pair of antennas is a very good and reliable indicator of human activities. Figure 2 shows the CSI phase difference variance of nine different human activities. Interestingly, it is observed that only several immobile human postures, such as *sitting still* and *lying*, result in very steady and stable signal patterns over the time. While most of the human activities, such as *walking*, *running*, *standing* and *falling*, all lead to obvious CSI phase difference fluctuation over time. Therefore, when people fall down, lie down or sit down, the variance of the CSI phase difference exhibits an obvious *transition from the fluctuation state to stable one*. To validate this observation, we recruit more people to conduct various daily activities, such as sweeping the floor, picking up objects, opening the window, etc. Through those experiments, *it is found that the state transition of the CSI phase difference variance is a robust feature to detect the fall and few other non-fall activities (i.e. lying down, sitting down).* We refer those few human activities which also result in obvious transition from fluctuation to stable state as *fall-like activities*. In this work, by using the state transition of CSI phase difference as the salient feature, we can automatically identify all the fall and fall-like activities in the continuously captured WiFi wireless signal streams.

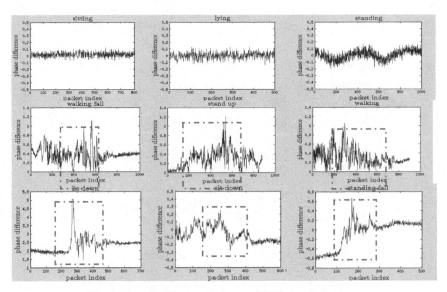

Fig. 2. Phase Difference Variance of Different Activities

In order to detect the ending point of fall and fall-like activities robustly, we need to detect the state transition of CSI phase difference by quantifying the stable state. We propose a *threshold-based sliding window method* to detect the stable state. First, we calculate the mean μ and the normalized standard deviation σ of CSI phase difference stream in stable state (e.g., *lying*) across multiple sliding windows off-line. Then, we compute the threshold value $\delta_{threshold}$ as follows:

$$\mu(V_{stable}) + 6\sigma(V_{stable}) <= \delta_{threshold}$$

Finally, we acquire the CSI phase difference variance in a sliding window and see if the whole sliding window lies in the stable state, by comparing the mean of CSI phase difference in the sliding window with the threshold $\delta_{threshold}$. Figure 3 shows the fall and fall-like human activity ending point identification results based on the state transition detection. It can be seen that *only the fall and fall-like activities are identified*, while other activities such as standing up and walking are left out.

Determine the Best Window Size for Fall Detection. Based on the CSI phase difference state transition detection, we can identify the ending point of fall and fall-like activities in the continuously captured WiFi signal streams. To differentiate the fall from fall-like activities, we need to find the best window size to capture the fall and fall-like activities for accurate fall detection. In this regard, we propose a *two-phase approach* to search the optimal window size. First, we change the window size with a large step and evaluation the fall detection performance. After identifying a "good" window size range, we conduct a finer window size search and compare the fall detection performance, and in the end we choose the optimal window size based on the training dataset. In the evaluation section, we will report the window size search result.

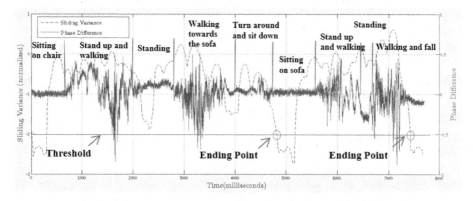

Fig. 3. Fall and Fall-like Activity Ending Point Identification ($\delta_{threshold} = -2$)

4.2   Fall Detection

After determining the starting point and ending point in the *Activity Segmentation* module, only the CSI phase and amplitude of fall and fall-like activities are singled out. The goal of *Fall Detection* module is to separate the fall from fall-like activities.

Feature Extraction. We choose the following seven features as [12] for activity classification: (1) the normalized standard deviation (STD) of CSI, (2) the median absolute deviation (MAD), (3) the period of the activity, (4) the offset of signal strength, (5) interquartile range (IR), (6) signal entropy, (7) the velocity of signal change. However, different from [12] that only extracts features from the CSI amplitude information, we extract each of the above features from both CSI amplitude and phase information. Furthermore, since human activities affect different wireless links independently whereas affect neighboring subcarriers in a similar way [12], we select four subcarriers that spread evenly among all available 30 subcarriers. So each link generates the above seven features on amplitude and phase information in four subcarriers respectively and they together constitute the input of the SVM Classifier.

SVM Classifier. To detect the fall activity, a one-class Support Vector Machine (SVM) [17] is applied using the features extracted above. In one-class SVM, all the samples are divided into objective class (i.e., the fall) and non-objective class (i.e., fall-like activities). To solve the non-linear classification problem, it maps input samples into a high dimensional feature space by using a kernel function and find the maximum margin hyperplane in the transformed feature space. SVM classifier requires a training dataset and test dataset. In the process of classification model construction, fall and fall-like activities are segmented in the continuously captured WiFi wireless signal streams in the activity segmentation phase. Then the extracted features along with the corresponding labels are injected into the SVM classifier to build the classification model. In the process of real-time fall detection, the classification results along with the data will be recorded. With the user feedback, the wrong classification results will be re-labeled correctly and the model updating process will be triggered in time to update the classification model. We build the classification model by utilizing LibSVM [18].

5   Evaluation

In this section, we present the evaluation results of our Anti-Fall system using off-the-shelf WiFi devices. First, we introduce the experiment settings and the dataset. Second, we present the baseline method and metrics for evaluating Anti-fall briefly. Third, we report how fall detection results are affected by the activity window size. Then, the detailed evaluation results of Anti-Fall with respect to the baseline method are presented and compared. Finally, we show the system robustness with respect to environment changes.

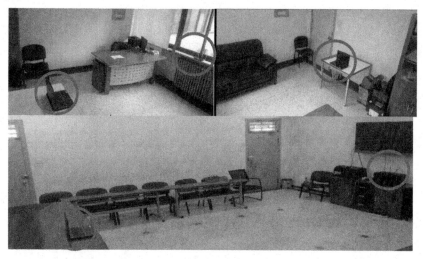

Fig. 4. Two Test Rooms: Office (upper) and Meeting Room (bottom)

5.1 Experimental Setups

We conduct experiments using an 802.11n WiFi network with one off-the-shelf WiFi device (i.e., a dell laptop with two internal antennas) connected to a commercial wireless access point (i.e., TP-Link WDR5300 Router with one antenna running on 5GHz). The laptop is equipped with an Intel WiFi Link 5300 card for measuring CSI [9]. The wireless data transmission rate is set to 100 packets per second.

   We conduct experiments in two rooms of different size to test the generality of our approach. The experimental setups in these two rooms are shown in Figure 4. The smaller room (i.e. office) has the size of about 3m × 4m, whereas the larger one (i.e. meeting room) is about 6m × 6m.

5.2 Dataset

We recruit five male and one female students to perform various daily activities in the two test rooms over two weeks. Each data record consists of a few continuous activities, mixing the fall, fall-like and other activities. We deploy a camera in each room to record the activities conducted as ground truth. Over the test days, the chairs were moved to different places and the items on tables, such as bottles and bags, were moved, as usually occurs in daily life. During the experiments, the door of the room kept closed, and there was no furniture movement. The collected data records are processed by our transition-based segmentation method. We label the segmentation results according to the video records, finding that all 230 fall activities (70 in the meeting room and 150 in the office room) and 510 fall-like activities (160 in the meeting room and 350 in the office room) are all segmented correctly.

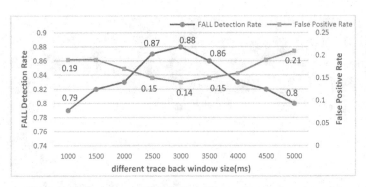

Fig. 5. Performance vs. Window Size (Coarse Search from 1s to 5s)

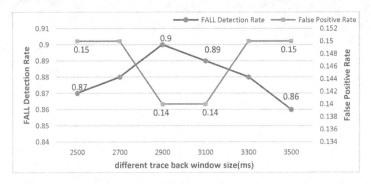

Fig. 6. Performance vs. Window Size (Fine Search from 2.5s to 3.5s)

5.3 Baseline Method and Metrics

In the experiments, we use the state-of-art fall detector WiFall proposed in [12] as the baseline. Since WiFall cannot segment the fall and other daily activities reliably, we thus leverage our proposed method to segment the fall and fall-like activities, subsequently we compare its activity classification method with our approach on our dataset. We use the following two standard metrics for performance comparison: **FALL Detection Rate (FDR)** indicates the proportion that the system can detect a fall correctly (true-positive). **False Positive Rate (FPR)** is defined as the proportion that the system generates a fall alarm when there is no fall happening.

5.4 Fall Detection Performance vs. Activity Window Size

Before we compare the fall detection performance of Anti-Fall with that of WiFall [12], we need to select the best activity window size using the method proposed in Section 4.1. We first use the dataset collected in the office room to show the relationship between the performance and window size. As shown in Figure 5, the best window size is between 2500ms to 3500ms using the coarse search method. The best window size is found to be 2900ms when a fine search is conducted between 2500ms and 3500ms, as shown in Figure 6. Then we use the dataset in the meeting room to repeat the same experiments, interestingly we get very similar optimal window size (3000ms). Thus, in all the evaluations we choose 3000ms as the test activity window size.

5.5   System Performance

In this part, we first compare the performance of Anti-Fall with that of the baseline method WiFall in terms of FDR and FPR. Then, we evaluate the system robustness of Anti-Fall system with respect to various environment changes.

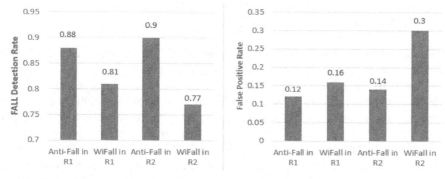

Fig. 7. FDR and FPR Results of Anti-Fall and WiFall in Two Test Rooms (R1 is the meeting room, R2 is the office room)

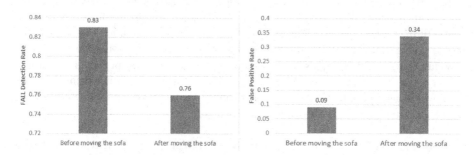

Fig. 8. Fall Detection Performance vs. Furniture (Sofa) Move

Performance Comparison. Figure 7 shows the performance of Anti-Fall with respect to the baseline method. Averaging the experimental results in both rooms, Anti-Fall achieves 89% detection rate and 13% false alarm rate. Compared to the baseline method WiFall, Anti-Fall gets 10% higher detection rate and 10% less false alarm rate.

Robustness to Environment Changes. As wireless signal is said to be very sensitive to environment changes, we thus evaluate the robustness of our approach against several common setting changes, including *opening the door and window, switching*

on/off the light, moving the furniture around. While the Anti-Fall system performance is not affected much by *the opening of windows/door* or *the light on/off* in the two test rooms, its performance deteriorates when the furniture, such as the sofa, is moved. Specifically, when the sofa is moved from the window side to the door side in the office room as shown in Figure 8, the FDR drops from 83% to 76% while the FPR increases from 9% to 34%. So it seems that the furniture movement has quite a big impact on the fall detection performance, as it leads to significant CSI change due to wireless signal propagation path change, which requests classification model reconstruction.

6   Conclusion

The availability of the Channel State Information (CSI) and multi-antenna capability in commodity WiFi devices has opened up new opportunities for activity recognition in recent years. In this work, we design and implement a non-intrusive, real-time and low-cost indoor fall detection system, called Anti-Fall, exploiting both the phase and amplitude information of CSI. To the best of our knowledge, **this is the first work** *to identify the CSI phase difference over two antennas as the salient feature to segment the fall and fall-like activities* reliably and *exploit both the phase and amplitude information of CSI for fall detection.* We have conducted extensive experiments and the evaluation results show that Anti-Fall is a very promising fall detection approach.

Fall detection has long been a research challenge in the public healthcare domain, especially for the elders. Although we implemented quite an effective fall detector using off-the-shelf WiFi devices, there are still many interesting problems that deserve further study. For example, can we apply the Anti-Fall solution in a multi-room home setting? How it works with the elders in real home setting where there are very few fall training data samples? Can we develop a very accurate personalized fall detector for an individual elder? How can we develop a fall detector which can adapt and evolve according to the environment change? We are working on these questions and expect to obtain promising results in near future.

Acknowledgment. This work is funded by the National High Technology Research and Development Program of China (863) under Grant No. 2013AA01A605. We would like to thank Wang Yibo, Wang Yuxiang, Li Xiang and Wu Dan for their help with experiments.

References

1. Lord, S.R., Sherrington, C., Menz, H.B., Close, J.C.T.: Falls in Older Peolpe: Risk Factors and Strategies for Prevention. Cambridge University Press, New York (2001)
2. CDC: Falls among older adults: An overview (April 2013). http://www.cdc.gov/HomeandRecreationalSafety/Falls/adultfalls.html
3. Alwan, M., Rajendran, P.J., Kell, S., Mack, D., Dalal, S., Wolfe, M., Felder, R.: A smart and passive floor-vibration based fall detector for elderly. In: Information and Communication Technologies. ICTTA 2006. 2nd, vol. 1, pp. 1003–1007. IEEE (2006)

4. Li, Y., Ho, K., Popescu, M.: A microphone array system for automatic fall detection. IEEE Transactions on Biomedical Engineering **59**(5), 1291–1301 (2012). International Conference of the IEEE, pp. 1663–1666. IEEE (2007)
5. Yu, X.: Approaches and principles of fall detection for elderly and patient. In: 10th International Conference on e-health Networking, Applications and Services. HealthCom 2008, pp. 42–47. IEEE (2008)
6. Bianchi, F., Redmond, S.J., Narayanan, M.R., Cerutti, S., Lovell, N.H.: Barometric pressure and triaxial accelerometry-based falls event detection. IEEE Transactions on Neural Systems and Rehabilitation Engineering **18**(6), 619–627 (2010)
7. Dai, J., Bai, X., Yang, Z., Shen, Z., Xuan, D.: Perfalld: A pervasive fall detection system using mobile phones. In: 2010 8th IEEE International Conference on Pervasive Computing and Communications Workshops (PERCOM Workshops), pp. 292–297. IEEE (2010)
8. Natthapon, P., Thiemjarus, S., Nantajeewarawat, E.: Automatic Fall Monitoring: A Review. Sensors, 12900–12936 (July 2014)
9. Halperin, D., Hu, W., Sheth, A., Wetherall, D.: Predictable 802.11 packet delivery from wireless channel measurements. SIGCOMM Comput. Commun. Rev. **40**(4), 159–170 (2010)
10. Kosba, A.E., Saeed, A., Youssef, M.: Rasid: A robust wlan devicefree passive motion detection system. In: Proceedings of IEEE PerCom, pp. 180–189. IEEE (2012)
11. Pu, Q., et al.: Whole-home gesture recognition using wireless signals. In: ACM MobiCom, pp. 27–38 (2013)
12. Han, C., Wu, K., Wang, Y., Ni, L.: WiFall: Device-free fall detection by wireless networks. In: Proc. of 33rd IEEE Int. Conf. on Computer Communications, Toronto, Canada, pp. 271–279 (2014)
13. Liu, X., Cao, J., Tang, S., Wen, J.: Wi-Sleep: Contactless Sleep Monitoring via WiFi Signals. In: IEEE RTSS (2014)
14. Nandakumar, R., Kellogg, B., Gollakota, S.: Wi-Fi Gesture Recognition on Existing Devices. arXiv:1411.5394v1
15. Wang, Y., et al.: E-eyes: device-free location-oriented activity identification using fine-grained WiFi signatures. In: Proceedings of the 20th Annual International Conference on Mobile Computing and Networking. ACM (2014)
16. Scholkopf, B., Platt, J.C., Shawe-Taylor, J., Smola, A.J., Williamson, R.C.: Estimating the support of a high-dimensional distribution. Neural computation **13**(7), 1443–1471 (2001)
17. Chang, C.-C., Lin, C.-J.: Libsvm: a library for support vector machines. ACM Transactions on Intelligent Systems and Technology (TIST) **2**(3), 27 (2011)
18. Shea, J.: An Investigation of Falls in the Elderly (July 2005). http://www.signalquest.com/master%20frameset.html?undefined

Smart Fall: Accelerometer-Based Fall Detection in a Smart Home Environment

Dennis Sprute[✉], Aljoscha Pörtner, Alexander Weinitschke,
and Matthias König

Department of Technology, University of Applied Sciences Bielefeld,
32427 Minden, Germany
dennis.sprute@fh-bielefeld.de

Abstract. The detection of falls in an elderly society is an active field
of research because of the the enormous costs caused by falls. In this
paper, Smart Fall is presented. It is a new accelerometer-based fall detection system integrated into an intelligent building. The developed system consists of two main components. Fall detection is realized inside a
small customized wearable device that is characterized by low costs and
low-energy consumption. Additionally, a receiver component is implemented which serves as mediator between the wearable device and a
Smart Home environment. The wireless connection between the wearable
and the receiver is performed by Bluetooth Low Energy (BLE) protocol. OpenHAB is used as platform-independent integration platform that
connects home appliances vendor- and protocol-neutral. The integration
of the fall detection system into an intelligent home environment offers
quick reactions to falls and urgent support for fallen people.

1 Introduction

The World Health Organization [1] states in its global report that 28-35% of
the 65+ year old people fall each year with an increasing rate for older people.
40% of injury deaths are caused by fatal falls. Falls are major health problems
that cause enormous costs to health systems. Due to the aging society, both,
the total amount of falls and the costs will increase in the future. The medical
consequences of a fall highly depend on the rescue time [2]. This statement
encourages the development of automatic fall detection systems to reduce the
reaction time. A reliable fall detection system can provide urgent support and
reduce the consequences of the fall.

Such a detection system is only of value if it is accepted by the concerned
people. A major point is the intrusion of the fall detection system because people want to stay independent and undisturbed. Another important aspect of
acceptance is the useability of the system that should be easy to install and use.
Additionally, a low-cost system is preferable.

In this paper, a new accelerometer-based fall detection system with integration into a Smart Home environment is proposed. The integration into an
intelligent building via Bluetooth Low Energy permits urgent support for fallen

© Springer International Publishing Switzerland 2015
A. Geissbühler et al. (Eds.): ICOST 2015, LNCS 9102, pp. 194–205, 2015.
DOI: 10.1007/978-3-319-19312-0_16

people with high battery lifetime. The system is characterized by its low costs and energy efficiency. Because of the small size of the customized wearable device, the system ensures minimal intrusion into the live of the concerned people.

The remainder of the paper is structured as follows: the next section gives an overview over existing fall detection algorithms and applications. In the following section, the Smart Fall system is described in detail considering the hardware, the fall detection algorithm and the integration into a Smart Home. The main section is followed by an evaluation of the system and conclusions.

2 Related Work

Due to the high importance of fall detection, it is an intensive field of research. There are several methods of detecting falls that can be categorized by their approach. Mubashir et al. [2] build an hierarchy of fall detection methods with three classes on top of the categorization. The top-layer consists of wearable sensors, vision system and ambient/fusion approaches. Wearable sensors are characterized by its cost-efficiency and easy installation. Camera-based methods feature low intrusion and high robustness but also higher costs and a more expensive installation than wearable sensors. The last category, ambient/fusion fall detection methods, mostly utilize pressure sensors for the detection of high vibrations. The intrusion is low, but the accuracy is stated to be not as good.

For reasons of low costs and easy useability of the device, a tri-axial accelerometer as basis of fall detection is used in this paper. Thus, approaches using accelerometers are summarized in the following section.

Igual et al. [3] distinguish between two fall detection techniques: TBM (threshold-based methods) and MLM (machine learning methods). TBM use predefined thresholds to distinguish between falls and ADL (activities of daily living). This technique is characterized by its simplicity and low computational costs. On the other hand, MLM apply supervised learning methods for fall detection. These methods are more computational intensive, and a dataset containing samples of falls and ADL is necessary to train a classifier.

Kangas et al. [4] determine thresholds for simple fall detection algorithms using a tri-axial accelerometer attached to either the waist, wrist and head. The results show that the waist and the head are the most suitable locations for placing the sensor. A fall is detected by comparing the vector sum of all three acceleration directions with a threshold and checking the body posture after fall. The authors claim that such a simple method can achieve high sensitivity and specificity up to 100%. The popular waist location is confirmed by Howcroft et al. [5] in a comprehensive literature review.

Another TBM approach is proposed by Ren et al. [6]. They developed an energy-efficient prototype that detects falls by considering the vector sum of the three acceleration axes and the BTA (Body Tilt Angle) after the fall. The fall sensor is connected to a home server using ZigBee protocol. An accuracy rate of 96% is achieved by the detection algorithm.

A location-independent fall detection algorithm is implemented by Mehner et al. [7]. They utilize a smartphone with integrated accelerometer and apply an energy-efficient detection method. It considers different phases of a fall: free fall, impact, post impact, stability and orientation check.

Kerdegari et al. [8] evaluate different machine learning classification algorithms. A sliding window technique is used to split the continuous acceleration data into overlapping, fixed-size windows and extract certain features. Data are recorded by a waist worn device, and the evaluation shows that Multilayer Perceptron is the best option with its high accuracy of 90%.

3   Smart Fall System

As stated in the previous section, there are already various robust fall detection approaches and algorithms, but in most cases there is a focus on the algorithmic realization instead of integration into a wider context. In this paper, a novel fall detection system with integration into an intelligent building is presented. This allows further processing of a fall event by the Smart Home. Another advantage is the indirect localization of the fallen person inside the house which permits fast support. The detection of a fall is based on an accelerometer integrated into a wearable device. It is focused on energy efficiency, low costs as well as easy usage. A small size of the customized wearable targets to enhance the acceptance.

This section describes the fall detection system. First, a high-level overview of the application is given and described in detail. The next subsection focuses on the hardware needed for realization, and the customized wearable device is presented. The following subsection considers the fall detection algorithm that utilizes the acceleration data. Finally, the integration into a Smart Home environment is explained.

3.1   System Description

The system consists of two main components: the wearable device that is attached to the user and a component that receives signals from the wearable and serves as connection to the home automation bus. Figure 1 illustrates the situation. The user is depicted in the bottom right of the draft with the Smart Fall device. If the wearable detects a fall, a signal is send to the receiver via BLE (Bluetooth Low Energy). In this case, a small low-cost computer board called Raspberry Pi with a BLE dongle is chosen as receiver. The Raspberry Pi is connected to the home automation bus and is able to forward the fall event. As reaction to the fall, urgent support for the fallen person can be provided. Both components are shaded in red in the figure.

The central unit of the Smart Fall system is the wearable device which mainly consists of an accelerometer, a microprocessor and a wireless communication module. The decision for a wearable device incorporating an accelerometer is made because of several reasons: (1) high accuracy can be achieved, (2) low costs and (3) small footprint yield to higher acceptance.

Another advantage over vision-based methods is the protection of the privacy because people do not feel comfortable if they are observed by cameras [9]. Due

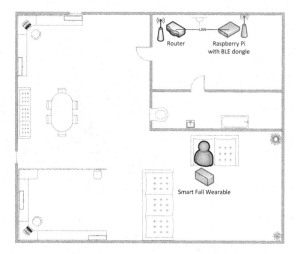

Fig. 1. Smart Fall environment

to this, accelerometers are more likely to be accepted by the user. The position of the attached device significantly influences the performance of the system. As a result of the literature research, the waist is chosen as position for the wearable because it is supposed to be the optimal position for fall detection.

The second component is an embedded system, a small computer. It serves as receiver for fall events emitted by the wearable and as binding to the Smart Home. This small computer is cost-effective and can be installed in the home unobtrusively.

3.2 Hardware

This section describes the newly developed hardware that is used for the system and explains the decision for several components. Figure 2 gives an overview over the structure of the device and the first prototype.

There are two main components that build the functional unit of the wearable. The NRF51822 by Nordic Semiconductor [10] is a ultra-low-power system on a chip that is build around a 32-bit ARM Cortex M0 with 256 KB flash and 16 KB memory. It incorporates a BLE transceiver which permits sending and receiving in 2.4 GHz frequency.

The second component is the sensor of the system, the Bosch BMI055 tri-axial accelerometer [11] which provides linear acceleration in three orthogonal directions. Its accelerometer is stated as ultra-low-power IC (Integrated Circuit) with a current consumption of 130 μA. This yields to an increasing lifetime of the battery power supply. The accelerometer is capable of a bandwidth up to 1 kHz and measures acceleration in a range up to $\pm$ 16 g with a resolution of 12 bit. For the fall detection algorithm a range of $\pm$ 4 g is chosen because it is sufficient to separate falls from ADL.

Smart Fall Wearable

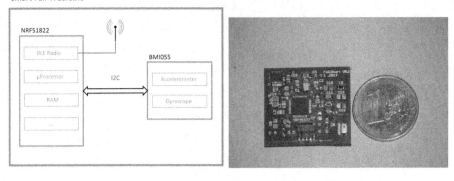

(a) Block diagram   (b) Hardware

Fig. 2. Smart Fall wearable

The fall detection is performed inside the wearable. NRF51822's microprocessor gets the acceleration values of the BMI055 using I²C communication protocol. The values are processed, and fall events are transmitted by BLE transceiver and antenna to the receiver station. It is obvious from the hardware description that the selection of the hardware components targets to low costs and energy efficiency.

3.3   Fall Detection Algorithm

The task of the fall detection algorithm is to distinguish between falls and ADL robustly. In this section, the algorithm for fall detection is presented. It is a TBM considering several states of a fall similar like in [7] or [4]. The decision is fallen onto a TBM to support the low-power requirements because TBM are less computational intensive than MLM. The method is based on acceleration data provided by a tri-axial accelerometer. An acceleration value measured in g is given for each dimension in space. These values are further referred to x-, y- and z- acceleration. The VSA (vector sum of acceleration data) is a scalar representing the total acceleration in all three directions. It is calculated as follows:

$$VSA = \sqrt{x^2 + y^2 + z^2} \ . \tag{1}$$

The first three graphs in Figure 3 give an overview over some ADL situations where x-, y-, z- acceleration and the VSA are visualized dependent on the time. Note that the time values are indices and no time unit. The most important graph is the VSA colored in red. In a situation with no acceleration, the axis parallel to the gravitation vector measures ±1 g, while the other axes are close to 0 g. Therefore, the VSA is 1 g in such a situation. In the setup for the example figures, the z-axis is positioned parallel to the gravitation which leads to the similarity of the z-axis graph and the VSA graph. Figure 3a shows acceleration values

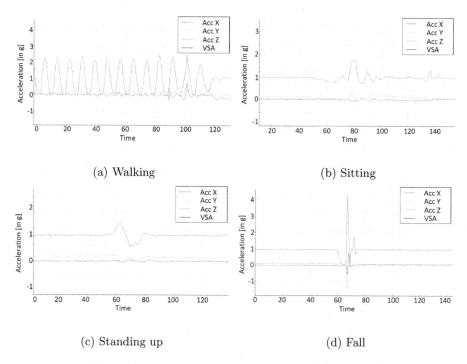

Fig. 3. Acceleration data during several ADL and a fall

for faster walking. The VSA is characterized by a periodic oscillation with peaks at about 2.3 g. Sitting down on a chair results in a different acceleration graph. The situation is featured by a decreasing VSA followed by a strong acceleration increase. This happens because of the movement towards the ground followed by the impact on the chair that yields to a higher VSA. The opposite action, standing up, leads to an increasing VSA followed by an acceleration decrease down to 0.6 g. These figures show that each action is characterized by its own graph.

In contrast to the graphs of ADL, Figure 3d illustrates a typical flow of a fall. The first indication for a fall is a decrease of the VSA. Compared to sitting down on a chair, this decrease is higher and deceeds a minimal value. This is caused by the free fall which tends to 0 g in an optimal situation. After reaching the local minimum, the VSA strongly increases with a peak up to 4 g. In comparison to a walking situation or sitting down, the peak has a higher value. This high peak is the result from the transition from a free fall to the impact on the ground which yields to high acceleration values. Finally, there is a stabilization after the fall that *can* differ from the situation before the fall if people fall from an upright posture into lying posture. If falls out of beds are considered, the acceleration values before and after the fall can be similar because of the similar body orientation.

From these observations, a fall detection algorithm and its features can be derived. The most discriminative characteristics are the free fall before the impact and the impact itself giving information about the intensity of the fall. These characteristics can be recognized by analyzing the VSA. Additionally, an orientation check after the fall makes the algorithm more robust.

The threshold-based fall detection algorithm can be represented by a state chart where each state corresponds to a well-defined state of a fall. Figure 4 gives an overview over the state machine. It consists of several states and transitions between states. A transition happens if the attached condition is satisfied. The default and starting state is called *Before Fall*. For each acceleration sample and VSA value, the state machine is updated according to the current state, the input and the transition. Each state, its meaning and transitions are described in the following paragraphs.

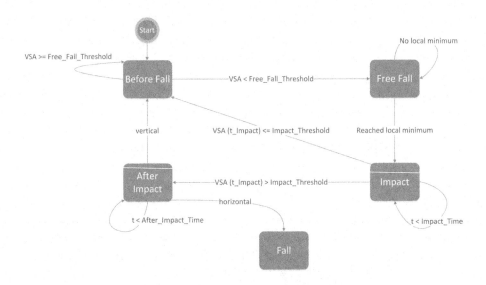

Fig. 4. Fall detection algorithm's state chart

Before Fall The first indicator for a fall is the free fall before the impact. A steady situation is characterized by a VSA that tends to 1 g because of the gravitation that effects the accelerometer. A free fall has a VSA close to 0 g. To determine a free fall, a threshold *Free_Fall_Threshold* is needed. Each VSA is compared against this value. If the VSA deceeds the threshold, the current state is updated to *Free Fall* state. Otherwise the current state remains the same. In the current implementation *Free_Fall_Threshold* is set to 0.7 g.

Free Fall This state represents the falling of the person. The VSA decreases until it reaches a local minimum which is the end of the falling process and the beginning of the impact. If the local minimum is reached, the current state is changed to *Impact* state.

Impact The impact of the falling person onto the ground is characterized by a strong increase of the VSA. Its value gives information about the intensity of the fall. This feature is the second import characteristic for distinguishing falls from ADL. In general, falls have greater impact intensities than ADL which can be seen comparing diagrams in Figure 3. The state machine remains in the current state for a time of *Impact_Time*, which is set to 300 ms. *t_Impact* is the time of the maximum in the time window and *VSA(t_Impact)* its acceleration value. A second threshold *Impact_Threshold* is used to distinguish falls from ADL. In the current implementation its value is set to 2.5 g. If the intensity of the impact maximum is smaller than the threshold, the current state is updated to *Before Fall*. This is the case in a walking situation as stated in Figure 3a where VSA undercuts the *Free_Fall_Threshold* and the following maximum does not reach the *Impact_Threshold*. If the impact maximum exceeds the threshold, it is assumed to be fall relevant. The current state is updated accordingly.

After Impact If a free fall is followed by a strong impact, the acceleration data are analyzed for a lying posture of the person. This is done in a time interval of the length *After_Impact_Time* after the impact. Three seconds for the time interval are chosen for the algorithm. Formula 2 calculates the absolute tilt angle with respect to the x-axis. $tilt = 0°$ corresponds to a horizontal posture, while $tilt = 90°$ is a vertical posture:

$$tilt = abs\left(arcsin\left(\frac{x}{VSA}\right)\right). \tag{2}$$

A sample is considered as horizontal if its tilt value is smaller or equal than 45°. In the current implementation, the tilt angles of all acceleration samples in the time interval are checked against its tilt value. If most of the samples (here: 70%) are horizontal, the posture is considered horizontal, otherwise vertical. A horizontal posture after the impact is classified as a fall. The transitions in the state diagram are visualized accordingly.

Fall This is the situation when a free fall is followed by a strong impact and a horizontal posture. In this case, a fall is detected. Because of the orientation check in the previous phase, only falls that end in a horizontal posture are considered.

3.4   Home Integration

A major contribution of this work is the integration of the fall detection system into a Smart Home environment. This environment is characterized by a high degree of interconnection between home appliances and entertainment devices. Its aims are an increasing quality of living, better security and energy efficiency due to the automatic and remote control of the connected devices. The Smart Fall system aims to increase the quality of living for elderly people in their home environment.

This section describes the chosen wireless technology and justifies the decision with regard to the requirements. Afterwards, the integration into the Smart Home is explained.

Bluetooth Low Energy. The integration of the Smart Fall system into an intelligent building is realized by a wireless connection between the wearable device and the receiver that serves as a binding to the home automation bus. The low-cost and energy efficiency demands of the system require a low-energy wireless communication protocol. Siekkinen et al. [12] compare BLE protocol with ZigBee/802.15.4 which is popular in home automation. It is concluded that BLE is very energy efficient compared to ZigBee. Also, Dementyev et al. [13] analyze the power consumption of three low-power standards in a cyclic sleep scenario. The results show that BLE achieved the best results followed by ZigBee and ANT. Therefore, BLE is chosen as wireless technology to connect the wearable device with the receiver in the home.

BLE [14] was introduced in 2010 as part of the new Bluetooth Core Specification Version 4.0. It is a short range wireless standard that enables BLE devices to run from a coin cell battery due to its low-power consumption. The specification uses a service-based architecture, called GATT (Generic Attribute Profile), to treat communication between server and client. In the case of the Smart Fall system, the receiver component acts as client and the wearable as server. A server provides data in form of characteristics representing one logical value respectively. Several related characteristics can be summarized to a service. The developed BLE server provides a service containing four characteristics: one characteristic for each acceleration direction and a characteristic indicating the detection of a fall. Additionally, GATT protocol offers notifications. It is possible to register a client at the server to receive notifications on a certain characteristic. This avoids the continuous polling of data and saves resources. The characteristic that indicates a fall supports notifications. The receiver component is able to observe the state of seven connected wearable devices which leads to easy scalability of the system.

OpenHAB. OpenHAB [15] provides an integration platform to connect several devices vendor- and protocol-neutral to the home automation bus. It is an open source Java software solution which is platform-independent and is able to run on low-cost targets like a Raspberry Pi. A powerful rule engine is integrated to accomplish automation tasks. The integration of the devices is realized by an event-based architecture which is illustrated in Figure 5. An asynchronous event bus is the base of OpenHAB's architecture. All devices are connected to each other via the bus, and information are transported from and to the devices. The different devices are linked to the event bus by specific protocol bindings. There are already a lot of bindings integrated into OpenHAB that allow an easy integration of devices into the system. An item repository is directly connect to the bus and keeps track of all devices' states. These states are used to represent the devices on the user interface and to inform the automation logic execution engine about current states.

To connect the Smart Fall system to the OpenHAB event bus, a new Smart Fall binding is implemented. The modular structure allows an easy and flexible integration of the binding. It offers direct access to the characteristics of the

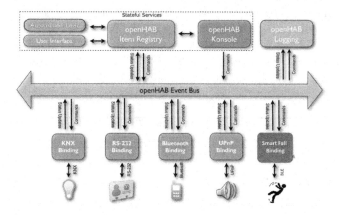

Fig. 5. OpenHAB architecture (Referring to [15])

BLE server on the wearable. Therefore, it is possible to view the provided data, like the detection of a fall, on OpenHAB's user interface.

OpenHAB's rule engine allows to react on incoming events easily. In the current implementation of Smart Fall, a smartphone notification is realized that informs a predefined person about the occurrence of a fall. The quick reaction to a fall in form of urgent support reduces the risks of serious consequences. Due to the high degree of networking in the home, lots of other reactions are imaginable. If a fall is detected, the home could automatically open the windows in the relevant room to provide fresh air for the fallen person. In another scenario, a service robot could be send to the fallen person to administer first aid. The utilization of OpenHAB as extensible integration platform allows fast development and effective interaction with the intelligent building.

4   Evaluation

The following section focuses on the evaluation of the fall detection algorithm. Ten healthy people were asked to wear a waist belt with the Smart Fall wearable device and perform ADL and falls. Falls were performed backwards, sidewards and forwards, each five times per participant. Walking, sitting, jumping and going stairs up and down were considered as ADL. Each action was performed five times by each person. While performing the activities, a supervisor monitored and documented the algorithm's results. Table 1 gives an overview over the evaluation results where the last row and column contain the sums of the corresponding column and row respectively. There are 136 (true positive classifications) out of 150 falls correctly classified, while 14 (false negative classifications) falls were classified as ADL and not detected. These misclassifications are mostly caused by the simulation of falls, especially by simulating forward falls. The participant intuitively absorbs the intensity of the fall by using his or her knees and hands. Therefore, the *Impact_Threshold* of 2.5 g is not exceeded, and no fall is detected.

Table 1. Fall detection confusion matrix

		Activity		
		Fall	ADL	
Algorithm's output	Fall	136 (TP)	0 (FP)	136
	ADL	14 (FN)	250 (TN)	264
		150	250	

On basis of the confusion matrix, the sensitivity and specificity can be calculated as follows:

$$Sensitivity = \frac{TP}{TP + FN} , \tag{3}$$

$$Specificity = \frac{TN}{FP + TN} . \tag{4}$$

These values result in a sensitivity of 91% and a specificity of 100%. This means that 91% of all falls are detected and all of the ADL are classified correctly. In comparison to other fall detection solutions, the results are reasonable. It shows that the Smart Fall system is a robust system for detecting falls. Especially, the specificity encourages a high acceptance by the user because there are no false alarms.

5   Conclusions and Future Work

In this paper, a new low-cost fall detection system inside a Smart Home environment has been presented. The system consists of two main components: a wearable device that is worn by people at the waist and a receiver component that acts as gateway to the home automation bus. The wearable device is able to measure linear acceleration in three axis and communicate over BLE protocol, which is stated to consume low energy. All components of the developed hardware system feature low-power consumption which yields to long lifetime. Additionally, a fall detection algorithm is implemented on the wearable device. The use of thresholds for fall detection results in low power consumption but still achieves high sensitivity and specificity. Finally, a software component that connects the wearable device with the Smart Home environment was developed. The combination of robust fall detection and intelligent building integration offers fast support for fallen people and lots of possibilities to react on falls.

Further work will focus on an improved interaction with the Smart Home, e.g. guiding a helping person through the house via programmable trail signs. Especially, this would be of great interest if the system is deployed in larger buildings like hospitals or nursing homes. Additionally, a more comprehensive evaluation with real falls is planned.

References

1. World Health Organization: WHO Global Report on Falls Prevention in Older Age, Nonserial Publication Series. World Health Organization (2007)
2. Mubashir, M., Shao, L., Seed, L.: A survey on fall detection: Principles and approaches. Neurocomputing **100**, 144–152 (2012)
3. Igual, R., Medrano, C., Plaza, I.: Challenges, issues and trends in fall detection systems. BioMedical Engineering OnLine **12**(1), 66 (2013)
4. Kangas, M., Konttila, A., Winblad, I., Jamsa, T.: Determination of simple thresholds for accelerometry-based parameters for fall detection. In: 29th Annual International Conference of the IEEE Engineering in Medicine and Biology Society, EMBS 2007, pp. 1367–1370 (2007)
5. Howcroft, J., Kofman, J., Lemaire, E.: Review of fall risk assessment in geriatric populations using inertial sensors. Journal of NeuroEngineering and Rehabilitation **10**(1), 91 (2013)
6. Ren, L., Zhang, Q., Shi, W.: Low-power fall detection in home-based environments. In: Proceedings of the 2nd ACM International Workshop on Pervasive Wireless Healthcare, MobileHealth 2012, pp. 39–44 (2012)
7. Mehner, S., Klauck, R., Koenig, H.: Location-independent fall detection with smartphone. In: Proceedings of the 6th International Conference on PErvasive Technologies Related to Assistive Environments, PETRA 2013, pp. 11:1–11:8 (2013)
8. Kerdegari, H., Samsudin, K., Ramli, A.R., Mokaram, S.: Evaluation of fall detection classification approaches. In: 2012 4th International Conference on Intelligent and Advanced Systems (ICIAS), pp. 131–136 (2012)
9. Ziefle, M., Rocker, C., Holzinger, A.: Medical technology in smart homes: exploring the user's perspective on privacy, intimacy and trust. In: 2011 IEEE 35th Annual Computer Software and Applications Conference Workshops (COMPSACW), pp. 410–415 (2011)
10. Nordic Semiconductor - nRF51822. http://www.nordicsemi.com/eng/Products/ Bluetooth-Smart-Bluetooth-low-energy/nRF51822 (online accessed January 2015)
11. Bosch Sensortec - BMI055. https://www.bosch-sensortec.com/en/homepage/ products_3/6_axis_sensors_2/inertial_measurement_unit_1/bmi055_1/bmi055 (online accessed January 2015)
12. Siekkinen, M., Hiienkari, M., Nurminen, J.K., Nieminen, J.: How low energy is bluetooth low energy? comparative measurements with ZigBee/802.15.4. In: 2012 IEEE Wireless Communications and Networking Conference Workshops (WCNCW), pp. 232–237 (2012)
13. Dementyev, A., Hodges, S., Taylor, S., Smith, J.: Power consumption analysis of bluetooth low energy, zigbee, and ant sensor nodes in a cyclic sleep scenario. In: Proceedings of IEEE International Wireless Symposium (IWS) (2013)
14. Bluetooth SIG - Developer Portal. https://developer.bluetooth.org (online accessed September 2014)
15. openHAB - empowering the smart home. http://www.openhab.org/ (online accessed September 2014)

Dead Reckoning with Smartphone Sensors
for Emergency Rooms

Ravi Pitapurapu[1], Ajay Gupta[1], Kurt Maly[1(✉)], Tamer Nadeem[1],
Ramesh Govindarajulu[1], Sandip Godambe[2], and Arno Zaritsky[2]

[1] Department of Computer Science, Old Dominion University, Norfolk, VA 23529, USA
{rpitapur,ajay,maly,nadeem,rgovinda}@cs.odu.edu
[2] Children's Hospital of the King's Daughters, 601 Children's Lane, Norfolk, VA 23507, USA
{Sandip.Godambe,Arno.Zaritsky}@CHKD.ORG

Abstract. 'Lean' principles are being applied to healthcare to optimize the operating processes. One such tool is the development of 'spaghetti diagrams' to track the movement of staff to expose inefficient layouts and identify large distances traveled between key steps in a hospital department or ward. In this paper we report on an automated tool based on smart phone sensors that will record and provide reports on the movement of staff in the emergency room of the Children's Hospital of The King's Daughters. Dead Reckoning also known as Deduced Reckoning, is a process of calculating one's current position by using a previously determined or known position, and advancing that position based upon known or estimated measurements over elapsed time and course. Most smart phones today come equipped with all the necessary sensors that allow us to design such a system. We have built a prototype system that can track a person from a known location indoors and continue to plot the user's position and can provide the number of strides the user has taken, the approximate length for each stride and direction of the user with each stride. The prototype system also includes a path correction module that considers the physical objects on a floor map and rules out corrects for paths that intersect physical objects. It has been successfully tested on a laboratory floor of the Computer Science Department of Old Dominion University and the emergency floor of the Children's Hospital.

Keywords: Indoors positioning · Lean process · Smartphone sensors · Error correction · Spaghetti diagram

1   Introduction

'Lean' principles have first been introduced in the Japanese car industry and first formalized in the 1980s [1]. A recent study [2] documents the evolving application of these principles to health care. In Fig.1 we show a spaghetti diagram that tracks the movement of staff members on a hospital floor. With such information administrators can rearrange workstations, rooms and pathways to minimize time spent walking

© Springer International Publishing Switzerland 2015
A. Geissbühler et al. (Eds.): ICOST 2015, LNCS 9102, pp. 206–217, 2015.
DOI: 10.1007/978-3-319-19312-0_17

from one station to another. Currently, the spaghetti diagram is created manually in which the movements of the staff member or patient are visually observed, and then, are manually drawn as lines on the layout diagram of the area under concern. This traditional way suffers from several challenges including: i) the layout of some areas (e.g., the emergency department (ED)) is not friendly to be visually surveyed; ii) layout consists of many isolated islands; and iii) workstation layout is not standardized.

Dead Reckoning also known as Deduced Reckoning, is a process of calculating one's current position by using a previously determined or known position, and advancing that position based upon known or estimated measurements over elapsed time and course. This methodology is used for Global Positioning System (GPS) navigation systems, auto-

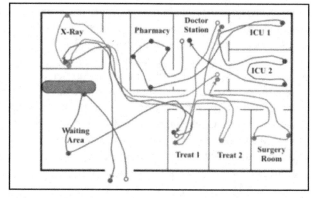

Fig. 1. Spaghetti diagram for hospital ward

motive navigation, and autonomous navigation in the field of robotics.

While GPS and cell tower signals can be used for navigation outdoors, indoor navigation remains mostly an unsolved problem. Making use of equipment such as active Radio Frequency Identification (RFID) tags may result in a high precision indoor positioning system but involves considerable infrastructure modifications and is not cost effective. With increasing use of smart phones as well as smart phones having more and more sensors built in and becoming computationally more powerful, we have developed dead reckoning algorithms to work with the inertial sensors on the smart phone to solve the spaghetti problem.

The system we developed provides a low cost, low maintenance indoor positioning system that makes use of smart phones inertial sensors. Section 2 covers the background of the problem domain and related research including our own previous work. Section 3 presents our dead reckoning algorithm that includes the module that detects the strides and keeps track of the number of strides taken by the user. Section three also covers the stride length model that is personalized to a user with a quadratic approximation function to calculate the heading or direction of the user with respect to his/her previous position. This section also includes the description of the error detection and correction module. Section 4 describes the application of the system to the spaghetti problem as tested on a as tested on the emergency floor of CHKD.

2   Background

The algorithms discussed in this paper are based on using an accelerometer and a gyroscope in human gait detection. A gyroscope is a device for measuring or maintaining orientation of the device when suspended in 3D space and a fixed origin, and works on the principles of angular momentum. The angular momentum measured along X-axis is called pitch, the one along the Y-axis is call roll and around the Z-axis is called yaw shown in Fig. 2. The output from this sensor is measured in radians per second and is very precise for short duration of time. An accelerometer is a device that measures proper acceleration. Proper acceleration is different from actual acceleration. Proper acceleration takes into account the force exerted on the device in all three axes that includes the constant acceleration caused due to earth's gravity. The current generation smart phones come equipped with a MEMS gyroscope that takes the idea of the Foucault pendulum and uses a vibrating element, known as MEMS.

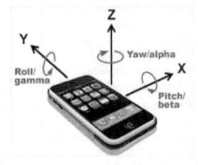

Fig. 2. The X, Y, Z, axes of a mobile phone. Source: http://hillcrestlabs.com

Accelerometers in smart phones measure the acceleration of the device relative to the three axes shown in Fig. 2. They are implemented by tethering thin strips of silicon to a housing that is fixed to the phone and measuring current flows through the tethered strips.

Accurate step counting, or rather detecting the beginning of a step and the end of a step, is a critical parameter for indoor positioning systems. The existing systems do not have the accuracy required in the solution to the spaghetti problem, especially, at low walking speeds observed in natural walking. In [3] an accelerometer was used based on an algorithm called Dynamic Time Wrapping (DTW) where a threshold was applied in the number of samples that cross a threshold per step. DTW showed better accuracy than other step detection algorithms at that time but still failed to detect some strides when the users changed their walking speed.

Lim et al. [4] have proposed a foot mounted gyroscope-based pedometer, they use specialized force sensitive resisters sensors to detect the toe and heel contacts that would be difficult to deploy in a hospital setting.   A gyroscope based step detection algorithm [5] was proposed to detect steps by inferring a relationship between the phone and the movement of the thigh. Emphasis was laid on detection of step at low speeds however they cannot achieve the accuracy desired for our hospital environment. Fan et al. [6] reported on a system that includes stride detection and estimation of stride length as well as turn detection. Although they report accuracy of 1-2 m per walk, their testing environment and experiments are very simple. Moreover, the paper did not consider any path correction scheme.

The second aspect of an accurate indoor positioning system is to estimate the length of each stride taking into account that strides will vary as the user will walk at different speed. In [7] a linear model was developed that reflected a user's personalized style of walking. It needed to be calibrated by having the user walk set distances at different speed. It was fairly accurate at normal and fast speed but did not handle slow walking well.

The third aspect concerns the direction a user is walking. In all our experimentations and algorithm development, this aspect has been the most volatile to control and to provide reliable, accurate data. In [7] a technique was developed that fused accelerometer and gyroscope sensors and mapped the phone's 3-D coordinate system into a global coordinate system. Despite using various filters to eliminate noise, the data introduced errors that accumulated to significant errors on walks lasting more than 100 feet.

3   Dead Reckoning Algorithm

Our proposed algorithm makes use of readings from both the accelerometer and the gyroscope sensors of the smart phone. We fuse the readings from both the sensors to make better decisions. The gyroscope and accelerometer sensors have their own advantages and disadvantages when used in isolation. But by fusing the data from both the sensors in a given time frame and relate their characteristics with respect to user's movements, it is possible for us to determine certain patterns that corresponds to the walking motion of the user. Gyroscopes drift over time and cannot be trusted for a longer time span. Accelerometers do not have any drift but they are unstable for short time spans. We shall make use of accelerometer data to eliminate noise from the gyroscope's data when tracking a user's movement.

For our dead reckoning system we will assume a known starting point. As a first approximation, we have chosen to enter into our system all fixed desktop computers' locations as possible starting points. When a person starts our application she will be asked to choose the right location. The three major steps of the algorithm that are used to estimate the user's position in time are: stride detection, stride length estimation, and change in user direction at each stride.

Stride detection involves the calculation of where in a sequence of reported data points a stride begins and where it ends. The duration of the stride is used to estimate the length of the stride using a model that is personalized to each user. Stride detection also triggers the users the calculation to estimate the change in direction a user is headed for. Combining the output from all the three modules we can plot a user's path taken when starting from a known position.

The dead reckoning system is then validated against a path correction module that checks the feasibility of the path against the physical world such as walls, corridors, doors and stationary objects on a map of the floor.

3.1   Stride Detection

The stride detection module is built on the basic signal processing techniques. If the readings from the sensors are plotted against time in a two dimensional coordinate plane ideally we would expect a sinusoidal wave. Now the characteristics of this wave are different for the accelerometer and the gyroscope. Since accelerometer is very sensitive we can observe a lot of noise in the accelerometer readings. The gyroscope has much smoother and finer readings when compared to the accelerometer.

In order to detect walking steps, we need to filter out the noise before understanding the characteristics of each wave and their relation with the users walking pattern.

The raw data from accelerometer can be seen in Fig. 3. The following data was collected with a sampling frequency of 60 samples per second and the data shown is recorded when the user walked for 10 seconds. The accelerometer data in its raw form is very difficult to process and therefore we move on to gyroscope data.

The raw gyroscope data can be seen in Fig. 4. The following data was collected with a sampling frequency of 60 samples per second with the device in pocket as discussed above. Each data point is a root mean square of pitch and roll experienced by the device.

Since Gyro data is sensitive to small movements we will use accelerometer data to validate the reported steps from gyro data. The signal processing involves two filters that will remove most of the noise from the gyro data. We use a 6th order Butterworth filter – experimentally determined to be optimal for our environment - with a cut-off frequency of 2Hz which serves as the low pass filter. This eliminates most of the noise from our gyro data. The higher the order of the equation is, the steeper is the drop of the wave as shown in Figure 5 which allows for clean determination of peaks.

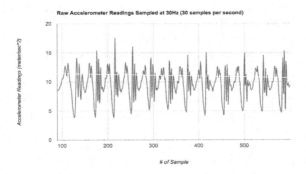

Fig. 3. Raw accelerometer readings plot

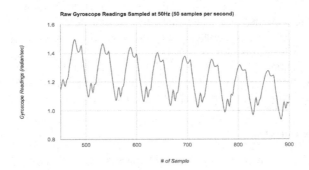

Fig. 4. Raw gyro readings plot

The processed output from the Butterworth filter is then passed through a Kalman filter to remove any erroneous readings which are completely higher or lower in magnitude from the actual set of readings. Kalman filtering, also known as linear quadratic estimation (LQE) is an algorithm that uses a series of measurements observed over time, containing noise (random variations) and other inaccuracies, and produces estimates of unknown variables that tend to be more precise than those based on a single measurement alone.

The algorithm works in a two-step process. In the prediction step, the Kalman filter produces estimates of the current state variables, along with their uncertainties. Once the outcome of the next measurement (necessarily corrupted with some amount of error, including random noise) is observed, these estimates are updated using a weighted average, with more weight being given to estimates with higher certainty. Because of the algorithm's recursive nature, it can run in real time using only the present input measurements and the previously calculated state and its uncertainty matrix; no additional past information is required.

The processed gyro data with root mean square of pitch and roll using Butterworth and Kalman filters is a much smoother wave which can be used for further processing and detection of stride. The Processed smooth data can be seen in Fig. 5.

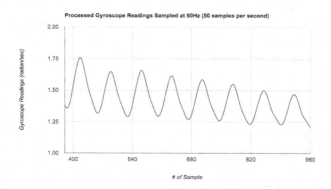

Fig. 5. Processed gyro readings plot

With the processed gyro data it is easy for us to relate the user movement while the phone is in a user's pocket. We can relate the thigh movement when walking to that of the phone. The forces acting on the phone, and measured by the gyro when the phone is in the pocket, are the pitch and roll. We are considering the following assumptions. A step is considered the duration between when the foot toes leaving the floor to the touchdown of the heel. Analysing the movement of the leg, we can see that when user walks forward the root mean square of pitch and roll is going to be at its peak when the user takes the step, and at its minimum when he takes the step with the other leg. This perfect motion wave of a minimum followed by a maximum and then again a minimum defines two steps or a stride. The algorithm takes into account this basic understanding and counts the steps from the readings. We also bring in a sampling threshold that makes sure that no false steps are detected. For example we cannot have two maximums in a span of 30 samples.

The algorithm reports a stride when it detects a minimum followed by a maximum followed by a minimum. This handle is used to trigger the stride length estimation and calculation of user direction.

3.2   Stride Length Estimation

It is very important for us to keep track of the distance traveled by each stride. Every individual has a unique stride length and it varies with the speed at which he/she is walking. The algorithm includes a personalized stride length estimation model which captures the characteristics of each user by gait analysis. The stride length estimation includes a training phase that captures the user gait characteristics.

The stride pattern and length per stride is different for different individuals. And with varying speeds of walk, the stride length is different for the same user. So an average distance per stride will not work for the accuracy we are looking. We have devised a personalization model that captures these characteristics and can estimate the stride length at varying speeds. From experiments we have inferred that slower walks generally have shorter stride lengths and longer stride durations – although it can be the opposite for some persons. Likewise faster walks include longer stride lengths and shorter stride duration. The personalized stride model is based on this observation and the relation between varying speeds and distance traveled is plotted in a two dimensional coordinate plane. The result is a quadratic function in time whose value decreases with increase in time.

The training phase captures the total distance travelled by the user, the number of strides taken to travel that distance and the time taken for covering the same. This is repeated for variable walking speeds and the average time taken per stride, average distance per stride are calculated for individual speeds. When these are plotted in a graph where x-axis measures the duration of stride and y-axis measures the distance covered in that time we have a quadratic curve as shown in Fig. 6.

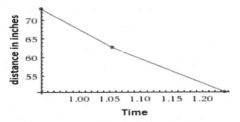

Fig. 6. Quadratic personal stride model

Using this data we can create a quadratic equation that represents the above curve and when a new time measured per stride is plugged in, we obtain the distance traveled in that stride. Table 1, Table 2, & Table 3 provide calibration experiments, estimated model paramteres, and results of walking experiment using the generated model repectively.

Table 1. Calibration data for User1

Walking Pace	No. of Strides	Distance(ft)	Distance(inches)	Time(secs)
Slow	20	83.589	1003	23.680148
Normal	15	71.802	861.625	16.441338
Fast	12	65.406	784.875	12.326791

Table 2. Quadratic Coefficients for User1 in equation $Y = A*X^2 + B*X + C$

Model Parameter	Value
A	-0.10715
B	-6.667098
C	12.223272

Table 3. Walk Experiment for User1

Walking Pace	No. of Strides	Distance Measured(ft)	Distance Actual(ft)	Error %
Slow	10	45.912	46.67	1.62
Slow	15	68.81	69.65	1.21
Slow	20	92.42	93.8	1.47
			Average Error %	1.43
Normal	10	47.297	47.875	1.21
Normal	15	74.04	74.4	0.48
Normal	20	97.076	97.6	0.54
Normal	25	121.319	120.75	0.47
			Average Error %	0.67
Fast	10	52.8	57.2	7.69
Fast	15	79.905	83.6	4.42
Fast	20	119.98	112.9	6.27
			Average Error %	6.13
Mixed Pace	15	71.044	77.57	8.41
Mixed Pace	25	122.2	130.65	6.47
			Average Error %	7.44

Table 4, Table 5 and Table 6 provide the calibration details and results for another person using the personalized quadratic model.

Table 4. Calibration data for User2

Walking Pace	No. of Strides	Distance(ft)	Distance(inches)	Time(secs)
Slow	20	84.417	1013	24.728147
Normal	20	104.365	1252.375	21.113796
Fast	20	121.635	1459.625	18.796116

Table 5. Quadratic Coefficients for User2 in equation $Y=A*X^2+B*X+C$

Model Parameter	Value
A	-0.180905
B	-5.104435
C	10.808544

Table 6. Walk Experiment for User2

Walking Pace	No. of Strides	Distance Measured(ft)	Distance Actual(ft)	Error %
Slow	10	42.9	43.75	1.94
Slow	15	63.22	61.31	3.12
Slow	20	85.45	84.63	1.29
			Average Error %	2.12
Normal	10	51.432	53.15	3.23
Normal	15	78.56	79.52	1.21
Normal	20	102.4	101	1.39
Normal	25	131.89	131.77	0.09
			Average Error %	1.48
Fast	10	58.47	61	4.15
Fast	15	86.21	89.5	3.68
Fast	20	115	119.5	3.77
			Average Error %	3.86
Mixed Pace	15	75.113	77.66	3.28
Mixed Pace	25	126.01	129	2.32
			Average Error %	2.80

The overall results are satisfactory and meet the required accuracies for indoor positioning with periodic correction mechanisms using an external means like a Bluetooth beacon.

3.3 Changes in User Direction with Each Stride

Along with the stride length estimation it is equally important to maintain the users direction or heading with each stride. We use quaternions [8] to represent the orientation of the phone in 3-D space using the roll, pitch and yaw of the gyro. We also take into account how these characteristics change over time and repeat themselves. Turn angles are then calculated from deviations from the observed pattern that repeats itself.

3.4   Path Correction

Given the system described so far, unfortunately, the path depicted by the data can produce errors when superimposed on a map, particularly, as the length of the path taken increases. Hence we have developed a module for path correction that will consider physical properties of objects represented by the map of the floor under consideration. For example, a path can enter a room only through a door and not intersect walls or a path cannot go through a fixed station but only around it.

Map Representation: we represent the map of a floor in a Cartesian coordinate system built from components such as walls, doors, and stations. Feasible paths are paths that do not intersect any physical objects. Clearly, for any reasonable sized floor the total number of feasible paths becomes very quickly too high to have any algorithm to compute in real time. Instead we store only feasible path segments such as corridor paths.

Error Detection: We use a simple geometric line intersection algorithm to identify a path segment making a collision. Once a collision is detected we do not make any decision on path correction immediately. We found it to be critical to know the course of path before and after the collision before applying any correction and ended up with an average of considering three segments before and after a collision.

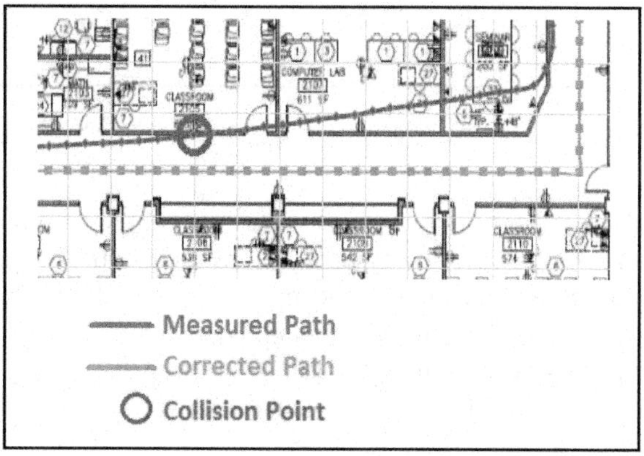

Fig. 7. Corridor correction

Error Correction: If the measured path is detected to have a collision then we consider a number of cases of types of collisions. Below we will illustrate a sample of these cases.

Corridor correction: if at the collision point the path segment is close (mean square distance) to an existing feasible corridor segment. We will replace the segment with the feasible corridor segment, see Fig. 7.

Door correction: if the measured path is detected to have a collision and continues with a turn of considerable angle (over 70 degrees threshold, then the corrected path will be either extended or shortened to the next door to accommodate the turn.

Backtracking: the decision making process for error correction is a best choice approach. If the wrong decision is being made the corrected path may lead to a dead end. In such circumstances, a backtracking mechanism is applied recursively to make an alternative choice at the previous node of correction, see Figure 8, resulting in a feasible path.

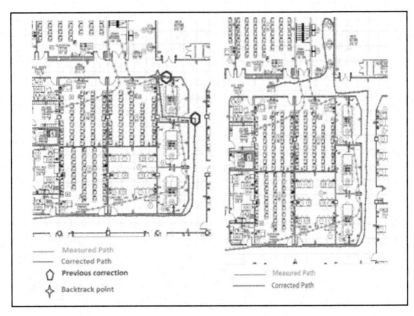

Fig. 8. Backtracking corrections

Known Point Correction: at some point of the path the user may encounter a location that is known to the system such as Bluetooth a beacon (in our environment visible light communication would not be a good alternative as we have no clear lines of sight and the phone would typically be in a pocket). The system will listen for such beacons and when it comes within range will determine its location by observing the signal strength. Once a location has been computed the path will be corrected to that location.

4   Application to CHKD Emergency Floor

We have applied the system we developed to the emergency floor at CHKD. In Fig. 9 we

Fig. 9. Measured and corrected path at CHKD

show the measured path and at the beginning no corrections are necessary, at the second corner the measured angle turns out to be slightly off and is corrected.

5   Conclusions and Future Work

The overall objective of the project was to lay a foundation for an accurate and robust indoor positioning system using inertial sensors of a mobile device. With the measuring components were unable to achieve correct paths but by adding a correction module, we were able to achieve correct paths in all experiments at ODU and CHKD.

Future work includes the addition of reporting modules that will allow the analyst to produce various plots selected from various users at various times and make that information available through the web to various devices.

References

1. Krafcik, J.F.: Triumph of the lean production system. Sloan Management Review **30**(1), 41–52 (1988)
2. Toussaint, J.S., Berry, L.L.: The Promise of Lean in Health Care. Mayo Clinic Proceedings **88**(1), 74–82 (2013)
3. Uddin, M., Gupta, A., Maly, K., Nadeem, T., Godambe, S., Zaritsky, A.: SmartSpaghetti: Accurate and Robust Tracking of a Human's Location. In: 2014 IEEE-EMBS International Conference on Biomedical and Health Informatics (BHI), Valencia, Spain, pp. 129–132 (June 2014)
4. Lim, Y.P., Brown, I.T., Khoo, J.C.T.: An accurate and robust gyroscope-based pedometer. In: 30th Annual International Conference of the IEEE Engineering in Medicine and Biology Society, EMBS 2008, Vancouver, BC, pp. 4587–4590 (2008)
5. Jayalath, S., Abhayasinghe, N., Jayalath, S.: A gyroscope based accurate pedometer algorithm. In: 2013 8th International Conference on Computer Science & Education (ICCSE), pp. 551–555 (April 2013)
6. Li, F., Zhao, C., Ding, G., Gong, J., Liu, C., Zhao, F.: A reliable and accurate indoor localization method using phone inertial sensors. In: Proceedings of the 2012 ACM Conference on Ubiquitous Computing, UbiComp 2012, pp. 421–430 (2012)
7. Uddin, M., Gupta, A., Maly, K., Nadeem, T., Godambe, S., Zaritsky, A.: SmartSpaghetti: use of smart devices to solve health care problems. In: International Workshop on Biomedical and Health Informatics, Shanghai, China, pp. 40–45 (December 2013)
8. Shuster, M.D.: The quaternion in Kalman filtering. In: AAS/AIAA Astrodynamics Conference (1993)

Health IT and Supportive Technology

A Kinematic Based Evaluation of Upper Extremity Movement Smoothness for Tele-Rehabilitation

Saiyi Li$^{(\boxtimes)}$ and Pubudu N. Pathirana

School of Engineering, Deakin University, Geelong, Australia
{saiyi,pubudu.pathirana}@deakin.edu.au

Abstract. Tele-rehabilitation has been widely studied in recent year, although a number of crucial issues has not been addressed. Quantitatively assessing exercise performance is vital in monitoring the progress in exercise based rehabilitation. This allows physiotherapists not only to refine rehabilitation plans, but also provides instant feedback to patients and facilitate the exercise performance in non-clinical setting. In this paper, we propose to evaluate the performance of upper extremity reaching tasks with in a kinematic perspective by assessing the smoothness of motion trajectories with the entropy of shape model, including curvature and torsion. The simulation result confirms that approximate entropy of shape model is consistent with the change of the smoothness in motion trajectory while it is capable of classifying six levels of the ability to perform upper extremity reaching tasks with higher accuracy.

1 Introduction

In recent decades, tele-rehabilitation has been extensively studied for its potential to deliver services at reduced cost and time and the assessment of rehabilitation services while in general it promotes regaining, acquiring and maintaining skills for patients with musculoskeletal and neurological movement disorders [1][2].

As defined in [4], one of the four potential priorities in tele-rehabilitation applications was to develop an approach to evaluate the progress of tele-rehabilitation. In other words, accurately assessing the improvement of subjects in a quantitative form is critical.

As for the traditional approaches in rehabilitation outcome assessment, there have been a number of assessment scales proposed for various conditions. For instance, the disabilities of the arm, shoulder and hand (DASH) questionnaire was proposed in [5] to assess disability and symptoms of upper extremities.

This work was supported by Deakin University and National ICT Australia (NICTA). NICTA is funded by the Australian Government as represented by the Department of Broadband, Communications and the Digital Economy and the Australian Research Council through the ICT Centre of Excellence program.

© Springer International Publishing Switzerland 2015
A. Geissbühler et al. (Eds.): ICOST 2015, LNCS 9102, pp. 221–231, 2015.
DOI: 10.1007/978-3-319-19312-0_18

Levine questionnaire [6] was utilised to assess the severity of symptoms of functional status of patients with carpal tunnel syndrome. Shoulder pain and disability index (SPADI) [7] was a 13 items self-administered index developed for assessing the pain and disability of the shoulder. More examples for musculoskeletal movement disorders can be found in [8]. A large number of assessment scales have also been developed for neurological rehabilitation. Wolf Motor Function Test (WMFT) and Fugl-Meyer Motor Assessment (FMA) [9] could be utilised for upper-extremity assessment for stroke patients. Unified Parkinsons Disease Rating Scale [10] was modified from Obeso dyskinesia scale for dyskinesia assessment during activities of daily living. As for Wilson's Disease, Global Assessment Scale (GAS) was proposed to capture its manifestations and track the progression.

Although these assessment scales have been extensively utilised in daily practices, they are not suitable for tele-rehabilitation. As can be seen, these questionnaire based assessment tools either are self-administered or likely to rely on human judgement. The former may lead to subjective results and the latter cannot be done without the presence of professional therapists, which is common occurance in tele-rehabilitation services.

To avoid these potential issues, as well as to stimulate patients to perform rehabilitation exercises more regularly at home by showing them their progress, it is vital to develop an approach to give patients using tele-rehabilitation services with instant performance feedback.

Though tele-rehabilitation has received considerable attention, only a few automated assessment methods have been explored. For example, [12] proposed a suite of tools for upper extremity motor impairments assessment, which included range of motion, tracking and system identification toolbox. Minimal number of movement repetitions were estimated in [13] as an automated approach to assess the post-stroke upper extremity movement impairment.

This paper was inspired by the observation that the majority of movement disorders were associated with jerky movements to certain extend, such as myoclonus [14], chorea [15], dystonia, tics [16] and so on. Therefore, assessing the ability of performing functional daily activities with upper extremity could be partially achieved by evaluating the smoothness of the motion trajectories.

In light of the above, the major contributions of this work are as follows:

- proposing a shape model [22] based approach to assess the ability to perform functional upper extremity movements from the trajectory smoothness perspective for tele-rehabilitation;
- comparing three commonly utilised entropies, including Shannon entropy [17], approximate entropy [18] and sample entropy [19] to select the most suitable method for evaluating the randomness of the shape model built for motion trajectories.

The rest of the paper is organised as follow. In Section 2, the methods utilised to extract features are introduced, followed by the simulation to confirm the performance of the proposed method in Section 3. The concluding remarks are given in Section 4.

2   Feature Extraction

To evaluate the smoothness of motion trajectories automatically, quantitatively and objectively, it is important to extract features to represent the trajectory. In this paper, we propose to utilise the shape model to encode human motion trajectory and compute the entropy to estimate the randomness in the shape model.

Before introducing the techniques used to process data, the raw data (motion trajectory captured from a joint on human body) is notated as $\mathbf{r}_t = [x_t, y_t, z_t]^\top$, where x_t, y_t and z_t are 3D positions of this joint on the X, Y and Z axes in a Cartesian coordinate system at time $t = [1, 2, \cdots, T]$ with temporal interval of δt.

2.1   Shape Model

In differential geometry, curvature and torsion has been utilised pervasively to encode trajectories. As for curvature, it represents the change rate of unit tangent vector along the trajectory with respect to the arc-length, while the torsion means the change rate of unit binormal vector along the trajectory with respect to the arc-length. However, due to the fact that data captured with motion capture devices is usually indexed by time, we computed the shape model involves the following steps.

Firstly, the velocity of the joint is computed with forward, backward and centered finite difference as

$$\mathbf{V}_t = \begin{cases} \frac{\mathbf{r}_{t+1} - \mathbf{r}_t}{\delta t}, & t = 1 \\ \frac{\mathbf{r}_t - \mathbf{r}_{t-1}}{\delta t}, & t = T \\ \frac{\mathbf{r}_{t+1} - \mathbf{r}_{t-1}}{2\delta t}, & 1 < t < T \end{cases} \tag{1}$$

Secondly, utilising the same approach, the acceleration $\mathbf{A}_t$ and jerk $\mathbf{J}_t$ of the trajectory can be computed by replacing $\mathbf{r}_t$ with $\mathbf{V}_t$ and $\mathbf{A}_t$ respectively.

Eventually, the curvature of the trajectory can be computed as

$$\kappa_t = \frac{\|\mathbf{V}_t \times \mathbf{A}_t\|}{\|\mathbf{V}_t\|^3}, \tag{2}$$

where $\times$ is the cross product of two vectors, and the torsion of the joint is

$$\tau_t = \frac{(\mathbf{V}_t \times \mathbf{A}_t) \cdot \mathbf{J}_t}{\|\mathbf{V}_t \times \mathbf{A}_t\|^2}, \tag{3}$$

where $\cdot$ is dot product of two vectors.

As can be seen from the process, κ and τ are very sensitive to noise in trajectories. If we treated the jerky movements in the trajectory as noise, then the change of jerky amplitude enormously influences the change of κ and τ, which leads the shape model to be consistent and sensitive to represent the jerks in motion trajectories. This is confirmed in the simulated examples.

2.2   Shannon Entropy

Before computing Shannon entropy of a variable, it is essential to have the probability density function (PDF) of the variable since the general form of entropy is defined as

$$ShE = -\int f(x)log_2 f(x)dx, \tag{4}$$

where $f(\cdot)$ is the probability density function (PDF) of variable x.

However, although histogram is widely utilised to estimate the PDF of a variable, how to automatically determine the number of bins for this variable is a problem. To solve this problem, Freedman-Diaconis rule [20] is used to optimise the number of bins used to construct the PDF. The rule is stated as

$$N_{bin} = \frac{(\max x - \min x) \times \sqrt[3]{n}}{2IQR(x)}, \tag{5}$$

where N_{bin} is the number of bins with same width, $IQR(\cdot)$ is interquartile range of the data and n is the number of samples. Eventually, the probability density function of variable x can be estimated with histogram. After that, the Shannon entropy for shape model $S = \{\kappa_t, \tau_t\}$ can be computed as.

$$E_\kappa = -\int f(\kappa)log_2(f(\kappa))d\kappa \tag{6}$$

$$E_\tau = -\int f(\tau)log_2(f(\tau))d\tau. \tag{7}$$

2.3   Approximate Entropy

Applying approximate on κ involving two parameters, namely m for segment length and r for similarity threshold. Pairs of segments of κ with length of $m < T$ and starting point of the ith and j^{th} sample ($i, j = [1, 2, \cdots, T - m + 1]$) in the whole series of κ are generated and notated as $P_{i,j} = [P_i, P_j]$, where P_i is the segment with length of m and start point of i. For each pair, the distance of kth sample ($k = [1, 2, \cdots, m]$) between two segments is computed as

$$D_{i,j}^k = \left|P_i^k - P_j^k\right| \tag{8}$$

These two segments are similar if $\forall k, \ D_{i,j}^k < r$.

For all segments with length of m in κ, a value is computed as $V_i^m = \frac{n_i^m}{T-m+1}$, where n_i^m is the number of similar segments in all segments with length of m with respect to i^{th} segment. Eventually, the approximate entropy can be computed as $E_\kappa = ln\frac{V_m}{V_{m+1}}$, where $V_m = \frac{1}{T-m+1}\sum_{i=1}^{T-m+1} V_i^m$ and V_{m+1} is computed with same steps.

The approximate entropy of τ can be calculated with the same process.

2.4 Sample Entropy

Similar to approximate entropy, sample entropy can also be utilised for complexity evaluation. The differences between sample entropy and approximate entropy is that when the distance between two segments is computed, sample entropy does not compute two segments starting from the same sample. In other words, in (8), $i \neq j$.

3 Simulation and Result

A simulated experiment was conducted to illustrate the performance of the proposed method and compare three entropies. Here, we simulated a reaching motion, which was commonly seen in functional upper extremity tasks.

3.1 Simulation Data Collection

An upper extremity reaching movement was simulated in Matlab 2014b ®as

$$\mathbf{r}_t = \{\cos(\pi t/(3 \times T) + \pi/3), \sin(\pi t/(3 \times T) + \pi/3), 0\} \qquad (9)$$

To simulate the different levels of ability to perform this task, six categories (the ability of performing this task reduces with the increase of the index) of trajectories were simulated with (9). In each level, the length of trajectories is in certain range (refer to the first row in Table. 3.1). For example, the length of trajectories in level one will be randomly selected in the range from 950 to 1050 because it is impossible for different people to have the same length of trajectory while doing the same activity. Due to our assumption that with the decrease of the ability to perform an upper extremity task, people tend to slow down their movement. Therefore, in the next level, the base length of trajectories will be increased by 100 samples with random range of 50 samples. In terms of the jerky movements in trajectories, we utilised Gaussian noise with various amplitude (increasing from 0.01 m to 0.06 m) and duration (20 samples to 70 samples). The detailed specifications for the parameters used to simulate motion trajectories are shown in Table. 3.1.

Furthermore, for each level, 55 trajectories were generated with the length uniformly and randomly generated from the range given in Table. 3.1 for further analysis and classification. In addition, to simulate the data captured from a

Table 1. Specification of trajectories in different categories

	Ability Level (high to low)					
	1	2	3	4	5	6
Length (samples)	1000±50	1100±50	1200±50	1300±50	1400±50	1500±50
Jerk Duration (samples)	20	30	40	50	60	70
Jerk Number	1	2	3	4	5	6
Jerk Amplitude (m)	0.01	0.02	0.03	0.04	0.05	0.06

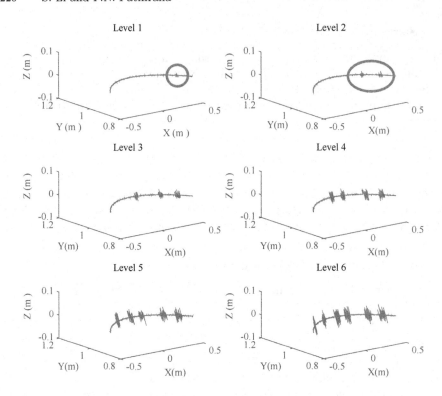

Fig. 1. Example of motion trajectories of various ability levels

motion capture device, Gaussian noise with amplitude of 0.001 meter was added to each trajectory as measurement noise.

Examples of trajectories in various levels were shown in Fig. 1. The red circles were the examples of jerky movements involving in these trajectories.

3.2 Simulation Data Analysis

Firstly, the entropies, including Shannon, approximate and sample entropy, of the shape model of each trajectory in all the levels was computed and denoted as E_i^j where $i = [1, 2, , \cdots, 6]$ indicating the ability levels and $j = [1, 2, \cdots, 50]$ is the trajectory index in this level.

Being a good assessment tool, it should be consistent to the change of smoothness in motion trajectories and also able to distinguish various ability levels to a high extent. Therefore, these two criteria were followed to evaluate the performance of the proposed method. For the first criterion, the maximum, minimum, mean, first and third quarters of the entropies in each level were computed and displayed (refer to Fig. 2). According to the hypothesis, with the decrease of the ability to perform upper extremity tasks, the motion trajectories tend to be less and less smooth, and the entropy of the shape model should show an increase trend. In addition, to evaluate the performance of the proposed approach for the second requirement, we utilised Gaussian mixture model (GMM) [21] to cluster all the entropies into six levels. GMM for each level were trained with five randomly selected trajectories in the simulated 55 trajectories, while the rest ones were used as testing datasets. Eventually, the number correctly classified trajectories for each level was counted to show the performance of various entropies.

3.3   Simulation Result

Fig. 2 shown the entropies of the shape model (the first and second column in the figure are for curvature and torsion respectively) computed with three different methods, including Shannon entropy, approximate entropy and sample entropy, in the first to the third row in the figure.

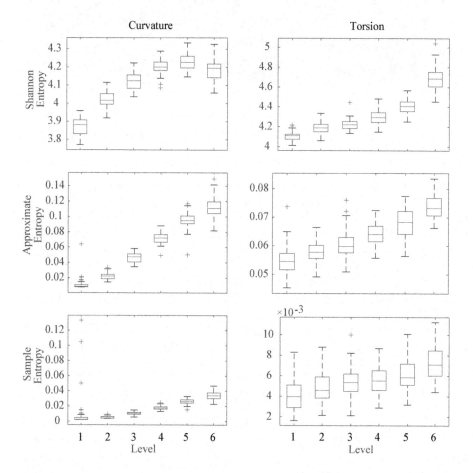

Fig. 2. The distribution of computed entropies of the shape model with various approaches. The parameters of approximate entropy and sample entropy were selected for the best classification result.

As can be seen, the majority of the them, except for the Shannon entropy of curvature, kept the same increasing trend when the ability level of performing functional upper extremity tasks deteriorated from level 1 to 6 (refer to 3.1). However, the Shannon entropy of curvature was not able to keep the trend for the last level showing a lower entropy, representing smoother curvature than the fifth level, which was not expected. Therefore, as for the criterion of consistency, approximate entropy and sample entropy outperformed Shannon entropy.

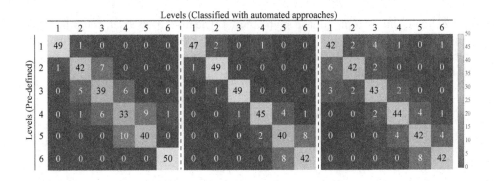

Fig. 3. Classification confusion matrix between the pre-defined ability levels and that classified with various approaches

The second figure (Fig. 3) show the result of automated classification with GMM. Three confusion matrices where included in this figure, and from left to right were for Shannon entropy, approximate entropy and sample entropy respectively. The values in cells shown the total number of trajectories classified into particular ability levels. For example, the 49 in the top left corner of the first matrix shown that 49 out of 50 trials pre-defined as ability level 1 were classified as ability level 1 by GMM, while the value 1 in the first row and second column represented that 1 trial pre-defined as ability level 1 was misclassified into level 2 by GMM.

As is observed, approximate entropy and sample entropy had higher correct classification rate than Shannon entropy for they had higher values in the diagonal in the confusion matrix. More specifically, the values of approximate entropy and sample entropy were all more than 40, while for Shannon entropy, there were only 39 and 33 trials correctly classified in level 3 and 4.

Although the correct rate for the sixth level of Shannon entropy was 100% (50 out of 50), the trend of this levels was not consistent to the change of ability level (refer to Fig. 2). Therefore, we generally deemed that Shannon entropy was not as good as approximate entropy and sample entropy with another reason for its low classification rate for the third and fourth level.

The comparison between the approximate entropy and sample entropy shown that the former outperformed the later for higher correct classification rate for the majority of levels. Specially, for the first to fourth ability levels, the number of correctly classified trials were 47, 49, 49 and 45, compared to 42, 42, 43, 44 for sample entropy. The possible reason for this was that there were more overlaps between these levels in sample entropy than approximate entropy in terms of curvature. As can be clearly observed from Fig. 2, it is easy to distinguish the range of entropies for two consecutive levels without much overlap. However, it is difficult for sample entropy for the range of entropies in these levels were too close to each other. As a result, it is difficult for GMM to classify trials in these levels to correct classes. As for the rest two levels, sample entropy shown a slightly higher correct classification rate (42 out of 50) than approximate entropy (40 out of 50) in level 5 and both correctly classified 42 trials for the last level.

4   Discussion and Conclusion

This paper proposes an approach to assess the ability to perform functional upper extremity tasks in terms of the smoothness of motion trajectories. The shape model (curvature and torsion) of the motion trajectories is computed to encode the trajectories. The reason for using shape model is for its ability to amplify the noise (jerks) in trajectories, thereby showing amplified differences between jerky trajectories and smooth ones. Since people with musculoskeletal or neurological movement disorders, as well as elderly people, usually have jerky motion trajectories, assessing the smoothness of motion trajectories can be one of the criteria for tele-rehabilitation systems to track the outcome of rehabilitation exercises.

The simulation results have confirmed that the propose method performed well as expected for its consistency with the change of the smoothness in motion trajectories. Additionally, the high correct classification rate confirmed again that approximate entropy outperformed sample entropy and Shannon entropy for trajectory smoothness evaluation.

However, this paper reports the simulated results for preliminary feasibility study. Therefore, further experiments should be done with patients and elderly people. In addition, due to the fact that lower extremities are less likely to have jerky movement compared to upper extremity, the performance of the propose method for lower extremities should be further investigated.

References

1. Hailey, D., Roine, R., Ohinmaa, A., Dennett, L.: Evidence of benefit from tel-erehabilitation in routine care: a systematic review. Journal of Telemedicine and Telecare **17**(6), 281–287 (2011)
2. Kairy, D., Lehoux, P., Vincent, C., Visintin, M.: A systematic review of clinical outcomes, clinical process, healthcare utilization and costs associated with telere-habilitation. Disability and Rehabilitation **31**(6), 427–447 (2009)
3. Winters, J.M.: Telerehabilitation research: emerging opportunities. Annu. Rev. Biomed. Eng. **4**, 287–320 (2002)

4. Natl. Inst. Disabil. Rehabil. Res. request for applications for Rehabilitation Engi neering Research Center on Telerehabilitation. Fed. Regist., 3252639 (June 12, 1998)
5. Gummesson, C., Atroshi, I., Ekdahl, C.: The disabilities of the arm, shoulder and hand (DASH) outcome questionnaire: longitudinal construct validity and measuring self-rated health change after surgery. BMC Musculoskeletal Disorders **4**(1), 11 (2003)
6. Levine, D.W., Simmons, B.P., Koris, M.J., Daltroy, L.H., Hohl, G.G., Fossel, A.H., Katz, J.N.: A self-administered questionnaire for the assessment of severity of symptoms and functional status in carpal tunnel syndrome. (1993)
7. Roach, K.E., Budiman-Mak, E., Songsiridej, N., Lertratanakul, Y.: Development of a Shoulder Pain and Disability Index. Arthritis & Rheumatism **4**(4), 143–149 (1991)
8. Dowrick, A.S., Gabbe, B.J., Williamson, O.D., Cameron, P.A.: Outcome instruments for the assessment of the upper extremity following trauma: a review. Injury **36**(4), 468–476 (2005)
9. Wolf, S.L., Catlin, P.A., Ellis, M., Archer, A.L., Morgan, B., Piacentino, A.: Assessing Wolf Motor Function Test as Outcome Measure for Research in Patients After Stroke. Stroke **32**(7), 1635–1639 (2001)
10. Goetz, C.G., Stebbins, G.T., Shale, H.M., Lang, A.E., Chernik, D.A., Chmura, T.A., Ahlskog, J.E., Dorflinger, E.E.: Utility of an objective dyskinesia rating scale for Parkinson's disease: Inter- and intrarater reliability assessment. Movement Disorders **9**(4), 390–394 (1994)
11. Aggarwal, A., Aggarwal, N., Nagral, A., Jankharia, G., Bhatt, M.: A novel Global Assessment Scale for Wilson's Disease (GAS for WD). Movement Disorders **24**(4), 509–518 (2009)
12. Feng, X., Johnson, M.J., Johnson, L.M., Winters, J.M.: A suite of computer-assisted techniques for assessing upper-extremity motor impairments. In: 27th Annual International Conference of the Engineering in Medicine and Biology Society, IEEE-EMBS 2005 (2005)
13. Olesh, E.V., Yakovenko, S., Gritsenko, V.: Automated Assessment of Upper Extremity Movement Impairment due to Stroke. PloS one **9**(8), e104487 (2014)
14. Caviness, J.N., Brown, P.: Myoclonus: current concepts and recent advances. The Lancet Neurology **3**(10), 598–607 (2004)
15. Clarke, J.M.: On Huntington's Chorea (1897)
16. Sanger, T.D., Chen, D., Fehlings, D.L., Hallett, M., Lang, A.E., Mink, J.W., Singer, H.S., Alter, K., Ben-Pazi, H., Butler, E.E., Chen, R., Collins, A., Dayanidhi, S., Forssberg, H., Fowler, E., Gilbert, D.L., Gorman, S.L., Gormley, M.E., Jinnah, H.A., Kornblau, B., Krosschell, K.J., Lehman, R.K., MacKinnon, C., Malanga, C.J., Mesterman, R., Michaels, M.B., Pearson, T.S., Rose, J., Russman, B.S., Sternad, D., Swoboda, K.J., Valero-Cuevas, F.: Definition and classification of hyperkinetic movements in childhood. Movement Disorders **25**(11), 1538–1549 (2010)
17. Shannon, C.E.: A mathematical theory of communication. SIGMOBILE Mob. Comput. Commun. Rev. **5**(1), 3–55 (2001)
18. Pincus, S.: "Approximate entropy (ApEn) as a complexity measure." Chaos: An Interdisciplinary. Journal of Nonlinear Science **5**(1), 110–117 (1995)
19. Richman, J.S., Moorman, J.R: Physiological time-series analysis using approximate entropy and sample entropy (2000)

20. Freedman, D., Diaconis, P.: On the Histogram as a Density Estimator - L2 Theory. Zeitschrift Fur Wahrscheinlichkeitstheorie Und Verwandte Gebiete **57**(4), 453–476 (1981)
21. Reynolds, D.: Gaussian mixture models. In: Li, S. Jain, A.(eds.) Encyclopedia of Biometrics. Springer, US, pp. 659–663 (2009)
22. Saiyi, L., Caelli, T., Ferraro, M., Pathirana, P.N.: A novel bio-kinematic encoder for human exercise representation and decomposition - part 1: indexing and modelling. In: 2013 International Conference on Control, Automation and Information Sciences (ICCAIS) (2013)

Home-Based Self-Management of Dementia: Closing the Loop

Timothy Patterson[1]([✉]), Ian Cleland[1], Phillip J. Hartin[1], Chris D. Nugent[1], Norman D. Black[1], Mark P. Donnelly[1], Paul J. McCullagh[1], Huiru Zheng[1], and Suzanne McDonough[2]

[1] School of Computing and Mathematics, University of Ulster,
Newtownabbey BT37 0QB,
Co. Antrim, Northern Ireland, UK
{t.patterson,i.cleland,cd.nugent,nd.black,mp.donnelly,
pj.mccullagh,h.zheng}@ulster.ac.uk, hartin-p1@email.ulster.ac.uk
[2] School of Health Sciences, University of Ulster, Newtownabbey BT37 0QB, Co.
Antrim, Northern Ireland, UK
s.mcdonough@ulster.ac.uk

Abstract. Within a technological home-based self-management of dementia paradigm there exists a nexus between a person with dementia, personalised reminding technology, detection of the adherence to reminders and an additional human-in-the-loop, for example a caregiver. To date, much work has focused on either the reminding technology per-se or monitoring adherence with less emphasis on integrating these aspects into a coherent self-management system for dementia. Within this paper, we present our current work on closing the remind-sense-reason-act loop. The proposed framework is outlined and we describe an early-stage prototype that incorporates; (i) mobile-based reminding technology, (ii) detection of adherence by using environmental sensors and (iii) the potential to contact a carer in the event of non-compliance.

1 Introduction

It is estimated that between the years 2010 and 2050 the number of persons with dementia (PwD)[1] will increase over threefold from 35.56 million to 115.38 million [1]. This projected rise in worldwide prevalence is, in part attributed to increased life expectancy [2] coupled with the increasing levels of middle-age obesity [3]. The promotion of self-management of chronic conditions is an emerging healthcare trend which aims to empower individuals to manage their illness in their own environment thereby, to some extent, alleviating the socio-economic burdens imposed by such conditions. In the case of dementia this empowerment is achieved via approaches such as education, social engagement, collaborative goal setting between a PwD and health-care professional and the capture and display of health-related metrics, for example levels of activity.

---

[1] Depending on context, PwD may also refer to a single person with dementia.

A. Geissbühler et al. (Eds.): ICOST 2015, LNCS 9102, pp. 232–243, 2015.
DOI: 10.1007/978-3-319-19312-0_19

In comparison to the other major chronic conditions such as Chronic Obstructive Pulmonary Disease, Coronary Heart Disease and Stroke, dementia primarily impacts upon a patient's mental ability by progressively reducing the capabilities of psychological functions such as the executive system and attention [4]. These symptoms may become increasingly severe eventually impacting upon the ability of a PwD to *remember* and *perform* Activities of Daily Living (ADLs). Consequently, one focus of our previous work [5] has been the development of mobile-based reminding technology to act as a *cognitive prosthetic* with the primary motivation of enabling a PwD to remain longer in their own homes.

There are two main reasons why a PwD should be afforded the opportunity to remain in their own home for as long as possible. Firstly, patients with *mild* dementia are likely to have a higher quality of life and level of social connectedness when receiving home-based as opposed to facility-based care [6]. Furthermore, where the caregiver is a family member the transition of a PwD between community and residential-based care may not decrease carer anxiety and in some cases actually leads to an increased risk of carer depression [7]. Secondly, from a financial perspective caring for a person with mild dementia in the community is considerably less expensive than the costs of care in a residential environment [8].

The system described in [5] reminds PwDs to perform ADLs such as taking medicine or eating regularly and requests that the user 'acknowledge' receipt of the reminder through simple interaction with the technology. Nevertheless, given the nature of dementia it is not sufficient to consistently assume that an acknowledged reminder is indicative of a PwD actually performing or completing the prompted task correctly. It is therefore necessary to consider alternative mechanisms for detecting reminder adherence for ADLs. Additionally, we consider the requirement of incorporating a human-in-the-loop, for example an informal caregiver, to provide intervention should episodes of non-compliance be detected.

The contribution of this paper lies in presenting a framework and an early stage prototype for facilitating home-based self-management of early-stage dementia. Specifically, we focus on closing the remind-sense-reason-act loop pertinent for our application resulting in a framework which contains mobile-based reminding technology, detecting adherence via environmental sensors and the potential to contact a human-in-the-loop, for example a caregiver. The remainder of this paper is structured as follows: in Section 2 we provide an overview of related work in the area of remind-sense-reason-act loop. The framework is presented in Section 3, with details of the early stage prototype discussed in Section 4. Finally, Conclusions and Future Work are outlined in Section 5.

2   Related Work

Whilst the problem of reminding a PwD to perform an activity is an active area of research, there has been less focus on integrating reminding technology, adherence detection and reasoning into a coherent self-management solution for dementia. Within this Section we provide an overview of related work pertinent to our target application specifically, reminding technology and detecting adherence.

2.1 Reminding Technology

Technological based reminding solutions have previously taken the form of pagers and voice reminders. NeuroPage [9] is an alphanumeric system, which sends short messages to a pager worn by a client. The pager is operated by a single button to acknowledge receipt of the reminder. Reminders are scheduled on a desktop PC which uploads the reminders to a central server where they are subsequently transmitted to the targeted pager device. Reminders are time and date based and usually relate to routine events such as taking medication, attending appointments, performing daily chores and meal preparation. Neuropage has been evaluated with over 200 patients with a range of cognitive impairments, including dementia and has been shown to be effective at assisting with perspective memory problems [10]. Due to technical limitations, however, such solutions have been criticised either for their lack of generalisability or the inability to modify the solution to suit the needs or preferences of the user [11].

More recently reminders have been delivered to a mobile platform in text format via email or Short Message Service (SMS). SMS reminders have been used within a number of health interventions with varying results. Previous studies have shown that SMS reminders can have a positive impact on medication adherence [12] and patient self-management [13]. A recent review by Kannisto et al. [14] found that although evidence for SMS application recommendations is still limited, the majority (77%) of the studies thus far had shown improved health outcomes which may support its use in health care. The authors did note, however, that additional well-conducted SMS studies are required particularly in cohorts with varying age, gender, socio-economic backgrounds and conditions.

Although the use of SMS reminder systems within healthcare is still a relatively new concept [14], mobile technology continues to progress rapidly with UK smartphone ownership amongst memory impaired users reflecting that of the wider population [15]. Within the literature there are a number of smartphone applications reported which focus specifically on people with cognitive impairments, such as dementia. O'Neill et al. [16] developed a Mobile Phone Video Streaming (MPVS) system which provides video-based reminders for everyday activities. Videos are recorded by the carer or family member using a touch screen display and software application. The carer can schedule the reminders for the appropriate time and set the frequency with which they repeat. Upon receiving the reminder, users are required to acknowledge receipt by pressing a large button on a modified handset. This initialises the playback of the pre-recorded video. The application was developed through an iterative design process and has been evaluated with a cohort of 40 PwD and their respective caregivers.

Reminder systems have attempted to improve reminder delivery by considering the context of the user (for example, user activity and location) in addition to time of delivery. Helal et al. [17] described a reminder system which uses data from sensors in the home to detect the location of the user and display reminder information, in the form of a video, on an appropriate display. Other reminder systems have attempted to utilise the user's location, detected from GPS or an indoor location system to deliver the reminder when the user is detected at a pre-defined location, for example escalate a reminder to buy milk when the user is at the local supermarket. The COGKNOW project [18] proposed a hybrid context-aware reminding framework for elders with mild Dementia (HYCARE). This architecture incorporated location and user activity as contexts, along with the time that the required activity was typically performed.

2.2 Adherence Detection

Few of the mobile reminder systems reported in the literature provide feedback on whether a task has been completed. A small number of the systems, for example Memojog [19] do provide functionality to alert a carer if the reminder is not acknowledged by the user. Nevertheless, user acknowledgement of a reminder does not necessarily mean that the user has interpreted the reminder and followed through and completed a task. Therefore methods to detect adherence to reminders has become an area of increased importance.

One solution to assess adherence of reminders is the use of activity recognition methods to accurately detect whether or not a scheduled activity has taken place. For example, computer vision algorithms make it possible to detect, where a person is and what they are doing within an environment. Radio-Frequency Identification (RFID) tags and accelerometer devices allow everyday objects such as cups and utensils to be uniquely labelled and then located. Data from environmental and body worn sensors can then be used to infer a user's activity. Systems have been developed which utilise environmental sensors to prompt the user during the completion of a task in order to aid task completion. The COACH system [20], for example, can monitor a user's progress washing their hands and prompt for completion only when necessary. These systems focus on complex step based activities, such as hand washing or preparing a meal and therefore differ in perspective from the reminder systems previously discussed.

Much of the work on adherence of reminders, assessing whether the individual has followed through and completed the task, has focused on medication reminders. In this research, the act of taking medication is typically inferred using either a simple binary result generated by a contact sensor or pressure sensor attached to a pill box, for example as described by Zhou et al. [21]. The indirect notion that a user takes their medication once it is removed from the container is largely naively accepted across these studies [22]. Asai et al. [23], designed a context aware medication reminder system. The system consisted of four modules: a sensing module, inferring module, ruling module and actuating module. The sensing module utilised a medication table consisting of a set of scales and an RFID receiver. When a medication bottle is removed from the scale, the system senses which bottle is moved using the RFID tags and can detect how many of the tablets are removed from the bottles by measuring the reduction in weight once the bottle is set back on the scales. The system uses a smartphone to deliver medication reminders and acts as a method for the user to self-report medication compliance whilst away from the home.

O'Neill *et al.* [16] proposed a method of monitoring adherence to reminders through the use of low cost off-the-shelf sensors embedded within the environment. Sensors included contact sensors on doors and drawers, accelerometers on kettles and food containers and a buzzer for monitoring attendance at meetings. Sensor data was uploaded to a server where it was later mined using a bespoke analysis tool for evidence of task completion within a specific time of acknowledging a reminder. Results showed that low cost off-the-shelf sensors could be used to assess task completion following reminders, with 87% of tasks being sensed correctly. The authors suggested that such a system could provide peace of mind to PwDs and their respective carers by providing assurance that scheduled tasks have been completed. This provides a strong rationale to provide an end-to-end system which utilises low cost off-the-shelf sensors to provide feedback on task completion following reminders for PwDs.

3   Framework

Within this Section we present a framework for the self-management of dementia which incorporates a remind-sense-reason-act loop in the form of mobile-based reminding technology, detecting adherence and where appropriate contacting a human-in-the-loop.

In Figure 1, an overview of the four main components pertinent for home-based self-management of dementia are illustrated with the sequence of events shown in Figure 2. The *'Remind'* component of our framework consists of a smartphone application (app) which enables a PwD or their caregiver to create, edit and delete reminders. When a reminder's date/time is reached a prompt is displayed on the smartphone with relevant details such as reminder type and description. There are two intuitive types of reminder response: acknowledged which indicates the PwD has read or conversely missed the reminder. The response is subsequently transmitted to cloud-based storage.

Giving consideration to the short-term memory impairment experienced by PwDs it is not sufficient to assume that the PwD has performed the displayed action. Therefore, taking into account the critical nature of specific types of reminders such as eating meals or taking medication upon a PwD's overall well-being it is necessary to detect adherence to the reminder. The *'Sensing'* module of the framework consists of environmental sensors which would be statically placed around a PwD's home. Each sensor will have an associated location, for example 'medicine cupboard door', type, for example 'contact switch' and metric which denotes the types of reminder that a sensor is associated with, for example 'medicine'. Upon a change, a sensor's state is transmitted to a receiver where it is subsequently timestamped and uploaded to cloud-based storage.

A cloud-based system is used for storage of data and for executing the *'Reason'* and *'Act'* components. Whilst this results in the requirement of an available internet connection for uploading data it yields two main advantages from an

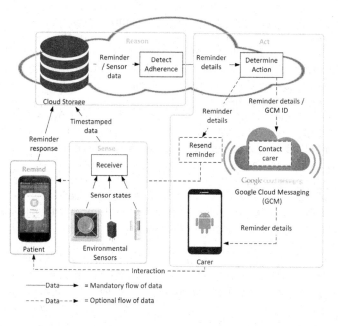

Fig. 1. Self-Management of Dementia framework highlighting the main components of the remind-sense-reason-act loop

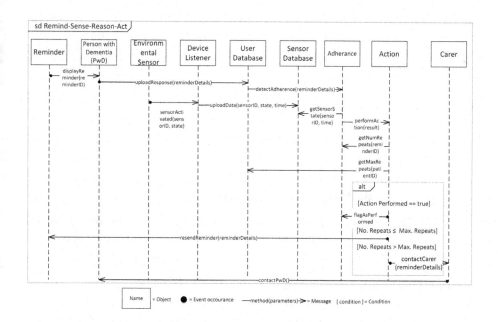

Fig. 2. Sequence of data flow between system components

extensibility perspective over performing the computation on hardware based in the PwD's home. Firstly, a cloud-based approach enables the *'Reason'* and *'Act'* modules to be extended without updating software on devices within a PwD's home. Secondly, the approach readily facilitates the incorporation of internet connected sensors which do not require a dedicated home-based receiver.

Upon a reminder response being uploaded the *'Detect Adherence'* module retrieves sensor observations for a given time frame and utilises the reminder type to determine reminder adherence. The *'Determine Action'* module is subsequently called with reminder details such as the time and type, in addition to a boolean value indicating if the reminder was performed and an integer denoting the number of times the reminder was displayed. There are three possible outcomes of the *'Determine Action'* module: flag reminder as performed, resend reminder and contact carer. Where the system has detected adherence, the reminder would be flagged as performed and the PwD would be oblivious to the cloud-based computation. Secondly, in the event of a missed reminder, or where it is detected that there has not been adherence, the reminder would be rescheduled for a user at a reminder-specific time in the future which reflects the estimated time required for the individual to perform the task.

Thirdly, upon detecting that there has been repeated (determined by an individual's condition) non-adherence of crucial reminders such as taking meals or medication a registered carer for the PwD would be contacted via a Google Cloud Message (GCM) delivered via a smartphone app. The carer would then interact with the PwD using, for example, a telephone call or personal visit. From a workflow perspective the primary advantage of incorporating a human-in-the-loop in this manner is that a human such as a carer can quickly collate, analyse and act upon contextual information, for example the type of reminder and the PwD's recent history and subsequently act in an empathetic and intuitive fashion. Furthermore, from a carer's perspective the knowledge that a PwD is being unobtrusively monitored may decrease carer burden and anxiety [24].

4   Prototype Implementation

In this Section we present details of an early-stage prototype implementation of the discussed framework.

4.1   Mobile-Based Reminding Technology

The smartphone reminder app has been developed to run on the Android platform, and acts as an assistive reminder tool for ADLs [5]. The developed app benefits from over 10 years of experience in the design, implementation and evaluation of assistive cognitive prosthetics, for example [16] [18]. An interdisciplinary team, consisting of computer scientists, psychologists, epidemiologists and statisticians designed the app through an iterative process and have evaluated its efficacy with a representative cohort [5]. The intended end users of the app are persons with the condition (in this case dementia) and their primary

A Reminder prompt displayed on PwD's smartphone

B Repeat reminder prompt displayed on PwD's smartphone

C Alert displayed on a registered carer's smartphone

Fig. 3. Example screens from the PwD and carer smartphone applications

carers. The users can set temporal based reminders for any of the ADL types, for scheduled delivery at a specific time and date. The app follows a wizard design pattern, which guides the user through 6 sub-steps to create a reminder. Functionality to record voice messages has also been included.

To enable integration with the *'Act'* component of the framework and to further promote the self-management of dementia the reminder app presented in [5] has been extended in two aspects. Firstly, we incorporate GCM enabling reminders to be automatically generated in response to non-adherence and pushed to the reminder app. Secondly, a characteristic of PwDs is that they may not be willing to acknowledge that they suffer from a memory impairment and therefore become agitated with a system that acts as a cognitive prosthetic [25]. With this in mind the reminder prompt is displayed as a question, for example instead of displaying "Remember to take your medication at 11:30" the reminder prompt would be rephrased to "Did you remember to take your medication at 11:30?" (Figure 3A).

The reminders can be configured to be repeated automatically on a daily or weekly basis. Repeat reminders are especially useful in scenarios in which a schedule is to be maintained, such as that imposed by a medication regimen [5]. A typical use case is a PwD living independently and having their carer or close family member set an array of reminders based on their understanding of the PwD's daily routine and needs. At the specified time, the reminder is delivered to the device as a popup accompanied by a melodic tone. The popup contains a textual description of the task to be performed, along with a graphic representing the ADL type (Figure 3A).

If the reminder is a voice message, the popup will indicate this to the user and a play button is presented. The message can be listened to as many times as is needed. In this application, the user has a default of 60 seconds in which to acknowledge the notification, before it is flagged as missed. This acknowledgement information is subsequently uploaded to cloud-based storage.

4.2   Detecting Adherence

The aim of the *'Detecting Adherence'* module is to determine if the action associated with a specific reminder has been executed and incorporates the *'Sense'* and *'Reason'* components in Figure 1. From a sensing perspective there are three types of Tynetec sensors [26] utilised within the prototype implementation: a wall mounted passive infrared (PIR) sensor; magnetic contact switches placed on the room's two doors and a 'medicine' cupboard and, a pressure-activated sensor. Upon a change, each of the sensors transmit their state to a listener which subsequently timestamps the data and forwards it to cloud-based storage.

The *'Detect Adherence'* module performs reasoning based on a specific reminder and relevant environmental sensor states. To accommodate the scenario where a PwD performs the task associated with a prompt before the reminder, an ADL and client-specific time duration is included when retrieving sensor states. Thus we consider sensor readings relevant if the state has changed in the time interval $[R_T - threshold, R_T] = \{X \in \mathbb{N} | R_t - threshold \leq X \leq R_t\}$ where X is a non-negative integer containing a Unix timestamp, R_T is the reminder time and *threshold* indicates an acceptable time for commencement of an activity before the reminder alert being displayed. At this stage in development the sensor states are combined in a rule-based manor resulting in a binary value indicating if the action associated with a reminder has been performed.

4.3   Act

The *'Act'* component of the framework accepts a binary value indicating if the action associated with a reminder was performed and determines an appropriate action of either: resend reminder, contact carer or flag reminder as performed.

Should the activity associated with a reminder not be executed the system would in the first instance, resend the reminder to the client's device with the original reminder time incremented by an ADL specific value (Figure 3B). This value would be chosen at registration and reflects the time required for the PwD to perform the specific ADL. The repeat reminder is subsequently pushed to the reminder app using GCM. The number of times that a reminder may be resent is a user-defined parameter. Should the PwD repeatedly fail to perform the action associated with a reminder a carer such as a family member is contacted via an Android Carer App (Figure 3C). The Carer App receives a GCM containing the missed reminder details and upon the notification being clicked displays the details on screen. A 'call' button is incorporated which enables the carer to quickly telephone the PwD. In the event of the ADL associated with a reminder being performed an 'adherence' log is updated and no further action is taken by the system.

4.4   Testing

The prototype implementation was tested using three example ADLs of 'take medicine', 'appointment' and 'go to bed'. Nine reminders were set for each type for one healthy participant (27 reminders in total). The participant was instructed to perform each ADL as follows: 'take medicine' consisted of {open door 1, enter room, open Medicine cupboard door}, attend appointment consisted of {enter room, open door 2, exit room} and 'go to bed' consisted of {open door 1, enter room, activate pressure sensor}.

The participant was instructed to perform the activity in advance of three reminders being displayed (i.e. Figure 2 condition 'Action Performed == true'), perform the activity after three reminders had been displayed (i.e. Figure 2 condition 'No. Repeats ≤ Max. Repeats') and not perform the activity for three reminders (i.e. Figure 2 condition 'No. Repeats > Max. Repeats'). The focus of testing was to verify that the appropriate system actions of 'flag reminder as performed', 'resend reminder' and 'contact carer' was executed as expected (Figure 2). This was a straight forward verification test of the three use cases. In these tests the system performed as expected with nine reminders flagged as acknowledged, nine reminders resent to the reminder app with the time incremented by a predetermined threshold and nine alerts sent to the carer app. Whilst these tests demonstrate the technical feasibility of the approach it is envisaged that future software development iterations will be validated using contemporary methodologies and tools orientated towards smart environments, for example the Spin based method presented by Augusto and Hornos [27].

5   Conclusions and Future Work

Within this paper we have presented a framework and early-stage prototype for the home-based self-management of dementia. In particular we have focused on closing the remind-sense-reason-act loop pertinent to our application resulting in an approach which incorporates reminding technology, environmental sensing, reasoning to detect adherence and an *'Act'* component which determines an appropriate action to take. Early tests have been discussed which demonstrate the technical feasibility and practical potential of the approach.

There will be two main focuses of future work: firstly identification of ethical considerations, parameter choices such as the time taken to perform a task and visual design requirements will be solicited from PwDs and carers via a workshop. Secondly, from an implementation perspective the *'Sense'* and *'Reason'* components will be extended to detect adherence for further ADL types such as 'making a meal' or 'taking a drink' in multiple occupancy scenarios with the complete system validated using a pre-pilot cohort in a representative Smart Living Environment [28]. After further refinement the system will be trialled with a small cohort of PwDs and their associated caregivers thus enabling the identification of further real-world challenges and capture of performance and usage metrics.

Acknowledgments. The authors gratefully acknowledge support from Invest Northern Ireland under Research and Development grant RD0513844. Additionally, we wish to thank Dr. Jonathan Synnott (Connected Health and Innovation Centre, University of Ulster) for assistance with the sensors used within this work.

References

1. Prince, M., Bryce, R., Albanese, E., Wimo, A., Ribeiro, W., Ferri, C.P.: The global prevalence of dementia: a systematic review and metaanalysis. Alzheimer's & Dementia: the Journal of the Alzheimer's Association **9**(1), 63–75.e2 (2013)
2. Aronson, M.K., Ooi, W.L., Geva, D.L., Masur, D., Blau, A., Frishman, W.: Dementia: Age-dependent incidence, prevalence, and mortality in the old old. Archives of Internal Medicine **151**(5), 989–992 (1991)
3. Whitmer, R.A., Gunderson, E.P., Barrett-Connor, E., Quesenberry, C.P., Yaffe, K.: Obesity in middle age and future risk of dementia: a 27 year longitudinal population based study. BMJ (Clinical research ed.) **330**(7504), June 2005
4. Stopford, C.L., Thompson, J.C., Neary, D., Richardson, A.M.T., Snowden, J.S.: Working memory, attention, and executive function in Alzheimer's disease and frontotemporal dementia. Cortex **48**(4), 429–446 (2010)
5. Hartin, P.J., Nugent, C.D., Mcclean, S.I., Cleland, I., Norton, M.C., Sanders, C., Tschanz, J.T.: A smartphone application to evaluate technology adoption and usage in persons with dementia. In: 36th Annual International Conference of the IEEE Engineering in Medicine and Biology Society, Chicago, USA, pp. 5389–5392. IEEE (2014)
6. Nikmat, A.W., Hawthorne, G., Al-Mashoor, S.H.: The comparison of quality of life among people with mild dementia in nursing home and home care-a preliminary report. Dementia, 1–12, July 2013
7. Schulz, R., Belle, S.H., Czaja, S.J., McGinnis, K.A., Stevens, A., Zhang, S.: Long-term care placement of dementia patients and caregiver health and well-being. JAMA: The Journal of the American Medical Association **292**(8), 961–967 (2004)
8. Crisp, H.: Spotlight on Dementia Care. Number October. The Health Foundation, London (2011)
9. Oliver Zangwill Centre Neuropsychological Rehabilitation. NeuroPage (2014). http://www.neuropage.nhs.uk/ (Accessed December 2014)
10. Wilson, B.A., Emslie, H.C., Quirk, K., Evans, J.J.: Reducing everyday memory and planning problems by means of a paging system: a randomised control crossover study. Journal of Neurology, Neurosurgery & Psychiatry **70**(4), 477–482 (2001)
11. Seelye, A.M., Schmitter-Edgecombe, M., Das, B., Cook, D.J.: Application of cognitive rehabilitation theory to the development of smart prompting technologies. IEEE Reviews in Biomedical Engineering **5**, 29–44 (2012)
12. Vervloet, M., van Dijk, L., Santen-Reestman, J., van Vlijmen, B., Bouvy, M.L., de Bakker, D.H.: Improving medication adherence in diabetes type 2 patients through real time medication monitoring: a randomised controlled trial to evaluate the effect of monitoring patients' medication use combined with short message service (sms) reminders. BMC Health Services Research **11**(1), 5 (2011)
13. de Jongh, T., Gurol-Urganci, I., Vodopivec-Jamsek, V., Car, J., Atun, R.: Mobile phone messaging for facilitating self-management of long-term illnesses. Cochrane Database Syst Rev **12**, (2012)

14. Kannisto, K.A., Koivunen, M.H., Välimäki, M.A.: Use of mobile phone text message reminders in health care services: A narrative literature review. Journal of medical Internet Research, **16**(10) (2014)
15. Migo, E.M., Haynes, B.I., Harris, L., Friedner, K., Humphreys, K., Kopelman, M.D.: mHealth and memory aids: levels of smartphone ownership in patients. Journal of Mental Health **00**(00), 1–5 (2014)
16. ONeill, S.A., Mason, S., Parente, G., Donnelly, M.P., Nugent, C.D., McClean, S., Scotney, B., Craig, D.: Video reminders as cognitive prosthetics for people with dementia. Ageing International **36**(2), 267–282 (2011)
17. Helal, S., Giraldo, C., Kaddoura, Y., Lee, C., El Zabadani, H. Mann, W.: Smart phone based cognitive assistant. In: UbiHealth 2003: The 2nd International Workshop on Ubiquitous Computing for Pervasive Healthcare Applications (2003)
18. Davies, R.J., Nugent, C.D., Donnelly, M.P., Hettinga, M., Meiland, F.J., Moelaert, F., Mulvenna, M.D., Bengtsson, J.E., Craig, D., Dröes, R.M.: A user driven approach to develop a cognitive prosthetic to address the unmet needs of people with mild dementia. Pervasive and Mobile Computing **5**(3), 253–267 (2009)
19. Morrison, K., Szymkowiak, A., Gregor, P.: Memojog – an interactive memory aid incorporating mobile based technologies. In: Brewster, S., Dunlop, M.D. (eds.) Mobile HCI 2004. LNCS, vol. 3160, pp. 481–485. Springer, Heidelberg (2004)
20. Mihailidis, A., Boger, J.N., Craig, T., Hoey, J.: The coach prompting system to assist older adults with dementia through handwashing: An efficacy study. BMC Geriatrics **8**(1), 28 (2008)
21. Zhou, S., Chu, C.H., Yu, Z., Kim, J.: A context-aware reminder system for elders based on fuzzy linguistic approach. Expert Systems with Applications **39**(10), 9411–9419 (2012)
22. Vurgun, S., Philipose, M., Pavel, M.: A statistical reasoning system for medication prompting. Springer (2007)
23. Asai, D., Orszulak, J., Myrick, R., Lee, C., Coughlin, J.F., de Weck, O.L.: Context-aware reminder system to support medication compliance. In: 2011 IEEE International Conference on Systems, Man, and Cybernetics (SMC), pp. 3213–3218. IEEE (2011)
24. Torkamani, M., McDonald, L., Saez Aguayo, I., Kanios, C., Katsanou, M.N., Madeley, L., Limousin, P.D., Lees, A.J., Haritou, M., Jahanshahi, M.: A randomized controlled pilot study to evaluate a technology platform for the assisted living of people with dementia and their carers. Journal of Alzheimer's Disease: JAD **41**(2), 515–523 (2014)
25. Mograbi, D.C., Ferri, C.P., Sosa, A.L., Stewart, R., Laks, J., Brown, R., Morris, R.G.: Unawareness of memory impairment in dementia: a population-based study. International Psychogeriatrics **24**(6), 931–939 (2012)
26. Tynetec. Tynetec - Telecare Devices 2015. http://www.tynetec.co.uk/telecare-devices (Accessed January 2015)
27. Augusto, J.C., Hornos, M.J.: Software simulation and verification to increase the reliability of Intelligent Environments. Advances in Engineering Software **58**, 18–34 (2013)
28. Nugent, C.D., Mulvenna, M.D., Hong, X., Devlin, S.: Experiences in the development of a smart lab. International Journal of Biomedical Engineering and Technology **2**(4), 319–331 (2009)

Patient Centric Ontology for Telehealth Domain

Daniel Bjerring Jørgensen[1](✉), Kasper Hallenborg[1], and Yves Demazeau[2]

[1] The Maersk Mc-Kinney Moller Institute, University of Southern Denmark,
5230, Odense, Denmark
{dbj,hallenborg}@mmmi.sdu.dk
[2] CNRS, LIG, 38000, Grenoble, France
yves.demazeau@imag.fr

Abstract. This paper presents an ontology for the telehealth domain, a domain that concerns the use of telecommunication to support and deliver health related services e.g. patient monitoring and rehabilitative training. Our vision for the future of telehealth solutions is that they adapt their behavior to the needs, habits, and personality of the patient through user modeling and context awareness. The ontology will be our foundation for user modeling of patients in the telehealth domain, and hence it is one of the initial steps toward our vision. Compared to other ontologies within the domain, ours has explicit focus on: 1) personality traits of the patient, which is vital for fulfillment of our vision in term of adaptability, and 2) use of international standards to describe diseases, functioning and physiological measurement – ICD, ICF and SNOMED respectively – to promote interoperability with external systems. Besides being the foundation for user modeling, the ontology is a component in the Patient@home infrastructure, where it will ease the integration of applications to the platform, and facilitate semantic interoperability between the applications.

Keywords: Ontology · Personalization · Telehealth infrastructure · User modeling

1   Introduction

Patient@home (www.patientathome.dk) is the largest welfare technology project in Denmark, running until 2018. Demographic changes have caused increased interest in the care of patients in their own homes. New technologies make this possible for increasing numbers of medical and non-medical procedures and treatments. The purpose of the Patient@home is to allow patients to be treated and monitored in their own home to a greater extent than it is currently possible through the development of new technologies and applications for patient monitoring and rehabilitation.

The background for this paper is the challenge of designing an ontology for the telehealth domain and Patient@home with the purpose of 1) forming a knowledge base that serves as a foundation for user modeling in the telehealth domain, 2) building the foundation enabling semantic interoperability for the heterogeneous applications and

© Springer International Publishing Switzerland 2015
A. Geissbühler et al. (Eds.): ICOST 2015, LNCS 9102, pp. 244–255, 2015.
DOI: 10.1007/978-3-319-19312-0_20

technologies that can be used, and 3) easing the integration of software and hardware components into the Patient@home infrastructure.

Aside from the technical purposes mentioned, a survey on the uses of ontologies for the telehealth domain uncovered three groups of features that will be used as criteria in the design of the ontology:

- Activity coverage: keep track of the patient's activities and daily habits.
- Health tracking: keep track of the patient's health, disabilities, and physiological measurements.
- User profiling: keep track of the patient's personality.

The following domain requirements from Patient@home will be considered in the design process as well:

- Collect context information to help healthcare professionals reach a more accurate determination of the necessity of hospital visits and other healthcare interventions.
- Increase patient empowerment and motivate the patient to participate and take responsibility (where possible) of her own health.
- The telehealth platform must be able to adapt its behavior to the patient using it, and thereby become a natural part of her everyday life and fit her needs.

To address the problem of designing a patient-centric ontology for the telehealth domain this paper is divided into five sections. Section 2 will present relevant ontologies that have previously been proposed for the telehealth domain. That leads to a discussion in Section 3 of the data sources and technologies that will be included in the ontology in order for it to meet the purposes, criteria, and requirements. Section 4 presents the designed ontology. The ontology is discussed in relation to the related works, criteria, and requirements in Section 5, and finally conclusions are drawn in Section 6 where the future work to be done is also outlined.

2   Related Work

An ontology forms a vocabulary for a certain domain through a set of objects and the relationships between them [1]. Ontologies can be used by software agents to exchange knowledge based on a shared and agreed upon semantic model [1]. A semantic model, which facilitates the sharing and reuse of contextual knowledge, is considered a key technology in context aware systems [2]. [2]–[5] are examples of ontologies previously designed for the telehealth domain.

In [2] Paganelli and Giuli present a context management system for patient and alarm monitoring that includes four ontologies describing the heterogeneous types of knowledge relevant in the home care domain. The four ontologies are: Patient personal domain (keeps track of monitored biomedical parameters), Home domain (keeps track of environment parameters), Alarm management (contains knowledge necessary to handle abnormal biomedical or environmental parameters), and Social context (keeps track of the people involved in the patient's network, both family and healthcare professionals). Besides these different parameters, each ontology contains corresponding evaluation conditions, which can be used to mine information and identify any deterioration in the patient's condition. The ontologies and system is highly focused on health tracking of the user, but important knowledge such as diagnoses and disabilities is not included in the system.

Latfi et al. [3] have designed an ontology based system for elderly people with loss of cognitive capabilities (e.g. patients diagnosed with Alzheimer). The system is intended to be used in TSHs (Telehealth Smart Homes), with focus on activity recognition and development of proper ways of communication between the system and its user. To fulfil its purpose, the system relies on seven different ontologies: Habitat (the housing of the patient), PersonAndMedicalHistory (information about the patient, her needs and medical history), Equipment (medical and environmental sensors and furniture), Software applications (describes the software modules of the deployment), Task (the tasks the patient is supposed to achieve), Behavior (habits and physiological measurements), and Decision (what needs to be done in critical situations). This system has a strong focus on the activity coverage of the user, knowledge that we find highly valuable in the development of future telehealth platforms.

Ongenae et al. [4] propose a self-learning, probabilistic, and ontology-based framework for building context aware applications for the healthcare domain, that are capable of adapting their behaviors at run-time to its users. The framework consists of multiple components ranging from ontologies to reasoners to a learning engine. The framework includes different ontologies such as a medical ontology, a context-aware ontology, and domain ontologies specific to the healthcare setting. For the medical ontology the Galen Common Reference Model (http://www.opengalen.org/) is used, and as the context-aware ontology the Continuous Care Ontology [6] is used. The system developed by Ongenae et al. is comprehensive with great focus on health tracking and environment of the user. The system, however, has little focus on activity coverage and personality of the user.

In [5] a two-layered ontology for the telemedicine domain is described. The purpose of the two layered ontology is to support the exchange of messages in telemedicine, and to ease the process of analyzing the data collected through a shared knowledge base and rules. The lower layer includes some general objects: Actor (e.g. patient doctor, hospital etc.), Resource (e.g. devices), Telemedicine task (the medical domain e.g. cancer, cardiology), Data (images, physiological measurements etc.), and Location. The upper layer is specific to the domain (hospital or home) where the ontology and system are deployed. The architecture proposed by Nageba et al. [5] has a fundamentally different focus (interoperability and data exchange among distributed systems and actors in healthcare) compared to the others systems. The data to exchange is only concerned with health tracking of the user.

Although all four instances are designed for the healthcare and/or telehealth domain, the examples show how differently ontologies can be used to:

- Exchange semantic interoperable messages between multiple settings [5].
- Develop intelligent user interfaces that are proper for its user both in terms of representation and communication [3].

With this related work in mind, the next section will discuss the data sources and standards that are considered when designing our ontology.

3   Relevant Data Sources and Standards

3.1   Monitoring of Physiological Measurements

Telehealth concerns the delivery of health-related services and remote monitoring of vital signs. Therefore knowledge about different physiological measurements is a natural element in an ontology for the telehealth domain. Many different solutions exist to facilitating collection of health related data, examples include: Continua Health Alliance (CHA) (http://www.continuaalliance.org), ANT+ alliance (www.thisisant.com) and the WellnessConnected system from A&D Medical (www.wellnessconnected.com).

The solutions mentioned can to a certain extent collect similar health related data (e.g. blood pressure, pulse and weight). But they do not use the same communication protocols or data models, and hence they cannot be used by the same software systems. To cope with these differences, data from different types of devices (e.g. blood monitors) must be abstracted to a higher level so they can be used in a uniform way regardless of the underlying technology and manufacturer.

3.2   Activity of Daily Living

Activities of daily living (ADL) cover a number of different activities such as eating, toileting, mobility, housecleaning, managing medications, and use of technology. Recognizing physical activities is a complex field, but according to [7] ADL can prove to be valuable for identifying deterioration of a patient's health. Therefore it is desirable to keep track of such knowledge in a telehealth platform. In addition to ADL, the activity types that are considered in the ontology are the primary activities used by The United States Department of Labor in their annual labor statistics called American Time Use Survey (ATUS) [8]. Besides the identification of deterioration of health, location and activity information can contribute in a number of different scenarios, of which two are described below.

1) The care providers get new information, which can help them to gain a better understanding of the physical capabilities of the patient. This information gives the care provider an improved knowledge base from which to decide the care and assistance most appropriate for the patient.

2) COPD (chronic obstructive pulmonary disease) patients are known to have low levels of oxygen in their blood. Let us consider the scenario where a patient has been out for a walk, and afterwards measures her O_2 saturation. The walk may have had a negative impact on the amount of oxygen in the blood, and because the value is low, a non-context-aware-system or the healthcare professional interpreting the measurement will sound the alarm. The low levels measured should not cause alarm in this case as they are explained by the patient's activity.

3.3   Classification of Health

To design and develop a personalized telehealth platform that can adapt its behavior dynamically to the user, knowledge about the health of the user will be a valuable source of knowledge. For this purpose classification systems can be used.

ICD [9] and ICF [10] are abbreviations for "International Statistical Classification of Diseases and Related Health Problems" and "International Classification of Functioning, Disability and Health" respectively. ICD and ICF are two complementary ways of classifying the health of a person. The classifications are maintained by the World Health Organization (WHO) and are used throughout the world. ICD is used in 117 countries to report mortality data, and as part of the "World Health Survey Program in 2002/2003" ICF was used in 71 countries.

ICD and ICF are internationally recognized methods for describing diagnosis, health condition, function, disability etc. Therefore it is natural to include the two classifications in an ontology for future telehealth platforms. The task of classifying a patient using ICD and ICF is naturally the job of healthcare professionals, and not a software system using the ontology.

3.4   Personality and Everyday Life of User

Like other sorts of technology, telehealth solution will add new activities to the everyday life of the user [4]. We believe that using a telehealth solution should be a natural part of the everyday life, and not a burden for the user. This implies that the telehealth system must adapt its behavior to the user. Therefore it will be necessary to incorporate a user model into the telehealth platform. The ontology will describe the knowledge of the user model, and thereby it constitutes the foundation for this user model. The user model will be based on a number of quantitative personality traits of the user, and over time the telehealth platform must adapt its behavior to the user's habits and everyday life. That means the system should learn patterns in the everyday life of the user, i.e. the user's habits (e.g. sleeping, eating etc.).

4   The Ontology

The different data sources presented and discussed in Section 3 have been included in an ontology for the telehealth domain, presented in Fig. 1. It includes the main concepts and the overall design that has been implemented in the ontology editor Protégé [11]. The ontology is followed by a textual description of its content and examples of how it will be used.

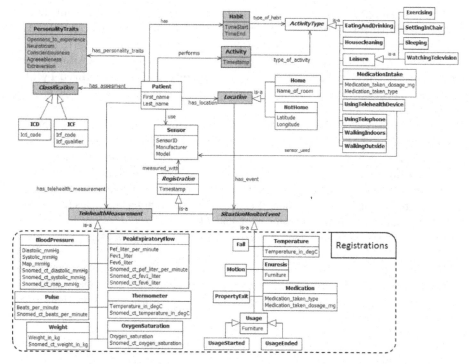

Fig. 1. Ontology for the telehealth domain

In Patient@home, we envision future telehealth solutions to be individualized to the patient based on her activities of daily living, physical abilities and personality. To fulfil this vision, a lot of customization of each deployment is necessary. However, the ICT infrastructure underlying the telehealth platform itself must have the capabilities to adapt its behavior to the patient.

Therefore the central concept of the designed ontology is the *Patient*. In itself the concept Patient is simple; however it is related directly or indirectly to seven other concepts, together providing very different and important knowledge pertaining to the patient. On Fig. 1 the seven concepts are highlighted in grey.

The *Classification* concepts i.e. ICD and ICF provide knowledge about the health of the patient in terms of diagnoses (the data property Icd_code of the ICD concept) and the impacts that follow (described in collaboration between the data properties Icf_code and Icf_qualifier (severity of the problem) of the ICF concept).

The knowledge pertaining to the patient's ADL in the ontology is covered by the concepts: SituationMonitorEvent, Location, Activity, and Habit.

SituationMonitorEvents occur at a specific *Location*. Locations are either a room of the patient's home or outside the home, specified by spatial coordinates. Situation-MonitorEvent cover different sorts of knowledge either directly pertaining to the patient (i.e. fall detection, usage of pill dispensers, usage of furniture, and enuresis) or knowledge used to reason about the location of the patient (i.e. detection of motion and property exit), or about the environment where the patient is (i.e. temperature).

Using SituationMonitorEvents and Location a software system will be able to reason about the patient's *Activities*. Examples of activities are when medication is taken and when the Patient is sleeping etc. Currently the ontology includes twelve different activity types, others may be added later. The activity types are also used by the *Habit* concept. Besides having a specific activity type, Habits are defined by time intervals (TimeStart and TimeEnd). This is a similar method to the one used in ATUS [8].

Besides SituationMonitorEvents the ontology contains *Registration* concepts for various types of physiological measurements (*TelehealthMeasurement*). This version of the ontology contains concepts for six different physiological measurements: peak expiratory flow, oxygen saturation, pulse, blood pressure, weight, and body temperature. Each of the concepts contain data properties corresponding to the data collected by the corresponding type of device. When new and relevant technologies (e.g. robots or vision systems under development in Patient@home) are developed, data from those technologies must be added to the ontology as well. All measurements will be supplemented with relevant SNOMED CT codes [12][1].

The final concept of the ontology is *PersonalityTraits*. The five data properties of PersonalityTraits comes from "Big Five personality traits" [13], a widely used psychological theory to study personality traits. The theory defines five dimensions of the human personality [13]:

- Openness to experience: people who are open to experience are curious, creative, have a vivid imagination etc.
- Conscientiousness: conscientious people are self-disciplined, and prefer planned as opposed to spontaneous behavior, and detailed oriented etc.
- Extraversion: extraverted people are talkative, enjoy and get energy from interactions with other people etc.
- Agreeableness: agreeable people are optimistic, interested in others, willing to compromise, helpful etc.
- Neuroticism: people with neurotic tendencies are typically easily disturbed, stressed, and in general experience negative emotions easily.

Considering the possible data sources available, aggregation of the concepts described in this section constitutes a complex, diverse, and extendible knowledge base for the telehealth domain.

The ontology has some limitations as well. 1) The ontology relies on software agents to reason about e.g. accuracy of sensor readings or rather the sensors (e.g. pill dispenser) have been used correctly by the user. 2) In terms of coding systems the ontology relies on (and is limited to) SNOMED CT, ICF, and ICD. To achieve interoperability with other coding systems, the telehealth platform using the ontology will need an agent with the ability to translate between different coding systems.

---

[1]   SNOMED CT is an internationally recognized and standardized coding system, which for example can be used to describe the type of physiological measurement collected.

4.1   Use of the Ontology

The ontology will be an important component in the ICT infrastructure under development in the Patient@home project. The infrastructure will facilitate integration between the applications (both software and hardware) being developed in the project. An application integrating to the ICT infrastructure will be "wrapped" in a software agent designed for the specific application. All software agents must register the designed ontology. The ontology will provide the agents with a shared vocabulary and meaning of the things about which they can communicate with each.

Some of the applications will be data providers, for example devices for health monitoring, robots used for rehabilitative training, environment sensors, systems for activity recognition and real-time positioning etc. The wrapper-agents for this type of applications will be focused on sending data to the Patient@home infrastructure, whereas they will have a very limited (if any) need for receiving data from the platform.

Like the data providing applications, there will be applications mainly using the ontology to identify and retrieve data from the platform using the ontology. Possible applications: intelligent user interfaces, health status reasoners, and personal assistants etc. The semantic properties of the ontology will be used by those applications to construct relevant queries to get the desired knowledge. A few examples of such knowledge could be:

1. Will the patient mind being asked to use a telehealth device when the news are on?
2. Get blood pressure and pulse measurements taken within the first hour of walks outside longer than 10 minutes.
3. Within the last week, how many times has the patient taken her asthma medication outside the intended timeslots (12 hours apart, +/- 1 hour), and has the peak expiratory flow been affected?
4. Has the patient any visual impairment making it hard to read text on a screen?

The list above illustrates the diversity of the possible uses of the ontology. Examples 1 and 4 can be used computationally by the platform to determine its behavior during runtime, examples 2 and 3 can be used by health status reasoners or by professional caregivers to identify trends and get a better understanding of how the patient is affected by her diagnoses, and additionally example 3 can be used to understand the patient's habits and everyday life.

Prior to deploying a telehealth system using the ontology, it will be necessary to acquire some data about the user that the system can use to determine its behavior. The user's personality traits can be identified using personality tests dedicated to the purpose. Appropriate ICD and ICF codes used to classify the health of the user should be included as well (e.g. to use for layout of user interface) – some medical records and caregiver documentation systems stores such information. Dataset from ATUS can be used to define a general daily time use model that fits the age of the user. The general daily time use model will most likely change over time to fit the everyday life of the specific user more accurately (to determine timing of possible interventions). Besides personality, classifications, and habits, the reminder of data necessary will depend on the use of the system using the ontology. For example, for health tracking, previous physiological measurements are needed. In order to act as a personal assistant, an agenda, e.g. with a medication plan, is needed.

5   Discussion

This discussion will compare the designed ontology to the ones in Section 2, and the ontology is evaluated against the three criteria found in the paper's introduction.

5.1   Comparison of Ontologies

Compared to the existing ontologies described, our ontology has a different focus in that it is intended to be part of an infrastructure where numerous different applications and data providers will integrate. Though different in focus, the ontology naturally has things in common with the other ontologies as well. Table I compares the features of five ontologies – the ones described in Section 2 and ours. Apart from our ontology which is placed in the column furthest to the right of the table, the other ontologies are arranged alphabetically in the table's first row. Below the table some of the features are discussed.

The list of the features in Table I arose through careful study of the content of the ontologies listed. In the table the features are related and organized in accordance with the three criteria stated in the introduction of this paper.

Table 1. Comparison of Content in Ontologies

	Latfi et al. [3]	Nageba et al. [5]	Ongenae et al. [4]	Paganelli et al. [2]	Our ontology
Activity coverage					
Activities	✔			✔	✔
Habits	✔				✔
Health tracking					
Evaluation parameters and/or alarms		✔	✔	✔	
Diagnoses, disabilities and functional status	✔		✔		✔
Physiological measurements	✔	✔	✔	✔	✔
User profiling					
Personality traits					✔
Relatives and contacts	✔		✔	✔	

The ontologies in Table 1 concern the same domain, and hence naturally there are some overlaps in terms of content. Our ontology has been described in the previous sections. Therefore the following two paragraphs will discuss the two features our ontology does not cover compared with the others.

Three of the other ontologies include information about relatives and contacts. Our ontology forms a knowledge base focused on the current health, capabilities, personality traits etc. of individuals, and in this context, information about relatives and contacts is not relevant.

Three of the other ontologies have "Evaluation parameter and/or alarms". The evaluation parameters (upper and lower threshold values) are not included in our ontology because the parameters are application specific, and the purpose of our ontology is to act as a shared knowledge base for multiple applications.

5.2   The Ontology Evaluated According to the Criteria Stated in Section 1

In the introduction, three evaluation criteria were given: Activity coverage, Health tracking, and User profiling.

Activity coverage: Through the Activity, SituationMonitorEvent and Location concepts the ontology contains knowledge pertaining to *activities* of the patient. A software system will use the knowledge about the activities as the basis for reasoning to understand the patient's *everyday habits*. Understanding the habits is essential to incorporate personalization and adaptability into the telehealth domain.

Health tracking: The ontology describes knowledge about the patient's *health, disabilities*, and *physiological measurements* through the Classification and Telehealt-Measurement concepts. The classifications are expected to become key components in the personalization and implementation of intelligence of the human-machine interaction bridging the Patient@home infrastructure and the patient. The concept of intelligent user interfaces was coined in [3] as well, but instead of designing a customized data model (i.e. the concepts Deficiency, Visual-deficiency, and Auditive-deficiency in [3]) to hold the necessary knowledge, we have chosen to use the ICD and ICF classifications, which are already used to a great extent in the healthcare sectors in Denmark and internationally.

User profiling: The "Big Five personality traits" is the foundation for keeping track of the patient's *personality* in the ontology. Interesting scientific questions can be asked based on the knowledge about the patient's personality traits, e.g.:

- Is there correlation between a person's personality and her willingness to use telehealth solutions in general?
- How does personality influence a patient's willingness to adapt her ADL to telehealth solutions?
- Is there correlation between the health of a patient (both diagnoses (ICD) and the severity of the problems (ICF)), and her willingness to adapt the ADL living to accommodate the rules set by telehealth solutions?
- How does the health status of a patient influence her personality?

The designed ontology contains diverse and relevant sources of knowledge for user modeling in the telehealth domain in the context of the Patient@home project considering the requirements stated in the introduction of this paper. The ontology not only considers the physiological measurements and smart home technologies, but also knowledge on the diagnoses, physical capabilities, and personality traits of the patient – sources relevant for the personalization and adaptability of the platform.

By presenting the physiological measurements appropriately and personalized by using the diagnoses and context information, we expect the measurements will become a tool that increases patient empowerment and motivation. Presenting the measurements appropriately and personalized refer to both the timing and the form of communication. E.g. the platform should not tell the patient to take her medicine if she is currently sleeping, or while she watches the news, if she prefers not to be disturbed while doing so. Instead, the patient should be asked to take her medication, when it fits her activities schedule. An example of an appropriately and personalized form of communication (intelligent user interface) could be, if the patient is diagnosed with dyslexia or blindness (ICD classifications), she cannot be expected to read information on a graphical user interface by herself. Instead, the information should be read out loud by the system.

6   Conclusion and Future Work

This paper has presented a new ontology for the telehealth domain, in the context of the large national R&D project Patient@home. The foundation for the designed ontology were three criteria concerning activity coverage, user profiling, and health tracking, and the domain requirements concerning patient empowerment, context information and adaptability. To comply with the criteria and requirements the designed ontology contains the following knowledge about a patient:

- Activities of daily living
- Context and location through smart home technologies
- Diagnoses (psychological and physiological) and functional status and disabilities
- Physical condition through various types of telehealth measurements
- Personality traits

The primary contribution of this paper is the ontology designed that constitutes a holistic knowledge base for user modeling. Compared to four existing ontologies for the telehealth domain, ours includes knowledge to describe patient's personality using the dimensions of "Big Five personality traits" and it uses the internationally recognized standards ICD and ICF for classifying the patient's diagnoses and functional status.

Our future work will focus on the implementation of a multi-agent system that will use the designed ontology in the context of the Patient@home project. The multi-agent system will be implemented in BDI4JADE [14], a Java based framework for developing BDI (Belief Desire Intention) based multi-agent systems. The multi-agent system is expected to consist of four different types of agents: *Sensor agents* (bridge between physical world and infrastructure), *Reasoning agent* (data mining and reasoning on physiological measurements to identify deterioration), *Hospital Information System agent* (facilitate the exchange of messages between infrastructure and other systems in the Danish healthcare sector), and *User agent* (identify and learn behavior and everyday habits, capabilities of patient, and know about personality traits). Our primary focus will be on the User agent. This component is expected to make telehealth solutions more focused on the individual patient, and thereby more adaptable to the everyday life of its user.

Acknowledgment. This paper has been conducted under the Patient@home project, which is supported by Danish Strategic Research Council, the Danish Council for Technology and Innovation, and Growth Forum in the Region of Southern Denmark.

References

1. Gruber, T.R.: A Translation Approach to Portable Ontology Specifications. Knowl. Acquis. **5**(2), 199–220 (1993)
2. Paganelli, F., Giuli, D.: An ontology-based system for context-aware and configurable services to support home-based continuous care. IEEE Trans. Inf. Technol. Biomed. **15**(2), 324–333 (2011)
3. Latfi, F., Lefebvre, B., Descheneaux, C.: Ontology-based management of the telehealth smart home, dedicated to elderly in loss of cognitive autonomy. In: 3rd International Workshop OWLED on OWL: Experiences and Directions (2007)
4. Ongenae, F., Claeys, M., Dupont, T., Kerckhove, W., Verhoeve, P., Dhaene, T., De Turck, F.: A probabilistic ontology-based platform for self-learning context-aware healthcare applications. Expert Syst. Appl. **40**(18), 7629–7646 (2013)
5. Nageba, E., Fayn, J., Rubel, P.: A model driven ontology-based architecture for supporting the quality of services in pervasive telemedicine applications. In: 3rd International Conference on Pervasive Computing Technologies for Healthcare, pp. 1–8 (2009)
6. Ongenae, F., Bleumers, L., Sulmon, N., Verstraete, M., Van Gils, M., Jacobs, A., De Zutter, S., Verhoeve, P., Ackaert, A., De Turck, F.: Participatory design of a continuous care ontology: towards a user-driven ontology engineering methodology. In: Proceedings of the International Conference on Knowledge Engineering and Ontology Development (KEOD), pp. 81–90 (2011)
7. Kuusik, A., Reilent, E., Lõõbas, I., Parve, M.: Software architecture for modern telehome care systems. In: 6th International Conference on Networked Computing, INC 2010, pp. 1–6 (2010)
8. Bureau of Labor Statistics - United States Department of Labor: American Time Use Survey (2014). http://www.bls.gov/tus/home.htm (accessed: November 05, 2014)
9. World Health Organization: International Classification of Diseases (ICD). http://www.who.int/classifications/icd/en/
10. World Health Organization: International Classification of Functioning, Disability and Health (ICF). http://www.who.int/classifications/icf/en/
11. Stanford University: Protégé (2014). http://protege.stanford.edu/
12. International Health Terminology Standards Development Organisation: SNOMED CT. http://www.ihtsdo.org/snomed-ct
13. McCrae, R.R., Costa, P.T.: Personality trait structure as a human universal. Am. Psychol. **52**(5), 509–516 (1997)
14. Nunes, I., de Lucena, C.J.P., Luck, M.: BDI4JADE: a BDI layer on top of JADE. In: International Workshop on Programming Multi-Agent Systems, pp. 88–103 (2011)

Invited Papers

Durable Plug and Play Device for Bed Tele-Monitoring

Hisato Kobayashi[✉]

Faculty of Design and Engineering, Hosei University, Fujimi,
Chiyoda, Tokyo 102-8160, Japan
h@hosei.ac.jp

Abstract. This paper describes a compact plug and play bed sensor that can detect in-bed/out-of-bed status, bed vibrations, room temperature, room illuminance, and foot movement. All detected data are stored on the cloud server in real time. The proposed system performs all basic tele-monitoring functions. Further, the system is entirely autonomous and can recover from any black outs, communication breakdowns, and computer failures.

Keywords: Health-tele-monitoring · Plug & Play device · Durable and robust system · Bed-monitoring · Environment-monitoring

1 Introduction

Currently, our world is moving towards an aging or super-aging society [1]. Therefore, we need to develop possible solutions to survive such a society. Tele-health monitoring is a basic issue that should be addressed in an aging society. Data that is collected remotely can be further analyzed to help caregivers construct accurate care plans and aid in preventing diseases or accidents [2] [3]. There are many commercial products and research results regarding this issue, for example, [5] [6] [7] [8]; however, they lack the following three important aspects required for real deployments [9] [10]. The first two aspects are closely related to the concept of autonomous computing [11]. If these aspects are accomplished, the device could be a good component for smart spaces [12].

- Plug and Play (quick and easy installation)
- 24-h 365-day Operation (running without human maintenance)
- Invisibleness (should not be obstructive)

Conventional monitoring systems often require hardware and software installations. In many cases, such systems are installed at rooms where people are already residing. In such scenarios, a long installation period is undesirable, thus, the factor "plug and play" is important.

Usually, such devices have power and/or reset switches. If the device has a power-on switch, someone may turn-off the device by accident. Therefore, we believe that such switches are not necessary and manual operation interfaces should be discarded. In any case, the devices should be operational throughout

© Springer International Publishing Switzerland 2015
A. Geissbühler et al. (Eds.): ICOST 2015, LNCS 9102, pp. 259–269, 2015.
DOI: 10.1007/978-3-319-19312-0_21

the year. Further, such conventional devices often enter an error-stop stage owing to errors such as communication and computer hang-ups. A "reset switch" then needs to be manually pressed to recover from such a scenario. However, this is not feasible in tele-monitoring scenarios. For example, in case of nursing homes, it is not always possible for the caregivers to take care of such devices, because they are often occupied with daily tasks. The device should be able to recover autonomously. Thus, an autonomously recovering system should be developed that would make "reset switches" obsolete.

In terms of bed monitoring, the in-bed/out-of-bed information is crucial. In general, conventional in-bed/out-of-bed sensing devices are floor-mat type, bed-sheet type, pillow type, and down-light type and all these devices are visible, thus being physically and mentally obstructive for the users. A bed-sheet type sensor may be invisible in a general situation; however, it may be obstructive when the bed-sheet is replaced, and it may cause discomfort when sleeping. Considering the above viewpoints, we designed a compact bed-monitoring device. In the next section, we present detailed information about the hardware design.

2   Hardware

The proposed device is compact and can be installed easily. The device has six basic sensors to detect the situations around the bed.

2.1   Sensors

In-Bed/Out-of-Bed Status. The most crucial information for bed-monitoring is the in-bed/out-of-bed status. Several methods have been proposed to obtain the status; however, these methods are not very accurate and often obtain miss-detections. These miss-detections are generally caused by human errors. For example, in the case of the bed-sheet type or pillow-type bed-monitoring devices, sensors might slip from the intended position; in the case of ultra-red (UR) thermo sensor, ultra-wide band (UWB) radar sensor, or video camera, the position of the sleeper may move away from the target area. To avoid such "shifting errors" and to enable easy installation, we adopt a basic approach of measuring the weight of the bed to detect in-bed/out-of-bed status. The principle is considerably simple; when someone sleeps on the bed, the overall weight of the bed increases. The sensor detects the difference between "bed only" and "bed with human being" weights to identify the in-bed/out-of-bed status. The sensor has a hammock-style structure; the metal plate is inserted below the bed leg. The metal plate is a cantilever-type plate hanged using another thin plate. On the thin plate, strain gages are pasted, which detect the extension of the thin metal as shown in Figures 1, 2 and 3.

The strain gages are connected to a conventional bridge circuit as shown in Fig. 5, and the output voltage is magnified electronically. A low-pass filter is used to retrieve only the low frequency component. We cannot use this value as accurate weight data, because we only measure the force on one leg and

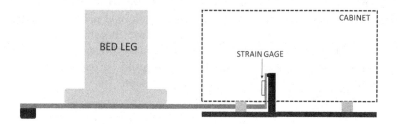

Fig. 1. Structure of Weight Sensor

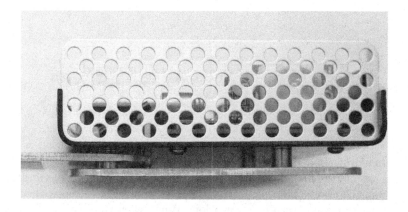

Fig. 2. Front-View of the Proposed Device

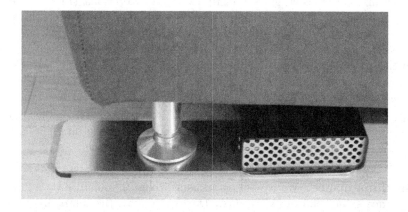

Fig. 3. Proposed Sensor Installed Beneath the Bed Leg

the characteristic of the strain gages may change over time. The threshold for classifying the in-bed and out-of-bed status is determined using past data. The device acquires the old data sequence for normal days. It calculates the average of the top 1000 data and bottom 1000 data. It sets the threshold in between the two averages, as shown in Fig. 4. This threshold could be renewed periodically to compensate the chronological change of the sensors.

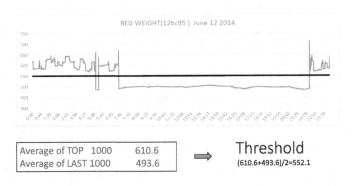

Fig. 4. Automatic Threshold Calculation

Bed Vibration. Bed vibration is another important data used to estimate the situation around the bed. Currently, we only check the magnitude of vibration to identify unusual events. Some doctors and nurses believe that sleeper's body may not move and may not turn over for a long time, when the sleeper experiences some brain trouble. In this case, the bed will not exhibit any vibrations even when the human is on the bed. However this is a rule of thumb; there is no statistical evidence. Our device may acquire such statistical data.

We utilize the same weight sensor to detect bed vibrations, (Fig. 5), because the strain gage has a sufficient frequency response. The signal from the strain gage is passed through a high-pass filter and magnified. The high frequency components of the signal denote the vibrations of the bed. Indeed, this value itself is not the accurate physical value; however, we only need to identify whether the situation is normal or abnormal. Therefore, to satisfy this requirement, the value obtained from the high frequency component of the signal is a good indicator.

The following four sensors have a uni-modular hardware interface, and we can add/replace any sensor with the same hardware interface.

Room Illuminance. We can easily measure room illuminance by adding an illuminance sensor shown in Fig. 6-A. During the day, the sensor may not be useful; however, at night, room illuminance information gives us an activity indicator of the residents.

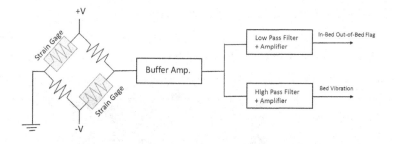

Fig. 5. Bed Vibration Signal from Strain Gage

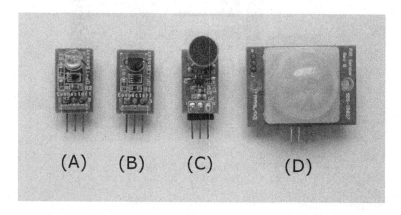

Fig. 6. Environmental Sensors with Same Hardware Interface

Room Temperature. We add a temperature sensor shown in Fig. 6-B. Room temperature is important information especially for the elderlies, because their temperature sensing capability often declines with age, which makes it difficult for them to set the air conditioners appropriately, and this may lead to illness such as dehydration and/or cold.

Sound Level. The device has a sound sensor shown in Fig. 6-C. A sound signal has a considerable amount of information; but currently, we retrieve only the amplitude of the signal. Using the amplitude of the sound signal, we can determine the residents' activity and detect abnormal events. By changing the firmware of the device, we may obtain more accurate data such as fast Fourier transform (FFT) data or sound recognition data.

Pyroelectric Motion Sensor Around Bed. We also added a pyroelectric motion sensor shown in Fig. 6-D to detect foot movement around the bed. However, this sensor covers a limited area, and therefore, it cannot detect foot motion beyond a particular range. Thus, the information obtained from this sensor is a type of ancillary data.

All sensors are installed in a compact cabinet as shown in Fig. 7.

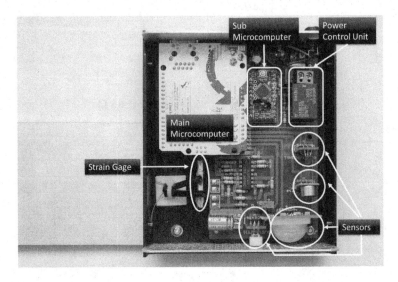

Fig. 7. Inside of Device

2.2   Communication

The device is designed to send data over the Internet, and therefore, the communication function is realized using an Ethernet connection, as shown in the schematic diagram in Fig. 8. All acquired data is stored on a cloud server.

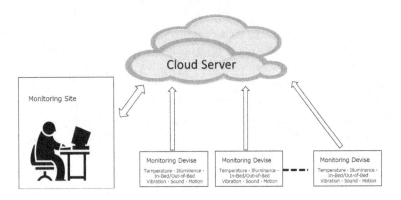

Fig. 8. Data Flow

Wired Internet Connection. The microcomputer has an Ethernet function, which can access any router using the DHCP protocol. It sends the data with the HTTP-Put protocol to the pre-assigned IP address of the cloud server. The microcomputer acquires data through the sensors, pre-processes the data, and sends this data periodically every 20 seconds. There is no essential reason to choose the communication period as 20 seconds; this communication interval will be revised after experiences over a long period. Ideally, the devise changes its communication interval based on the situation by itself.

Wireless Internet Connection. If the environment where the device is to be installed does not provide a wired Internet connection, we use a Wi-Fi adapter to connect the device to a wired Ethernet. The device also provides a power supply for this adapter. This implies that the device can reset the Wi-Fi adapter by switching its power on and off. In case even Wi-Fi connection is not available, we have to set up a cellular 4G router, for example [13], somewhere in the facility. This router is plug & play and ideal for any situations where a wireless network is needed.

3 Three Important Aspects

In this section, we explain the three aspects described in the Introduction.

3.1 Plug and Play Function

The device is governed by the microcomputer, which has a "power-on-reset" firmware. Thus, when power is supplied, the microcomputer starts with the specified firmware. The device does not need a power-switch; the AC-plug of the power adapter functions as the power switch. The necessary information, including the cloud server's IP address is already stored on the microcomputer's memory, and therefore, the device does not need to configure any switch. The threshold and other environment-dependent parameters are adjusted autonomously, and therefore, there is no need to use switches.

3.2 Dependable Operation

To realize a dependable throughout-the-year operation, we adopt another microcomputer to control the power supply, i.e., the additional microcomputer turns off and turns on when any communication error occurs. As shown in the schematic diagram in Fig. 9, the two microcomputers perform a watchdog function, where each one always checks the microcomputers' soundness, and if the microcomputer freezes, the watchdog resets the microcomputer. On the other hand, if the main computer identifies some communication error, it sends a signal to the second microcomputer. Then, the second microcomputer turns off the power of the first microcomputer as well as the Wi-Fi adapter (in case of a Wi-Fi connection), and waits for one minute before turning the power on again. This implies that the first computer, the Ethernet function, and the Wi-Fi adapter are reset and rebooted from the initial state.

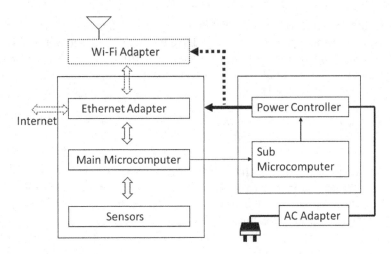

Fig. 9. Two Microcomputers

3.3 Invisibleness

The device is sufficiently compact and can be installed under the bed. The device stays in a fixed location and cannot be moved after installation. The location is inconspicuous, and the device does not obstruct the daily routine of the user. The device generates no sound (noise) or blinking lights such as power-on light and/or communication progressing light. Therefore, the device is not obstructive either mentally or physically.

4   Deployment

We installed four prototypes in the beginning of 2013: two prototypes were installed at a group home for dementia patients, one was installed at an apartment with nursing care, and the last one was installed on the author's bed. These four prototypes worked for more than 10 months without any maintenance issues. However, two breakdowns were caused by human errors. Once, a caregiver accidentally unplugged the AC cord. The AC-plug should be firmly plugged, or should be locked. In the other case, a caregiver accidentally turned off the Wi-Fi router of the apartment room. The Wi-Fi router too should be invisible, or installed at an isolated place where a person cannot access it easily. The prototype sent data as shown in Fig. 10, which is the data for the author's bed. The data shows the bed-in time and bed-out time, illuminance, temperature, and the sound level of the bedroom. It also shows the foot movement when the author moved away from the bed to use the bathroom. For the data that is sent from the device to the cloud server, Fig. 11 shows the communication time or interval at which the cloud server receives the data. The transmission period is not accurate, and it is often delayed because of communication conjunction. However, such a delay does not significantly affect the monitoring function. At

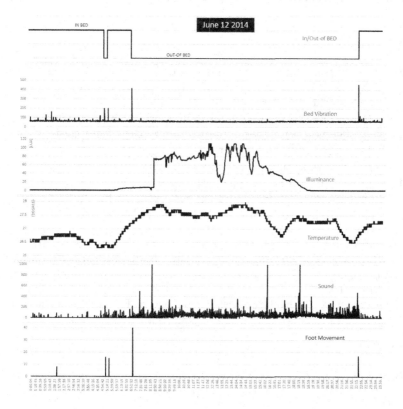

Fig. 10. Data from Device

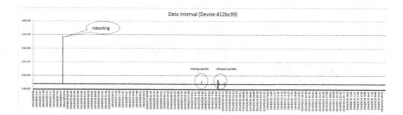

Fig. 11. Communication Interval

around 9:00 on 8 April, the interval was longer than 3 min, which implies that the device was not operating correctly and was autonomously rebooted.

5   Conclusion

In this paper, we presented a new design for a bed-monitoring system considering three aspects: "Plug and Play," "24-h 365-day Operation," and "Invisibleness." In terms of these three aspects, our new design works well. However, there are still many improvements required in terms of information processing. In particular, the "bed vibration" and "sound" signal is not utilized effectively. These data may include rich information about the living environment, but the microcomputers do not have enough computational power to analyze the signal in detail. Our future tasks are to improve the data processing method and to determine relationships between these data and the real events, which requires analyzing extensive data acquired for a sufficiently long period.

Acknowledgments. This project is being carried out with Mr. Yoshiyuki Hino, Mr. Ivan Ho, and Mr. Billy Pham. I appreciate Mr. Hino's help with the installation and management, and the server side operation carried out by Mr. Ho and Mr. Pham. Further, I acknowledge I-care Group Co. Ltd., for providing us with the test sites. I also would like to thank Editage(www.editage.jp) for English language editing.

References

1. Kinsella, K.W.H.: The U.S. Census Bureau. International Population Reports, P95/091. An Aging World 2008. US Government Printing Office, Washington DC (2009)
2. Lee, Y., Bien, Z., Mokhtari, M., Kim, J.: Aging Friendly Technolgogy for Health and Independence, vol. 6159, pp. 263–266. Springer, Heideberg (2010)
3. Ianculescu, M., Lupeanu, E., Alexandru, A., Tudora, E., Coman, O.A., Coman, L.: Strenthening the role of medical infromatics in promotin a successful positive aging. In: Proceedings of the 11th WSEAS International Conference on Applied Informatics and Communications, Florence, Italy, pp. 305–310, August 23–25 (2011)
4. AbuDagga, A., Resnick, H.E., Alwan, M.: Telemedicine and e-Health **16**(7), 830–838, September 2010
5. S+ Sleep Sensor. https://sleep.mysplus.com
6. Beddit Sleep Monitor. http://www.beddit.com
7. MIT Technology Review. http://www.technologyreview.com/news/426073/sleep-sensor-hides-beneath-the-mattress/
8. Withings Aura. http://postscapes.com/wireless-sleep-sensors-withings-aura
9. Kobayashi, H., Hino, Y., Ho, I., Pham, B., Watanabe, S.: Information and communication technology-based tele-monitoring for elderly care houses. In: Proceedings of the 12th International Conference on Control, Automation, Robotics and Vision ICARCV, pp. 662–667 (2012)
10. Kadouche, R., Mokhtari, M., Giroux, S., Abdulrazak, B.: Personalization in smart homes for disabled people. In: 2008 Second International Conference on Future Generation Communication and Networking, 13–15 December 2008

11. Kephart, J.O., Chess, D.M.: The vision of automatic computing. IEEE Computer **36**(1), 41–50 (2003)
12. Gouin-Vallerand, C., Abdulrazak, B., Giroux, S., Mokhtari, M.: A self-configuration middleware for smart spaces. International Journal of Smart Home **3**(1) (2009)
13. 4G Router. http://www.netgear.com/home/products/mobile-broadband/lte-gateways

Serious Games and Personalization
of the Therapeutic Education

Jacques Demongeot[1(✉)], Adrien Elena[1], Carla Taramasco[2], and Nicolas Vuillerme[1]

[1] AGIM, Faculty of Medicine, University J. Fourier Grenoble, 38700, La Tronche, France
{Jacques.Demongeot,Adrien.Elena,Nicolas.Vuillerme}@agim.eu
[2] Escuela de Ingeniería Civil en Informática, Un. de Valparaíso, Av. Gran Bretaña 1091,
Playa Ancha, Valparaíso, Chile
carla.taramasco@uv.cl

Abstract. Therapeutic education uses currently serious games techniques, to have more impact on persons with a chronic disease at their place of living. This requires to customize the game so that the person attempts to change in his lifestyle and dietary habits, according to the specific advices given at relevant moments by the therapeutic monitoring. Thus, taking better account of alimentary and sedentary own habits, and those of his family or professionnel environment, it is possible to build a personalized educational tool, which evolves according the transformations of the pathotology (toward stabilization or to complication), taking into account an actimetry objectified by sensors, complementing and overlapping the information obtained by subjective reporting declarative procedures of dialogue with the virtual coach, during the game. We take as an example the sequence obesity/type 2 diabetis, which affects between 4% and 10% of older people in most developed and developing countries.

Keywords: Therapeutic education · Serious game · E-health · Chronic disease · Type 2 diabetes

1 Introduction

After [1], 34.9% (with 0.95 Confidence Interval equal to [32,38]) of the US adults (aged more than 20 years) were obese in 2011-2012, with a Body Mass Index (BMI=weight/size^2) more than 30 (an adult with a BMI between 25 and 29.9 being considered overweight). This percentage was equal to 16.9% (95 CI = [15,19]) for children and teenagers (aged from 2 to 19 years). As co-morbidity of obesity, type 2 diabetes represents about one third of obese adults, with complications like retinitis, sores (diabetic foot), nephropathy,... The estimated cost of obesity was $147 billion in 2008 in US (1,43 times higher than for normal weight population), and the percentage of obese children aged 6–11 years (resp. teenagers aged 12-19 years) increased from 7% in 1980 to 18% in 2012 (resp. from 5% in 1980 to 21% in 2012) [1,2]. This dramatic increase involves an urgent progress in preventive and therapeutic education, especially in the domain of alimentation and physical activity, because overweight and obesity result mainly from a caloric imbalance (too few calories ingested for calories consumed) and depend on genetic, behavioural and environmental factors, many of which can be compensated by correct habits learned through proper targeted education Both type 2 diabetes and obesity share same risk factors(notably race, age, and family history) and modern life

A. Geissbühler et al. (Eds.): ICOST 2015, LNCS 9102, pp. 270–281, 2015.
DOI: 10.1007/978-3-319-19312-0_22

with sedentary and high fatty and energetic diet habits is known to lead to obesity, then to diabetes: demographic projections show that one in three of the children born in 2000 will develop diabetes, which justifies the development of preventive serious games [3-7] based on the observation of the lifestyle of the person at home. We present successively in the following three serious games allowing the prevention of type 2 diabetes complications, in which the actimetry, objectified by sensors, complements and overlaps the information obtained by reporting subjective declarative procedures in the dialogue with a virtual coach, whose aim is to help to prevent complications of vision (diabetic retinitis), locomotion (diabetic foot) and nutrition (obesity).

2 Serious Game on Vision

The objective of the serious game devoted to vision is to detect early defects in the perception of visual illusions by the type 2 diabetic patient. We present successively 6 examples of such illusions based on different features of their perception and allowing the measure of threshold psycho-physical variables related to their recognition [8,9]:

2.1 Geometric Illusions

They concern artifactual perception of geometric properties like parallelism or equality of size or area of simple objects, like in the illusion by Zöllner, showing apparently non parallel lines on a dashed ground, in which the threshold variable is the critical angle of dashed lines giving the non parallelism feeling. We have also selected among the set of geometric illusions Fraser's, Hering's, Jastrow's, Poggendorff's, ... illusions.

2.2 Contrast Illusions

They concern artifactual perception of virtual objects due to a high contrast between real objects of different colours, certain objects having tendency to propagate their colourover the others. We have selected among this set of illusions the classical Hermann's illusion, whose threshold variable is the thickness of the network of perpendicular black and white lines giving the feeling to have white or gray squares at their intersections, and also the Bergen's, White's, Mach's, Munker's,... illusions.

2.3 Contour Illusions

They concern artifactual perception of virtual objects due to the prolongation of contours from vertices giving the feeling to see a real frontier delimitating these objects. We have selected the Ehrenstein's illusion, whose threshold variables are theradius value of the virtual circles and the number of afferent rays causing viewing these circles. We have also selected the classical Kanizsa 2D and 3D illusions.

2.4 Motion Illusions

They concern artifactual perception of objects moving at different velocities on a contrasted ground due to their different colours and intensities. We have selected among this set of illusions the "Rotating cylinders" illusion, showing the artefactual

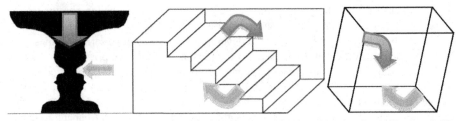

Fig. 1. Game searching for the threshold of object identification: Vase vs faces illusion (left), Schroeder's scale descending or ascending (middle) and Necker's cube open or closed (right)

rotation of a yellow central cylinder with blue spots, whose threshold variable is the value of the size of the blue spots, for which we search for the critical value causing first the feeling that the cylinder rotates.

2.5   Persistence Illusions

They concern artifactual perception of objects due to the retinal persistence of highly contrasted scenes, with in some cases the inversion of colours, one colour being replaced by its complementary colour. Among this set of illusions, we have the Jesus or Che's face illusion in which we perceive the complementary black and white face from its white and black version, whose threshold variable is the intensity of the black and white contrast, the French flag illusion from the inverted (in colour) flag, the moving pink points illusion, in which one of the pink points becomes green.

2.6   Cognitive Illusions

They concern artifactual perception of different objects or of a unique object but moving in different directions, from the same view but interpreted in function of the context. The most known such illusions are the Vase vs face illusion, in which we perceive a vase or two faces depending on the attention given on the central or peripheral part of the picture (Fig. 1). The cognitive perception depends often on the attention given on the central or peripheral part of the picture, *e.g.*, with the Vase vs faces illusion, Schroeder's scale descending or ascending and Necker's cube open or closed. Cognitive illusions are numerous, and among them we can notice "Old woman", Schroeder's scale, Necker's cube, "Cow-boy riding" illusions (in which his horse seems to be coming towards the viewer or away) and Ballerina illusions (in which she seems rotate clock- or anticlockwise).

3   Serious Game on Locomotion

The game consists to record pressure data at the level of foot sole, basin and shoulder with help of smart socks and web sensors (pressure sensing mat placed on a wheel chair, armchair, bed or optionally at ground level) done with a sensitive textile made by Texisense®, recording continuously pressure and after displaying these data on devices related to the patient like the smartphone [10-19] in case of alert at a critical levels for the genesis of sores (including shoulders, iliac crest, sacrum and foot sole). The pressuredata are monitored especially for persons lying supine or working in a standing or sitting posture. The loss (due to vascular complications type II diabetes) of pressure-sensitive organs indeed often causes local anoxia, due to the constant position of the patient on the same side. The alert (usually non conscious) is given by the cutaneous corpuscles pressure sensitive: Meissner corpuscles (superficial dermal), Pacini (median dermal) and Ruffini (deep dermal). The latter variety corresponds to free nerve endings associated with the Merkel cells, which arrive until the epidermis.

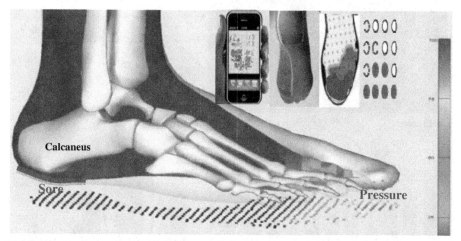

Fig. 2. Locomotion game showing different devices of recording and display (smartphone, sock and sole with discretization of the signal on thumbnails). The confrontation between bone densitometry data (X Rays or Ultra Sound) and sole pressure map allows preventing calcaneus osteoporosis during bone reconstruction highly depending on pressure of the heel on the ground.

The type II diabetes keeps functional nociceptive sensors of the cutaneous pain due to pressure, called mechanical nociceptor and located in the skin, muscles and joints. The analgesic response often leads to a vicious circle of postures that gradually induce; to escape the pain, other ulcerative locations in new pressure zones as well as trouble in bone reconstruction in the zones avoided (Fig. 2).

4   Serious Game on Nutrition

The risk of a bad alimentation, too rich in carbohydrates and sugar, during the early phase of type 2 diabetes, is to increase the imbalance of insulin control and cause a pre-prandial coma, due to a poor use of glycogen. It is therefore appropriate to advise the diabetic, avoiding snacking and an excessive load of fast sugars. A healthy diet, balancing carbohydrate and sugar intake for an energy balance corresponding to a given physical activity is recommended: the player disposes of several menus he composes entirely in his own way, and a virtual coach reminds him food mistakes he made and advises other virtuous behaviors, corresponding to a nutrition adapted to his diabetic condition (Fig. 3). Depending on the quality of patient's responses, exercises are proposed in order to build a collection of tailored menus for all periods of the year and all sedentary conditions or physical activities motivating the patient and allowing him to avoid accidents of hypo- or hyperglycemic types.

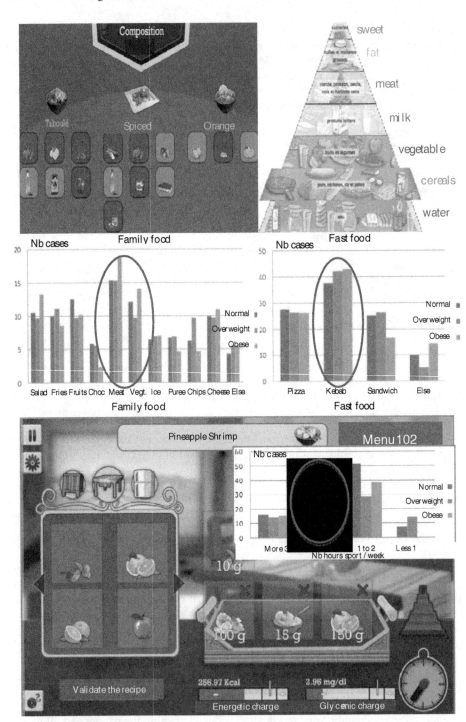

Fig. 3. Nutrition game allowing a personalized choice based on physical and social status

Depending on the quality of the patient's responses, progressive exercises are proposed offering the opportunity to build a collection of tailored menus for all periods of the year and all sedentary conditions or physical activities motivating the patient and allowing him to avoid accidents hypo- or hyperglycemic types. Two levels of game are proposed, the first for the early diabetes patient, who ignores the mechanism of the disease and the consequences of a bad nutrition, and the second for the complicated diabetes, which takes into account complications already installed (like retinitis or nephropathy) proposing more than dietary advises, *i.e.*, an actual combined Adapted Alimentation and Physical Activity (AAPA) diminishing the effects of the evolution of the disease to the complications. On Fig. 3, we see a summary of observations done in a class of a French high school, reporting some factors of way of life (diet, physical or sedentary lifestyle) characterizing individuals in their intra- and extra-familial environment allowing the game personalization.

5   Results: Personalization of the Alimentation Game

A way to personalize a serious game through its first dialogue with the coach, is to know better users in their familial and professional environment, *e.g.* (Fig. 4), the weight status of the whole college is obtained to propose to it an adapted alimentation.

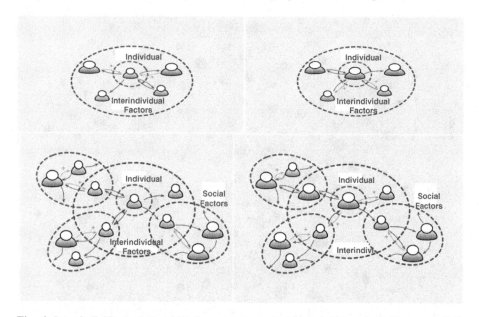

Fig. 4. Inter-individual relationships between obese (in blue) and non obese (in green) individuals in their social context

The corresponding study has been performed in classes of a French high school. In 2010, 211 (89%) of Joeuf college students responded to our questionnaire. Of the 211 college students surveyed, 82% (173) had a normal weight and 18% (38 students)

were overweight. Overweight students were divided into four categories (representing the importance of their overweight): overweight, obvious obesity, severe obesity and morbid obesity. From these four categories, we distinguish only students overweight and obese students. Throughout the college, 6% of students become overweight and 12% obese. Students are represented in Fig. 5 by nodes of different colors: blue represents the normal weight adolescents, while red represents overweight adolescents. The in-degree value of a node corresponds to the size of the circle representing an individual as the level corresponding to incoming students who have been appointed as friends of this individual, which means that the circle is big if the corresponding student was named as a friend by many other students in his promo. Normal weight students can be appointed as a friend by overweight and obese students. For out-degrees (Fig. 6), we draw the same type of graph, where size of the circle varies so the more the circle is big plus student named other students as friends.

Students overweight and obese call, on average, less friends than others. This result, however, can be quantified. Indeed, the median out-degree of overweight and obese students is higher than that of normal-weight students. As against the median of in-degrees of overweight and obese students is lower than that of normal-weight students.

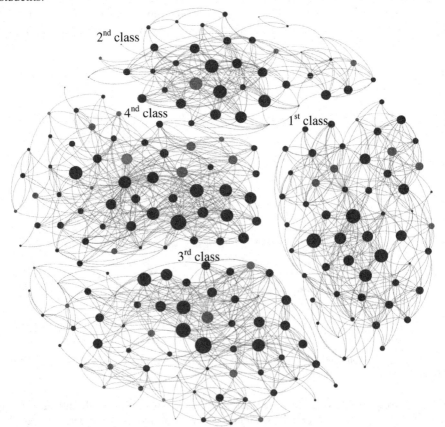

Fig. 5. Interaction graphs representing the in-degree of an individual (equal to the number of students having chosen him as friend) proportional to the size of the circle representing him

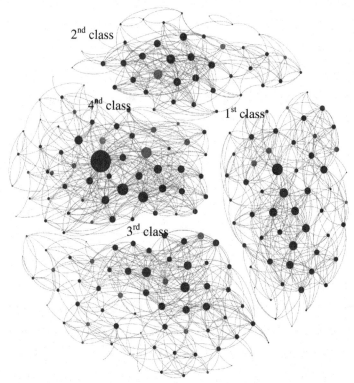

Fig. 6. Interaction graphs representing the out-degree (equal to the number of students having chosen him as friend) of the individuals from classes of increasing level, proportional to the size of the circle representing them

Overweight and obese children appear in most choices unless appointed as a friend but they call as many friends as others. This finding departs from that of previous studies [25] who affirmed that obese and overweight students chose a smaller number of friends. The interaction graphs of Fig. 5 and 6 represent a summary for the entire college. These graphs do not show large differences between people in overweight and normal weight. These graphs (in-degree) seem to confirm the observation that obese and overweight adolescents are not necessarily choosing fewer friends than normal ones. From the observation of the whole sample of the students n the selected French high school, we can propose adapted collective menus taking into account all the sensitivities and needs expressed by students through the questionnaire and the game practice. Such a study could be also done in a residency of elderly people, in order to increase both the collective empowerment and engagement of the persons with respect to the alimentation in their community. On Fig. 7, we see a wide distribution of the students among the different histograms and interaction graphs presented. To summarize, the most useful observations of the students sample for improving their collective alimentation are:

1) histograms a) to d) show an influence of age on the occurrence of obesity, which justifies an early practice of serious games devoted to alimentation, in order to change lifestyles and food habits, already highly varying among the student population, notably because the influence of the family's opinion seems very biased and weak,

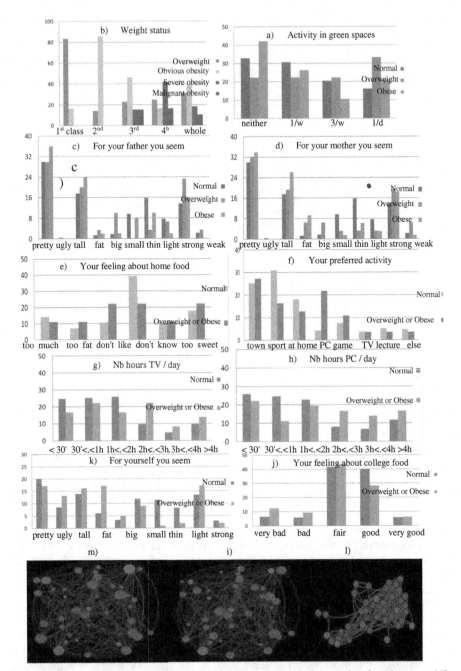

Fig. 7. Histograms and graph from the observation of the whole sample of students used for personalizing Alimentation game: a) distribution of students among weight classes; b) activity in green spaces; c) feeling of the father; d) feeling of the mother; e) home food; f) preferred activity; g) and h) TV and PC activity; i) self-esteem; j) college food; k) out-degree interaction graph for second class students (12 yrs); l) in-degree interaction graph; m) friends group graph

2) histograms e) to j) prove that there is already a big difference between the chosen activities and expressed opinions by the two categories of students (normo- and overweight adolescents) showing well the crucial point of the personalization of the food game, to better fit the needs of the player (detecting his knowledge gaps in nutrition and tracking his behaviors), and, then, have an appropriate preventive action,

3) the graphs k), l), m) of Fig. 7 use the Atlas Force® method which represents through spatial networks the students the most related to the others as nodes appearing next to each other, with a size depending on their connectivity. The distance between the individuals will be correlated with the amount of links that they share. This spatial method strengthens links between students who form a group whose members are friends. The graphs do not show a dichotomy (separated clusters) overweight-obese vs normal, but college students overweight or obese (in red) seem to be more isolated than normal students (in blue), because they are usually not inserted in a large group of friends (see graph m)). This may indicate that overweight or obese adolescents have more difficulties to belong to a friends group than others, hence must be individually taken into account, *e.g.*, through the alimentary serious game, when menus and physical activities have to be planned.

6   Conclusion

The aim of the paper was to describe the first results of a research about serious games, with biofeedback techniques and personalization inside the social network of a chronic patient, used i) in their dimension of elaboration of therapeutic education scenarios, ii) in their dimension of information capture using specific sensors at home allowing the customization of the game, with the visualization of social networks to which the patient belongs, to bring him to an awareness of belonging to a community sharing same pathology and therapy. We built three game scenarios aiming the detection and monitoring of i) diabetic retinitis, ii) diabetic foot ulcers and iii) obesity.

The coupling with individual identification techniques in a social group for the visualization and customization of the game using new educational methods of therapeutic education, combined with the recognition of the presence of the patient in his local social network, will maximize the effectiveness of serious games and biofeedback necessary to the educational personalization [20-25].

Acknowledgments. We acknowledge the Project Investissements d'Avenir VHP (Visual Home Presence inter@ctive)supported by the French BPI® (Banque Pour l'Investissement).

References

1. Ogden, C.L., Carroll, M.G., Kit, B.K., Flegal, K.M.: Prevalence of Childhood and Adult Obesity in the United States, 2011–2012. JAMA **311**, 806–814 (2014)
2. National Center for Health Statistics: Health, United States, 2011: With Special Features on Socioeconomic Status and Health. US Dept Health & Human Serv, Hyattsville, MD (2012)

3. Joubert, M., Gaudinat, A., Boyer, C., Geissbuhler, A., Fieschi, M.: Hon Foundation Council Members:WRAPIN : a tool for patient empowerment within EHR. Studies in health technology and informatics **129**, 147–151 (2007)
4. McCallum, S.: Gamification and serious games for personalized health. Studies in health technology and informatics **177**, 85–96 (2012)
5. Diehl, L.A., Souza, R.M., Alves, J.B., Gordan, P.A., Esteves, R.Z., Jorge, M.L., Coelho, I.C.: InsuOnline, a Serious Game to Teach Insulin Therapy to Primary Care Physicians: Design of the Game and a Randomized Controlled Trial for Educational Validation. JMIR Res. Protocols **21**, e5 (2013)
6. Rizzo, A.S., Lange, B., Suma, E.A., Bolas, M.: Virtual Reality & Interactive Digital Game Technology: New Tools to Address Obesity and Diabetes. J. Diabetes Sci. & Tech. **5**, 256–264 (2011)
7. Kahol, K.: Integrative Gaming: A Framework for Sustainable Game-Based Diabetes Management. J Diabetes Sci Technol **5**, 293–300 (2011)
8. Yoshino, A., Kawamoto, M., Yoshida, T., Kobayashi, N., Shigemura, J., Takahashi, Y., Nomura, S.: Activation time course of responses to illusory contours and salient region: A high-density electrical mapping comparison. Brain Research **1071**, 137–144 (2006)
9. Demongeot, J., Fouquet, Y., Tayyab, M., Vuillerme, N.: Understanding Physiological & Degenerative Natural Vision Mechanisms to Define Robust Contrast and Segmentation Operators. PLoS ONE **4**, e6010 (2009)
10. Demongeot, J., Virone, G., Duchêne, F., Benchetrit, G., Hervé, T., Noury, N., Rialle, V.: Multi-sensors acquisition, data fusion, knowledge mining and triggering in health smart homes for elderly people. C. R. Biologies **325**, 673–682 (2002)
11. Virone, G., Noury, N., Demongeot, J.: A system for automatic measurement of circadian activity deviation in telemedicine. IEEE Trans. BME **49**, 1463–1469 (2002)
12. Chenu, O., Payan, Y., Hlavackova, P., Demongeot, J., Cannard, F., Diot, B., Vuillerme, N.: Pressure sores prevention for paraplegic people: effects of visual, auditive and tactile supplementations on overpressures distribution in seated posture. Appl. Bionics & Biomechanics **9**, 61–67 (2012)
13. Franco, C., Fleury, A., Guméry, P.Y., Diot, B., Demongeot, J., Vuillerme, N.: iBalance-ABF: a smartphone-based audio-biofeedback system. IEEE Trans. BME **60**, 211–215 (2013)
14. Fouquet, Y., Franco, C., Diot, B., Demongeot, J., Vuillerme, N.: Estimation of Task Persistence Parameter from Pervasive Medical Systems with Censored Data. IEEE Trans. Mobile Comput. **12**, 633–646 (2013)
15. Virone, G., Vuillerme, N., Mokhtari, M., Demongeot, J.: Persistent behaviour in healthcare facilities: from actimetric tele-surveillance to therapy education. In: Mellouk, A., Fowler, S., Hoceini, S., Daachi, B. (eds.) WWIC 2014. LNCS, vol. 8458, pp. 297–311. Springer, Heidelberg (2014)
16. Demongeot, J., Hansen, O., Hamie, A., Hazgui, H., Virone, G., Vuillerme, N.: Actimetry@home: actimetric tele-surveillance and tailored to the signal data compression. In: Bodine, C., Helal, S., Gu, T., Mokhtari, M. (eds.) ICOST 2014. LNCS, vol. 8456, pp. 59–70. Springer, Heidelberg (2015)
17. Vuillerme, N., Chenu, O., Pinsault, N., Fleury, A., Demongeot, J., Payan, Y.: A plantar-pressure based tongue-placed biofeedback system for balance improvement. Comp. Methods in Biomech. & Biomed. Eng. **10**, 63–64 (2007)
18. Fleury, A., Mourcou, Q., Franco, C., Diot, B., Demongeot, J., Vuillerme, N.: Evaluation of a smartphone-based audio-biofeedback system for improving balance in older adults - a pilot study. In: IEEE EMBS 2013, pp. 1198–1201. IEEE Press, New York (2013)

19. Franco, C., Diot, B., Fleury, A., Demongeot, J., Vuillerme, N.: Ambient assistive health-care and wellness management – is "the wisdom of the body'' transposable to one's home? In: Biswas, J., Kobayashi, H., Wong, L., Abdulrazak, B., Mokhtari, M. (eds.) ICOST 2013. LNCS, vol. 7910, pp. 143–150. Springer, Heidelberg (2013)
20. Vukadinovic Greetham, D., Hurling, R., Osborne, G., Linley, A.: Social Networks and Positive and Negative Affect. Procedia Social and Behavioral Sciences **22**, 4–13 (2011)
21. Christakis, N.A., Fowler, J.H.: The spread of obesity in a large social network over 32 years. New England journal of Medicine **357**, 370–379 (2007)
22. Taramasco, C., Demongeot, J. (2011) Collective intelligence, social networks and propagation of a social disease, the obesity. In: EIDWT 2011, pp. 86–90. IEEE Press, New York
23. Demongeot, J., Elena, A., Taramasco, C., Vuillerme, N.: Serious game as new health telematics tool for patient therapy education: example of obesity and type 2 diabetes. In: Biswas, J., Kobayashi, H., Wong, L., Abdulrazak, B., Mokhtari, M. (eds.) ICOST 2013. LNCS, vol. 7910, pp. 187–197. Springer, Heidelberg (2013)
24. Demongeot, J., Taramasco, C.: Evolution of social networks: the example of obesity. Biogerontology **15**, 611–626 (2014)
25. Strauss, R., Pollack, H.: Social marginalization of overweight children. Archives of Pediatrics & Adolescent Medicine **157**, 746–752 (2003)

Australian Community Care Experience on the Design, Development, Deployment and Evaluation of Implementing the Smarter Safer Homes Platform

Elizabeth Dodd[1(✉)], Paul Hawting[2], Eleanor Horton[3],
Mohanraj Karunanithi[4], and Anne Livingstone[1]

[1] Global Community Resourcing, Office 17, Building 1,
747 Lytton Road, Murarrie, QLD 4172, Australia
{liz,anne}@globalcommunityresourcing.com.au
[2] Bromilow Home Support Services, 14/102 Burnett Street,
Buderim, QLD 4556, Australia
paul.hawting@bromilow.com.au
[3] The University of the Sunshine Coast, Locked Bag 4, Maroochydore,
QLD 4558, Australia
ehorton@usc.edu.au
[4] CSIRO Digital Productivity Flagship, Office Level 5, HQ Health Sciences,
Building 901/16, RBWH, Herston, QLD 4029, Australia
Mohan.Karunanithi@csiro.au

Abstract. By 2040, the Australian population is predicted to have 20% of its citizens aged 65+. The country is working now to reduce costs of associated health and aged care with a strong emphasis on developing innovative assistive technologies to support older people to stay safer and keep living at home, independent and healthy, for longer. Following a review of the literature and initiatives of Smart home technology, in 2012, Australia's leading research organisation took advantage of recent advances lifestyle technologies and sensor-network to develop novel approach to an innovative solution to support people living in their homes, called the Smarter Safer Homes (SSH) platform. The SSH platform has the capability to capture measure of functional independence and health from sensors and home health monitors to deliver data and ready interaction for self-management, engage family or carer in the support, and also social and clinical services. This paper explores the interface and translation of research and development into mainstream service delivery through a project deploying the platform in a community based setting in regional Australia.

1 Introduction

The provision of Community Care is changing. Government reform processes are in place and, like most other countries; Australia is facing funding shortfalls and challenges [1]. This paper explores the translation of research and development into mainstream service delivery through a project deploying the platform in a community based setting in regional Australia. It outlines a case study of a recent successful

© Springer International Publishing Switzerland 2015
A. Geissbühler et al. (Eds.): ICOST 2015, LNCS 9102, pp. 282–286, 2015.
DOI: 10.1007/978-3-319-19312-0_23

partnership between older people and their carers, an aged care service provider, a private company supporting innovation and a leading national research entity.

The paper explores the policy and funding setting in Australia, details the deployment of the Smarter Safer Homes platform in a regional setting, outlines the experiences of clients and carers on the use of the platform via a narrative, as well as outlining some of the policy and funding challenges which are present and impact on large scale mainstream deployment of Smart Assistive Technologies in Community Care Settings.

Smarter Safer Homes Platform

As the leading Australian national research agency, Commonwealth Research and Industrial Organisation (CSIRO) is focused on research that improve the lives of Australian population. One of its flagships goals are to improve productivity using digital technologies in the area of health and wellbeing and the care for aging population, in particular independent living in the community.

From a recently recognised research on the first validated innovative home care delivery for cardiovascular disease management using smartphones and the internet [2], CSIRO developed an innovative platform called the Smarter Safer Homes (SSH) to support independent living [3]. The novelty of this platform is its ability to support self-management and engage informal/family and aged care services from a sensor networked home environment. The design of the SSH platform leverages on wireless sensor network and depart from the burden of wearable sensors to provide monitoring for support. Moreover, information delivered through the platform to the consumer and the carers was developed through engagement of senior networked workshop and a user-interface design company.

The SSH platform features simple sensors deployed in a home environment, for gathering activity, physiological sensors to gather health profile, mobile devices for self-management/feedback, and web portal (via internet cloud services) to engage consumers, family/informal carers and clinical services for support and care of the older person living in the community

The sensor-network on the SSH platform uses sensors such as motion, contact, power, temperature, humidity, etc. specific to capture information that contribute to the measure of functional independence, using the activities of daily living (ADL) framework [4]. In particular, the key domains of the activities of daily living that relate to mobility, transfer, hygiene, meal preparation/intake and dressing/grooming. The physiological monitoring were gathered mainly through wireless monitoring devices to gather vital signs to assess the health profile of the person. This included blood pressure, weight, and temperature, and also the option of blood glucose for people living with diabetes. Information from these sensors and devices were transmitted via high speed broadband to a server in which smart algorithms that extracted ADL domains and score [5] and health assessments.

The SSH platform presented the ADL and health assessment information from the server to an App, designed according to older person's needs of interpretation, on a tablet mobile device. This enabled the person cared for to self-manage their everyday living activities that keeps them functionally able and healthy through information, reminders, and appointments. The same information and presentation were also available on an internet portal for the family or the carer engaged to continuously monitor and record daily activity levels and a variety of health checks and triggers for timely support interventions determined by unexpected variations. A separate Internet clinical portal was designed to cater for the needs of aged and clinical care provision. The objective of the portal was to tailor health monitoring and alerts to correspondence with their ADL, which is a more comprehensive approach to chronic care and disease management such as in cardiovascular and diabetes health management.

The Project Collaboration and Rationale

This project was collaboration between:

- Bromilow Home Support Services Pty Ltd a regional Australian Community Care Provider;
- Global Community Resourcing Pty Ltd an Australian innovation company assisting Community Care Providers to transform their business operations; and
- CSIRO- Commonwealth Science and Industry Research Organisation Australia's preeminent Research entity.

The impact of technological advances such as that of the SSH platform on service organisations, the service model, service users and their families will be profound.

The appropriate use of a diverse range of technologies has the potential to:

- improve levels of client mobility
- allow more independent and autonomous management of the activities of daily living
- allow clients to maintain or reestablish connections with their past and improve their mental wellbeing
- allow case managers to remotely link with clients to carry out reviews, engage socially and monitor a client's health and wellbeing
- allow case managers and care staff to more effectively interact remotely about client issues and support options
- allow clients to maintain or reestablish links with family, friends and the local community via mobile platforms to enhance their social inclusion
- improve client health outcomes such as nutrition, stress levels and personal hygiene
- empower clients to take greater control of their lives
- enhance service delivery by enabling positive risk taking and encouraging greater levels of independence
- reduce carer stress, provide reassurance that their family member is safe and allow family carers time out to enhance their own lives
- enhance the roles of care staff provide more effective and efficient use of government funding, thereby offering the potential to reach greater numbers of clients and providing funding bodies with real value for money

Case Study -Narrative Relating to Implementation of Strategy and Health Maintenance

This is a narrative about how the practical use of the platform can help a stroke survivor to stay in their own home for as long as possible and promote more independence in partnership with their carer and/ or care provider.

My partner had a very severe and dense stroke 15 years ago- he was 51 at the time. He was an academic who enjoyed talking, reading, writing, philosophizing, riding his mountain bike, playing the guitar and piano and the social red wine. As a result of the stroke he can no longer do most of these things as he is hemiplegic on the right side of his body. This has resulting in him not being able to use his right arm at all and now walks with a splint on his leg and with the aid of a stick. The stroke has also affected his speech. He is aphasia and apraxia which makes communication quite challenging, however he continues to improve the use of his words. Post stroke my partner has also developed epilepsy, has depression and some cognitive impairment.

His life changed significantly since the stroke. From being a very independent person to having to accept that you need help to perform basic daily functions is a challenge and not one readily accepted. Our life has been focused on mobility as the months he spent in a wheel chair were hard and we found that accessing places in the community was a challenge. After about eleven years of physiotherapy and hydrotherapy we stopped as we decided he could maintain his own mobility program from home with the use of some assistive technologies. During this time his speech and mobility has continued to improve.

Eight years ago we faced the realisation that to meet some socialisation needs and to maintain independence at home, an outside care provider could help us. We engaged Bromilow Home Support Services to assist with my partners care and also helped share the duties as I am a working carer.

The relationship with Bromilow Home Support Services has provided the opportunity to be involved in the trial of this platform. The focus of the platform has unlimited potential for those who are disabled or ageing in their own home. The platform does not replace the face-to-face interaction with carers, but it enhances the level of care that can be provided and supports social interaction. It enables my partner and I to video conference when I am at work or a call to Bromilow Home Support Services. The platform allows for goals to be set for example steps for mobility, and then they can be monitored and attained or assistance provided if needed. Blood pressure and weight recording are two components that we use regularly and are valuable tool for health maintenance and promotion. We also use the sleep efficiency tool that also monitors heart rate during sleep. This is important for people with chronic health conditions in relation to sleep apnea and in our case epilepsy.

This platform uses everyday items so that it is congruent with primary healthcare being affordable and accessible. For myself as a working carer this is important, as government pensions are often not available to us. Organisations such a CSIRO developing technologies that assist working carers are invaluable.

The Future of Technology Enhanced Community Care in a Rapidly Ageing Population

All governments face the challenge of providing care that is based more on the consideration of the needs of the person than the drivers of the economy, but this is strongly influenced by the population projections.

The current Australian population is ageing, but it is not ageing as fast as many OECD countries such as Japan. The proportion of Australian people ageing is much less than many countries such as the United Kingdom.[6] Commonwealth of Australia, 2015:10) However, the projected changes in the ageing population have raised economic considerations for the government, and this has meant a revision of the model of service provision.

The role of technology in all its forms will be a critical component of both operational developments of service provisions, new service models and also in the provision of care within community care service organisations. The aged and community care industry is entering a period of significant change. If community care providers are to grow and prosper into the future, let alone remain successful, they must respond to the changing dynamics of the industry and the preferences of the client base. Equally, they must embrace and create new opportunities.

One new transformed model of care embracing technological innovations is utilising the CSIRO's 'Smarter Safer Homes platform' as an example of the way in which sensor technology is being developed to enhance provision of care and complement health maintenance.

Conclusion

This project which has translated research and development into practice is in early stages of being trialled. As the project progresses the collaboration hopes to be able to measure improvements in respect to :

- the health and wellbeing of clients and carers of community care programs;
- service providers capacity to reform service models and workforce design;
- opportunities for researchers and developers the opportunity to refine further research directions; and
- the opportunities for governments to view the transformational effects smart assistive technologies applied in practice can have.

References

1. Aged Care in Australia, Part 1 – Policy, Demand and Funding, CEPAR Research Brief 2014/01
2. Varnfield, M., Karunanithi, M., Lee, C-K., Arnold, D., Ding, H., Smith, C., Walters, D.: Smartphone-based home care model improved utilisation of cardiac rehabilitation in post-myocardial infarction patients: Results from a randomized controlled trial. HEART, June 27, 2014. doi: 10.1136/heartjnl-2014=305783
3. Zhang, Q., Karunanithi, M., Rana, R., Liu, J.: Determination of activities of daily living of independent living older people using environmentally placed sensors. Conf. Proc. IEEE Eng. Med. Biol. Soc. 2013, 7044–7047 (2013)
4. Katz, S.: Assessing self-maintenance: activities of daily living, mobility, and instrumental activities of daily living. J. Am. Geriatr. Soc. 31, 721–727 (1983)
5. Zhang, Q., Karunanithi, M., Bradford, D., van Kasteren, Y.: Activity of Daily Living assessment through wireless sensor data. Conf. Proc. IEEE Eng Med. Biol. Soc. 2014, 1752–1755 (2014). doi:10.1109/EMBC.2014.6943947
6. Commonwealth of Australia (2015) 2015 Intergenerational Report Australia in 2055, Commonwealth of Australia, Canberra ISBN: 978-1-925220-41-4

Short Contributions

Measurement and Assessment of Hand Functionality via a Cloud-Based Implementation

Hai-Trieu Pham$^{(\boxtimes)}$ and Pubudu N. Pathirana

School of Engineering, Deakin University, Geelong,
Victoria 3216, Australia
{hph,pubudu.pathirana}@deakin.edu.au

Abstract. Measurement of hand functionality is vital for the rehabilitation process as a result of hand injuries. However, patients in remote areas are experiencing difficulties with frequent visits to clinics and hospitals for therapy. This research proposes a novel framework involving a cloud-based implementation based on finger function measurement and tele-assessment employing an affordable optical sensor. Creative Senz3D allows patients to measure and monitor their hand function in non-clinical settings without affecting the quality of treatment. The underlying system includes a subsystem of non-contact ROM measurement of the hand and a cloud-based application which provides web interface for authorised users and a web API for hospital and healthcare professionals. Phalangeal measurement data is regularly sent to data centres that it is conveniently accessible for clinicians to monitor the progress and advise patients the suitable time to visit the hospital. The proposed system is aimed at addressing and providing an e-health solution to a crucial short coming in phalangeal rehabilitation.

1 Introduction

Hands play an important role in performing daily activities and can be considered an an intrinsic interface lane has with the rest of the world. Measuring the range of movement (ROM) of the hand is an essential part in clinical practices and rehabilitation. Most of clinical settings are currently using goniometers, inclinometers, or electro-goniometers as major instruments to measure the declination of hand joint angles which encode joint movement range [17]. Limitations of the current practice include that the assessment tools physically in contact with the injured (i.e burns, wounds, lacerations and dermetalogical conditions) finger. Other significant challenges include limited intra and inter-rater reliability [6] as well as time and financial cost involved in commuting for regularly assessments [3]. All these aforementioned problems can be eliminated by using an automatic non-contact measurement system. In recent years, a range of optical based 3D sensors are introduced to the market, hence they enforce variant projects to develop optical based measurement systems. Although these sensors such as Kinect, Senz3D, and Leap Motion Controller were not initially developed for medical purposes, these are adopted in e-health projects as in [7,13–15]. Measurement data from these system are not influenced by human subjectivity and does not require direct contact during use.

© Springer International Publishing Switzerland 2015
A. Geissbühler et al. (Eds.): ICOST 2015, LNCS 9102, pp. 289–294, 2015.
DOI: 10.1007/978-3-319-19312-0_24

The trend in healthcare in recent years focused on e-health and tele-health applications. Medical services delivered remotely by using telecommunication technologies to provide treatment and therapy is an important and meaningful step in the delivery of modern medication and healthcare. The contribution of e-health and tele-health applications not only reduces the cost of treatment particularly for patient in rural areas [3] but also increase the frequency of medical examination for better diagnosis with less visits to the hospital. E-health solutions also stimulate innovation in clinical data exchange to allow researchers, businesses and clinicians to collaborate on deploying better healthcare services, understand current diseases and find cures for incurable illnesses. The kernel of implementation of e-health and tele-health applications is cloud computing. There are number of technological companies offering cloud computing solutions, such as Microsoft Azure, Google Cloud Platform, Amazon EC2, IBM Cloud. These services not only deliver sound computational capabilities but also are affordable for small businesses and start-ups [1]. Another great characteristic of cloud services is an ability of dynamically allocating resources depending on processing demands [2]. Therefore, cloud service users are freed from deploying and managing hardware system and can focus on software solutions.

2   System Infrastructure

Our system can be divided to 4 components depending on their functions. The first component is the measurement component which includes an optical sensor Creative Senz3D and a computer, and this system is located at patient's home clinic settings, or hospital. This component undertakes the task of measurement the phalangeal declination joint angle. The second component is cloud service. Cloud service ensure the interoperability within components, and is also a place to host and backup data. The third component is a web application allowing authorized users access patient's data through a computer or a mobile device. Authorized users include patient who is mainly possess the data, clinicians who directly treat that patient. Measurement data are protected by user account system and is encrypted. A report of measurement records is automatically generated to help clinicians assess the status of the treatment and advise the patient the suitable date to visit the hospital. The last component is a Web API package which undertake the role of communicating with existing hospital enterprise system. This interface enables the interoperability feature of the system, allows hand data integrate to medical profile of the patient in the hospital, and open a chance for small business and medical organization to access anonymous data for research purpose and better healthcare services. The software system overview is depicted in Figure 1.

2.1   Measurement Component

The measurement component includes an affordable optical sensor Creative Senz3D, a computer to control the optical sensor and communicate with cloud

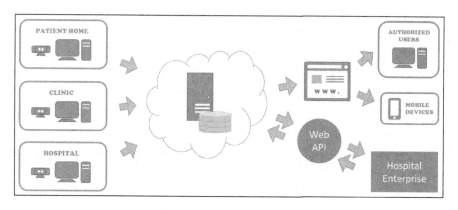

Fig. 1. System Infrastructure Overview

services. The Creative Senz3D is a commercial product which is capable of acquiring depth image for human tracking and gesture tracking. Point cloud of the Creative Senz3D has the resolution of 640 × 480 pixels and refresh frequency of 30 Hz. The Intel Perceptual Computing SDK was employed to track the motion of the hand using Melax's tracking algorithm [12]. This algorithm matches each phalangeal bone of the hand to a convex rigid body and estimate the position of the rigid body in computer virtual environment associating with the position of that bone in reality. The rigid hand model is adjustable in term of width and length of each bone so that it is optimized for all user hand to improve the accuracy. The model of the hand is optimized by our optimization algorithm based on patient's bone length information. This information should be measured at the first time when the patient visit the hospital and demand a telehealth system set up. The recommended configuration for the computer used in the measurement component is a computer running a 64-bit Operating System Microsoft Windows® 7 installed .NET framework and Intel Perceptual Computing SDK. The computer also need to be equipped an internet connection to send measurement data to cloud service.

For the best measurement results, the environment at patient's site should be set up as following: The patient seats at a table with their arm on the hand elevator and elbow supported on the table. This position should put their shoulder in approximately 45-80° flexion, their elbow in approximately 40-60° flexion and their wrist in a neutral, pronated position. The Creative Senz3D camera should be mounted on a tripod or any support equipment so that it is placed below, slightly in front of the patient hand as depicted in Figure 2. The measurement components are set up at patient's home, clinic and hospital.

2.2   Cloud Service

This component is crucial to the whole system due to its functions of data storage, processing and communication between other components. In cloud computing concept, there are three levels of architectures: Infrastructure as a Service

Fig. 2. Measurement System Overview

(IaaS), Platorm as a Service (PaaS) and Software as a Service (SaaS). Our system is deployed at SaaS level using Amazon EC2 services. Amazon EC2 services provide dynamically computing resources for easily expanding and shrinking depending on the demand. Database of the system is implemented using Apache Cassandra which is a type of NoSQL databases. As the ehealth is still in the early state of development, the system may evolve to meet new requirements and standards in the future, using of NoSQL database instead of traditional relational database enables an easy and smooth transition later.

2.3   Web Interface and Web API

A web application was implemented to provide an interface of data analysis and monitoring for authorized users. The web system, which is implemented in ASP.NET MVC 5 framework for building scalable, standards-based web applications, has one version for desktop and one version for mobile device. Only authorized users, i.e. patient and clinician of that patient, have the privilege to access the reports of the measurement. The contents of reports include a visualisation of ROM of the hand comparing to the functional ROM of daily activities

The Web API for this system is in developing stage to enhance the ability of interoperability for communicating with other systems and hospital enterprise. Medical data and rehabilitation progress are useful for hospital to further studies and help developing better therapeutic method as well as better healthcare services.

3   Implementation and Results

The project is developed under trademark name Artimen. A clinical trial was conducted to examine the reliability of the system in term of measurement.

The ethics has been approved for this experiment. The procedure was conducted following the American Society for Hand Therapists clinical recommendations. There are 40 subjects participating to the trial. Measurement of the system was compared to measurement of hand physiotherapists. A correlation of 0.94 between manual rating and automatic rating was found. In the experiment stage, our system was deployed on Amazon t2.micro server.

4   Conclusion

This paper introduced a new cloud-based measurement and tele-assessment framework for the hand. The system is a combination of a measurement system and a tele-assessment system. These sensing and measurement technologies can assist the clinicians to provide an improved healthcare system at a reduced cost. This system enables patient to have their hand measured and monitored with less visits clinics or hospitals. Indeed clinicians have a better insight into the additional information of exercise performed at home and manage the treatment process with better control and efficiency with better measurement records of patients, advises as well as appointment invitation to keep the treatment process planned and structured. Another advantage of the system is clinician evaluation with less subjectivity and misjudgement. As future work, more experiments with larger group of subjects will be conducted to extensively examine the reliability of the system to ensure the best healthcare service being delivered.

References

1. Armbrust, M., Fox, A., Griffith, R., Joseph, A.D., Katz, R., Konwinski, A., Lee, G., Patterson, D., Rabkin, A., Stoica, I., Zaharia, M.: Above the Clouds : A Berkeley View of Cloud Computing Cloud Computing : An Old Idea Whose Time Has (Finally) Come. Computing **53**, 07–013 (2009)
2. Armbrust, M., Stoica, I., Zaharia, M., Fox, A., Griffith, R., Joseph, A.D., Katz, R., Konwinski, A., Lee, G., Patterson, D., Rabkin, A.: A view of cloud computing (2010)
3. Burns, R.B., Crislip, D., Daviou, P., Temkin, A., Vesmarovich, S., Anshutz, J., Furbish, C., Jones, M.L.: Using telerehabilitation to support assistive technology. Assistive Technology : The Official Journal of RESNA **10**, 126–133 (1998)
4. Clark, P.G., Dawson, S.J., Scheideman-Miller, C., Post, M.: TeleRehab: Stroke teletherapy and management using two-way interactive video. Journal of Neurologic Physical Therapy **26**, 87–93 (2002)
5. Cobos, S., Ferre, M., Sanchez Uran, M., Ortego, J., Pena, C.: Efficient human hand kinematics for manipulation tasks. In: 2008 IEEE/RSJ International Conference on Intelligent Robots and Systems, pp. 2246–2251. IEEE, September 2008
6. Ellis, B., Bruton, A.: A study to compare the reliability of composite finger flexion with goniometry for measurement of range of motion in the hand. Clinical Rehabilitation **16**(5), 562–570 (2002)
7. González-Ortega, D., Díaz-Pernas, F.J., Martínez-Zarzuela, M., Antón-Rodríguez, M.: A Kinect-based system for cognitive rehabilitation exercises monitoring. Computer Methods and Programs in Biomedicine **113**, 620–631 (2014)

8. Hume, M.C., Gellman, H., McKellop, H., Brumfield, R.H.: Functional range of motion of the joints of the hand. The Journal of Hand Surgery **15**(2), 240–243 (1990)
9. Kuch, J., Huang, T.: Human computer interaction via the human hand: a hand model. In: Proceedings of 1994 28th Asilomar Conference on Signals, Systems and Computers, vol. 2, pp. 1252–1256. IEEE Comput. Soc. Press (1994)
10. Liu, L., Miyazaki, M.: Telerehabilitation at the University of Alberta. Journal of Telemedicine and Telecare **6**(Suppl 2), S47–S49 (2000)
11. Marx, R., Bombardier, C., Wright, J.: What do we know about the reliability and validity of physical examination tests used to examine the upper extremity? The Journal of Hand Surgery (1999)
12. Melax, S., Keselman, L., Orsten, S.: Dynamics based 3D skeletal hand tracking. In: Proceedings of the ACM SIGGRAPH Symposium on Interactive 3D Graphics and Games - I3D 2013, p. 184. ACM Press, New York, New York, USA (2013)
13. Metcalf, C.D., Robinson, R., Malpass, A.J., Bogle, T.P., Dell, T.A., Harris, C., Demain, S.H.: Markerless motion capture and measurement of hand kinematics: validation and application to home-based upper limb rehabilitation. EEE Transactions on Bio-medical Engineering **60**(8), 2184–2192 (2013)
14. Pham, H.T., Kim, J.J., Won, Y.G.: A Low Cost System for 3D Motion Analysis Using Microsoft Kinect. Applied Mechanics and Materials **284–287**, 1996–2000 (2013)
15. Pham, H.T., Pathirana, P.N., Member, S., Caelli, T., Ieee, F.: Functional Range of Movement of the Hand : Declination Angles to Reachable Space, pp. 6230–6233 (2014)
16. Popescu, V.G., Burdea, G.C., Bouzit, M., Hentz, V.R.: A virtual-reality-based telerehabilitation system with force feedback. IEEE Transactions on Information Technology in Biomedicine : A Publication of the IEEE Engineering in Medicine and Biology Society **4**, 45–51 (2000)
17. Reese, N., Bandy, W.: Joint range of motion and muscle length testing. Saunders (2009)
18. Reinkensmeyer, D.J., Pang, C.T., Nessler, J.A., Painter, C.C.: Web-based telerehabilitation for the upper extremity after stroke. IEEE Transactions on Neural Systems and Rehabilitation Engineering **10**, 102–108 (2002)
19. Russell, T.G., Jull, G.A., Wootton, R.: The diagnostic reliability of Internet-based observational kinematic gait analysis. Tech. rep. (2003)
20. Simonsen, D., Hansen, J., Spaich, E., Andersen, O.S.: Kinect-based telerehabilitation system for hand function. In: Jensen, W., Andersen, O.K.S., Akay, M. (eds.) Replace, Repair, Restore, Relieve Bridging Clinical and Engineering Solutions in Neurorehabilitation SE - 122, Biosystems & Biorobotics, vol. 7, pp. 871–872. Springer International Publishing (2014)
21. Simonsen, D., Irani, R., Nasrollahi, K., Hansen, J., Spaich, E., Moeslund, T., Andersen, O.S.: Validation and test of a closed-loop tele-rehabilitation system based on functional electrical stimulation and computer vision for analysing facial expressions in stroke patients. In: Jensen, W., Andersen, O.K.S., Akay, M. (eds.) Replace, Repair, Restore, Relieve Bridging Clinical and Engineering Solutions in Neurorehabilitation SE - 103, Biosystems & Biorobotics, vol. 7, pp. 741–750. Springer International Publishing (2014)
22. Stam, H.J., Ardon, M.S., den Ouden, A.C., Schreuders, T.A.R., Roebroeck, M.E.: The compangle: a new goniometer for joint angle measurements of the hand. A Technical Note. Europa Medicophysica **42**, 37–40 (2006)

Influencing Factors in the Design of Smart Homes for Persons with Disabilities

Kris Doelling[✉], Jonathan Kretz, and Mike McNair

The University of Texas at Arlington Research Institute (UTARI), Fort Worth, TX 76118, USA
{kdoelling,kretz,mcnairmk}@uta.edu

Abstract. This paper discusses factors that influenced our approach to the design of advanced smart homes for persons with unique disability needs. Our project was formed to address the needs of veterans with disabilities; however we believe the knowledge gained is applicable more broadly to the aging population and other persons with disabilities. In this paper, we discuss components in the smart home design context and key features of our approach. We also identify challenges observed in the design process and offer several recommendations to streamline the process for future initiatives.

Keywords: Smart home · Assistive technology · Robotics · Automation · Disability · Needs assessment

1 Introduction

Several organizations in the U.S. have provided homes at no or low cost to U.S. military service members in recognition of their service and to help meet the needs of the service members and their families. In 2013, the authors contributed to a collaboration with objective to design and construct smart homes for disabled U.S. veterans. A goal for these homes was to push the frontier by including the most advanced architectural and technological features available to help meet needs. This was an ambitious project aimed at developing a scalable, repeatable, and economically extensible design with the intent to correlate the benefits to the aging population and other persons with disabilities.

This paper discusses components in the smart home design context, several key aspects of our approach for the first home, observations of design challenges, and recommendations to streamline the process for future initiatives. Our research is a work in progress.

2 Toward a Holistic Approach

It was quickly recognized that the design effort would require a holistic approach and consideration of numerous factors beyond the immediate home. Figure 1 illustrates a context for some of these considerations.

© Springer International Publishing Switzerland 2015
A. Geissbühler et al. (Eds.): ICOST 2015, LNCS 9102, pp. 295–300, 2015.
DOI: 10.1007/978-3-319-19312-0_25

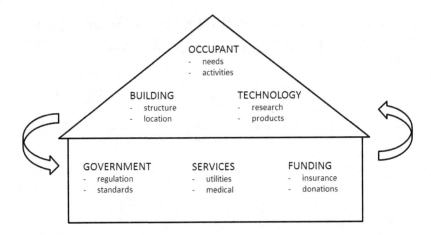

Fig. 1. Key components in the smart home design context

There is an implicit relationship and inherent set of expectations between an occupant and their living environment. For instance, the occupant assumes their home will provide protection from adverse weather conditions. Due to the availability and affordability of technology and services, the occupant also assumes a level of comfort beyond basic shelter. Technology and services, for example, enable control of temperature and provide other conveniences.

Additional factors have direct and indirect influences. As suggested by Figure 1, Government entities, for instance, define a standard of quality and other considerations for home construction, service provision, and technology development. Some applicable regulations are geographically-driven, driving seismic loading requirements for example, while others are imposed through zoning regulations, historic preservation districts, or other stipulations. Regulations drive the development of standards; implementing these standards often influences the home's design and requires funding.

Technologies within the home are often the result of extensive research efforts that culminate in the production of commercial products. These products, like the home they may eventually be included in, may be subject to regulations and clearly require funding for development and production.

2.1 Key Features of the Approach

Our design process involved many technical and non-technical considerations. In this section we discuss a few key features of the initial approach.

Goals and objectives for the home were outlined early in the project and refined as the project progressed. The project aimed to create a home environment that promoted independence, encouraged healing, and enhanced quality of life. Although the design would integrate accessible design features, encompassing barrier free and universal (or inclusive) design practices and state of the art technology, a key focus was an architecturally and aesthetically pleasing design. The finished home would need to feel like a home, rather than a hospital or rehabilitation facility.

The project was tailored to the specific needs of the veterans and their families, incorporating architectural and technological components driven by their expressed needs. The initial home design would address the needs by applying accessible design features as well as sustainable practices. Where design practices alone could not fully meet the needs, the design would integrate assistive technologies. Technologies would be carefully evaluated prior to design integration to maximize usability of the home and avoid unnecessary complexity. As reflected by Dewsbury et al. [1], "technology for technology's sake like inappropriate design can be debilitating and disempowering."

A multi-disciplinary collaborative team supported the project. The candidate for the home was informed of selection for the home early in the process. This was done intentionally to include the veteran, their family, caregivers, clinicians, and other experts who could advise on the candidate's and other stakeholders' specific needs in the design process.

Understanding the needs of the occupant was of primary importance. This included not only identifying and understanding any disability needs and its effect, but, among other considerations, how the person perceived assistive options and the reaction of others to those options. For example, a mobility impaired person may find a powered wheelchair an acceptable solution while someone else may wish to use a wearable exoskeleton. Some persons wish to have a solution remain as inconspicuous as possible, while others relish the obvious use and display of technology innovation. Interviews with the occupant, knowledge of the disability, consultation with family and caregivers, and other tools and assessments help provide insight for selecting and tailoring potential solutions.

As needs were identified and understood, we found it important to understand the range of technological and architectural options. We did not find a current or comprehensive repository of potential options; as such, we began constructing our own. Having this information available and current helped provide a concrete means of discussing and exploring solutions.

In the course of our project, we found it useful to segregate options into three categories as identified below:

Category 1: Commercial-Off-The-Shelf (COTS) technology. Some examples of this category may include refrigerators, ovens, home automation and security systems, robotic systems such as robotic vacuum cleaners, and assistive solutions such as automated shelving and transfer aids.

Category 2: Near-term future technology - products less than 2 years from product launch. Whether this references existing products with new capability or new products, the near-term commercialization potential is recognized.

Category 3: Future technology more than 2 years from product launch, possibly in research and early development. Examples of such technology may be known through product roadmaps, announcements at technology trade shows, or other venues.

We learned that understanding the solution space required a multi-disciplinary and inclusive approach. Including clinicians, technology experts, family members and others helped to provide an understanding of the range of possible solutions.

Additionally, we solicited involvement from foundations, charitable organizations, product and service providers, and others, through special events, mailings, personal contacts, and other avenues.

2.2   Observations and Recommendations

In this section, we discuss several challenges observed in the design process and offer recommendations that may help streamline the process for future initiatives.

A wide variety of architectural and technological options are available and may become available that could benefit persons with disabilities. We observed that information about these options today, however, is very fragmented. As a result, it could be difficult for designers, clinicians, persons with disabilities, caregivers, and others to readily identify the range of available and emerging options and assess the option's maturity along with other important factors. Understanding available international options may additionally be challenging due to factors such as language differences and international regulations. Due to these and other considerations, many people today may not be aware of the range of available and emerging options.

Advancing resources to help designers, clinicians, persons with disabilities, caregivers, and others more readily identify and assess the range of options could facilitate the design process and implementation of successful solutions. We suggest that to maximize the effectiveness, resources should include means to readily keep the information up to date with rapid and global advancements.

We observed that persons and groups designing and building assistive homes are gaining valuable knowledge as a result of their experiences. Additionally, end users, clinicians, caregivers, and others using and/or observing the use of assistive options, are gaining valuable insight into the effectiveness of the options. Advancing means to facilitate and improve the ability to capture and share knowledge gained could additionally be helpful.

We noted that understanding the range and type of potential options for assistances with costs may be challenging. Options may be self-paid, partially self-paid, or provided by others. Organizations that may provide assistances include insurances, foundations, and service providers. As part of our efforts, we found people and organizations with interests in donating funds, products, services, and other resources. It was our observation that some of these groups were difficult to find and some did not seem to connect, as there did not appear to be a ready conduit to identify and connect them.

We also noted differences in eligibility criteria for assistances, approval processes, and types of assistances among the various providing organizations. We noted that criteria and processes for some organizations were more complex than others.

Some organizations, for example, may provide assistance with specific types of architectural and technological options. Some options may require physician or other approvals. Assistances may not be provided until an option has achieved a certain stage of maturity and been approved through the organization's processes. Options may be reimbursed but assistance with related costs, such as upgrades and maintenance, may be limited. In addition, assistances could be limited or not available for some options, such as technologies that enable persons to continue some types of hobbies.

The design process and use of options could be facilitated by advancing means to help persons more readily identify and understand options for assistances with costs, eligibility criteria for these assistances, and processes for application and approval. Further development of means to help people and organizations who want to provide assistances find each other and recipients who may benefit could also be helpful.

Further, we suggest that advancement of resources to help people more readily understand the potential need for assistive options and potential associated costs as people age, with illness, or other factors, may be helpful. We observed that many homes today are not designed for persons with disabilities. We additionally note that homes with features to assist persons with disabilities may not always meet the need.

An occupant of a home may experience a disability due to age, illness, injury or other factors. Occupants may additionally care for children, elderly persons, or others with a disability in the home. Important questions could arise when architectural and technological changes to the home may be beneficial. As the prevalence of disability and potential need for assistance increases with age [2], these questions may become increasingly important over time. Further advancement of tools and resources which help people include these considerations in their life and retirement planning may be beneficial.

We suggest that processes could be facilitated by bringing together involved groups. These groups may include, among others: home building organizations, technology experts, clinicians, and parties with interests in providing funds, products, and services. Centralizing the organization may help:

- Provide a multi-disciplinary collaborative platform for design and development
- Facilitate sharing of knowledge gained and best practices
- Identify expertise
- Provide resources that help with understandings of technology advancements and trends
- Identify and facilitate collaboration between various persons and organizations with interests in providing funds, products, and services
- Assist stakeholders in more readily understanding available resources and the range of options

3   Conclusions

This paper discusses aspects of our smart home design approach for persons with unique disability needs, observations of design challenges, and recommendations to streamline the process for future initiatives.

The project aimed to create a home environment that promoted independence, encouraged healing, and enhanced quality of life. We noted that long term success required a holistic approach, taking into consideration the viewpoints of the stakeholders as part of an integrated team.

We encountered challenges along the way. Stakeholders need information in order to make informed decisions and find effective solutions. There is a clear need to advance tools and resources to assist with identification and assessment of options and costs. Cost is typically a significant constraint and must be taken into consideration as solutions are developed. Donations, subsidies, insurance, and other funding sources may help to ease the cost impact. All of these factors point to the need for increased awareness and action among the stakeholders.

Smart homes can make a difference - not just in conveniences they embody, but also for the potential benefit to persons who are disabled and/or elderly. Successful implementation will be a combined and integrated effort with great potential reward as we seek to improve quality of life.

Acknowledgement. The authors would like to extend a special thanks to Janey Carman at H-E-B for sharing her architectural and accessible design insights and offering many helpful comments on this paper.

References

1. Dewsbury, G., Taylor B., Edge, M.: The process of designing appropriate smart homes: including the user in the design. In: Equator IRC Workshop on Ubiquitous Computing in Domestic Environments, pp. 131–146. University of Nottingham, UK (2001)
2. Brault, M.: Americans with Disabilities: 2010 Household Economic Studies. Publication P70–131. U.S. Census Bureau (July 2012). http://www.census.gov/prod/2012pubs/p70-131.pdf

Multimodal Recognition of Emotions Using Physiological Signals with the Method of Decision-Level Fusion for Healthcare Applications

Chaka Koné[1(✉)], Imen Meftah Tayari[2], Nhan Le-Thanh[3], and Cecile Belleudy[1]

[1] University of Nice Sophia Antipolis, LEAT Laboratory CNRS UMR 7248,
Sophia Antipolis, France
{chaka.kone, Cecile.belleudy}@unice.fr
[2] REGIM Laboratory, University of Sfax, Sfax, Tunisia
imentayari@gmail.com
[3] University of Nice Sophia Antipolis, I3S Laboratory CNRS UMR 7271,
Sophia Antipolis, France
nhan.le-thanh@unice.fr

Abstract. Automatic emotion recognition enhance dramatically the development of human/machine dialogue. Indeed, it allows computers to determine the emotion felt by the user and adapt consequently its behavior. This paper presents a new method for the fusion of signals for the purpose of a multimodal recognition of eight basic emotions using physiological signals. After a learning phase where an emotion data base is constructed, we apply the recognition algorithm on each modality separately. Then, we merge all these decisions separately by applying a decision fusion approach to improve recognition rate. The experiments show that the proposed method allows high accuracy emotion recognition. Indeed we get a recognition rate of **81.69%** under some conditions.

Keywords: Signal fusion method · Basic emotions · Multimodal detection · Physiological signals

1 Introduction

Historically, emotions have had a great impact on our behavior, our feelings and we are constantly trying to manage our emotions as well as the people that surround us, in order to live together in harmony. Indeed emotions enable us to communicate with our environment but also to adapt, innovate, succeed, and to flourish. A lot of research based on video application or speech analysis [9], [10] (EMOTIENT, Eurospeech, Nice Speech) has emerged to analyze emotions, with the aim amongst other, to provide a real-time, aggregate view of users feelings and in general to identify customer dissatisfaction. The solution proposed in this article targets the healthcare domain in that it monitors biological signals, but in a non-intrusive manner for the benefit of patients. In the future, emotion detection tests will be very challenging because they

© Springer International Publishing Switzerland 2015
A. Geissbühler et al. (Eds.): ICOST 2015, LNCS 9102, pp. 301–306, 2015.
DOI: 10.1007/978-3-319-19312-0_26

constitute a key point to analyze the impact of all medical treatments, and the resulting device market will probably be substantial. Indeed, new technologies benefiting people's health have emerged and have allowed, for example, developing the bases of affective computing, defined by Rosalind Picard in 1995 [8], [17].

Our goal is to collect the physiological signals of a person under different conditions of real life to detect emotions automatically. We propose a method for a multimodal detection of emotions using physiological signals. The paper is structured as follows. In section 1, a brief state of the art on the multimodal recognition of emotions and different methods to merge signals are shown. In section 2, all the steps of the proposed methods are explained in details; later on in section 3, a comparison between obtained results of the state of the art and ours is highlighted; finally, conclusion and future work are reported in section 4.

2   State of the Art

Many works were focused on the detection of emotions using facial expressions, vocal expressions or physiological signals [14], [15], [16]; however fewer studies are focused on the multimodal recognition [2] of emotions. The use of a multimodal approach allows not only enhancing the recognition rate but it gives more strength to the system when one of these modalities is acquired in a noisy environment [3]. In theory, there are three methods [12] to merge the signals from various sensors.

↓ **Fusion of signals [4]:** It is directly performed on raw data from each physiological signal sensors; it can be applied only when signals are similar in nature and have the same temporal resolution. This technique is therefore rarely used on account of the difficulty of merging the different signals and the noise due to the sensor's sensitivity.

↓ **Fusion of features [5], [6], [7]:** This fusion method that is most often used aims at forming a multimodal vector from features vectors extracted for each sensor. MIT's hybrid method SFFS-FP (Sequential floating forward search - Fisher projection) allowed to have an **83%** recognition rate. Nevertheless, the SFFS-FP method allows to determine emotions during a fixed time interval. Unlike MIT's method that does not permit an instantaneous detection of emotions, our method allows automatic and instantaneous detection of emotions. In the following section, we focus our study on the instantaneous detection of emotions.

↓ **Fusion of decisions** [4], [5]**:** After having classified separately from each sensor signals, we merge these different decisions in order to obtain a global vision of the emotion. Unlike features level fusion, this fusion technique is independent of the nature of the low level features used for decision making [4].

3   Methodology

A   Learning phase

This phase consists of four steps (signal splitting, filtering, feature extraction, creation of the basis for learning) in order to provide a learning base which will then be used in the detection phase for the automatic detection of emotions.

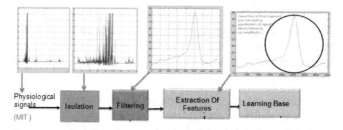

Fig. 1. Synoptic of the learning phase

⁙ In the signal splitting step, after having acquired the physiological signal (here we use the physiological signals provided by MIT). We isolate the part of the signal corresponding to a given emotion because we have information on the period in which each of the eight emotions is expressed. Therefore, this step divides the input signal into eight portions of signal corresponding to eight emotions.

⁙ After having isolated the signal, we filter it to remove the noise of the useful signal, which will facilitate the extraction of the features. This method is less computationally expensive in calculations.

⁙ For each isolated and filtered signal, we proceed to the detection of peaks, which is done by calculating the gradient of the signal and then finding the sign changes in the gradient. Once a peak is isolated, we calculate a feature vector composed of five features.

⁙ After extraction of the features vectors, we create a learning base for each modality. 40% of the signals available for each modality were used for the creation of the learning base and the remaining 60% were used for detection (test).

B   Detection Phase

Our research is based on Imen method [8], she has developed a new vector method to represent emotions. Therefore, each emotion is written as a linear combination of the 8 basic emotions we considered. Indeed, each emotion e can be written as:

$$(e) = a1 * (\text{No emotion}) + a2 * \text{Anger} + \cdots + a8 * \text{veneration} \qquad (1)$$

Where (a1, a2... a8) are the probabilities of the feature vector extracted belonging to each emotional class of our base. This phase consists of two steps. The first step consists in the extraction of features, requiring the same steps as in the learning phase, without going through the splitting step since in this phase. The remainder of our process will be based on this features extraction step that means while before pass to classification step, detecting an emotional activity (peak detection) is necessary. Indeed, thanks to this condition on the necessity of detecting an emotional activity, our method allows an instantaneous recognition of emotions. The second step is classification, the purpose of which is to predict the emotional class of the features vector extracted using our learning base, which was developed in the learning phase. We opted for the classification using the K-nearest neighbors (KNN) algorithm.

This allows determining the K nearest emotions in our database of extracted feature vector. Studies in [8] have allowed to determine the optimal value of K = 10 and the size of the Hanning window **n = 500** which enable better detection.

a.   Fusion method of signals through voting: In this section, we studied 2 voting techniques of formalisms:

- The first technique consists in constituting a matrix made up of the emotional vectors for each modality. We calculate a vector average from which we choose the most probable emotional class. This technique is a better measurement of the center around which the values of the probabilities of each emotional class for each modality tend to concentrate. However, it does not allow a detection of the most probable emotional classes.
- In the second approach, starting from each monomodal vector, we take the most probable emotional class. Thus, we will have as many decisions as there are modalities. The final decision will be the class having been decided by the maximum of modalities. This allows one side to take the most probable partial decisions for each modality, and on the other hand it allows a measure of the central tendency as in the first technique. We opted for this technique on account of the two advantages that we have just enunciated.

Our objective being thereafter to put these algorithms in mobile devices which do not have a great memory size, it is thus necessary to set up simple algorithms. That is the reason why we chose this fusion approach on the decisions level.

4   Results

For these results, we use as data base the signals provided by the MIT. This physiological data collection, the process of which is well described in [1], was carried out on an actor during 32 days for a period of 25 minutes per day, with a sampling frequency of 20 Hz. For this collection, four physiological sensors were used: sensor for the blood volume and pulse (BVP), the respiration (RESP), the electromyography (EMG) and the galvanic skin response (GSR). During this collection, eight emotions were taken into account. The results obtained by our algorithm when the unimodal recognition of emotions approach is used are grouped on the histogram below. This approach allows having a mean recognition rate of **57.24%**.

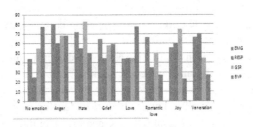

Fig. 2. Monomodal recognition rate

As observed in the above figure, certain emotions are better detected with certain modalities than others. This characteristic of modalities is very important because it will allow putting weight on each of the modalities, depending on whether it can better detect an emotion or not for the purpose of a more efficient detection. Subsequently, we have expanded our method to the multimodal approach to increase the emotion recognition rate. Indeed, this multimodal approach allowed having a recognition rate of **81.69%**, which is a considerable improvement of the recognition rate compared to the unimodal approach which presented a recognition rate of **57.24%**.

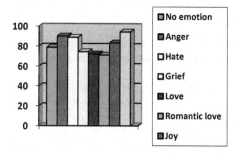

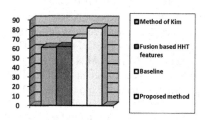

Fig. 3. Multimodal approach result   **Fig. 4.** Comparison of results

We note that in figure 3, our method allows to detect each of the eight emotions with a good recognition rate, where the minimum of 71.18% is obtained for the emotion "Romantic Love". The figure 4 allows doing a comparison between our results and the different results of the methods of the state of the art that allow an instantaneous detection of emotions. The method we have proposed presented a better rate of correct classification of emotions than all the other methods found in the above table.

5   Conclusion and Perspectives

We have developed a novel method of multimodal recognition of emotions based on the processing of physiological signals. The physiological signals of 4 modalities were used for the recognition of 8 basic emotions. A new method for multimodal recognition based on the fusion decision level has been defined and developed. The different results show a marked improvement in the recognition rate of emotions.

In our future work, we will study physiological signals acquisition platforms in order to generate our own recognition base and on the other hand set up a complete system from the acquisition of physiological signals for emotions detection. Moreover this system will allow creating more appropriate recognition base for a wide range of people.

References

1. Healey, J.: Wearable and automative systems for a affect recognition from physiology, these doctorale MIT soumis le 18 Mai 2000
2. Sebe, N., Bakker, E., Cohen, I.: Theo Gevers et Thomas Huang. Bimodal Emotion Recognition (2005)
3. Shan, Shaogang Gong, Peter, W.: McOwan : Facial expression recognition based on Local Binary Patterns: A comprehensive study Caifeng. Image and Vision Computing 27, 803–816 (2009)
4. Hamdi, H.: Plate-forme multimodale pour la reconnaissance d'émotions via l'analyse de signaux physiologiques : Application à la simulation d'entretiens d'embauche. Modeling and Simulation. Université d'Angers. French. <tel-00997249> (2012)
5. Sharma, R., Pavlovic, V.I., Huang, T.S.: Toward multimodal human-computer interface. Proceedings of the IEEE 86(5), 853–869. 29, 30, 32, 167 (1998)
6. Noureddine Aboutabit. Reconnaissance de la Langue Française Parlée Complété (LPC) : décodage phonétique des gestes main-lèvres.. domain stic. Institut National Polytechnique de Grenoble - INPG. French (2007)
7. Zhi, Q., Kaynak, M.N., Sengupta, K., Cheok, A.D., Ko, C.C.: Hmm modeling for audio-visual speech recognition. In: Proceedings of the IEEE International Conference on Multimedia and Expo (ICME 2001), p. 136 (2001)
8. Meftah,I.T.: Modélisation, détection et annotation des états émotionnels à l'aide d'un espace vectoriel multidimensionnel. Artificial Intelligence. Université Nice Sophia Antipolis. French. <NNT : 2013NICE4017>. <tel-00908233> (2013)
9. Park, Hyung-Bum, Han, Ji-Eun, Hyun, Joo-Seok: You may look unhappy unless you smile: The distinctiveness of a smiling face against faces without an explicit smile. Acta Psychologica 157, 185 (2015)
10. Busso, S.L., Narayanan, S.: Analysis of Emotionally Salient Aspects of Fundamental Frequency for Emotion Detection in IEEE transactions on audio, speech and language processing vol 17 n°4, 4 Mai 2009
11. Kim,K.H., Bang, S.W., Kim, S.R.: Emotion recognition system using short-term monitoring of physiological signals in medical & biological engineering and computing 2004, vol 42, pp. 419–427, 17 February 2004
12. Wagner,J., Andre, E., Lingenfelser, F., Kim, J.: Exploring fusion methods for multimodal emotion recognition with missing data in Affective computing IEEE Transactions on vol 2, issue 4, pp. 206–218, 12 January 2012
13. Zong, C., Chetouani, M.: Hilbert Huang transform based Physiological signals analysis for emotion recognition. In: 2009 IEEE International Symposium on Signal Processing and Information Technology(ISSPIT), pp. 334–33, 14 Decembre 2009
14. Monte-Moreno, E., Chetouani, M., Faundez-Zanuy, M., SoleCasals, J.: Maximum likelihood linear programming data fusion for speaker recognition. Speech Communication 51(9):820–830. 68 (2009)
15. Mahdhaoui, A., Chetouani, M.: Emotional speech classification based on multi view characterization. In: IAPR International Conference on Pattern Recognition, ICPR. 51 (2010)
16. Mahdhaoui, A.: Analyse de Signaux Sociaux pour la Modelisation de l'interaction face à face.Signal and Image processing. Université Pierre et Marie Curie - Paris VI. French. <tel-00587051> (2010)
17. Meftah1, I.T., Le Thanh, N., Amar, C.B.: Detecting depression using a multidimensional model of emotional states: Global Health 2012: The First International Conference On Global Health Challenges

Feature Sub-set Selection
for Activity Recognition

Francisco J. Quesada[1]([⊠]), Francisco Moya[1], Macarena Espinilla[1],
Luis Martínez[1], and Chris D. Nugent[2]

[1] Department of Computer Science, University of Jaén, Jaén, Spain
{fqreal,fpmoya,mestevez,martin}@ujaen.es
[2] School of Computing and Mathematics,University of Ulster, Jordanstown,
Coleraine BT37 0QB, UK
cd.nugent@ulster.ac.uk

Abstract. The delivery of Ambient Assisted Living services, specifically relating to the smart-home paradigm, assumes that people can be provided with help, automatically and in real time, in their homes as and when required. Nevertheless, the deployment of a smart-home can lead to high levels of expense due to configuration requirements of multiple sensing and actuating technology. In addition, the vast amount of data produced leads to increased levels of computational complexity when trying to ascertain the underlying behavior of the inhabitant. This contribution presents a methodology based on feature selection which aims to reduce the number of sensors required whilst still maintaining acceptable levels of activity recognition performance. To do so, a smart-home dataset has been utilized, obtaining a configuration of sensors with the half sensors with respect to the original configuration.

Keywords: Activity recognition · Smart-homes · Feature selection

1 Introduction

The knock-on effects on ageing in society have now become widely appreciated. Health services, pension services and informal care provision are all experiencing increased levels of burden. A key focus, from a research perspective, has subsequently been identified in the area of healthy ageing and wellbeing with goal to deliver services which extend the period of time older persons can remain in their own homes.

One of the most common diseases within this cohort are cognitive related such as dementia. These illnesses are currently incurable, hence efforts are focused towards delaying their progression. In the early stages of dementia, it is useful to provide support in the form of prompting through the completion of activities of daily living (ADL) in addition to offering a series of reminders for tasks such as medication management, eating and grooming.

The advance in the miniaturization of electronic devices in addition to a reduction in their cost, has created an environment whereby we are surrounded

© Springer International Publishing Switzerland 2015
A. Geissbühler et al. (Eds.): ICOST 2015, LNCS 9102, pp. 307–312, 2015.
DOI: 10.1007/978-3-319-19312-0_27

by embedded sensing technology. Ambient Intelligence (AmI) characterizes a vision where humans are surrounded by computers [1]. The notion of a smart-home follows this vision with an environment of embedded technology and processing units with the ability to ascertain the behavior of its inhabitants.

At the core of this paradigm is the process of *Activity Recognition (AR)*, which gleans data from sensors embedded within the environment. Its main aim is to identify the different actions and/or activities which are taking place at that particular moment in time. Once the process recognizes the underlying activity automated assistance, in for example the form of a prompt or warning can be delivered through the smart environment itself.

Although there has been significant progress within the domain with promising results offer improvements in quality of life, it still remains expensive to deploy a full configuration of sensors within the home environment. For this reason, it is important to know which type of sensors and in which configuration are essential to detect the key ADLs. Thus, optimizing the configuration of sensors has the benefit to reduce costs from a technology perspective whilst having the additional benefit of reducing computational complexity.

In this work we focus on identifying an optimal set of sensors capable of detecting an inhabitants ADLs without a reduction in performance of the process of AR.

The remainder of the paper is structured as follows: in Section 2, the basic concepts of feature selection are reviewed. Section 3 presents the proposed methodology and a case study is presented in Section 4. The paper concludes with a Summary in Section 5.

2   Feature Selection

It is difficult to know, *a priori*, the relevant features which should be considered in a classification problem. It is therefore usual to gather information from multiple sources each having many features, in an effort to represent the domain as best as possible. Such an approach produces redundant or irrelevant information [2]. In addition it has the effect of increasing the size of the dataset to be processed hence increasing the computational complexity and potentially hindering the learning processes and generalization capabilities of the classifier.

Reducing the number of irrelevant or redundant features, clearly improves the time taken to deploy a learning algorithm and assists in obtaining a better insight into the concept of the underlying classification problem [3]. Thus, *Feature selection* methods aim to select a subset of relevant features to reduce the dimensionality of the classification problem without having a negative impact on classification accuracy. So, feature selection attempts to select the minimally sized subset of features according to the following criteria [4]: i) the classification accuracy does not significantly decrease; ii) the resulting class distribution, given only the values for the selected features, is as close as possible to the original class distribution, given all features.

Dash and Liu categorized the two major steps of feature selection as being the generation procedure and the evaluation function [4]:

1. **Generation Procedure** The total number of competing candidate sub-sets to be generated is 2^N if the original feature set contains N number of features. There are different approaches for solving this problem:
   - *Complete* that carries out an exhaustive search for the optimal subset according to the evaluation function used.
   - *Heuristic* in which each iteration all remaining features yet to be selected (rejected) are considered for selection (rejection).
   - *Random* that sets a maximum number of possible iterations and usually search fewer number of subsets than 2^N.

2. **Evaluation Functions** Normally, an evaluation function attempts to measure the discriminating ability of a feature or a subset to distinguish the different class labels. There are several types of evaluation functions:
   - *Distance Measures* have the idea that in a two-class problem, the most preferred features are those which induce a higher difference between the conditional probabilities of two classes. An example of this type of measure is the Euclidean distance measure.
   - *Information Measures* are based on the information gain. A feature is preferred to another if the information gain from the first feature is higher than the second.
   - *Dependence Measures* in which a feature is preferred to another if the correlation between the feature with a class is higher than the correlation between another feature and the same class.
   - *Consistency Measures* that deal with to find out the minimally sized subset that satisfies the tolerable inconsistency rate, that is normally set by the user.
   - *Classifier Error Rate Measures* that depend on the classifier itself in order to perform the feature selection.

3   Sensor-Based AR Optimisation

In this Section the method used in the current study to optimize the configuration of sensors within a smart environment to improve AR performance is presented. The motivation to reduce the number of sensors is two fold: firstly to reduce costs from a technology perspective and second to reduce the computational complexity of the AR process.

First of all, it is necessary to clarify that the AR method to be consider is sensor-based and data-driven [5]. Under the premise, the assumption is that a sensor network will generate an interpretable dataset, which is then used as the source to apply data mining and machine learning algorithms to recognise the activities that have been recorded in the dataset.

In this contribution it is proposed a method, which initially applies feature selection and subsequently the process of AR. Regarding the data-driven activity recognition, this proposal adds a pre-processing phase which applies feature selection to the original dataset. This pre-processing aims to remove all sensors that are irrelevant or redundant, hence avoiding unnecessary data. Once it is generated the sensor-reduced dataset, it is applied the activity recognition procedure as in the general scheme, generating the results of the process.

The application of feature selection techniques, has a knock-on effects with the process of AR. This is due to the fact that depending on the characteristics of the data there are some algorithms which are more appropriate than others.

The most popular classifiers for AR have been described by Wu et al. describe in [6] and include Naive Bayes (NB) [7], Support Vector Machines (SVMs) [8] and Nearest Neighbor (NN) [9].

4   Case Study

This Section details the dataset used in the current study and the effects of the feature selection on the overall accuracy of the AR process.

4.1   Activity Recognition Dataset

The case study presented in this contribution is based on a popular activity recognition dataset [10]. The dataset was collected in the house in which 14 state-change sensors were installed. Each sensors had the ability to provide two possible discrete values: 1 and 0, representing ON and OFF, respectively. Locations of sensors where on the doors of the apartment, cupboards, refrigerator and a toilet flush sensor. Seven different activities were annotated.

4.2   Applying Feature Selection

We have applied feature selection using Weka[11]. In practice, the way to apply feature selection is combining a generation procedure and an evaluated function as outlined in Section 2.

In the current work a complete generation method, specifically *Exhaustive Search*[12] has been used. This generation method produces an optimal result instead of the considerable computational cost.

Regarding the evaluation functions, *Dependence* and *Consistency Measures*, were used generating one dataset from each function. We have used the dependence function *CFsSubSetEval*[12], given that it produces a minimum subset of sensors and a high correlation with the class to be classified. Furthermore, the consistency function that we have used is *ConsistencySubSetEval*[12], because this evaluator seeks the smallest subset with a consistency that is equal or less as the consistency of the full attribute set.

Thus, applying the *Exhaustive Search* and the *ConsistencySubsetEval*, 10-sensors dataset was produced and, applying the *Exhaustive Search* and *CfsSubsetEval*, it is produced a 7-sensors dataset.

4.3   Classification Algorithms, Results and Discussion

A set of test were run using some popular classifiers used for AR. Among them, we used NB, SVMs and NN classifiers as reference methods (refer to Section 3). Apart from that, there are also used R+DRAH [13] and Decision Table (DT)[14] were also considered, given these algorithms have been previously used to perform a process which reduces the number of sensors[15].

To evaluate the classifiers' performance in different situations, we have executed with a 10 fold Cross-Validation the original dataset (14 sensors) as well as the two datasets resulting from the two optimizations: the dataset with 10 sensors and the dataset with 7 sensors. The obtained results are presented in Table 1.

We can see how SVM has the highest level of accuracy with the full range of sensors. Nevertheless, in the case of the 7 sensor dataset, the highest level of classification was achieved for the R+DRAH. The approaches based on NN, DT and R+DRAH improved their rates regarding the 10 sensors configuration. This improvement is caused by cutting of the sensors that produce irrelevant or redundant information, which act as noise, confusing the classifier.

Table 1. Results following 10 fold Cross-validation

Method	Original Dataset %	10 Sensor Dataset %	7 Sensor Dataset %
NB	96.33	96.33	95.51
NN(k=10)	94.69	92.65	93.88
DT	95.51	94.69	95.92
SVM	**96.73**	**97.14**	95.1
R+DRAH	93.47	95.51	**98.37**

5   Concluding Remarks

This contribution presents a method to optimize the number of sensors required to inform the process of activity recognition in a smart environment. Applying this technique, the number of sensors was reduced, however the level of accuracy in the process of AR was maintained. This approach therefore provides a potential reduction in cost from a technology perspective and secondly reduces the computational complexity of the AR process. Regarding future works, we aim to focus on the classification with unbalanced datasets, in order to know how unbalanced data affects the process of AR.

Acknowledgments. This contribution was supported by Research Projects TIN-2012-31263, ERDF and CEATIC-2013-001. Invest Northern Ireland is acknowledge for partially supporting this project under the Competence Centre Program Grant RD0513853 - Connected Health Innovation Centre.

References

1. Streitz, N., Nixon, P.: The disappearing computer. Communications of the ACM **48**(3), 32–35 (2005)
2. John, G.H., Kohavi, R., Pfleger, K., et al.: Irrelevant features and the subset selection problem. ICML **94**, 121–129 (1994)
3. Koller, D., Sahami, M.: Toward optimal feature selection. Stanford InfoLab (1996)
4. Dash, M., Liu, H.: Feature selection for classification. Intelligent data analysis **1**(3), 131–156 (1997)
5. Chen, L., Hoey, J., Nugent, C.D., Cook, D.J., Yu, Z.: Sensor-based activity recognition. IEEE Transactions on Systems, Man, and Cybernetics, Part C: Applications and Reviews **42**(6), 790–808 (2012)
6. Wu, X., Kumar, V., Quinlan, J.R., Ghosh, J., Yang, Q., Motoda, H., McLachlan, G.J., Ng, A., Liu, B., Philip, S.Y., et al.: Top 10 algorithms in data mining. Knowledge and Information Systems **14**(1), 1–37 (2008)
7. van Kasteren, T., Krose, B.: Bayesian activity recognition in residence for elders. IET (2007)
8. Vapnik, V.: The nature of statistical learning theory. Springer Science & Business Media (2000)
9. Cherkassky, V., Mulier, F.M.: Learning from data: concepts, theory, and methods. John Wiley & Sons (2007)
10. Van Kasteren, T., Noulas, A., Englebienne, G., Kröse, B.: Accurate activity recognition in a home setting. In: Proceedings of the 10th International Conference on Ubiquitous Computing, pp. 1–9. ACM (2008)
11. Hall, M., Frank, E., Holmes, G., Pfahringer, B., Reutemann, P., Witten, I.H.: The weka data mining software: an update. ACM SIGKDD explorations newsletter **11**(1), 10–18 (2009)
12. Hall, M., Witten, I., Frank, E.: Data mining: Practical machine learning tools and techniques. Kaufmann, Burlington (2011)
13. Calzada, A., Liu, J., Wang, H., Kashyap, A.: Dynamic rule activation for extended belief rule bases. In: International Conference on Machine Learning and Cybernetics (ICMLC), vol. 4, pp. 1836–1841. IEEE (2013)
14. Kohavi, R., Sommerfield, D.: Feature subset selection using the wrapper method: Overfitting and dynamic search space topology. In: KDD, pp. 192–197 (1995)
15. Calzada, A., Liu, J., Nugent, C., Wang, H., Martinez, L.: Sensor-based activity recognition using extended belief rule-based inference methodology. In: 2014 36th Annual International Conference of the IEEE Engineering in Medicine and Biology Society (EMBC), pp. 2694–2697. IEEE (2014)

Reducing the Response Time for Activity Recognition Through use of Prototype Generation Algorithms

Macarena Espinilla[1]([✉]), Francisco J. Quesada[1], Francisco Moya[1],
Luis Martínez[1], and Chris D. Nugent[2]

[1] Computer Sciences Department, University of Jaén,
Campus Las Lagunillas s/n, 23071 Jaén, Spain
{mestevez,fqreal,fpmoya,martin}@ujaen.es
[2] School of Computing and Mathematics, University of Ulster,
Jordanstown, Coleraine BT37 0QB, UK
cd.nugent@ulster.ac.uk

Abstract. The nearest neighbor approach is one of the most successfully deployed techniques used for sensor-based activity recognition. Nevertheless, this approach presents some disadvantages in relation to response time, noise sensitivity and high storage requirements. The response time and storage requirements are closely related to the data size. This notion of data size is an important issue in sensor-based activity recognition given the vast amounts of data produced within smart environments. A wide range of prototype generation algorithms, which are designed for use with the nearest neighbor approach, have been proposed in the literature to reduce the size of the data set. These algorithms build new artificial prototypes, which represent the data, and subsequently lead to an increase in the accuracy of the nearest neighbor approach. In this work, we discuss the use of prototype generation algorithms and their effect on sensor-based activity recognition using the nearest neighbor approach to classify activities; reducing the response time. A range of prototype generation algorithms based on positioning adjustment, which reduce the data size, are evaluated in terms of accuracy and reduction. These approaches have been compared with the normal nearest neighbor approach, achieving similar accuracy and reducing the data size. Analysis of the results attained provide the basis for the use of prototype generation algorithms for sensor-based activity recognition to reduce the overall response time of the nearest neighbor approach.

Keywords: Activity recognition · Data-driven · Nearest Neighbor (NN) · Prototype Generation (PG) · Response time

1 Introduction

Sensor-based activity recognition is an important research topic that involves multiple fields of research including pervasive and mobile computing [1], context-aware computing [2] and ambient assistive living [3].

© Springer International Publishing Switzerland 2015
A. Geissbühler et al. (Eds.): ICOST 2015, LNCS 9102, pp. 313–318, 2015.
DOI: 10.1007/978-3-319-19312-0_28

The process of activity recognition aims to recognise the actions and goals of one or more people within the environment based on an observation series of actions and environmental conditions. Therefore, it can be deemed as a complex process that involves the following steps: i) to choose and deploy the appropriate sensors to objects within the environment in order to effectively monitor and capture a user's behavior along with the state change of the environment; ii) to collect, store and process information and, finally, iii) to infer/classify activities from sensor data through the use of computational activity models.

The k-nearest neighbour (k-NN) approach [4] is a Data-Driven Approach that is used for sensor-based activity recognition. It is considered to be one of the most popular algorithms among all machine learning techniques, mainly due to its simplicity and overall good levels of performance [5]. This approach is based on the concept of similarity due to the fact that patterns which are similar, usually, can be allocated to the same label class. K-NN have been used successfully in the past for the purpose of activity recognition [6].

The k-NN approach does, however, suffer from several shortcomings in response time, noise sensitivity and high storage requirements [7]. The response time and storage requirements are closely related to the size of the data. In the application domain of activity recognition, the size of the data is an issue given the vast amount of sensor data generated within smart environments. In order to take advantage of the main benefits provided by the k-NN approach and to avoid the drawback associated with the size of the datasets, this work proposes to use prototype generation (PG) algorithms to reduce the data size and, as result, reducing the response time in the k-NN approach.

PG algorithms [8] are focused on the identification of an optimal subset of representative samples from the original training data. This is achieved by removing noisy and redundant examples in order to generate and replace the original data with new artificial data [9]. The use of PG algorithms to improve the process of activity recognition can be viewed as an advance given that sensor data can be annotated and used to directly inform the training process. So, training data are increased and, proportionally, the response time. Therefore, a reduction in the number of stored instances, training samples, has the ability to reduce the response time of the k-NN.

Currently, there are a wide range of PG algorithms, which are categorized by the mechanism for prototyping [8]. It is therefore necessary to evaluate which of the available approaches are best suited for the problem domain of activity recognition considering the use of k-NN as the underlying classification model.

As a starting point, this work focuses on PG algorithms based on the mechanism of *positioning adjustment*. This type of PG algorithms is usually well adapted to numerical datasets and has been shown in the past to provide good levels of performance [8]. An evaluation is undertaken to consider of the effects of reduction rate and accuracy rate for activity recognition based on sensor data gleaned from smart environments.

The remainder of the paper is structured as follows: Section 2 reviews an overview of PG algorithms, focusing on the mechanism of positioning adjustment.

Section 3 presents an empirical study that analyzes PG algorithms. Finally, in Section 4, Conclusions and Future Work are discussed.

2 Prototype Generation Algorithms

In this Section, we present an overview of the notion of PG algorithms with a particular emphasis on the mechanism of positioning adjustment. The PG algorithms are a kind of data reduction technique [10] that aim to identify an optimal subset from the original training set, by discarding noisy and redundant examples and modifying the value of some features of the samples to build new artificial samples that are known as prototypes [9].

PG algorithms are therefore designed to obtain a prototype generate set, which has a smaller size than the original training set. The cardinality of the prototype generate set is sufficiently small and has the subsequent effect to reduce both the storage and response time spent by the k-NN approach. A wide range of PG algorithms have been designed for the k-NN approach to reduce the data size which have been categorized into a taxonomy based on the following four mechanisms of prototyping [8]: *Positioning adjustment, Class relabeling, Centroid based* and *Space splitting.*

In this work, we focus on PG algorithms based on the mechanism of *positioning adjustment* to generate prototypes. The rationale for this choice of technique is due to the fact that the approach of positioning adjustment is usually well adapted to numerical datasets and has an accuracy rate close to k-NN. Based on the use of this technique an evaluation is conducted to consider the reduction rate and accuracy rate for activity recognition based on data gleaned from binary sensors in smart environments.

The mechanism of *positioning adjustment* is usually associated with two types of reduction: *fixed* or *mixed*. The *fixed* type of reduction establishes the final number of prototypes for the prototype generate set using a user's previously defined parameter related to the percentage of retention of original training set [8]. The *mixed* type of reduction begins with a preselected subset prototype generate set and then, additions, modifications, and removals of prototypes are undertaken in the prototype generate set.

3 Case Study

This Section details the evaluations under taken to investigate the effects of the performance of the PG algorithms based on positioning adjustment to enhance the response time when using the k-NN as a mean so of classification for activity recognition.

3.1 Activity Recognition Dataset

The case study presented in this contribution is based on a popular activity recognition dataset [11]. The dataset was collected in the house in which 14 state-change sensors were installed. Each sensor had the ability to provide two possible discrete values: 1 and 0, representing ON and OFF, respectively. Locations of sensors where on the doors of the apartment, cupboards, refrigerator and a toilet flush sensor. Seven different activities were annotated.

3.2   Evaluation of PG Algorithms

Eight PG algorithms based on positioning adjustment were considered. Six of them operated with fixed reduction and two of them with mixed reduction.

Table 1. PG algorithms based on positioning adjustment with fixed reduction

Acronym	Name
DSM	Decision Surface Mapping
HYB	Hybrid LVQ3 algorithm
LVQ3	Learning Vector Quantization 3
LVQPRU	Learning Vector Quantization with pruning
LVQTC	Learning Vector Quantization with Training Counter
VQ	Vector Quantization

Table 2. PG algorithms based on positioning adjustment with mixed reduction

Acronym	Name
MSE	Means of gradient descent and deterministic annealing
PSCSA	Prototype Selection Clonal Selection Algorithm

The name and acronym of each PG algorithm based on positioning adjustment is shown in Table 1 for fixed reduction and Table 2 for mixed reduction. In [8] is showed the paper in which each algorithm that is used in this paper was proposed and its optimal configuration.

3.3   Analysis and Empirical Results

Due to its simplicity and successful application, the classification rate is used as an accuracy rate. This is defined as the proportion of true results among the total number of class examined. To assess the performance of the PG algorithms, a 10-fold Cross-Validation was used to evaluate the accuracy rate of each PG algorithm. The main advantage of this validation is that all the samples in the dataset are eventually used for both training and testing. So, it matters less how the data gets divided.

The PG algorithms were implemented using Keel software [12]. Table 3 presents the average results obtained by the PG algorithms over the dataset with the 1-NN approach, indicating the reduction type in addition to the reduction rate. Furthermore, the accuracy rate is indicated together with the ranked order of approaches.

In view of the results, we can note that the k-NN approach achieves the maximum accuracy rate. Nevertheless, as already introduced, this approach presents problems of storage and, consequently, response time. The PG algorithms obtain acceptable results and dramatically reduce the training data size. As result, the response time to classify a new activity is reduced proportionally given a reduction in the number of stored instances, training samples, implies a reduction in

Table 3. Average results with 10-fold Cross-Validation obtained by the PG algorithms

Approach	Reduction Type	Reduction Rate	Accuracy Rate	Acc. Ranking
1-NN	-	1	0.963	1
PG algorithms	Reduction Type	Reduction Rate	Accuracy Rate	Acc. Ranking
DSM			0.726	9
HYB			0.934	3
LVQ3	Fixed	0.05	0.775	7
LVQPRU			0.942	2
LVQTC			0.893	5
VQ			0.743	8
PG algorithms	Reduction Type	Reduction Rate	Accuracy Rate	Acc. Ranking
MSE	Mixed	0.03	0.890	6
PSCSA		0.06	0.918	4

the response time, which is necessary to search through these training samples and classify a new activity.

The PG algorithms with a fixed reduction of 5% significantly reduces the initial training data size which has 245 samples. So, the training data size is reduced to around 12 or 13 prototypes. Therefore, the response time will be clearly reduced in the same proportion, i.e., 5%, to classify a new activity.

Among PG algorithms with a fixed reduction, it is noteworthy that LVQPRU, HYB and LVQTC achieve a very good accuracy rate that is very close to the k-NN approach. In this group, LVQ3, VQ and DSM obtain acceptable results in the accuracy rate, though slightly far from the accuracy rate of k-NN approach due to the fact that these methods preserve the accuracy over the training set. However, the generalization accuracy over the test set can be negatively affected as in this case.

The PG algorithms with a mixed reduction obtain a very good performance in terms of accuracy rate. In this group of PG algorithms, the reduction rate is not fixed, however, they achieve a reduction rate very similar to 5%. On the one hand, the PSCSA algorithm obtains the greatest reduction ratio, 3%, which is translated into 8 prototypes, obtaining a high accuracy rate. On the other hand, the PSCSA algorithm obtains the lowest reduction ratio which is 6%, which is translates into 15 prototypes.

Analyzing the results, we can point out that PG algorithms based on positioning adjustment obtain acceptable results in terms of accuracy rate, reducing the number of instances to be stored. Therefore, the PG algorithms based on positioning adjustment for activity recognition can be deemed as being very useful given that a reduction in the number of stored instances corresponds to a reduction in the response time, which is necessary to search through these training samples and classify a new sample.

4   Conclusions and Future Works

This work has been focused on the use of prototype generation algorithms for the purpose of activity recognition through use of the k-NN approach in order to reduce the response time of classification, taking into appreciation that this is closely related with the size of the set of samples stored. Eight prototype generation algorithms have been reviewed with the mechanism of positioning adjustment; Six with a fixed reduction approach and two with a mixed reduction approach. Results from the evaluation demonstrated the ability of the approach to provide a good performance and a percentage reduction of approximately 5% of the instances stored which is directly proportional to the reduction in response time. Future work will be directed towards evaluating other kinds of mechanism to generate prototypes such as *Class relabeling, Centroid based* and *Space splitting*.

Acknowledgments. This contribution has been supported by research projects: TIN-2012-31263, CEATIC-2013-001, UJA2014/06/14. Invest Northern Ireland is acknowledged for partially supporting this project under the Competence Centre Program Grant RD0513853 - Connected Health Innovation Centre.

References

1. Satyanarayanan, M.: Pervasive computing: Vision and challenges. IEEE Personal Communications **8**(4), 10–17 (2001)
2. Emmanouilidis, C., Koutsiamanis, R.-A., Tasidou, A.: Mobile guides: Taxonomy of architectures, context awareness, technologies and applications. Journal of Network and Computer Applications **36**(1), 103–125 (2013)
3. Alam, M., Hamida, E.: Surveying wearable human assistive technology for life and safety critical applications: Standards, challenges and opportunities. Sensors (Switzerland) **14**(5), 9153–9209 (2014)
4. Cover, T., Hart, P.: Nearest neighbor pattern classification. IEEE Transactions on Information Theory **13**, 21–27 (1967)
5. Wu, X., Kumar, V.: The Top Ten Algorithms in Data Mining. Chapman & Hall/CRC, 1st ed. (2009)
6. Moayeri Pour, G., Troped, P., Evans, J.: Environment feature extraction and classification for context aware physical activity monitoring, pp. 123–128 (2013)
7. Kononenko, I., Kukar, M.: Machine Learning and Data Mining: Introduction to Principles and Algorithms. Horwood Publishing Limited (2007)
8. Garcia, S., Derrac, J., Cano, J., Herrera, F.: Prototype selection for nearest neighbor classification: Taxonomy and empirical study. IEEE Transactions on Pattern Analysis and Machine Intelligence **34**(3), 417–435 (2012)
9. Lozano, M., Sotoca, J., Sanchez, J., Pla, F., Pekalska, E., Duin, R.: Experimental study on prototype optimisation algorithms for prototype-based classification in vector spaces. Pattern Recognition **39**(10), 1827–1838 (2006)
10. Wilson, R.D., Martinez, T.: Reduction techniques for instance-based learning algorithms. Machine Learning **38**(3), 257–286 (2000)
11. Van Kasteren, T., Noulas, A., Englebienne, G., Krse, B.: Accurate activity recognition in a home setting, pp. 1–9 (2008)
12. Alcala Fdez, J., Fernandez, A., Luengo, J., Derrac, J., Garcia, S., Sanchez, L., Herrera, F.: Keel data-mining software tool: Data set repository, integration of algorithms and experimental analysis framework. Journal of Multiple-Valued Logic and Soft Computing **17**(2–3), 255–287 (2011)

Multi–Occupant Movement Tracking in Smart Home Environments

Masoud Vatanpour Azghandi, Ioanis Nikolaidis[✉], and Eleni Stroulia

Department of Computing Science, University of Alberta, 2-21 Athabasca Hall,
Edmonton, Alberta T6G 2E8, Canada
{mvatanpo,nikolaidis,stroulia}@ualberta.ca

Abstract. Recognizing the movement and activities of an individual in an indoor space is a key functionality of smart homes, as a prerequisite to providing services in support of the occupant. Focusing on the particular case of smart homes with multiple occupants, we developed a location-and-movement recognition method using many inexpensive passive infrared (PIR) motion sensors and, a small number of, more costly RFID readers. In our method, PIR sensors, placed throughout the space, recognize movement while RFID readers, placed in key locations, recognize tags worn by individuals as they pass through their coverage area. The RFID readings are used to disambiguate the trajectories constructed based on PIR sensor readings. We evaluate through simulations the effectiveness of our method under different occupancy conditions.

Keywords: Tracking · Activity recognition · Smart homes

1 Introduction

In previous work [4] we used inexpensive wireless passive infrared (PIR) sensors to determine the path of a single occupant in a "smart home" setting. Simple "anonymous" sensors such as PIR sensors are clearly inadequate when more than one individual are to be tracked and their trajectories need to be separated and labeled. In order to track multiple individuals, we are expanding our sensor toolkit to include RFID tag(s) worn by each individual and, correspondingly, RFID readers. The question addressed in this paper is whether a combination of PIR sensor deployment in an indoor space, coupled with the judicious use of RFID readers deployed at certain points in space, is an effective solution to multi-occupant localization.

RFID reader deployment is challenging and a significant contributor to total deployent costs. RFID readers need to be deployed at locations where they can be supplied by a continuous power source, i.e., powering them from batteries is not a viable option. Additionally, the use of relatively large antennas, to produce reliable readings, increases the per-reader cost and results in cumbersome placement. Hence, we are interested to reduce the number of RFID readers and deploy them in locations that are as effective as possible, i.e., where they can add the most in terms of improving the localization accuracy.

© Springer International Publishing Switzerland 2015
A. Geissbühler et al. (Eds.): ICOST 2015, LNCS 9102, pp. 319–324, 2015.
DOI: 10.1007/978-3-319-19312-0_29

Abstractly, the problem at hand is one of sensor fusion for the purposes of tracking individual trajectories, in a mixed environment of anonymous (PIR) and identity (RFID) sensors. The motion sensors are used to determine paths for (possibly groups of) individuals roaming the indoor space, but their paths mix and become ambiguous even if the original locations of each individual was known. The RFID readers help mitigate the ambiguity but are limited because the readers are only present in certain locations and have limited coverage. This leads us to develop a model that can assist the placement of readers using a "skeletal" tree of the paths of motion individuals follow in an indoor space.

Multi–object tracking is a well studied topic in computer vision, e.g., [2], including the fusion with other sensor data [6], but the use of cameras is perceived as privacy–intruding when compared to motion sensors and/or RFID tags and readers. RFID-based sensor fusion (usually with IMU data) solutions have been proposed [1,3], but, contrary to our approach, require individuals to carry cumbersome portable readers. In the following, Section 2 introduces the basic model and metrics used, while Section 3 provides sketches the RFID reader placement heuristic. Section 4 presents some early simulation results and Section 5 concludes with a summary of the main points of the paper.

2   System Model and Performance Metrics

We assume we know the geometry of the indoor space and the geometry of coverage of each sensor type. We also assume the existence (and use) of a heatmap of the *visitation frequency* of each point in the environment, as in [4]. The heatmap is constructed by simulating in advance the paths followed by a potential occupant between areas of interest in the space. This two-dimensional map, includes the location of the walls (W) and obstacles (O). Each of the remaining points is associated with an information utility (I), which is the probability of a person being present at that point. Overall, the heatmap contains N points, (x_1, y_1, l_1), ..., (x_N, y_N, l_N). l_i indicates the group, W, O or I, to which the point belongs. The objective of our method is, given k ($k > 1$) individuals present in and moving around the environment, to reduce the error in inferring the location of each individual in the space at any point in time.

The coverage of PIR motion sensors is modelled as a boolean rectangle, assuming that such sensors are placed on the ceiling, facing vertically down, projecting a rectangular base pyramid on the floor. We consider both the 0 degree and the 90 degree rotation rectangular footprints. To address the occlusion caused by, e.g., walls and doors, we use complex polygons to represent sensor footprints (Figure 1(a)). The coverage of RFID readers is a directed boolean sector model, in the sense of [5] (Figure 1(b)). ϕ_0 is called the *orientation angle*, ω is the *angle of view*, r is the *sensing range* resulting in a coverage represented by a circular sector.

In general, there exist locations within the environment, i.e., kitchen counter, one's own bed, etc., that tend to be *destinations* of the occupants' movement. These destinations are potential starting/ending points of paths. Considering

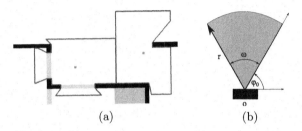

Fig. 1. Sensor coverage for (a) PIR sensors [4], and, (b) RFID readers

the set $\mathcal{P}$ representing the k individuals ($\mathcal{P} = \{P_1, P_2, \ldots, P_k\}$), the sequence of destinations chosen by each occupant, i.e., their trajectory T_{P_i}, is the sequence of the person's locations-at-time, $l_{P_i, t_n} = (x_{P_i, t_n}, y_{P_i, t_n})$. A *collision* between P_i and P_j means that there exists a timestamp t_{col} when the distance between $(x_{P_i, t_{col}}, y_{P_i, t_{col}})$ and $(x_{P_j, t_{col}}, y_{P_j, t_{col}})$ is less than δ (as a convention we set δ to two times the radius of a circle representing a person's body). The definition of collision is generalized to three or more people. Past a collision point, trajectories reconstructed purely by PIR sensors can be ambiguous, since it is not possible to identify which of the colliding individual(s) continue to which "branch". It is up to the readings from RFID readers to provide the authoritative unambiguous *IDs* as individuals cross the reader's range; unambigusously recognizing an occupant, at some location, at some point in time, allows us to revisit previous ambiguous trajectories and infer the corresponding individuals. The process is not perfect as certain segments of the trajectories can remain ambiguous. Nevertheless, we are interested to decide on an RFID reader placement that reduces ambiguity of trajectories.

Specifically, we consider two metrics: *ambiguity* and *tracking error*. The ambiguity metric in an indicator of the extent to which the occupants' locations have been incorrectly inferred. The ambiguity for each tracked individual is the fraction of time that the invividual's *ID* belongs to ambiguous trajectory segments (i.e., segments containing two more more candidate *IDs* including the *ID* of the particular individual and we call the sets of two or more candidate *IDs* the *ambiguity sets*). The ambiguity metric is the average over all individual ambiguities.

The tracking error metric is influenced by the ambiguity metric. It consists of a lower and an upper bound for the localization error. For each individual, there are ambiguous segments that this individual has likely traversed (based on its participation on trajectories that are ambiguous and include the particular *ID*). Of those, the two paths with most and least Euclidean distance from the person's actual (ground truth) path are considered to describe an upper bound (Tracking Error Upper-bound, TEU) and a lower bound (Tracking Error Lower-bound, TEL) error. The TEU and TEL errors are calculated on a per-individual basis and averaged across time.

3   RFID Reader Placement

We introduce a *skeleton* of the heatmap (Figure 2(c)), which is the result of a three step process: a) thresholding the heatmap, b) iterative thinning the binary values created by thresholding, and (c) removal of short branches and cycles. The end result is an undirected n-ary tree, $T = (V_t, E_t)$. The vertices of T are also called the branching points and the edges are the actual paths (*i.e.,* they correspond to a sequence of real spatial points, and are not just logical links between vertices). Figure 2 illustrates the conversion of the heatmap to a n-ary tree. Having computed T, all its vertices become potential coverage points for RFID readers as they indicate busy gateways towards different locations, but only some of them will be chosen for reader placement.

We consider the branching points of T as candidate locations for reader placement. The placement heuristic is based on a score function $\mathcal{F}$ that captures (via their product, $\mathcal{F}_v = H_v \times D_v$) two factors. First, the *heat factor* H_v is expressed as the sum of heatmap values of the locations covered by placing a reader at a particular vertex, thus favoring coverage of heavier traffic areas. Second, the *distance factor* D_v expresses the path distance from already placed readers, thus biasing in favor of readers further apart, as placing them near each other results in coverage overlaps producing no noticable advantage.

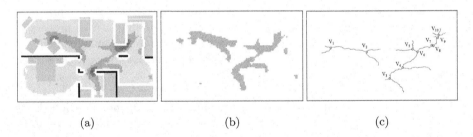

| (a) | (b) | (c) |

Fig. 2. The skeletonization process: (a) heatmap, (b) thresholding, and, (c) skeleton

4   Simulation Results

We produced a number of test cases simulating different numbers of occupants moving in the smart home with the floorplan in Figure 2(a) which corresponds to an actual space with an area of $10.60 \times 6.29\,m^2$. In total, we considered 14 different activity patterns, and we simulated the movement of the occupants assuming that each occupant randomly chooses three activities out of the possible 14. On average, each activity takes the occupant 15 seconds of simulated time. In order to emphasize the ability to distinguish trajectories, no pause times were simulated, that is, an individual would be simulated starting a new activity as soon as the previous one had ended. We conducted simulations for $k = 2$, $k = 3$ and $k = 5$ occupants. First, the PIR motion sensor placement by [4] was followed, producing an optimal solution consisting of 11 PIR sensors.

Table 1. Comparing different placement methods for five RFID readers

k=2	Tree-Based	Manual	Random
a_2^* (%)	3.097	3.458	3.864
TEU(m)	0.617	0.621	0.632
TEL(m)	0.613	0.613	0.613

k=3	Tree-Based	Manual	Random
a_2^* (%)	6.075	5.669	7.930
a_3^* (%)	5.073	6.062	6.085
TEU (m)	1.251	1.313	1.389
TEL (m)	0.748	0.755	0.776

k=5	Tree-Based	Manual	Random
a_2^* (%)	0.844	1.746	2.096
a_3^* (%)	3.471	4.389	5.339
a_4^* (%)	7.816	8.987	9.915
a_5^* (%)	11.059	12.190	12.492
TEU (m)	3.768	4.020	4.067
TEL (m)	1.016	1.051	1.056

We compare the placement determined from our heuristic against an "expert" manual placement and a random one. The manual placement aims to cover as much as possible of the entire space but places at least one reader in every room. For the randomized placement, points with a non-zero utility score in the heatmap were randomly chosen. For each RFID reader point, the closest point on a wall was determined and assumed to be the reader's mounting point (the same process was used for mounting points of readers in the tree-based method). For randomized placement we report the average of 10 randomized placements.

The results presented in Table 1 are averages over 100 runs for each reader placement. To properly appreciate the results, we note that even in the ground truth there is a small probability that individual trajectories collide (same location at the same time). The ground truth for the case $k = 2$ shows 2.986% collision between the two occupants. For $k = 3$, two people trajectories are colliding 10.547% of the time, and three colliding 0.301% of the time. The percentages for $k = 5$ are 14.627%, 1.209%, 0.137% and 0.001%, for collisions involving 2, 3, 4 and 5 trajectories, respectively.

In each sub-table of Table 1, two rows present the TEU and TEL. An additional $k-1$ rows show the average ambiguity (a_2^* to a_k^*) for an individual's trajectory, as a function of the cardinality (from 2 to k) of the *ambiguity set* (defined earlier). In all cases the tree-based method surpasses the other two methods: it exhibits smaller tracking error and smaller ambiguity. However, while the merits of the tree-based method become increasingly apparent as k increases, the absolute tracking error deteriorates quickly from approximately 60cm for two occupants, to between 75cm and 120cm for three occupants, to 3.5m in the case

324   M.V. Azghandi et al.

of five occupants (making it virtually unusable). Note that as k increases the value of a_k^* is inflated, because disambiguating ("teasing apart") the trajectories of each individual in a large group is less likely to accomplish, than from a small group. Additionally, for large populations of occupants, given a budget limitation to five RFID readers only, it is increasingly likely that, after approaching (and read by) an RFID reader, an individual's trajectory will collide with some other trajectory before it gets a chance to be read again by an RFID reader, hence ambiguous trajectories abound in large occupant population scenarios.

5   Conclusion

We introduced and evaluated through simulations an indoor multiple-person tracking system based on a combination of PIR and RFID technologies. The ambiguity of PIR-based tracking for mutiple occupants is mitigated by the use of information from RFID readers. Due to the relatively costly and challenging deployment of multiple RFID readers, we devised a RFID reader placement heuristic aiming to produce good tracking results. A reading from an RFID tag worn by an occupant provides unambiguous location information, subsequently used to disambiguate segments of occupants' trajectories that were, up to that point, unknown to which occupant they corresponded. The proposed heuristic favorably compares against random as well as naive manual placements that attempt to cover the whole space.

Acknowledgments. This work has been partially funded by IBM, the Natural Sciences and Engineering Research Council of Canada (NSERC), Alberta Innovates - Technology Futures (AITF), and Alberta Health Services (AHS).

References

1. House, S., Connell, S., Milligan, I., Austin, D., Hayes, T.L., Chiang, P.: Indoor localization using pedestrian dead reckoning updated with rfid-based fiducials. In: 2011 Annual International Conference of the IEEE Engineering in Medicine and Biology Society, EMBC, pp. 7598–7601. IEEE (2011)
2. Milan, A., Schindler, K., Roth, S.: Detection-and trajectory-level exclusion in multiple object tracking. In: 2013 IEEE Conference on Computer Vision and Pattern Recognition (CVPR), pp. 3682–3689. IEEE (2013)
3. Ruiz, A.R.J., Granja, F.S., Prieto Honorato, J.C., Rosas, J.I.G.: Accurate pedestrian indoor navigation by tightly coupling foot-mounted imu and rfid measurements. IEEE Transactions on Instrumentation and Measurement **61**(1), 178–189 (2012)
4. Vlasenko, I., Nikolaidis, I., Stroulia, E.: The smart-condo: Optimizing sensor placement for indoor localization. IEEE Transactions on Systems, Man, and Cybernetics: Systems **45**(3), 436–453 (2015)
5. Wang, B.: Coverage problems in sensor networks: A survey. ACM Computing Surveys (CSUR) **43**(4), 32 (2011)
6. Yu, C.R., Wu, C.L., Lu, C.H., Fu, L.C.: Human localization via multi-cameras and floor sensors in smart home. In: IEEE International Conference on Systems, Man and Cybernetics, 2006. SMC 2006, vol. 5, pp. 3822–3827. IEEE (2006)

Improving User Engagement by Aggregating and Analysing Health and Fitness Data on a Mobile App

Peter Leijdekkers[✉] and Valerie Gay

Faculty of Engineering and Information Technology, University of Technology, Broadway 2007, P.O. Box 123, Sydney, NSW, Australia
{Peter.Leijdekkers,Valerie.Gay}@uts.edu.au

Abstract. Nowadays, health, fitness and contextual data can be ubiquitously collected using wearable devices, sensors and smart phones and be stored in various servers and devices. However, to engage users in active monitoring of their health and fitness, it is essential to personalise the monitoring and have all the relevant data in one place. It is also important to give users control on how their data is collected, analysed, presented and stored. This paper presents how those important features are integrated in myFitnessCompanion®, an Android Health and fitness app developed by our team. The app is able to aggregate data from multiple sources, keep it on the phone or export it to servers or Electronic Health Records (EHR). It can also present the aggregated data in a personalised manner. A mobile app such as myFitnessCompanion® is a solution to the personalisation, interoperability and control issues that are key to user engagement.

Keywords: Connected health · Wearable devices · Wireless sensors · Health and fitness apps · Chronic disease management

1 Introduction

The fast adoption of wearable devices comes at a time where chronic diseases are increasing in developed countries and where those countries struggle with their healthcare budgets. Chronic disease is an increasing problem and, for most cases, some hospitalization or doctor visits can be avoided by prevention and self-monitoring. Wearable devices are becoming part of normal life and are able to collect some data needed for the self-monitoring. Other health data is collected using medical grade devices such as wireless blood pressure monitors and blood glucose meters.

There is an abundance of health and fitness apps available from the Apple store and Google Play. At the time of writing, there are 40,000 health related smartphone apps [1] and HIS [2] forecasts that the sales of wearable technology that can link to the Internet or work with mobile apps will grow from $8.6 billion in 2012 to almost $30 billion by 2018.

Physical activity promotion is a priority and a lot of research and mobile Apps address this issue and focus on motivating users towards a more active and healthy lifestyle (e.g.: [3-5]). Many Apps use a specific sensor or only deal with a particular

© Springer International Publishing Switzerland 2015
A. Geissbühler et al. (Eds.): ICOST 2015, LNCS 9102, pp. 325–330, 2015.
DOI: 10.1007/978-3-319-19312-0_30

chronic condition. (e.g. Asthma Coach). Mobile apps like Fitbit and Jawbone UP [8] only support their own activity trackers and mainly display data that is collected from their devices. Data collected from these wearable devices are stored on separate servers. Some fitness servers such as Google Fit claim to be an aggregator of health data but are limited to fitness data only, which makes them unsuitable as a complete Electronic Health Records (EHR) system. Government controlled EHR systems, on the other hand, focus on health data provided by health professionals. There is a need to combine these 'informal' fitness data and 'formal' health data in one system and make it easily available to the users.

For chronic disease patients, there is often a need to monitor several physiological parameters and not just their activity level or calories burned. Lack of device interoperability, and the presence of data silos prevent these users from obtaining an overall view of their health. To engage these users in active monitoring and controlling their condition, it is important to have all health & fitness data in one place and give them a personalized overview on trends and progress.

Several mobile apps already exist to play the role of health data aggregator. They have been named the *'connected mHealth app elite'* by Research2Guidance [6], a consultancy and market research company focussing on mobile app economics.

myFitnessCompanion® developed by our team is in the top five list of this exclusive group of connected apps'. It interacts with a wide range of sensors (20+) and wearable devices (e.g. MIO link, Polar, Zephyr) and aggregates data from third party apps and connects with public servers such as Microsoft HealthVault, Google Fit, Fitbit, Jawbone, Withings, and iHealth, as well as non-public EHR systems. It offers a user-centred solution and analyses and presents the aggregated data in a personalised and engaging manner.

This paper is structured as follows: Section 2 describes how we collect and aggregate the data from a variety of sources. Section 3 presents how the data is analysed and presented to the user. Section 4 concludes with a discussion on our work in progress and open issues.

2   Health and Fitness Data Aggregation

myFitnessCompanion® collects health & fitness data from different sources. It uses wearable devices and wireless sensors but also manual entries by the user. It gives the user the possibility to aggregate data from different sources and stores it on the mobile device and in the cloud using one or more servers as illustrated in Fig. 1.

myFitnessCompanion® collects data from wireless devices supporting open standard protocols such as the Google Android Wear smart watches and fitness trackers that allow third party developers to retrieve the data directly from the device (Fig.1, box 1). They are open in the sense that they use standard open protocols to transfer health data using either Bluetooth or ANT+. These devices are connected a server such as Google Fit and can then be retrieved by myFitnessCompanion®.

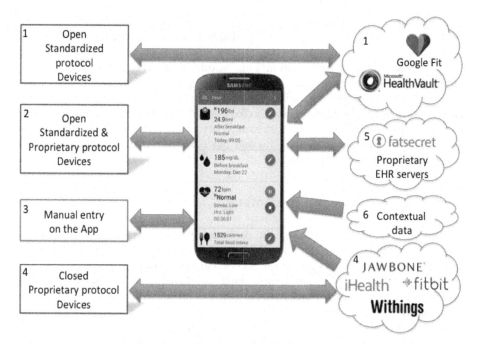

Fig. 1. myFitnessCompanion®'s eco system

myFitnessCompanion® can also collect data from devices paired with the user's mobile device (Fig.1, box 2) via Bluetooth or ANT+. These include Bluetooth Smart heart rate monitors and blood pressure monitors. The devices implement an open standard and work seamlessly with myFitnessCompanion® without making modifications for a specific vendor. Unfortunately, the majority of wireless devices implement a vendor specific protocol. Sometimes the vendor makes the protocol available which allows the integration but, for each device, specific software has to be written to communicate and interpret the data transmitted by these devices.

Closed and proprietary wireless devices (Fig.1, box 4) do not allow third party developers to communicate directly with the device. Although those devices use standard Bluetooth to communicate with a mobile device the actual protocol and data format are not public. This makes it near impossible for third party developers to integrate the device directly in their mobile app. Fitbit, Jawbone, Withings and many other vendors follow this strategy and only allow third party developers to obtain the data via their server through an open API.

Websites such as myFitnessPal and Fatsecret collect health data by allowing users to input data directly or via their mobile app (Fig.1, box 5). These sites then allow third party developers to retrieve the data via an open API. Some servers like Microsoft HealthVault allow 2-way communication whereas others like Withings do not allow uploading data from a third party app.

The objective is to collect as much relevant data as possible in order to offer the best overview for a user regarding his/her chronic condition. In future versions of myFitnessCompanion® we will also collect contextual data (e.g. location) that can be useful to offer more fine-grained analysis (Fig.1, box 6). For example, an asthma user could benefit from a pollution forecast for his/her area to take preventative action.

The users are in control of the data they want to collect and how it is collected. They can enter data manually into myFitnessCompanion® (Fig.1, box 3). This is the case when they have a non-compatible device or conditions for which no sensor exists (e.g. ostomy or stool tracking). Users can annotate a reading by adding comments and contextual information, such as extra coffee consumption or performed activities before and after a blood glucose measurement. They can also manually enter health data in Microsoft HealthVault, Google Fit and others, which is then automatically imported into myFitnessCompanion®.

3   Data Analysis and Presentation[1]

myFitnessCompanion® analyses health & fitness data in real time and presents the personalized information to the user. We opted for a user-centred approach where the user is in control of the way the data is analysed and presented.

myFitnessCompanion® deals with a wide variety of users. Some only need to monitor their weight and blood pressure whereas others suffer from asthma or obstructive sleep apnoea. Presenting the data is a major challenge, especially taking into account that some users exhibit the white coat syndrome when taking a reading. Based on feedback from customers and health professionals, we do show all data collected in various formats.

To accommodate this user variety, myFitnessCompanion® allows enabling or disabling analysis in real-time. If real-time analysis is activated, threshold levels can be set for several biometric monitors. The assessment for several health metrics such as blood pressure and blood glucose adhere to internationally accepted guidelines. For other health metrics, such as heart rate, the user can set max and min thresholds based on advice from a health professional or personal trainer. Some monitors such as stool and ostomy offer a more discreet feedback and do not show all details.

The analysis is performed on the mobile device and instant feedback is given to the user using either voice, textual or colour rating. Assessment is currently available for weight, blood pressure, blood glucose, oxygen level, asthma, heart rate (training zone, stress level), respiration, body temperature and urine osmolality.

Depending on the user's choice, we display the 'live' data, the user's history, the activity summary or a trend analysis. The live data is presented to the user on the dashboard and some data can be displayed on the smart watch. An important feature of myFitness-Companion® is exercise monitoring using a heart rate sensor. Showing the heart rate zones, together with other exercise information gives the user instant insight on how he or she performs. At the end of an exercise the data is analysed and presented in heart rate zones and it allows them to stay in their targeted heart rate zone.

Users can see their history under the form of tables and graphs. The data is colour-coded. Colours ranges from light green (good) to dark red (severe problem) and comes together with a description (e.g. normal, prehypertension, stage 1 hypertension etc.). Similar feedback is provided to obstructive sleep apnoea users using

---

[1] Screenshots can be viewed on myFitnessCompanion.com.

myFitnessCompanion®. Using a pulse-oxygen device (e.g. Nonin WristOx2) they record heart rate and oxygen saturation level during a night's sleep.

Other powerful features include the activity summary and the trend analysis of the collected readings. Users can quickly see how they progress over a certain time frame. Users can export or print the data for later viewing by health professionals and personal trainers.

4   Conclusion: Future Work and Open Issues

The ultimate goal of myFitnessCompanion® is to empower users and help them monitoring their health and fitness a personalised way with a clear overview of their data and activities. There are a lot of benefits in aggregating the health and Fitness data especially for chronic disease users, as their condition needs a long term monitoring and depends on a complex set of factors. With the aggregation, the silos can also be limited and users, their carers and health professionals can get more control on their health and fitness data.

Our objective is to keep adding new wearable devices and sensors as they come on the market, as well as, connecting to more health and fitness servers. In particular, there is a gap in the market for secure and well-designed EHR that combine health and fitness data. Companies are jumping on this market segment and we are currently integrating myFitnessCompanion® with these types of servers since it can deal with 'informal' and 'formal' health and fitness data.

The context of a user can be important and one of the challenges is to identify and collect the data that is important for a particular user and provide timely feedback. An example, for users with asthma, myFitnessCompanion® will capture location-based information about the Air Quality Index (AQI), alert the user when the air quality deteriorates (AQI > 100) and raise an alarm if it gets hazardous (AQI > 200). A similar approach will be taken for the pollen level since the information is widely available and using the location of the user a tailored advice can be given.

Location-based information such as the likelihood of flu, rheumatism and migraine is already available from various websites. The data can be used together with the health data collected to provide a more detailed analysis and alert the user if needed.

In future versions, we will use data mining and data analytics to offer a more personal and accurate assessment for each user. We are interested in making correlations between context and conditions (e.g. altitude, weather and blood pressure or location and stress level). We also looking at the possibility to make an assessment based on several input parameters (e.g. calorie intake, activity level and blood pressure).

Currently, myFitnessCompanion® stores all data locally on the mobile device or on a server chosen by the user. However, for more complex data analysis we will need the data to be stored on a server in order to provide more intelligent feedback based on long-term user's history and possibly comparing it to other users with similar conditions. Some users will accept that in order to get better insights while others will opt for less feedback and keep their data private. We will cater for both.

There are a lot of wireless sensors and activity trackers (e.g. Fitbit, Jawbone UP, Withings) on the market with different quality and accuracy. Many health professionals discard self-collected health and fitness data due to the unreliability of the data and prefer to use their own data for diagnosis. We believe that over time more health professionals will accept the data if the source is properly tagged so that they know which device, or which app, generated the data.

Apps like myFitnessCompanion® have the potential to change healthcare by empowering users and by helping them taking control of their health. This could lead to fewer visits to the doctor and fewer additional measurements. It also has the potential to give health professionals an overall view on their users' health and fitness data and help them making a more accurate and personalised assessment.

References

1. IMS Health Institute. Patient Apps for Improved Healthcare: From Novelty to Mainstream (2014) www.imshealth.com
2. IHS technology, Wearable Technology Intelligence Service. technology.ihs.com/ Services/511880/wearable-technology-intelligence-service, viewed January 2015 (2014)
3. Middelweerd, A., Mollee, J., van der Wal, N., Brug, J., te Velde, S.: Apps to promote physical activity among adults: a review and content analysis. International Journal of Behavioral Nutrition and Physical Activity 11(97), 2014 (2014). doi:10.1186/s12966-014-0097-9
4. Conroy, D., Yang, C-H., Maher, J.: Behavior Change Techniques in Top-Ranked Mobile Apps for Physical Activity (2014). doi: http://dx.doi.org/10.1016/j.amepre.2014.01.010
5. Hermens, H.J., op den Akker, H., Tabak, M., Wijsman, J.L.P., Vollenbroek-Hutten, M.M.R.: Personalized Coaching Systems to support healthy behavior in people with chronic conditions. Journal of electromyography and kinesiology 24(6), 815–826 (2014). ISSN 1050-6411
6. Research to Guidance, mHealth App Developer Economics 2014, The State of the Art of mHealth App Publishing (2014). http://www.mHealthEconomics.com (Accessed January 2015)

Ambulatory Energy Expenditure Evaluation for Treadmill Exercises

Gareth L. Williams[✉], M. Sajeewani Karunarathne,
Samitha W. Ekanayake, and Pubudu N. Pathirana

Deakin University, 75 Pigdons Road, Waurn Ponds, Victoria, Australia
g.williams@deakin.edu.au

Abstract. This paper introduces an ambulatory energy expenditure technique using a single inertial sensor, and compares the performance with an industry standard metabolic measurement system. Wearable energy expenditure estimation systems are key instruments in athlete evaluation. The cost and size of traditional oxygen intake measurement systems (VO2 systems) limits usage of such technology in everyday athlete training and evaluation events. This project describes a method of estimating energy expenditure during treadmill exercise, from limb angular velocity and metabolic measurements. The feasibility of using such a system was evaluated using experimental results.

Keywords: Wearable sensors · Ambulatory measurements · Energy expenditure · Activity monitoring

1 Introduction

In sports science, the measurement of how much energy someone has expended through exercise is recognized as a hard problem to solve. A common form of exercise that would involve energy estimation is walking. Knowing this, the experiment performed involved using healthy subjects between the ages of 20 to 45 and were put on a treadmill at various speeds for some time for each speed. A wireless system utilising an inertial measurement unit, and an oxygen intake measurement device were used to measure limb movement and oxygen consumption levels. Using the data collected, a correlation was sought and a linear model derived so that energy estimation for running or similar activities can be measured accurately. Inertial data acquisition is prone to errors but as a first step to gaining energy expenditure information [1]. The system utilizes a single tri-axial accelerometer and is called the Move II sensor. The one weakness it is that it is indoor based and does not have any GPS based sensors to measure any outside movements. Steps using a sensor placed on the chest in [2] utilized a full angular speed ratio unit that comprised of accelerometer, gyroscope and magnetometer (although the former two were used). The same issue was raised where a sensor using an angular speed ratio, albeit different model from [1], and was placed on the hip. [3,4] found that utilising acceleration and rotation data as

© Springer International Publishing Switzerland 2015
A. Geissbühler et al. (Eds.): ICOST 2015, LNCS 9102, pp. 331–336, 2015.
DOI: 10.1007/978-3-319-19312-0_31

well as using a O2 breath sensor apparatus to confirm energy measurement was accurate in some combinations but not others. Vathsangam *et al.* go on further, using statistical analysis to gain a better understanding of the results. It was evident from the paper that a different implementation of energy measurement capture, although [3] was important to help realize that if the number of sensors were increased, results would look a little different. A new approach was looked at in [5], where the angle of the knee was taken by using gyroscopes on two sensors on the leg, where one would be on the knee and other positioned on the lower leg, and the results were then used to estimate energy levels. It should be noted that all of the papers surveyed looked at indoor walking whilst [3] also considered outdoor walking using a GPS system. Walking can be considered a common enough activity that should be used for the purposes of gait analysis and energy expenditure measurement and is easy to model. In [3,4], the authors constantly used Bayesian Linear Regression and Gaussian Process Regression throughout their experiments as well as coupling both gyroscopic and acceleration measurements. In [3], the authors used Hierarchical Linear Models. This was used to supplement the energy expenditure estimation model by looking at the variations from user to user. It includes the user's height, weight, and age as parameters for the model as inputs. From this, a gap in the literature covered was found, and taking the experiment from [5] and [6] and instead of using the knees - it was found that using the angular velocity of the legs could be used to measure energy expenditure.

2   Energy Expenditure in Activities

The gold standard in evaluating the energy expenditure in a human body is by means of a metabolic measurements system [7]. Energy expenditure from the rate of oxygen consumption data is calculated using the following equation [8]:

$$E_m = \frac{\dot{v}_o \times 20900}{60} \tag{1}$$

where $\dot{v}_o$ represents the oxygen consumption during the activity in l/min and energy rate that is being measured E_m is in watts.

The energy calculation from the inertial measurement system does not have a direct relationship with energy expenditure via a rate of change of limb angles. The major disadvantage in such a system is the inability to measure energy or activity level while the subject is at rest or performing non-mobile exercises whereas the metabolic measurement systems can measure energy expenditure during any activity.

In this study we are using angular rate of the lower limb to estimate the energy expenditure during the activity as follows:

$$E_r = \frac{k}{T} \sum \left(\|\omega\|^2 \right). \tag{2}$$

Here T is the duration of the activity in seconds, energy rate of the activity level E_r is in watts, $\omega = [\omega_x \; \omega_y \; \omega_z]$ represents the raw gyroscope measurements around the respective local coordinate axis from the ankle mounted sensor (see Fig. 1b) and k is a scalar function to transform the angular rates into the energy.

Another method to evaluate energy in walking or running based exercises is based on the assumption that the energy consumption is linearly proportionate to the speed of walking or running [9]. The following empirical formula has been employed in calculating energy using speed of motion,

$$E_s = \frac{(v_L \times m)}{1000},$$ (3)

where v_L represents the linear velocity of motion (i.e. the treadmill speed) , energy rate of the activity level E_s is in watts and m represents the weight of the subject in kilograms.

3   Experimental Setup

The experiment was conducted in a laboratory environment with a speed regulated treadmill for precise control of the activity intensity. The experiment was performed with six subjects (five male and one female) without any history of orthopedic or intramuscular impairments. All subjects were recruited from the general population within the age bracket of 20 to 45 years.

Inertial measurements, in particular the angular speed of the limb which is of interest to this study, were recorded via a BioKin-WMS sensor attached to ankle of the subject as shown in Fig. 1b. BioKin is a purpose built wearable bio-kinematic motion capture sensor (www.biokin.com.au) consists of real-time wireless data collection with a 140Hz update rate.

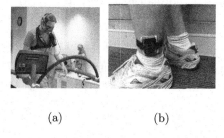

(a)   (b)

Fig. 1. (a)- Experimental Setup: Metamax metabolic measurement system was attached to the subject while performing the treadmill based exercises. (b) - Capturing inertial data: BioKin-WMS inertial measurement sensor was attached to the subject's ankle while performing the treadmill based exercises.

The activity level of the experiment was controlled by means of the speed of the treadmill the subject is walking/running. Before the exercises, subject's metabolic rate was measured for the resting state.

Each subject was asked to perform walking/running activities for five activity levels at treadmill speeds $3, 5, 7, 9$ and $11 km/h$ with each activity lasting for 2 minutes. For the VO2 measurements, they were taken in the final minute of recording.

In addition to the logging of gyroscope, accelerometer and rate of oxygen consumption measurements, we measured their height and weight in order to use older models/equations to roughly estimate their energy expenditure. The participants were also asked to give their consent for the use of their data after personal details relating to them was removed prior to publication.

4   Results and Discussion

In the study, a correlation was sought using a gold standard and the proposed energy expenditure system introduced in equation (2). The system uses angular rate measurements recorded by a IMU sensor worn on the ankle. We investigated the subject based variation of the energy expenditure relationships estimated with different methods. We employed an additional energy expenditure estimation method using speed of walking or running as introduced in equation (3).

4.1   Relationship of Gyro Based Proposed Energy Expenditure with Gold Standard Metabolic Rate

In this section, we compare the proposed energy expenditure technique (see equation (2)) with the gold standard oxygen consumption based system. In order to maintain generality and comparability between two energy expenditure calculation techniques we used the normalized energy expenditure compared to the first level of activities. The normalized energy at i^{th} activity level is calculated as,

$$\psi_i = \frac{E_i}{E_1}. \tag{4}$$

Here, E_1 is the energy for the base activity level of $3 km/h$ walk and E_i is the estimated energy at i^{th} activity level. The mean energy across five subjects for

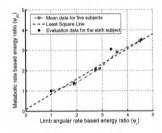

Fig. 2. Variation of treadmill speed derived, normalized energy expenditure (ψ_r) with activity levels for all test subjects

each activity level was calculated and Fig. 2 illustrates the comparison of the proposed approach with gold standard.

4.2 Variation of Energy Expenditure Pattern with the Subject

In this section, we investigate the variations in the normalized energy-activity level relationship within each subject. Table 1 provides the weight and height data collected from the participants of this study. We evaluated the energy expenditure calculated from each method introduced in Section 2 and are shown in Fig. 3a, 3b and 3c. The normalized energy-activity level has been represented as a ratio ψ_i with ψ_r being the ratio of limb based movements, ψ_m is VO_2 based Energy Expenditure and ψ_s is running speed. The ratio is useful as it allows to see these variations and allows the observation of abnormalities in the individual ψ_s, ψ_m and ψ_r readings that are unitless. The running speed based energy estimation ratio ψ_s does not demonstrate any difference among the subjects as ψ_s only depends on the speed.

Table 1. Weight and height of subjects

Subject	Weight(kg)	Height(cm)
1	100.8	1.795
2	92.4	1.704
3	70	1.755
4	62.5	1.564
5	86.5	1.834
6	53.5	1.709

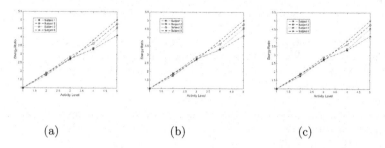

| (a) | (b) | (c) |

Fig. 3. (a)- Variation of rate gyro derived, normalized energy expenditure (ψ_r) with activity levels for all test subjects, (b)- Variation of metabolic measurement based, normalized energy expenditure (ψ_m) with activity levels for all test subjects, (c)- Variation of treadmill speed derived, normalized energy expenditure (ψ_s) with activity levels for all test subjects

5   Conclusion

In this paper, we investigated the feasibility of employing a single inertial sensor based energy expenditure estimation technique for treadmill based exercises. Although we have limited the study to treadmill based exercises to maintain a controlled experimental setup the same technique could be used in out-door walking and running based exercises.

Furthermore, we investigated the variations in energy expenditure between the activity levels across the participants, which demonstrated a distinguishable differences using both metabolic rate and angular rate based approaches.

References

1. Panagiota, A., Layal, S., Stefan, H.: Assessment of human gait speed and energy expenditure using a single triaxial accelerometer. In: 2012 Ninth International Conference on Wearable and Implantable Body Sensor Networks(BSN), pp. 184–188 (2012)
2. Panahandeh, G., Mohammadiha, N., Leijon, A., Handel, P.: Continuous hidden markov model for pedestrian activity classification and gait analysis. IEEE Transactions on Instrumentation and Measurement **62**(5), 1073–1083 (2013)
3. Vathsangam, H., Emken, A., Schroeder, E.T., Spruijt-Metz, D., Sukhatme, G.S.: Determining energy expenditure from treadmill walking using hip-worn inertial sensors: An experimental study. IEEE Transactions on Biomedical Engineering **58**(10), 2804–2815 (2011)
4. Vathsangam, H., Emken, B.A., Schroeder, E.T., Spruijt-Metz, D., Sukhatme, G.: Energy estimation of treadmill walking using on-body accelerometers and gyroscopes. In: 2010 Annual International Conference of the IEEE Engineering in Medicine and Biology Society (EMBC), pp. 6497–6501 (2010)
5. Schulze, M., Calliess, T., Gietzelt, M., Wolf, K.H., Liu, T.H., Seehaus, F., Bocklage, R., Windhagen, H., Marschollek, M.: Development and clinical validation of an unobtrusive ambulatory knee function monitoring system with inertial 9dof sensors. In: 2012 Annual International Conference of the IEEE Engineering in Medicine and Biology Society (EMBC), pp. 1968–1971 (2012)
6. Schulze, M., Tsung-Han, L., Jiang, X., Wu, Z., Wolf, K.-H., Calliess, T., Windhagen, H., Marschollek, M.: Unobtrusive ambulatory estimation of knee joint angles during walking using gyroscope and accelerometer data - a preliminary evaluation study. In: 2012 IEEE-EMBS International Conference on in Biomedical and Health Informatics (BHI), pp. 559–562 (2012)
7. Luinge, H.J., Veltink, P.H.: Measuring orientation of human body segments using miniature gyroscopes and accelerometers. Medical and Biological Engineering and Computing **43**(2), 273–282 (2005)
8. The American College of Sports Medicines: Guidelines for Exercise Testing and Prescription, 7th edn. Lippincott Willims & Wilkins, Philadelphia (2006)
9. Margaria, R., Cerretelli, P., Aghemo, P., Sassi, G.: Energy cost of running. Journal of Applied Physiology **18**, 367–370 (1962)

Facilitating Delivery and Remote Monitoring of Behaviour Change Interventions to Reduce Risk of Developing Alzheimer's Disease: The Gray Matters Study

Phillip J. Hartin[1]([✉]), Ian Cleland[1], Chris D. Nugent[1], Sally I. McClean[1], Timothy Patterson[1], JoAnn Tschanz[2], Christine Clark[2], and Maria C. Norton[2,3]

[1] Computer Science Research Institute, University of Ulster, Coleraine, Northern Ireland, UK
{pj.hartin,i.cleland,cd.nugent,
si.mcclean,t.patterson}@ulster.ac.uk
[2] Department of Psychology, Utah State University, Logan, UT 84322-4440, USA
{joann.tschanz,maria.norton}@usu.edu,
christine.clark@aggiemail.usu.edu
[3] Department of Family, Consumer, and Human Development, Utah State University, Logan, UT 84322-2915, USA

Abstract. Alzheimer's disease (AD) is a recognised global health concern, with currently no cure. Research is now focusing on risk factors and prevention methods associated with AD. Many of these risk factors can be attributed to lifestyle choices and environmental factors. In this paper, we present a smartphone app designed to facilitate, encourage and monitor behaviour change as part of a 6-month randomized control trial with 146 participants. The app provided a convenient, scalable and cost effective method of allowing participants to monitor and review behaviour change data. 94.5% of users entered, and 91.8% reviewed, their performance daily. Over 141,800 individual behaviour logs were submitted across the six-month trial. Analysis of these logs has shown positive trends in behavioural change across all domains, with particular emphasis on efforts to decrease stress, higher sleep promotion and increased social engagement. Respondents' rating of the app's effect on their health improvement: 31% reported "a great deal of effect", 48% reported somewhat of an effect, and 3% said the app was the key factor.

Keywords: Behaviour change · Intervention · Mobile computing

1 Introduction

Alzheimer's disease (AD) is recognised as a global health concern, however, there is currently no cure and research is now focusing on risk factors and prevention methods associated with AD. Almost two thirds of the risk of developing AD can be attributed to one's lifestyle choices and environment. As such international experts have called

© Springer International Publishing Switzerland 2015
A. Geissbühler et al. (Eds.): ICOST 2015, LNCS 9102, pp. 337–342, 2015.
DOI: 10.1007/978-3-319-19312-0_32

for a concentrated effort to study modifiable risk factors related to AD [1]. Cardiovascular factors (sedentary lifestyle, hypertension and high cholesterol) [2], dietary factors (food choices, body-mass index, endocrine disorders and diabetes) [3] and psychosocial factors (education, higher work complexity, social participation and intellectual activities) [4] have all been linked to cognitive decline and the onset of AD. Behaviour change interventions targeting similar factors for other conditions, such as obesity [5] and cardiovascular disease [6] have shown positive results and indicate that multi-factorial interventions, targeting several risk factors simultaneously pose the greatest likelihood of being effective [7]. Given that the behavioural risk factors associated with AD are modifiable and pose the greatest risk to the development of the disease [8], they are appropriate targets for the prevention of cognitive decline and AD through a behavioural change program.

2   Background

Whilst it is becoming more widely accepted that the neuropathological processes involved in AD begin decades before symptoms emerge, currently other behaviour intervention trials relating to AD have focused on an elderly population (65-80 years) [9], rather than introducing preventative interventions in mid-life (40-64 years). Middle-aged adults are increasingly avid consumers of smartphones devices [10], which enable instantaneous access to internet-based services and apps. Mobile (SMS) and internet-based technologies (Email and Websites) have been used successfully as methods to deliver intervention material in various studies [11]. As such there is an opportunity to deliver a behaviour change intervention to middle-aged persons at risk of developing AD, via their smartphones.

The Gray Matters study, a collaboration between Utah State University (USA) and Ulster University (UK), seeks to assess the effect of lifestyle changes on the risk of developing AD, that in the shorter term promote vascular health, in middle aged persons, supported via the use of everyday technology. It is hypothesized that motivations for lifestyle change may be different within a middle-aged group given that there is no known cure for AD and many middle-aged persons have experienced first-hand substantial dementia caregiving burden. To build upon this existing intrinsic motivation, an interdisciplinary team of computer scientists, biomedical engineers, mathematicians, psychologists, gerontologists, epidemiologists and statisticians designed the Gray Matters smartphone app; an app designed to supplement intrinsic motivations with external rewards and a means to quantify behaviour change effort [12].

3   Methods

To evaluate an evidence-based multi-domain lifestyle intervention designed to promote brain health among middle-aged persons (40-64 years) with normal cognition, a 6 month randomized controlled trial (RCT) was conducted with 146 participants, assigned to treatment (n=104) and control (n=42) groups. Primary outcome measures included a set of anthropometric measures, blood-based biomarkers, objective cognitive testing, and behaviour in targeted domains. Secondary outcome measures included metacognition, motivation, readiness-for-change, sleep quality, social engagement and depression.

For further detail on the RCT study design, inclusion criteria and CONSORT diagram, please refer to [13]. The intervention provided participants with health education material, derived from evidence-based literature, based on six core domains: Food, Physical, Cognitive, Social, Sleep and Stress. The intervention also tracked the behaviour in these domains over the duration of the study, to monitor for changes and trends. The treatment group had access to the following resources: Smartphone Application, an Activity Monitor, Booster Events, a Personal Coach and a supporting study website. This paper describes, in detail, how the smartphone application was successfully used to both deliver and monitor, the intervention.

3.1   Smartphone Application

As the primary means to deliver health education material and track behaviour change across the treatment group, a smartphone app was developed for iOS and Android and installed onto the participant's personal smartphone [12] (refer to Fig. 1). The app facilitated the delivery of the health education material through the form of 'factoids'. Each factoid comprised a fact and suggestion pair relating to AD and preventative strategies, e.g. "Low dietary sodium is protective against cognitive decline; Use your favourite spice instead of salt to flavour food" (refer to Fig. 1a). In total 164 factoids were produced for the study. A different factoid was delivered to the participant each morning via the app, accompanied with a notification on the smartphone at 8am. To monitor behavioural changes, the participants were requested to self-report their behaviours in a 'log' by answering 12 questions daily (refer to Fig. 1b). Each question related to one of the core domains and had a recommended value, based on the Centre for Disease Control and Prevention's (CDC) minimum daily targets. Using these recommended values it was possible to provide the participant with immediate feedback as to their efforts in the form of a 5 star rating (refer to Fig. 1c), designed to encourage and reinforce their efforts [12].

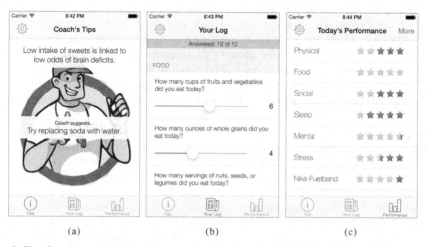

(a)   (b)   (c)

Fig. 1. Key functions of the Gray Matters smartphone app: (a) The factoid delivery screen. (b) Behavioural data entry screen, which displays 12 scrolling questions and facilitates behaviour logging. (c) Daily feedback for each domain with star ratings.

Participants could also review their aggregated weekly performances for each domain in a variety of graphs. In order to maximise adherence to the self-reporting, a notification was delivered at 6pm as a reminder; the users could also change this time manually. In addition to the 6 core behaviour domains, the participants also used the app to report the values generated by their wrist worn activity monitors.

3.2   Remote Monitoring of Intervention Components

In real time, upon the log being updated, the self-reported values are transmitted to a central repository via mobile data or Wi-Fi in the open-standard JSON format. This allows for immediate analysis of the data, which is already in a predefined and structured format, due to its ordinal nature. This almost-instant transmission of behavioural information allows the remote observation and monitoring for trends or significant changes, which may be due to internal or external components of the intervention. For example, a resource available to the participants is booster events, which were organised and delivered throughout the six-month period (n=39). Each booster event was designed to emphasize the link between a specific domain and the risk it poses to developing AD, accompanied by preventative measures that the participants can apply in their daily lives (i.e. the food domain hosted cooking classes that promoted sustainable healthy eating choices). Booster events are considered an internal component of the study, in addition to the activity monitors and personal coaches, whilst an external study factors are considered to be factors outside of the study's protocol, such as local weather conditions, public holidays and vacations.

4   Results

Typically, in behavioural studies such as this, participant data collection would be facilitated through the administration of online questionnaires or paper-based postal service, both of which require a large degree of human processing and interaction [14]. The Gray Matters app used within the current study provided a convenient, scalable and cost effective method of allowing participants and the study investigators to monitor and review behaviour change data. Analysis of in-app behaviours indicated that 94.5% of users entered, and 91.8% reviewed, their performance daily. In total over 141,800 individual logs were uploaded to the central online repository over the six-month trial. Analysis of these logs has shown positive trends in behavioural change across all domains, with particular emphasis on efforts to decrease stress, higher sleep promotion and increased social engagement. For the purposes of visualisation all individuals' self-reported behaviours for all domains results have been aggregated and normalised across the study duration, showing a steady increase of desirable behaviours for all domains (refer to Fig. 2a).

A post-study exit questionnaire was administered to glean attitudes towards various study components. Regarding the app's effect on their health improvement 31% reported "a great deal of effect", 48% reported somewhat of an effect, and 3% said the app was the key factor. Regarding monitoring the effectiveness of internal intervention components, a Paired-sample t Test relating to the booster events and their attendees highlighted a significant change ($p < 0.05$) in domain relevant behaviours, post-attendance across 7 days, for 7 events. One such event was the 'Intro to Pilates' class, a booster even designed to encourage participation in physical activity. For the 9 attendees, their pre and post attendance logs, in the physical domain, were analysed in a paired sample t-test and the booster event was found to have had a significant effect on their behaviours for 7 days (p: 0.0468, mean: -5.097 Std Dev: 6.5108, Std Err: 2.17). In addition, analysis of external factors of the study showed a positive correlation in physical activity, both moderate and vigorous, to the local temperature, R=0.585, R=0.725, respectively (Fig. 2b).

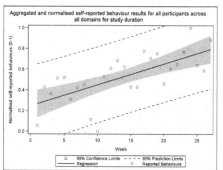 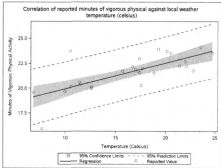

Fig. 2. (a) Scatter graph showing normalised average results (0-1) for self-reported behaviours for all participants in all domains across study duration. Regression shows steady increase of average scores over 27 weeks (R=0.684, p=<.0001,). (b) Scatter graph showing correlation analysis of participant's self-reported vigorous exercise against the external factor local average temperature in degrees Celsius (R=0.725, p=<.0001).

5   Conclusions

This project aims to assess the effect of lifestyle behaviour change on the risk of developing dementia by educating participants on strategies that promote better vascular health, improved sleep quality and lower perceived stress levels, all associated with lower risk. This behaviour change is monitored through a bespoke smartphone application. Results, reported within this paper have shown the mobile application to be a suitable method of delivery, capable of informing participants and the intervention investigators, of their performance and progress in real-time. In addition, data collected through the application is currently being examined to assess the effectiveness of internal components of the study, such as booster events. In the future, this data may be combined with external data sources, such as local weather, to assess the effect that these factors have on participants' behaviour. Future work will include additional analysis to assess the app's effect on altering both primary and secondary outcome measures in the RCT, such as behaviours, motivations and readiness-for-change, of those in the treatment group, against those who did not have the app in the control groups.

References

1. Smith, D., Yaffe, K.: Dementia (including Alzheimer's disease) can be prevented: statement supported by international experts. J. Alzheimers. Dis. **38**, 699–703 (2014)
2. Justin, B.N., Turek, M., Hakim, A.M.: Heart disease as a risk factor for dementia. Clin. Epidemiol. **5**, 135–145 (2013)
3. Morris, M.C.: Nutritional determinants of cognitive aging and dementia. Proc. Nutr. Soc. **71**, 1–13 (2012)
4. Wang, H.-X., Jin, Y., Hendrie, H.C., Liang, C., Yang, L., Cheng, Y., Unverzagt, F.W., Ma, F., Hall, K.S., Murrell, J.R., Li, P., Bian, J., Pei, J.-J., Gao, S.: Late life leisure activities and risk of cognitive decline. J. Gerontol. A. Biol. Sci. Med. Sci. **68**, 205–213 (2013)
5. Wadden, T.A., Webb, V.L., Moran, C.H., Bailer, B.A.: Lifestyle modification for obesity: New developments in diet, physical activity, and behavior therapy. Circulation **125**, 1157–1170 (2012)
6. Spring, B., Moller, A.C., Colangelo, L.A., Siddique, J., Roehrig, M., Daviglus, M.L., Polak, J.F., Reis, J.P., Sidney, S., Liu, K.: Healthy lifestyle change and subclinical atherosclerosis in young adults: Coronary artery risk development in young adults (CARDIA) study. Circulation **130**, 10–17 (2014)
7. Solomon, A., Mangialasche, F., Richard, E., Andrieu, S., Bennett, D.A., Breteler, M., Fratiglioni, L., Hooshmand, B., Khachaturian, A.S., Schneider, L.S., Skoog, I., Kivipelto, M.: Advances in the prevention of Alzheimer's disease and dementia. J. Intern. Med. **275**, 229–250 (2014)
8. Ridge, P.G., Mukherjee, S., Crane, P.K., Kauwe, J.S.K.: Alzheimer's disease: analyzing the missing heritability. PLoS One **8**, e79771 (2013)
9. Mangialasche, F., Kivipelto, M., Solomon, A., Fratiglioni, L.: Dementia prevention: current epidemiological evidence and future perspective. Alzheimers. Res. Ther. **4**, 6 (2012)
10. PEW Research Center Mobile Technology Fact Sheet. http://www.pewinternet.org/fact-sheets/mobile-technology-fact-sheet/, March 15, 2015
11. Buhi, E.R., Trudnak, T.E., Martinasek, M.P., Oberne, A.B., Fuhrmann, H.J., McDermott, R.J.: Mobile phone-based behavioural interventions for health: A systematic review. Health Educ. J. **72**, 564–583 (2012)
12. Hartin, P.J., Nugent, C.D., McClean, S.I., Cleland, I., Tschanz, J., Clark, C., Norton, M.C.: Encouraging behavioral change via everyday technologies to reduce risk of developing Alzheimer's disease. In: Pecchia, L., Chen, L.L., Nugent, C., Bravo, J. (eds.) IWAAL 2014. LNCS, vol. 8868, pp. 51–58. Springer, Heidelberg (2014)
13. Norton, M., Clark, C., Tschanz, J., Hartin, P., Fauth, E., Gast, J., Dorsch, T.E., Wengreen, H., Nugent, C., Robinson, D., Lefevre, M., McClean, S., Cleland, I., Schaeffer, S., Aguilar, S.: A multi-domain lifestyle intervention to lower Alzheimer's disease risk in middle-aged persons: the Gray Matters randomized trial. Alzheimer's Dement. Transl. Res. Clin. Interv. (2015) (manuscript in review)
14. Schueller, S.M.: Behavioral intervention technologies for positive psychology: Introduction to the special issue. J. Posit. Psychol. **9**, 475–476 (2014)

Preco Framework: A Predictive Approach for Comorbidities Risk Assessment

Mehdi Snene[✉], Manel Sghir, and Dimitri Konstantas

Information Science Institute, Rte de Drize7 1227, Carouge, Switzerland
{mehdi.snene,manel.sghir,dimitri.konstanas}@unige.ch

Abstract. The overall objective of the PRECO framework is to investigate comorbidities' patterns, based on the historic of comorbidities evolution, patient centric data and tele-health monitoring, for a predictive evaluation of comorbidity development risk and to determine the most probable one(s) the patient could declare.

Keywords: Predictive analytics · Comorbidities · Risk assessment

1 Introduction

From 2001 to 2012 the percentage of European citizen aged 65 years and more has increased from 15.6% to 17.4%. According to several studies, this percentage will reach 24% in 2030 and 35% in 2050 [1]. Public health and medical advances are credited of the improvement of life expectancy. However European health Indicators show that the life expectancy values are growing faster than healthy life years. This difference can be explained by the fact that elderly people are more prone to chronicle diseases and thus for co-morbidities. Many studies attempt to analyze and structure comorbid conditions, impact and weight. Those studies are based on statistical indicators such as Davis Index and Charlson Index [2], administrative data as Elixhauser Index [3] or sampling data as used in Khan Index [4]. Those indexes aim to predict the patient mortality percentage upon the declared comorbidities or the mostly probabilistic co-morbidities they could develop. Despite the existence of several methods of comorbidity assessment, the comorbidity diagnostic complexity and comorbid factors' evolution involves intensive clinical exams and regular admissions. Moreover, obtained results require a continuous update and regular adjustment for a quick consideration of patient state evolution. It is important also to note that those methods are rarely used in prevention of comorbidities but intervene during chronicle symptoms diagnostic. This diagnostic delay can be explained by the absence of preventive methods that exploit available patient's data (social, demographic, chronicle comorbid patterns, medical.) to calibrate the risk level of the patient suffering from a diagnosed chronicle disease to develop a comorbid condition and to predict the most likely comorbidity he will develop. In summary, the current methods of comorbidity assessment are not designed to support real time comorbidity evaluation of patients under remote medical monitoring. The PRECO framework tackle this issue by investigating several

© Springer International Publishing Switzerland 2015
A. Geissbühler et al. (Eds.): ICOST 2015, LNCS 9102, pp. 343–348, 2015.
DOI: 10.1007/978-3-319-19312-0_33

analytic approaches to integrate social and demographical data, real time monitoring parameters, and historical medical data to evaluate the risk of appearance of comorbid conditions.

2   Field of Study

The comorbidity risk assessment is usually carried by statistic indexes based on static data and thus it does not fit into the real patient's environment. Moreover, although comorbidity studies have increased population sample size, several clinical recommendations underline the importance to extend the study of comorbidity pattern to general pattern samples. The common claim is that it is not possible to know that patterns observed in clinical will reflect those in general community, because significant biases may be present [5]. Beyond the size extension of the population sampling size, the integration in the data collection of fragmented and multidimensional large scale data provided by heterogeneous sources (Broader social, environmental, and medical factors such as access to care, social support, substance abuse, and functional status) with real time monitoring data and medical history will contribute to the compilation of a complete schematic view of studied population.

Secondly, the Identification of comorbidity patterns based on health conditions is critical for evidence-based practice to improve the prevention, treatment and health care of relevant diseases. Existing approaches focus mainly on either using descriptive measures of comorbidity in terms of the prevalence of coexisting conditions, or addressing the prevalence of comorbidity based on a particular disease (e.g. psychosis) or a specific population (e.g. hospital patients) . By extending the sampling population (to patients with comorbid diseases and risky patient but with no comorbid diseases diagnosed yet), new approaches of population clustering for comorbidity pattern extraction can be designed. The size extension provides a more granular and accurate reference point for patterns structuring and for multidimensional patterns that extend their focuses to the complete patient's environment.

Finally, the comorbidity relationship between two illnesses exists whenever they appear simultaneously in a patient more than chance alone [5]. The comorbidity relationships between diseases could be exploited to build a model that predicts the diseases a patient could have in the future [6] based on the patient's comorbid conditions [7]. A vector of diagnosed diseases characterizes a patient and a prediction is made on the base of other similar patients. Major prediction methods and algorithms are designed to predict the mortality rate and its related risk, which makes the approach reactive, i.e. a medical treatment is undertaken only after the patient has already developed the disease, rather than proactive. An emerging viewpoint aims at identifying prospective health care models to determine the risk for individuals to develop particular diseases [7]. So, a proactive prediction models could improve efficiency and effectiveness of health care strategy by identifying which patients would benefit most from care transition interventions and to risk-adjust comorbidity development level [5].

2.1   Preco Use Case

For our framework, we have selected elderly persons that have developed comorbidities (mainly 65 years old and more, as this accounts for the major part of hospitalization and the major part of people under tele-health protocol). Although elderly can develop several forms of comorbidities, we concentrate on physical disease and patient with at least two declared chronicle diseases so excluding healthy subject. Between the set of co-existing comorbid conditions, we focus on patients suffering from arthritis and heart disease or diabetes. Arthritis is very common in elderly population and heart disease and diabetes are two of the most common comorbidities among patient suffering from arthritis. Other comorbidity that is common among those patients is chronic respiratory conditions. The main purpose of PRECO is to predict the health status evolution of patient and the risk of the development of diabetes, and respiratory chronic conditions if the patient suffers from arthritis and heart disease, or the risk of development of heart disease and chronic respiratory conditions if he suffers from arthritis and diabetes.

3   Preco Functional Architecture

The Preco architecture is designed based on a multi-layered approach. It facilitates the integration of new component and the interaction between them. The framework is structured around collected data and their related services. The purpose of the chosen architecture is to enable the exploitation of the results in varied contexts ranging from Medical to business decision. Mainly, three levels can be distinguished: the Data level (source), the predictive analytics level (interpretation) and the risk assessment level (exploitation).

3.1   Data Sources Identification

With more and more information sources available via inexpensive network connections, either over the Internet or in company intranets, the desire to access all these sources through a consistent interface has been the driving force behind much research in the field of information integration. Furthermore, the expansion of monitoring devices and the widespread of multisensory application, have contributed largely to the increased complexity and amount of collected data [8]. Thus, two data varieties co-exist in health care systems, which can be categorized in: static data (administrative databases, statistical databases, medical files...) and dynamic data (monitoring data, real time assessment data, geo-localization...).

3.2   Data Architecture

The first step of integration serve for the establishment of a unified data model exploitable within a big data structure. This model will encompass static data under a common index (basically a timestamp index). A first cycle of data clustering will be carried out for a preliminary profiling that will be then exploited as a contextual environment for the sensors' data fusion. It will identify and select sensors' data required depending on the patients' situation and their related contexts. Then, the collected data is stored in the same model. The major advantage of such model is the reduction of data complexity, the data storing and querying cost and data redundancy and therefore reduce the complexity of predictive analytics tasks.

3.3   Predictive Models

The comorbidity's sequential pattern design is mainly based on the data collected that have an inherent sequential structure. The discovery of the sequential relationships or patterns is useful for various purposes such as prediction of events or identification of sequential rules, conditions, states that characterize different clusters of data. Obtained patterns serve as data analysis and knowledge discovery algorithms. Giving temporal nature of patient's data, a big data analysis approach (usually structured in 3 layers: key, timestamp, event) is applied to our existing data frameset. Furthermore, existing patterns and indexes commonly used and widely known in comorbidities assessment are uniformed according to a generic form of sequential pattern. Since predictive factors span different domains such as life style, medical records and real time data, combining these resources into a coherent assessment of patient status requires taking into account in the model different granularities of their respective evolution and the different nature of their effect on the outcome. An important novelty in the framework is that outcomes are defined as combinations of occurrences of various diseases. As some combinations are more likely than others - for example diabetes are associated with heart disease - the correlations among outcomes is considered in the proposed model. We employed a structured prediction approach, which is a machine learning process, using conditional random fields [9]. The obtained models are composed from two main results:

- **Predictions model:** prediction model covers the entirety of the data space. It runs from global predictions based on statistical data merged with patients' data to be used for management and business purpose, to patients' health status predictions that cover the patient health pathway based on his private medical data and finally a risk assessment prediction for the patient's risk adjustment based on health sensors data.
- **Predictions accuracy metrics:** since the predictions generated have various level and various sources of data, metrics employed are adapted to each of them. A combination of two metrics is mainly defined: PPV predictions for financial and strategic goals that will measure the impact of the results on these two dimensions, and the C-statistic for the prediction oriented patients, which will measure the effectiveness of the models to each case.

3.4   Risk Assessment Method

The risk assessment model entails feeding patients' clustered data to profile the patient into a risk category. This step identifies patients who are likely to develop new comorbid diseases based on the correlation between their risk level and the comorbidities sequential pattern exploited or discovered in the system. The confidence rate assessment acts as a risk adjustment model. It mainly determines the level of confidence granted to prediction results by comparing the effectiveness and correctness of the prediction with former predictions done in a similar situation and it will also consider parameters of data quality and integrity. In addition to providing alerts, the integrated model allow prediction of the effect of specific interventions on patients' status. Disentangling such effects from spurious correlations, inquires incorporation of methods that reduce potential bias from confounding factors such as propensity score modelling [9] or causal modelling approaches [10]. Based on results of the risk assessment, a medical decision simulation process is implemented for decisions impact evaluation on the health pathway process. It predicts the most likely impact on patients based on former medical decisions in order to assist physicians to decide for the most suitable medical pathway. It also consider the decision taken for an update of the risk level according to the expected impact.

4   Limitations and Conclusion

Comorbidity is a relatively new concern in home healthcare. So far, elderly are monitored for specific symptoms related to a previously diagnosed disorder or disease, but no use is made of the collected data other than for the primary disease indicated. Indeed, using the data beyond this is a complex matter. Symptoms can be concealed, undeclared and easily confused, hence requiring different assessment and different monitoring depending on the secondary diseases of interest. The proposed Preco Framework, presents an innovative approach for data integration and real time risk assessment. The implementation of such framework requires an extensive use of health sensors, open data and medical data. The used predictive models are based on sequential patterns that require a logic and an ordered pathway of events and results. Such sequencing is not a natural element in the outbreaks of diseases. The integration of other predictive models taking into account fortuity such as gaming models could improve the accuracy and the confidence of the Preco results.

References

1. http://epp.eurostat.ec.europa.eu/statistics_explained/index.php/Healthcare_statistics
2. Fried, L., Bernardini, J., Piraino, B.: Comparison of the Charlson Comorbidity Index and the Davies score as a predictor of outcomes in PD patients, Pubmed (2003)
3. Elixhauser, A., Steiner, C., Harris, D.R., Coffey, R.M.: Comorbidity measures for use with administrative data. Med Care (1998)
4. Khan, I.H., Catto, G.R., Edward, N., Fleming, L.W., Henderson, I.S., MacLeod, A.M.: Influence of coexisting disease on survival on renal-replacement therapy. Lancet (1993)
5. Jack, M., Barbara markham, S.: Chronic Disease Management: Evidence of Predictable Savings. Health Management Associates (2008)
6. Health Care Cost Drivers: Chronic Disease, Comorbidity, and Health Risk Factors in the U.S. and Michigan. http://www.chrt.org/publications/price-of-care/issue-brief-2010-08-health-care-cost-drivers/

7. Marrie, R.A., Horwitz, R., Cutter, G., Tyry, T., Campagnolo, D., Vollmer, T.: Comorbidity delays diagnosis and increases disability at diagnosis in MS. Neurology Journal, January 2009
8. Pearl, J.: Causality: Models, Reasoning, and Inference. CambridgeUniversity Press, Second Edition (2009)
9. Ng, S.K., Holden, L., Sun, J.: Identifying comorbidity patterns of health conditions via cluster analysis of pair wise concordance statistics. Stat. Med. (2012)
10. Hidalgo, C.A., Blumm, N., Barab´asi, A.L., Christakis, N.A.: A dynamic network approach for the study of human phenotypes. PLoS Computational Biology (2009)

SNS Based Predictive Model for Depression

Jamil Hussain[1], Maqbool Ali[1], Hafiz Syed Muhammad Bilal[1], Muhammad Afzal[1],
Hafiz Farooq Ahmad[2], Oresti Banos[1], and Sungyoung Lee[1(✉)]

[1] Department of Computer Engineering, Kyung Hee University Seocheon-dong,
Giheung-gu, Yongin-si, Gyeonggi-do 446-701, Republic of Korea
{jamil,maqbool.ali,bilalrizvi,muhammad.afzal,
oresti,sylee}@oslab.khu.ac.kr
[2] Department of Computer Science,
College of Computer Sciences and Information Technology (CCSIT), King Faisal University,
Alahssa 31982, Kingdom of Saudi Arabia
hfahmad@kfu.edu.sa

Abstract. Worldwide the Mental illness is a primary cause of disability. It affects millions of people each year and whom of few receives cure. We found that social networking sites (SNS) can be used as a screening tool for discovering an affective mental illness in individuals. SNS posting truly depicts user's current behavior, thinking style, and mood. We consider a set of behavioral attributes concerning to socialization, socioeconomics, familial, marital status, feeling, language use, and references of antidepressant treatments. We take advantage of these behavioral attributes to envision a tool that can provide prior alerts to an individual based on their SNS data regarding Major Depression Disorder (MDD). We propose a method, to automatically classify individuals into displayer and non-displayer depression using ensemble learning technique from their Facebook profile. Our developed tool is used for MDD diagnosis of individuals in additional to questioner techniques such as Beck Depression Inventory (BDI) and CESD-R.

Keywords: Mental illness · Depression · Social networking sites · Facebook · Content analysis

1 Introduction

Recently, use of a social network increased exponentially as according to pew [24] report of 2014, 74% of online adult use SNS beyond them 40% use mobile. SNS provides a platform through which people share information in very cost effective way and easily express their opinions that enable research groups to investigate a numerous aspects of human behaviors and psychological concerns [16]. Among these platforms, Twitter and Facebook are mostly used as social sensor for collection of individual's daily life activities, feelings, and emotions. Changes in individual's life events can easily be detected from the recorded human behavior data of several years on these platforms, which leads to reveal the mental illness.

Mental illness, the major contributor in disability worldwide. It disrupts the individual's mood, cognitive and language styles, ability to work, and routine activities.

© Springer International Publishing Switzerland 2015
A. Geissbühler et al. (Eds.): ICOST 2015, LNCS 9102, pp. 349–354, 2015.
DOI: 10.1007/978-3-319-19312-0_34

Some individuals might not even know what's going on, especially in initial episode of psychosis.

Mental illnesses classified into depression, anxiety, bipolar disorder, obsessive-compulsive disorder (OCD), borderline personality disorder, schizophrenia, and post-traumatic stress disorder (PTSD) and others. Depression is the most common mental illness having symptoms like sadness, depressed mood, tiredness, sleep problem, losing interest in activities, poor concentration, reduce energy in work, guilt feeling, and suicidal attempt. Mostly adults are effected by depression that declines individual's working capabilities and recurrent episodes lead to suicidal attempt. Annually almost 1 million lives are lost due to suicide, which translates to 3000 suicide deaths every day and on average every 40 seconds 1 person dies from suicide. More than half of all suicides occur below the age of 45 years[1].

Globally, medical resources are utilize to overcome the consequences of mental illness. Recently, WHO and its members take actions to cope with mental illness and conducted survey in 17 countries which highlighted more than 450 million people are the victims of mental illness [1]. The annual statistical results revealed from multiple reports show that only in North America males have 3 to 5 % and females have 8 to 10% depression cases [2]. Still, there is insufficient global support and service for exposing the mental illness [3].

A comprehensive assessment to diagnose the episodes of psychosis and symptoms of depression is the foremost step towards plotting a recovery strategy. However for assessment of depression, medical science is still incompetent and no trustworthy techniques have been formulated that should be relied upon. The traditional approaches are questionnaire based, patient's self-reported or behaviors mentioned by their closed ones; care providers are unable to get the complete picture of depressed person using patients' self-reporting in one place at one time. For example questionnaires depend on a person's memory which are subject to high degree of inaccuracy [21].

To address these challenges, currently SNS are used as a tool, to find and predict behaviors and disorders in individuals [4-13][16-17][21], which overcome the problems of patients' self-reportingunintentionally.SNS recodes the routine activities and happening in a naturalistic way and hence is less vulnerable to memory bias or experimenter demand effects [16]. It provides a means for capturing behavioral attributes that are relevant to an individual's thinking, mood, communication, activities, and socialization. The emotion and language used in SNS postings may indicate feelings of worthlessness, guilt, helplessness, and self-hatred that characterize major depression. By mining the SNS user's activities, we get closer to the natural behavior of the users, way of thinking, and mental state of health.

We propose a tool that analyze users Facebook activities in automated manner, to detect and diagnose depression. Through their Facebook activities over a period preceding the onset of depression.

Existing approaches don't cover all the SNS influencing attributes. Usually a subset of attributes have been used to identify the sign and symptoms of depression. To get an accurate and precise diagnoses of causes and illness we proposed a comprehensive tool which cover all majors SNS inducing attributes related to depression risk factors. Attributes like gender, marital status, socioeconomic status, familial factors, personality, life events, and others are directly related to Facebook features [22].

The proposed tool classifies individuals using ensemble learning technique that identifies depressive symptom–related features from user's Facebook activities. The tool can be utilized by individuals in order to track their daily life activities to reveal depression at initial stages. It can also be used by Psychologists/Psychiatrist for depression detection and diagnosis of patient, additional to questioner techniques such as Beck Depression Inventory (BDI) [14], CESD-R [15].

2   Methodology

A brief description of eachmodules of our system architecture that shown in Fig.1 are described in below section.

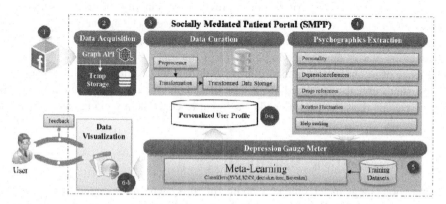

Fig. 1. System Architecture

2.1   Data Acquisition Module (DCM)

It gathers data from Facebook using graph API. It has data fetching engine and store data temporary using session variable. In order to collect data, a Facebook APP is created and registered, called Socially Mediated Patient Portal (SMPP). It is a PHP-based web tool that uses the Facebook Graph API, which uses URL-based queries to return result sets such as status updates, gender, comments, likes, photo, video and many more.

2.2   Data Curation Module (DCrM)

Data transformations are done by DCrM that is used by Psychographics Extraction Module. Sub modules are preprocessor and transformed-data storage. Preprocessor used temporary data stored in session variables and transformed it into normalized form that have no noisy, missing information and errors.

2.3   Psychographics Extraction Module (PEM)

PEM consists of many sub-modules, which used third party APIs such as Apply Magic Sauce (AMS)API [19],AlchemyAPI [20] and own Sentiment classifiers for Personality, Religious Views, Sexuality, Profession, Depression reference, Drugs references, Ego-network, Engagement and Help seeking information's extraction. AMS API predicts users' psycho-demographic traits based on Facebook Like IDs as input data along with our own personality model that based on Facebook like ID's , status updates, photos, demographics, videos, friendlist and others. Through AMS API we can predict the personality of a user using Big5 model, where Big5 model has correlation with personality disorder [18] and personality disorder is a subset of mental illness.

According to DSM-V criteria for depression, we classify the user posting into 9 categories in order to predict the depression references. The ego-network focuses on number of friends, number of followers and communication through comments. The fluctuation alarms the change in condition of the user which ultimately indicates the presence of or chances of mental illness. Multimedia classifier uses the uploaded images, status updates and user likes as input to predict the drug related references. The help seeking classifier gets user likes as input to check help seeking pages related to depression.

2.4   Depression Gauge Meter (DGM)

Depression Gauge meteris the key module in our system that accumulate the information extracted from PEM. Ensemble Learning technique, a type of meta-learning technique, is used in conjunction with other learning algorithms i.e. SVM, KNN, decision tree, Bayesian, to improve the performance.

Training datasets were made manually then labeled it according to DSM-V criteria against 9 features. Firstly we train the model using train dataset, and then applied the train model on users' Facebook profile through web application. To predict the existence of depression, our tool fetches the values of 9 features from user's Facebook profile and then trained model predicts.

2.5   Data Visualization Module (DVM)

It is used to portrait intellectual knowledge from classified data. It uses many Javascript data visualization libraries such as Google Graph, D3.js, JQuery for visualization. It visualizes analyzed data as map, chart, graph and tables. It reveals many hidden patterns regarding the user lifestyle. We also provide a user feedback functionality in order to validate the classified results.

3   Implementation of Socially Mediated Patient Portal (SMPP)

A web based tool is developed, in order to perform depression test according to DSM-V criteria, user must be subscribed to Facebook SMPP APP to fetch its profile data based on login permissions. The home page of portal gives the Facebook personal analytics based on user's Facebook profile data to assess on the basis of DSM-V criterion for a depression symptoms or Major Depressive Disorder (MDD).

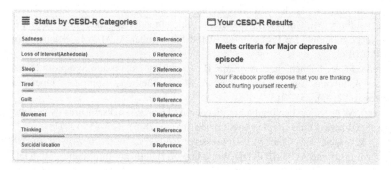

Fig. 2. User posting classification by CESD-R Categories and CESD-R result

The results in Fig. 2, reflects that subject user's posting have many depressive references. To cross check the results of the tool we perform peer review of the subject on the basis of well-defined standard questionnaires designed by [15]. It depict that the 53.66% of postings are in the category of sadness. The sleeping category is on the basis of usage of late night activities on Facebook which is 13.33%. The 26.66% posts represent that subject is confused about its rational while 6.66% characterizes the exhaustion state of the subject.

4   Conclusion and Future Work

We developed a tool that potentially used Facebook as a trustworthy source for detecting depression patterns in individuals. It is an individual-centric predictive model that analyze a subject's Facebook activities, and provide onset alerts if there is abnormalities in subject behavior. It considered multiple attributes of Facebook that are directly associated with depression risk factors. The evaluation indicates that depressed subject posts many depression references and also have small ego-network. To extend the current work we will consider multimedia posting as well as drug usage references to get more precise and accurate diagnosis of mental illness.

Acknowledgments. This work was supported by the Industrial Core Technology Development Program (10049079, Development of Mining core technology exploiting personal big data) funded by the Ministry of Trade, Industry and Energy (MOTIE, Korea).

References

1. World Health Organization: WHO-Incidence and prevalence of mental illness. World Health Organization (2014). http://www.who.int/mental_health/en
2. Andrade, L., Caraveo, A.: Epidemiology of major depressive episodes: Results from the International Consortium of Psychiatric Epidemiology (ICPE) Surveys. Int J Methods PsychiatrRes. **12**(1), 3–21 (2003)
3. Detels, R.: The scope and concerns of public health. Oxford University Press (2009)
4. De Choudhury, M., et al.: Predicting Depression via Social Media. ICWSM (2013)
5. De Choudhury, M., Counts, S., Horvitz, E.: Social media as a measurement tool of depression in populations. In: Proceedings of the 5th Annual ACM Web Science Conference. ACM (2013)
6. Moreno, M.A., Jelenchick, L.A., Kota, R.: Exploring Depression Symptom References on Facebook among College Freshmen: A Mixed Methods Approach. Open Journal of Depression **2**(03), 35 (2013)
7. Moreno, M.A., et al.: Feeling bad on Facebook: Depression disclosures by college students on a social networking site. Depression and anxiety **28**(6), 447–455 (2011)
8. Park, M., Cha, C., Cha, M.: Depressive moods of users portrayed in twitter. In: Proceedings of the ACM SIGKDD Workshop on Healthcare Informatics, HI-KDD (2012)
9. De Choudhury, M.: Role of social media in tackling challenges in mental health. In: Proceedings of the 2nd International Workshop on Socially-Aware Multimedia. ACM (2013)
10. Farnadi, G., et al.: How well do your facebook status updates express your personality? In: Proceedings of the 22nd Edition of the Annual Belgian-Dutch Conference on Machine Learning, BENELEARN (2013)
11. Rahman, M.M.: Mining Social Data to Extract Intellectual Knowledge. arXiv preprint arXiv:1209.5345 (2012)
12. Troussas, C., et al.: Sentiment analysis of Facebook statuses using Naive Bayes classifier for language learning. In: 2013 Fourth International Conference on Information, Intelligence, Systems and Applications (IISA). IEEE (2013)
13. Moreno, M.A., et al.: Associations between displayed alcohol references on Facebook and problem drinking among college students. Archives of pediatrics & adolescent medicine **166**(2), 157–163 (2012)
14. Steer, R.A., et al.: Use of the Beck Depression Inventory for Primary Care to screen for major depression disorders. General hospital psychiatry **21**(2), 106–111 (1999)
15. Center for Epidemiologic Studies Depression Scale Revised Online Depression Assessment. http://cesd-r.com/cesdr/ (accessed November 14, 2014)
16. De Choudhury, M.: Can social media help us reason about mental health?. In: Proceedings of the Companion Publication of the 23rd International Conference on World Wide Web Companion. International World Wide Web Conferences Steering Committee (2014)
17. Qiu, L., et al.: Putting their best foot forward: Emotional disclosure on Facebook. Cyberpsychology, Behavior, and Social Networking **15**(10), 569–572 (2012)
18. Costa Jr., P.T., McCrae, R.R.: Personality disorders and the five-factor model of personality. Journal of Personality Disorders **4**(4), 362–371 (1990)
19. Apply Magic Sauce. http://applymagicsauce.com (accessed October 15, 2014)
20. AlchemyAPI. http://www.alchemyapi.com (accessed: January 2, 2015)
21. Gannon, M.: Facebook profile may expose mental illness (2013)
22. Dobson, K.S., Dozois, D.J.A. (eds.): Risk factors in depression. Academic Press (2011)
23. Pew Research Center's Internet and American Life Project. http://www.pewinternet.org/ (accessed December 20, 2014)

An Interactive Case-Based Flip Learning Tool for Medical Education

Maqbool Ali[1], Hafiz Syed Muhammad Bilal[1], Jamil Hussain[1],
Sungyoung Lee[1]([⊠]), and Byeong Ho Kang[2]

[1] Department of Computer Engineering, Kyung Hee University,
Gyeonggi-do, Seoul 446-701, Korea
{maqbool.ali,bilalrizvi,jamil,sylee}@oslab.khu.ac.kr
[2] School of Engineering and ICT, University of Tasmania, Hobart, Australia
byeong.kang@utas.edu.au

Abstract. Legacy Case-Based Learning (CBL) medical educational systems aim to boost the learning and educational process but lacks the support of *Systematized Nomenclature of Medicine* (SNOMED) and flip learning concepts. Integrating these vocabularies can exploit the learning outcomes and build confidence in students while making decision to rehearsal in advance before attending the actual CBL. The scope of this research covers delivering of medical education in interactive and intelligent way, efficient knowledge sharing, promoting team work environments, and building a knowledge-base for future to support automated computerized feedback. To achieve these goals, we propose a tool called *Interactive Case-Based Flip Learning Tool* (ICBFLT) that covers formulation of CBL case summaries, getting standard computerized help from both SNOMED vocabulary and state of the art solutions, and finally getting feedback from concerned tutor. In order to evaluate the ICBFLT, a scenario from the *School of Medicine, University of Tasmania, Australia* has been considered. This is an ongoing work and this paper gives an overview of the ICBFLT architecture with some intermediate results. The evaluation shows that the system has satisfied its users in term of interaction upto 70%.

Keywords: Flip learning · Case-based learning · Natural language processing · SNOMED

1 Introduction

Medical education is experiencing one of the deepest revisions that has practiced in recent decades. In medical education, most of the literature is describing the Problem-Based Learning (PBL). The Case-Based Learning (CBL) is a kind of teaching in which PBL principles are followed. CBL proceeds on many forms, from simple hands-on, in-class exercises to semester long projects and/or case studies [1]. This approach promotes the learning outcomes and build confidence in the students while making decision to practice in real life [2],[3]. We have to

© Springer International Publishing Switzerland 2015
A. Geissbühler et al. (Eds.): ICOST 2015, LNCS 9102, pp. 355–360, 2015.
DOI: 10.1007/978-3-319-19312-0_35

take care about their learning systems so that medical students can easily grasp and memorize the knowledge. In order to boost the learning capabilities, we preferred the *flip learning* approach [4] as latest research recommend this approach [5], [6]. Kopp [7] defines that "a flipped class is one that inverts the typical cycle of content acquisition and application so that students gain necessary knowledge before class, and instructors guide students interactively to clarify the problem and then apply that knowledge during class".

There exists a large number of case-based tutoring and learning systems like COMET [8], MR Tutor [9], Reflective Learner [10], eCASE [11], and Turfgrass Case Library [12] that aim to boost the learning and educational process but from our best knowledge, none of them supports the formulations of cases summaries using SNOMED and flip learning concepts. Similarly, Batool et al. [13] described a mapping and transformation system for hospital discharge summaries using natural language processing without flip learning concepts. The motivations to build this system are to : 1) improve brainstorming skills, 2) retain knowledge in interactive and easy way, 3) formulate the case summaries with the help of standard SNOMED vocabulary and domain knowledge, and 4) provide the right information at the right time to right student. To achieve these goals, we proposed a solution called *Interactive Case-Based Flip Learning Tool* (ICBFLT). The online flip learning concept with incorporation of an expert system will provide standard terminologies from SNOMED vocabulary during formulations of cases summaries and will capture new knowledge. This new knowledge will provide automatic computerized feedback to help the students for solving their CBL. With the evolution of knowledge stored in database, this tool hold better clinical competence and will provide intensive learning in future [14].

In order to evaluate the ICBFLT, a scenario from the *School of Medicine, University of Tasmania* (UTAS), *Australia* has been considered.

2   Proposed System Architecture

For interactive formulation of cases summaries, an architecture is proposed as shown in Fig.1 that consists of two major components called *CBL Portal Interface* and *Expert System*. In our proposed system, there are three types of users. (i) Administrator/Coordinator: which manage the cases data, (ii) Tutor: which manage CBL cases, evaluate the CBL students' solutions, and provide feedback, and (iii) Medical Student: which solve the CBL case and get feedback. The outputs of this proposed tool are the cases summaries formulated by students and tutors, assessments of students solutions, and tutors' feedbacks. The *CBL Portal Interface*, a web application where multiple types of users are managed according to their roles and privileges.

2.1   CBL Portal Interface

This component acts as an intermediate layer between user and expert system. This component manages four subcomponents named *Case Management,*

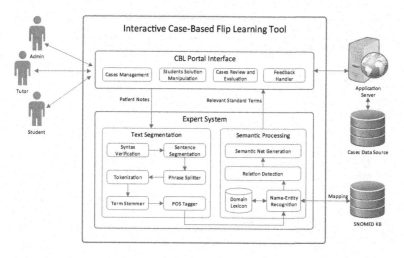

Fig. 1. Interactive case-based flip learning tool architecture

Students Solution Manipulation, Cases Review and Evaluation, and *Feedback Handler.* The *Case Management* subcomponent is used to add, view, edit, and delete the CBL case. Similarly, the *Students Solution Manipulation* subcomponent is used to add, view, edit, and delete own CBL solution, and also view other students solutions to get help and for better analysis during CBL solution. While, the *Cases Review and Evaluation* subcomponent is used to review and evaluate the students solution. Similarly, the *Feedback Handler* subcomponent provides feedback to student.

2.2   Expert System

This component is an intelligent part of the system that will provide relevant standard medical terms from SNOMED or domain lexicon during cases formulations. This component uses the *Natural Language Processing* and *Ontologies* concepts. This component is divided into two main components *Text Segmentation* and *Semantic Processing.* The basic functionality of *Text Segmentation* component is to divide the text into useful terms. Then *Semantic Processing* component takes the chunks and finds the semantics and finally sends related standard medical terms to user. The work flow for this component is described by *Relevant Standard Data Extraction Algorithm* as shown in Algorithm-1.

3   Evaluation Methodology

In this section, *CBL Portal Interface* of proposed system is evaluated. This section is divided into three categories called *Experimental Design, Experimental Execution, Experimentation Results.*

Algorithm 1. Relevant_Standard_Data_Extraction($D = pn$)

Data: $D = pn$: Input dataset (patient note)
Result: Relevant standard medical terms
1 **if** $Verify(D)$ **then**
2   DataSegmenter(D) : $D = s_1, s_2, s_3, ..., s_n$;
3   **for** $\forall\ s_i \in D$ **do**
4   PhraseSplitter($D.s_i$) : $s_i = ph_1, ph_2, ph_3, ..., ph_n$;
5   **for** $\forall\ ph_j \in s_i$ **do**
6   Tokenizer($D.s_i.ph_j$) : $ph_j = tkn_1, tkn_2, tkn_3, ..., tkn_n$;
7   **for** $\forall\ tkn_k \in ph_j$ **do**
8   stemmedword = TermStemmer($D.s_i.ph_j.tkn_k$) ;
9   taggedword = POSTagger($stemmedword$) ;
10   **return** $taggedword$
11   **end**
12   **end**
13   **end**
14   StopwordRemoval($taggedword$) ;
15   NameEntityRecognizer($taggedword, SNOMED$) ;
16   **if** $Mapping == null$ **then**
17   NameEntityRecognizer($taggedword, DomainLexicon$) : ;
18   **end**
19   relatedtuples = RelationDetection($listoftuples$) ;
20   SemanticNetGeneration($relatedtuples$);
21 **else**
22     $Error(message)$;
23 **end**
24 **return** $relevantstandardterms$

In **Experimental Design**, we select the survey process. For this purpose, a case scenario is built and then after selecting evaluating variables [15] as shown in Fig.3, multiple questions are prepared for survey.

In **Experimental Execution**, some important functionalities of *CBL Portal Interface* is shown in Fig.2. Fig.2 representing tutor and student views. The tutor view describes the details of CBL case, in which tutor can add, edit or delete any information that he/she has already added. Similarly, student view describes that student can edit or delete any information that he/she has already added. Moreover, while solving the CBL case, the student can also view other students solution like patient notes of *Presenting Complaint* information. Moreover, timer concept to count the time to complete this task helps tutor to assess the student and find the difficulty level of case in future for that particular group of students.

In **Experimental Results**, after performing survey, we get feedback from nearly 54 persons regarding the system usability under multiple criteria. We classify our users into 3 groups on the basis of their responses, into poor, average, and excellent. The analysis of chart as shown in Fig.3 represents the comparison of the evaluation under different categories to reflect the perfection of system in comparable aspects. Nearly 70% of the users show confidence on system capabilities and interface interaction. They are quite satisfied with respect to interaction with the system. About 50% of users are satisfied with the consistency, screen flow and learning aspect. The alarming indication is that less than 40% of users are satisfied with load on human memory and number of actions performed for a particular task. On average 42% of users registered their level of satisfaction as medium level for the evaluating criteria of the system.

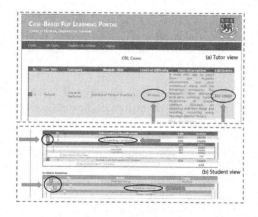

Fig. 2. Tutor and student views

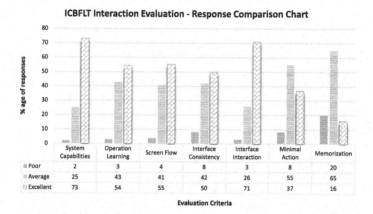

Fig. 3. ICBFLT interaction evaluation - response comparison chart

4   Conclusion and Future Work

The work describes a tool for case-based learning using new concepts including
flip learning, incorporation of SNOMED vocabulary, and *role of expert system
using Natural Language Processing (NLP) techniques.* The tool will help medical
students to solve their CBL case intelligent and interactive manner and will
boost the learning and educational process. The tool can work as a framework
for managing the learning in any subdomain of medicine. In future work, flip
learning and incorporation of SNOMED knowledge base will be done that will
support computerized standard help regarding solving the CBL case.

Acknowledgments. This work was supported by the Industrial Core Technology
Development Program (10049079 , Develop of mining core technology exploiting personal big data) funded by the Ministry of Trade, Industry and Energy (MOTIE, Korea).

References

1. Shepherd, M., Martz, B.: Problem based learning systems and technologies. In: Proc. of the 38th Annual Hawaii Int. Conf. on System Sciences, HICSS 2005, vol. 39 (2005)
2. Ottawa: A guide to case based learning, Faculty of Medicine, University of Ottawa (2010). http://www.med.uottawa.ca/facdev/assets/documents/TheCaseBasedLearningProcess.pdf (accessed August 20, 2014)
3. Cardiff University: What is Case Based Learning. http://medicine.cf.ac.uk/medical-education/undergraduate/why-choose-cardiff/our-curriculum/what-case-based-learning-copy/ (accessed August 24, 2014)
4. Sams, A., Bergmann, J.: Flip your students' learning. Technology-Rich Learning, Educational Leadership 70(6), 16–20 (2013)
5. Marwedel, P., Engel, M.: Flipped classroom teaching for a cyber-physical system course - an adequate presence-based learning approach in the internet age. In: 10th IEEE European Workshop Microelectronics Education (EWME), pp. 11–15 (2014)
6. Kiat, P.N., Kwong, Y.T.: The flipped classroom experience. In: 2014 IEEE 27th Conference Software Engineering Education and Training, pp. 39–43 (2014)
7. Kopp, S.: What is the Flipped Classroom (2004). http://ctl.utexas.edu/teaching/flipping-a-class/what (accessed August 25, 2014)
8. Suebnukarn, S., Haddawy, P.: Comet: A collaborative tutoring system for medical problem-based learning. Intelligent Systems 22(4), 70–77 (2007)
9. Sharples, M., Jeffery, N.P., Boulay, B.D., Teather, B.A., Teather, D., Boulay, G.H.D.: Structured computer-based training in the interpretation of neuroradiological images. International Journal of Medical Informatics 60(3), 263–280 (2000)
10. Turns, J., Newstetter, W., Allen, J.K., Mistree, F.: Learning essays and the reflective learner: Supporting reflection in engineering design education. In: Proc. American Society for Engg. Education Annual Conf. and Exposition (1997)
11. Papadopoulos, P.M., Demetriadis, S.N., Stamelos, I.G., Tsoukalas, I.A.: Online case-based learning: Design and preliminary evaluation of the ecase environment. In: 6th IEEE Inter. Conf., Adv. Learning Tech., pp. 751–755 (2006)
12. Jonassen, D.H., Serrano, J.H.: Case-based reasoning and instructional design: Using stories to support problem solving. Educational Technology Research and Development 50(2), 65–77 (2002)
13. Batool, R., Khattak, A.M., Kim, T.S., Lee, S.: Automatic extraction and mapping of discharge summary's concepts into SNOMED CT. In: Conf. Proc. IEEE Eng. Med. Biol. Soc., pp. 4195–4198 (2013)
14. Kilroy, D.A.: Problem based learning. Emergency Medicine Journal 21(4), 411–413 (2004)
15. Chin, J.P., Diehl, V.A., Norman, K.L.: Development of an instrument measuring user satisfaction of the human-computer interface. In: Proceedings of the SIGCHI Conference on Human Factors in Computing Systems, pp. 213–218 (1988)

Interactive Fridge: A Solution for Preventing Domestic Food Waste

Van Nhan Nguyen$^{(\boxtimes)}$, Thi Hoa Nguyen, Tai Tien Huynh, Van Hai Nguyen,
and Susanne Koch Stigberg

Faculty of Computer Science, Ostfold University College,
PO Box 700, 1757 Halden, Norway
{nhan.v.nguyen,hoa.t.nguyen,tai.t.huynh,hainv,susannks}@hiof.no

Abstract. This paper presents a design study of an interactive fridge aimed at encouraging people to prevent domestic food waste. The project implemented a prototype which consists of three main objects: i) Stickers help grouping similar food together; ii) Sliders visualize food expiration date into colors in order to help people be aware of food states; iii) LCD Screen provides graphic and sound feedback when people use their fridge to make the fridge more fun to use. To ground our design, we used design thinking as a guideline process. We evaluated the prototype using qualitative analysis of interview data. The findings show that the prototype motivated people grouping food and increased their awareness of the availability of food items in the fridge, the prototype also encouraged people in using food before expiration date. This paper offers three main contributions. Firstly, we identified three major problems that lead to domestic food waste. Secondly, we proposed a new design to address the problems. Thirdly, we applied design thinking as a design method to solve problems that related to domestic food waste.

Keywords: Food waste · Interactive fridge · Consumer behavior · Visualization · Design thinking · Human-computer interaction · Interaction design

1 Introduction

Nowadays, food waste is becoming a crucial issue. A report by Institution of Mechanical Engineers [10] has found that 30-50% (or 1.2 - 2 billion tonnes) of all food produced ended up waste. In the developed countries, the largest quantities of food are wasted at the consumer end of the supply chain [10][7]. For example in the UK, about seven million tonnes (worth about £10.2 billion) of food is thrown away from homes every year [10]. The United Nations predicts that the world population is set to reach around 9.5 billion by 2075, which could mean an extra three billion mouths to feed by the end of the century. With current practices wasting 30-50% of all food produced, it creates an urgent need about sustainable ways to reduce food waste, especially for consumers at the end of the supply chain. So in this paper, we focus on finding solutions to prevent food waste at household level.

© Springer International Publishing Switzerland 2015
A. Geissbühler et al. (Eds.): ICOST 2015, LNCS 9102, pp. 361–366, 2015.
DOI: 10.1007/978-3-319-19312-0_36

2   Background and Related Work

By 2015, lot of research about preventing domestic food waste has been conducted. Most of the research projects focused on changing consumer's behaviors or supporting consumers store food and consume food more effectively. A study which applied eco-feedback on household food waste with the prospective to increase awareness and explore its impact on food related decision-making was conducted by [8]. Using social networks to enhance relationships in communities or to enable sharing food and cooking experiences is a food waste preventing strategy that has been received focus from many researchers [6][12]. EUPHORIA, a mobile application being developed to reduce food waste in households by recommending recipes to a group of connected people via social network [15]. In addition, some research about intelligent fridge applications has also been conducted. PerFridge, an augmented refrigerator that detects and presents wasteful usage for eco-persuasion, focus on sensing wasteful behaviors [9]. To investigate the usefulness of grouping similar food types together, [4] conducted a study using paper-based color schema for increasing the awareness of available foods for consumers. They suggested that participants wasted less during the study period of a month.

2.1   Design Thinking

Design Thinking is a specific method, which is introduced and shaped by the design consultancy IDEO [2], to solve wicked problems and foster creativity. The method has become more and more popular among companies as well as educational institutions around the world. Design thinking process consists of six main steps: Understand, Observe, Point of View (POV), Ideation, Prototyping and Testing [13]. Design thinking is making its way into food industry. It has also been used to solve many food related problems (Ifooddesign.org, thinking-fooddesign.com, ideo.com/expertise/food-beverage). Following that vision, we use design thinking as a design process in order to help us identify what are the main causes of domestic food waste and foster the problem-solving process.

2.2   Information Visualization Using Colors

Visualization is a powerful way to convey data and visually represent abstract data (geographic information, text, number, etc.) to reinforce human cognition. Color, in particularly, is a very effective way for information coding so it is usually used for displaying data in categories, labeling, measuring and enlivening data [14]. There are four psychological primary colors − red, blue, yellow and green. Each color affects mood, feelings and emotions of people in very different ways. For example, green is a cool color that symbolizes nature and the natural world, it represents health, safety or good condition. Yellow is an intention getter, while red is a bright, warm color that evokes strong emotions. Based on the meaning of the colors and how they affect mood, feelings and emotions of users, we chose red, yellow and green for visualizing food expiration date.

3 Design Process

3.1 Understanding and Ideation

We use design thinking [2] as a guideline to ground our design. The process starts with understanding and ideation. In order to understand what are the main causes of food waste in domestic environment, a survey was conducted using a 10-question questionnaire, which comprised five question categories (shopping habits, eating habits, cooking style, food sharing and wasting behaviors). 27 participants was recruited to participate in the survey as well as semi-structured interviews. The main goal of the survey and the interviews is to investigate users' behaviors and habits on storing food, which are practices tied up with food waste by consumers [5]. The collected data was analyzed using selected methods from grounded theory [11]. The results showed that there are three major reasons that lead to food waste in domestic environment:

- **Consumers are not aware of the availability of their food.** There are two possible explanations for this. Firstly, people usually forget about the food that they bought long time ago. Secondly, people are not aware of the food that bought by other members in their family.
- **Consumers are not aware of the state of their food.** According to our survey, vegetable is the food kind that is thrown away the most. The reason is vegetable does not has exact expiration day and people usually forget when they bought them.
- **Consumers have no interest in consuming left-over and old food.** Many participants confessed that although they have no interest in consuming left-over food, they still want to keep it in their fridge because they do not want to have the feeling that they are wasting food or they do not know what to do with the food.

3.2 Prototyping

With the aim of solving the three listed problems above, we developed a prototype which comprises three objects: Stickers, Slider and LCD Screen. Stickers and Slider are developed in order to help user categorize food and be aware of the availability as well as the state of food, while the main goal of the LCD Screen is to make the fridge more fun to use and encourage users cooking.

Stickers. There are four types of stickers which were designed for four types of food: Meat, Fish and Eggs; Dairy products; Cereals; Vegetables and Fruits. Users are free to choose how use the stickers, however it is recommended that each layer in a fridge should be used for storing only one type of food and an appropriate sticker will be used to mark that layer.

Sliders. Sliders divide layers of a fridge into blocks (Fig. 1) based on expiration date of food in the layers. We recommend that each layer should have no more than three blocks in order to prevent fragmentation and make it easier to find food. When users buy new food, they can store the food in a new block and then set the timer of the block correspond to the expiration date of food in that block. The timers will help users "remember" when did they buy the food and remind users about the condition of the food by changing its color. The Sliders have two separate timers for both sides, so it removes the effort to move food from one block to another. The Sliders have four states based on food expiration day: Green (safe mode) is for food over seven days. Yellow (medial mode) is for food from three to seven days. Red (warning mode) is for food under three days. The last state is when food is expired, the Red-Blinking mode alerts user that it is dangerous to consume. The Slider was built using an Arduino board two rows of RGB LEDS.

The Front LCD Screen. The LCD Screen was designed as a "living creature" (Fig. 1). The creature has two emotional states: Happy State will be activated when all blocks are green. Cooking State will be activated when there is red or yellow block. In this case, the "living creature" will "think" and show suggestions how to cook with food from the blocks and when users consume food in the blocks, the "living creature" will responses with applause sound.

Fig. 1. The prototype with Sliders, Stickers and LCD Screen

3.3   Testing

According to [3], perceived usefulness and perceived ease of use can lead users to accept or reject a novel information technology product. We evaluated the two dimensions using qualitative interviews with 10 participants (ages 20-35) to learn more about user intentions in using the prototype. Our findings are limited by intention to use and can not give implications on user experience of real usage or technology acceptance. We first demonstrated the prototype to participants and then conducted semi-structured interviews. Finally, we used coding method [1] to analyze the collected data and discuss four assumptions below.

- **The prototype helps users to categorize their food.** All users thought that using the prototype will help them to categorize their fridges, find food easier because of well-organizing and remarkableness. In addition, some users said that the prototype would be useful when they share fridge with others.
- **The prototype makes the fridge interesting to use.** "The colorful fridge is interesting" - they thought but one user complained "Lights are good but I prefer no flashing". Many users said that the "living creature" is cute but not all of them think that the prototype will affect them.
- **The prototype makes people aware of their food state.** Users were familiar with the color scheme and its meaning, but sometimes the flashing mode caused the negative effects.
- **The prototype motivates people to reduce food waste.** Users agreed that food waste would be reduced when they are reminded about their food states. Because they can remember and consume it before expiration date.

4   Conclusion

This paper has presented a design called interactive fridge which is a set of objects (Stickers, Slider and LCD Screen) that help people in organizing food in their fridge, remind them about the availability of their food as well as motivate them to use their food before expiration date. We built a prototype and tested it with four assumptions: The prototype helps users to categorize their food, the prototype makes the fridge more interesting to use, the prototype makes people aware of their food state and the prototype motivates people to reduce food waste. The findings show that the prototype motivated people grouping food and increased their awareness of the availability of food items in the fridge, the prototype also encouraged people in using food before expiration. This paper offers three main contributions. Firstly, we identified three major problems that lead to domestic food waste. Secondly, we proposed a new design to address these problems. Thirdly, we applied design thinking as a design method to solve problems that are related to domestic food waste. The paper described a design process and a new concept that is not completely functional yet. Therefore we could not evaluate real use or even behavioral changes in domestic food waste. Instead we focused on investigating perceived usefulness and perceived ease-of use as two strong indicators from the technology acceptance model. Further research includes improving prototype in order to deploy it in real-life and explore how the design can help people preventing food waste as well as gathering new using experience. Our findings so far give us confidence that emotional and friendly interactions can motivate people changing behaviors which lead to negative effects. We believe that design thinking is a good candidate to develop new technology use cases in the future.

Acknowledgments. The project is part of "user-driven innovation in smart homes for energy and health" and we would like to thank Østfold University College for providing the MakerSpace, a creative lab environment for IT students.

References

1. Basit, T.: Manual or electronic? the role of coding in qualitative data analysis. Educational Research **45**(2), 143–154 (2003)
2. Brown, T.: Design thinking. Harvard Business Review **86**(6), 84 (2008)
3. Davis, F.D.: Perceived usefulness, perceived ease of use, and user acceptance of information technology. MIS Quarterly, 319–340 (1989)
4. Farr-Wharton, G., Foth, M., Choi, J.H.-J.: Colour coding the fridge to reduce food waste. In: Proceedings of the 24th Australian Computer-Human Interaction Conference, OzCHI 2012, pp. 119–122. ACM, New York (2012)
5. Ganglbauer, E., Fitzpatrick, G., Molzer, G.: Creating visibility: understanding the design space for food waste. In: Proceedings of the 11th International Conference on Mobile and Ubiquitous Multimedia, MUM 2012, pp. 1:1–1:10. ACM, New York (2012)
6. Gross, S., Toombs, A., Wain, J., Walorski, K.: Foodmunity: designing community interactions over food. In: CHI 2011 Extended Abstracts on Human Factors in Computing Systems, pp. 1019–1024. ACM (2011)
7. Gustavsson, J., Cederberg, C., Sonesson, U.: Global Food Losses and Food Waste. Food and Agriculture Organization of the United Nations, Technical report (2011)
8. Lim, V., Jense, A., Janmaat, J., Funk, M.: Eco-feedback for non-consumption. In: Proceedings of the 2014 ACM International Joint Conference on Pervasive and Ubiquitous Computing: Adjunct Publication, UbiComp 2014 Adjunct, pp. 99–102. ACM, New York (2014)
9. Murata, S., Kagatsume, S., Taguchi, H., Fujinami, K.: Perfridge: An augmented refrigerator that detects and presents wasteful usage for eco-persuasion. In: 2012 IEEE 15th International Conference on Computational Science and Engineering (CSE), pp. 367–374, December 2012
10. Institution of Mechanical Engineers: Global Food - Waste Not. Want Not. Technical report 01 (2013)
11. Strauss, A., Corbin, J.M.: Basics of qualitative research: Grounded theory procedures and techniques. Sage Publications Inc. (1990)
12. Svensson, M., Höök, K., Cöster, R.: Designing and evaluating kalas: A social navigation system for food recipes. ACM Trans. Comput.-Hum. Interact. **12**(3), 374–400 (2005)
13. Thoring, K., Müller, R.M., et al.: Understanding design thinking: A process model based on method engineering. In: International Conference on Engineering and Product Design Education (2011)
14. Ware, C.: Information visualization: perception for design. Elsevier (2013)
15. Yalvaç, F., Lim, V., Hu, J., Funk, M., Rauterberg, M.: Social recipe recommendation to reduce food waste. In: CHI 2014 Extended Abstracts on Human Factors in Computing Systems, CHI EA 2014, pp. 2431–2436. ACM, New York (2014)

MonDossierMedical.ch: An Efficient Tool for Sharing Medical Data Between Patients and Doctors

Aurélie Rosemberg and Olivier Plaut[✉]

Direction générale de la santé, 24, Avenue de Beau-Séjour, 1206 Geneva, Switzerland
information@mondossiermedical.ch,
olivier.plaut@etat.ge.ch

Abstract. MonDossierMedical.ch is a project led by the canton of Geneva, making it possible for every patient to access his own electronic health record (EHR) and to share the medical files with his doctors. It was introduced across the canton in mid-2013, and provided to all patients free of charge. It is based on the first Swiss-wide eHealth-compliant pilot project "e-toile". The canton of Geneva developed "e-toile" as a public-private partnership together with Swiss Post and it was launched in 2011 in few municipalities. Back then, Geneva's EHR represented the first Swiss attempt to link all healthcare professionals in the treatment chain. Today, it serves more than 4,000 patients and 380 physicians. This number is growing regularly, as well as the health care institutions (private hospitals, labs) joining the community.

Keywords: Electronic health record · Geneva · MonDossierMedical.ch · Shared care plan · Shared medication list

1 History

"MonDossierMedical.ch" project, originally named e-Toile, was born in Geneva in a context of public health costs higher than the national average and development of information technologies. Following issues initiated a thorough reflection:

— Placing the patient at the center of his medical care ("patient empowerment")
— Ensuring the quality of care and avoiding errors
— Ensuring data security
— Improving the efficiency and thus meeting up with the challenges of an aging population.

This project started in 1998. In 2001, the foundation IRIS-GENEVA was created to enable the networking of all health partners. This foundation is now in charge of monitoring the network and promotes its use. This pioneering project required a legal basis, then non-existent in Switzerland. In 2008, the law on the EHR community network was adopted in Geneva, entering into force in 2009. The Swiss federal law on the patient's EHR is forecast to be ready by 2018.

To realize the sharing of medical information according to the patient's will, a concept of technical architecture and access rules has been developed. It is now being implemented throughout the canton as "MonDossierMedical.ch". The project is conducted by the Directorate General for Health of the Canton of Geneva.

© Springer International Publishing Switzerland 2015
A. Geissbühler et al. (Eds.): ICOST 2015, LNCS 9102, pp. 367–372, 2015.
DOI: 10.1007/978-3-319-19312-0_37

2   Today

Access to online medical record is free of charge. Patients can register at specific places at the hospital and in some pharmacies and medical cabinets. No on-line registration is available till now because ID check is required as well as proper information of the patient, regarding configuration and access rights. The patient can then access his EHR using a smartcard and a USB card reader. A new way of connection has been introduced recently. The patient can use a user name, a password and a single-use code received via SMS, known as mTan. This procedure allows freeing oneself from soft and hardware installations and permits the patient to access to his EHR from any computer, including smartphone and tablets. The dual-security elements (smartcard/PIN code or password/mTan) provide a "strong authentication" and contribute to increasing the security level. The platform successfully underwent IT security audits.

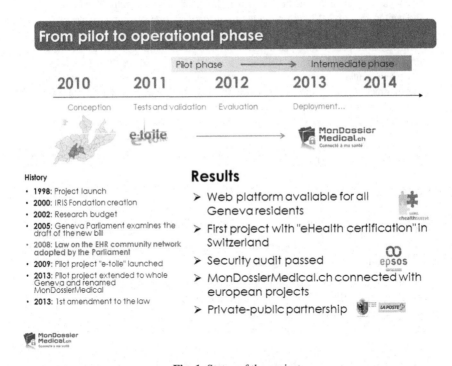

Fig. 1. Status of the project

Patients have an easy access to their medical documents from the University Hospitals of Geneva (HUG), home care services, some medical cabinets, connected pharmacies and laboratories. The patient gives access rights to his attending physicians, pharmacist or specialists. Those rights can be finely tuned by the patient in order to give restricted access to some health professionals and enlarged access to others, including access to stigmatizing documents. The patient can include or exclude some professions as well as defining systematically specific documents (i.e. published by the psychiatric hospital) as stigmatizing or even secret.

Physically, the information is stored on several servers in Geneva, whereas the MPI (Master Patient Index) is hosted at the Swiss Post which manages the platform through a private-public partnership with the Canton of Geneva.

3   Obstacles and Opportunities

Geneva has been pioneering this approach in Switzerland which allows physicians and other stakeholders to access, with the patient's permission, to essential information for its health management. Conducting this type of project requires overcoming technical and "business" obstacles.

From a technical point of view, after a pilot phase, the system was stabilized to allow wider deployment with improved access times to medical documents. It was also necessary to simplify the connection process for all users by replacing smart card connection with more modern technologies. As the documents may not be concentrated at one place, several repositories are equipped with physical and virtualized servers that had to be replaced after the pilot phase was over in order to provide higher speed access.

From a business point of view, the challenge is now to implement greater use of MonDossierMedical.ch for information sharing in the Geneva care network. For this purpose we are working on the management of complex patients with the implementation of a shared care plan and a shared medication list. Those issues require interoperability between the tools and avoiding double data entries. Complex patients require coordinated treatment between doctors and nurses. The shared care plan will provide a dashboard allowing nurses to see physician's diagnostic and orders. On the other hand, the doctor will be able to see nurses' observations. The patient will have access to his documents which will enable him to be aware of the doctor's intentions and improve accordingly his treatment.

We will also target more precisely population groups, according to age, conditions, interests, and provide services that are of particular interest to develop connections.

4   Perspectives

Registration of patients and professionals to MonDossierMedical.ch is no longer an anecdote. The platform use is today concrete and registrations increase regularly with 300 to 400 new patients per month - a total of more than 4,700 active records - and over 400 physicians connected. Those records contain more than 800,000 documents which are dispatched on five different repositories, according to the source of data. The specific law forbids the concentration of medical data at one place. When one accesses an EHR, the data is downloaded from the corresponding servers and consolidated at one place during a session.

We also work with various structures such as associations, municipalities, etc. to promote the use of "MonDossierMedical.ch". Public sessions will be held later this year for presenting "MonDossierMedical.ch" and to register interested citizens.

Targeted actions are conducted in various locations among the hospitals (HUG): enrollment is proposed at the main hospital, at the pediatric and geriatric hospitals, and at the emergency room, while patients are waiting, to help them pass the time. Patients doing administrative admission at the hospital will soon have the possibility to be registered in MonDossierMedical.ch at the same time.

As the network of involved partners is extending, we now hope family physicians, private clinics, and laboratories to join the community.

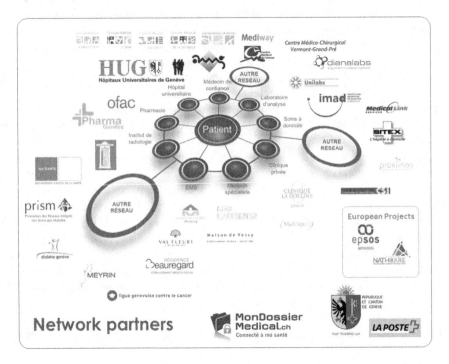

Fig. 2. Network Partners

The 2015 outlook is the improvement of complex patients care in the care network with the commissioning of a shared medication list, the upload of documents by the patient himself, and the pilot project of the shared care plan in partnership with PRISM (an association promoting integrated care to complex patients) and imad (home care services). Granting the patient to import his own data opens possible integration with *quantified self* devices such as fitness bands and their *actimetric* data, diabetic surveillance data, and other monitoring tools.

Today only health professionals are allowed to add documents to the EHR. Integrated clinical information systems add automatically data to the record. Other systems require the physician to choose which documents are to be uploaded. Doctors who don't have integrated systems are able to add pdf files to the EHR. This requires of course every document do be added separately and metadata to be introduced manually.

4.1 An Added Value Tool: Shared Medication List

The objective of the shared medication plan is to perform medication reconciliation in order to get a picture as comprehensive as possible of the drugs taken by the patient. This view allows the physician to have full vision and to avoid prescribing dual or interfering drugs.

Detection tools to prevent adverse effects in connection with other drugs or the patient's condition (weight, age, pregnancy, allergies, etc.) will also be introduced gradually.

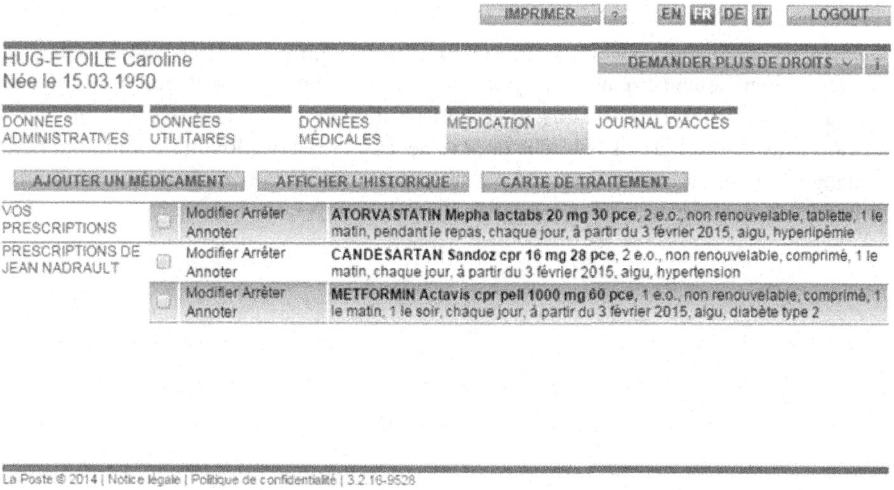

Fig. 3. Screenshot of a treatment list (test patient)

The shared treatment plan also allows to easily produce and print a treatment card, sort of "menu" for the patient showing him which dose to take, at what time, and with the reason of the treatment. An image of the tablet will be added for people having difficulties to recognize the different drugs.

This essential tool in the continuity of care is currently only available in "MonDossierMedical.ch". There are however many other prescription systems: HUG, a number of private doctors, clinics and pharmacies all have their own prescribing tools. A priority task in 2015 is to allow those different software means to communicate in order to have a complete shared treatment plan while avoiding dual entries. Among other things, pharmacists will be able to reprint the patient's treatment card with updated information, which may be different, i.e. in case of generic substitution.

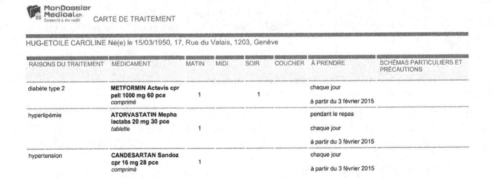

RAISONS DU TRAITEMENT	MÉDICAMENT	MATIN	MIDI	SOIR	COUCHER	À PRENDRE	SCHÉMAS PARTICULIERS ET PRÉCAUTIONS
diabète type 2	**METFORMIN Actavis cpr pell 1000 mg 60 pce** comprimé	1		1		chaque jour à partir du 3 février 2015	
hyperlipémie	**ATORVASTATIN Mepha lactabs 20 mg 30 pce** tablette	1				pendant le repas chaque jour à partir du 3 février 2015	
hypertension	**CANDESARTAN Sandoz cpr 16 mg 28 pce** comprimé	1				chaque jour à partir du 3 février 2015	

Fig. 4. Example of treatment card

5   Conclusion

After 15 years of development, Geneva's EHR is now on its way. Thanks to political, medical, scientific and financial support the canton's e-health unit is building a strong foundation on which added value tools will be implemented. The completion of the development of the federal law will lay the necessary basis allowing communities to exchange compatible documents and permitting any Swiss citizen to access and transfer its record to any place in Switzerland.

SmartHealth and Internet of Things

AbdulMutalib Wahaishi[1](✉), Afshan Samani[2], and Hamada Ghenniwa[2]

[1] College of Information Technology, UAEU, Al Ain, United Arab Emirates
amasuad@uaeu.ac.ae
[2] University of Western, London, Canada
{asamani5,hghenniwa}@uwo.ca

Abstract. The "Internet-of-Things" (IoT), is a new computation platform, in which "Things" are the fundamental computational elements that are characterized with some form of digital-based capabilities and utilizes various embedded technologies to connect through the Internet with the external environment through standard protocols. Healthcare services and systems become very complex and encompass a vast number of entities (software systems, doctors, patients, devices, etc.) that are characterized by shared, distributed and heterogeneous devices, sensors, and information sources with varieties of clinical and medical settings. This paper presents an agent-based architecture that supports adhoc system configurations emphasizing the strategies for achieving real-time smart monitoring in SmartHealth environments with privacy based interaction protocol to protect privacy of entities while sharing information in the environment.

Keywords: Internet of things · SmartHealth · Agent technology · Ontology · Privacy

1 Introduction

The computation platform has been drastically evolved to include massive number of diverse an ever-growing network of conventional computing systems, sensors, devices, equipments, software and information services and apps. This new form of computing platform is known as the "Internet-of-Things" in which "Things" are the fundamental computational elements. Each "thing" is characterized with some form of digital-based capabilities and utilizes various embedded technologies to connect through the Internet with the external environment through standard protocols. The rapid advancement and the evolution of IoT offers a great promise in the healthcare domain. The term SmartHealth refers to "the practice of medicine and public health supported by smart devices such as mobile phones, patient monitoring devices, handheld computers (PDAs) and other wireless devices". The combination of technologies such as WSN, digital home technologies, cognitive assistance, advanced robotics along with the RFID, NFC (near field communication), Bluetooth, ZigBee, and WiFi, shall permit substantial improvements SmartHealth. This paper presents an agent-based privacy architecture for monitoring SmartHealth environments.

© Springer International Publishing Switzerland 2015
A. Geissbühler et al. (Eds.): ICOST 2015, LNCS 9102, pp. 373–378, 2015.
DOI: 10.1007/978-3-319-19312-0_38

2   Internet of Things: Issues and Challenges

The tremendous shift in healthcare from being a clinic-centered environment to a remote ubiquitous patient-centered, knowledge-intensive enterprise will evidently revolutionize the way that medical and healthcare systems modeled and developed to fulfill and meet the broad objectives of various healthcare applications. Tiny sensors and actuators, flourishing at amazing rates are expected to explode in massive numbers over the next decade, potentially linking over 50 billion physical "entities" as costs plummet and networks become more pervasive [11]. Cisco estimates that the potential impact of the increased rate of connectivity created by the Internet of Everything could reach 19 trillion dollars in terms of "potential value" that can be generated over the next nine years, between private and public sector [7]. IoT will make it possible to create an environment in which health status is constantly monitored, and therefore easing the burden for those who are not able to have an effective access to sophisticated health monitoring devices and very expensive onsite medical equipment. However; the SmartHealth involves a various challenges and issues that need to be addressed such user engagements, the quality of care, efficiency, security, privacy, medical Big Data, safety and ethical considerations.

3   Literature Review

The remarkable increase in smart devices' users (there are about 6 billion subscribers in the world) has encouraged the growth of Healthcare domain [8]. The convergence of smart medical devices and wireless technologies has created new business opportunities for the provision of new venues of caregiving such as the so-called promising "Silver Economy" [18]. It is estimated that within the next decade the personal data from sensors will fall from 10% to 90% of all archived information [14]. Several approaches were proposed for integration of distributed information sources in healthcare [17]. In one approach [2], the focus was on providing management assistance to different teams across several hospitals by coordinating their access to distributed information. Using the ZigBee protocol between sensors and mobile phones for ECG and blood glucose measurements was reported in [19]. Other approaches attempts to provide wearable technologies to monitor indoor/outdoor activities [9][16] [12]. Agent-based medical appointments scheduling were reported in [1]. In previous work [5], agent architecture was proposed to facilitate privacy-based information brokering for various healthcare cooperative distributed systems.

4   Agent-Based Architecture for SmartHealth in IoT

The dynamic nature of the healthcare activities requires real-time monitoring and control of the various "things" conditions. The absence of a separate medium that deals exclusively with the coordination aspects means that the *"things"*, in addition to other computational activities, have to carry out the "interaction work" themselves to satisfy common or local tasks and hence participate in facilitating relevant decisions-making.

In open dynamic environments, a more complex degree of interaction would include "things" that can react to observable events. Within this context, the IoT SmartHealth is modeled as a Cooperative Distributed Systems (CDS) [3], in which the *"things"* are able to exercise some degree of authority in sharing their capabilities. The architecture is viewed as multi-layered system that comprises the various network layers. The conceptual model of SmartHealth as a whole is accomplished through three main modules: (1) The automatic real-time collection of various medical data and vital signs, (2) Identification and interpretation of variability in data and readings to take meaningful decisions and (3) Managing site-specific medical practices and activities. The open dynamic nature and the non-determinism aspect of the "things" participating in different real-time monitoring and control activities requires that they be able to change their configuration according to their roles. We strongly believe that agent-orientation is an appropriate design paradigm for providing monitoring and coordination services in such settings. As shown in Fig. 1, the SmartHealth environment is comprised of a collection of economically motivated software agents that interact cooperatively, find and process information, and disseminate valuable data and provide directive decisions to humans and other agents. The representative agents of the SmartHealth environment are built on the foundation of CIR-agent architecture [4] [8]. The proposed architecture comprises three types of intelligent agents: The Personal Assistant Agent (PAA), the Ontology Agent (OA) and the Data Collection Agent (DCA). The following describes the roles and the architecture of these agents.

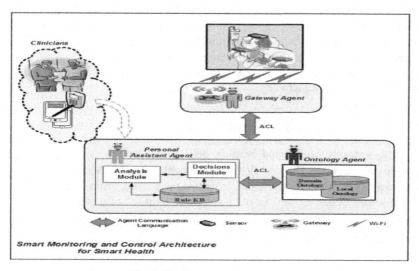

Fig. 1. The Proposed Architecture

4.1   The Personal Assistant Agent (PAA)

The Personal Assistant Agent (PAA) possesses the capability of consists of three major modules: communication module, analysis data module, and decision-making module. The PAA is a collection of knowledge and capabilities components. The knowledge component includes the agent's self-model, model of other agents available in the SmartHealth environment, and the local history. The main capabilities of the PAA include communication, reasoning and domain actions components. Upon receiving these readings, the PAA analyzes the information and determines the ideal outcome and the recommended actions.

4.2   The Ontology Agent (OA)

The Ontology Agent (OA) possesses the capability of capturing the domain ontology, which defines the set of activities and domain events. It provides various abstract levels of domain knowledge within the SmartHealth related applications and hence derives the decision–making process. In this work, the formal SmartHealth Ontology (denoted as SHA_Onto) can be defined formally as: $SHA\_Onto = (Ont\_Des, SH\_Concept, SH\_Relation, Axioms)$. The Ont_Des is a tuple that consists of the following elements: $Ont\_Des \equiv \langle OntID, DevId, ver, md \rangle$, where OntID is the ontology name, DevId defines the developer name, ver specifies the time of relevant to ontology creation and md represents the source and the purpose of the ontology metadata information. The SH_Concept represents the SmartHealth set of concepts and terminologies; SH_Relation defines both the set of hierarchal and non-hierarchal relationships between the SmartHealth concepts and Axioms are these assertions (including rules) in a logical form.

In this work, the knowledge representation of ontology adheres to the five-elements ontology approach, which is as follows: $Ont \equiv \{C, Attr^c, Rel^c, Attr^{Rel}, H^c\}$. The C defines the set of healthcare concepts and terminologies; $Attr^c$ is the set of attributes of each concept; Rel^c is the set of relationships among concepts; $Attr^{Rel}$ defines the various attributes of specific relationship which can be viewed in terms of a generalization relation such as $(is - a)$ relation or $(part - whole)$ dependency; H^c specifies the concept hierarchy.

4.3   The Data Collection Agent (DCA)

The DCA supports on-demand reading delivery as well as the full pre-defined measurement lifecycle. The knowledge component of the DCA includes the sensors model available in the SmartHealth environment starting from the registration of physical sensor nodes as well as the addition or removal of a physical sensor. The DCA capability component has the ability to dynamically identify and select the appropriate sensor and accordingly retrieves and processes readings data.

4.4   Privacy Protection

In many of medical settings, the sensors connecting to patients' bodies collect information and share with collaboration platforms such as "lab of things" [10]. One of the approaches to protect privacy in open environments such as IoT is to incorporate protection mechanism at the architecture level [13], [15]. In this work in [3], we propose an architectural privacy model for IoT in the context of sensitive information that deals with privacy concerns as a form of sensitive information management at the interaction level and hence defines appropriate interaction protocols. The interaction protocol (IP) is based on "request" and "response" scenarios and is represented formally as : *IP=<{<Request,req>,<Response,res>},{[<Request,req>,<Response,res>]}>.*

To protect the sensitive information such as the identity of patients, the anonymization techniques can be used [6]. The interaction protocol can be further defined to accommodate authorized access. and formally reptresnted as: $IP = < \{<Requst, req>, <Response, res>, <Anonymized, msg>, <AuthorizeAccess, acc>, <AuthorizeModify, mod>\}, \{[<Request, req>, <Response, res>], [<Request, req>, <Anonymized, msg>], [<Request, req>, <AuthorizeAccess, acc>], [<Request, req>, <AuthorizeModify, mod>]\}$

5   Conclusion

The proposed architecture promotes innovative technologies and innovative model that aims to manage and control real-time medical activities. The increasing demand and dependency on information and medical data such as genome information, medical records, and other critical personal information has brought the issue of finding new paradigms that has the ability to control the accessibility of the right information from the appropriate source whenever required in a real-tome manner. Home care practices can be highly improved for patients with diabetes in their homes. Any attempt to control the disease requires perseverance on the individual's part. The day-to-day nature of such illness makes it impractical for patients to constantly seek professional help and guidance of medical clinicians and therefore it is the sole patient's responsibility to not only monitor the status of their own health but to also act upon any findings. Ontologies play significant role to provide schemata or intelligent' view over information resources and can be a vital asset for developing and representing efficient of healthcare knowledge. The proposed privacy protection framework defines a generic privacy structure for the entities interaction, express many fundamental and essential characteristics in building adequate privacy-based specifications for CDS-based IoT applications.

References

1. Moreno, A., Isern, D.: Accessing distributed health-care services through smart agents. In: The 4th IEEE Int. Workshop on Enterprise Networking and Computing in the Health Care Industry - HealthCom 2002, France (2002)
2. Moreno, A., Valls, A., Bocio, J.: Management of hospital teams for organ transplants using multi-agent systems. In: Quaglini, S., Barahona, P., Andreassen, S. (eds.) AIME 2001. LNCS (LNAI), vol. 2101, pp. 374–383. Springer, Heidelberg (2001)
3. Samani, A., Ghenniwa, H.H.: Privacy in IoT: A model and protection framework, London Ontario, Tech. Rep. CDS-EnG-reportPrivacy in IoT: A Model and Protection Framework-TR -08272014 (August 2014)
4. Masaud-Wahaishi, A., Ghenniwa, H.H.: Privacy Based Information Brokering for Cooperative Distributed e-Health Systems. JETWI - Journal of Emerging Technologies in Web Intelligence (2010)

5. Masaud-Wahaishi, A., Ghenniwa, H.: Integration in Cooperative Distributed Systems: Privacy-Based Brokering Architecture for Virtual Enterprises. Virtual Enterprise Integration: Technological and Organizational Perspectives. IGI Global (2005)
6. Dwork, C.: Differential privacy: a survey of results. In: Agrawal, M., Du, D.-Z., Duan, Z., Li, A. (eds.) TAMC 2008. LNCS, vol. 4978, pp. 1–19. Springer, Heidelberg (2008)
7. Evans, D.: The Internet of Things: How the Next Evolution of the Internet Is Changing Everything, April 2011
8. ITU, Measuring the Information Society (2012). http://www.itu.int/en/ITUD/Statistics/Documents/publications/mis2012/MIS2012_without_Annex_4.pdf
9. Ouchi, K., Doi, M.: Indoor-outdoor activity recognition by a smartphone. In: Proceedings of the 2012 ACM Conference on Ubiquitous Computing, September 05-08 (2012)
10. Lab of Things (2013). http://www.lab-of-things.com
11. Chui, M., Löffler, M., Roberts, R.: The Internet of Things. McKinsey Quarterly (2) (2010). www.mckinsey.com
12. Ouchi, K., Doi, M.: Smartphone-based monitoring system for activities of daily living for elderly people and their relatives etc. In: Proceedings of the 2013 ACM Conference on Pervasive and Ubiquitous Computing Adjunct Publication. ACM (2013)
13. Schwartz, P.M., Solove, D.J.: The PII problem: Privacy and a new concept of personally identifiable information (2011)
14. Pentland, A, et al.: Improving Public Health and Medicine by use of Reality Mining. Robert Wood Johnson Foundation (2009)
15. Spiekermann, S., Cranor, L.F.: Engineering privacy. IEEE Trans. Software Eng. **35**(1) (2009). http://doi.ieeecomputersociety.org/10.1109/TSE.2008.88
16. Maekawa, T., Yanagisawa, Y., Kishino, Y., Ishiguro, K., Kamei, K., Sakurai, Y., Okadome, T.: Object-Based activity recognition with heterogeneous sensors on wrist. In: Floréen, P., Krüger, A., Spasojevic, M. (eds.) Pervasive 2010. LNCS, vol. 6030, pp. 246–264. Springer, Heidelberg (2010)
17. Shankaraman, V., Amorosiadou, V., Robinson, B.: Agents in medical informatics. In: Proc. of IASTED International Conference on Applied Informatics, Austria (2000)
18. WHO, New horizons for health through mobile technologies. http://www.who.int/goe/publications/goe_mhealth_web.pdf
19. Yu, S.H., et al.: Effects of' ubiquitous healthcare on the ability of self-management in elderly diabetic patients. Korean Diabetes Journal 33(1) (2009)

Genome Mining Using Machine Learning Techniques

Peter Wlodarczak[⊠], Jeffrey Soar, and Mustafa Ally

University of Southern Queensland, Toowoomba, Australia
wlodarczak@gmail.com

Abstract. A major milestone in modern biology was the complete sequencing of the human genome. But it produced a whole set of new challenges in exploring the functions and interactions of different parts of the genome. One application is predicting disorders based on mining the genotype and understanding how the interactions between genetic loci lead to certain human diseases.

However, typically disease phenotypes are genetically complex. They are characterized by large, high-dimensional data sets. Also, usually the sample size is small.

Recently machine learning and predictive modeling approaches have been successfully applied to understand the genotype-phenotype relations and link them to human diseases. They are well suited to overcome the problems of the large data sets produced by the human genome and its high-dimensionality. Machine learning techniques have been applied in virtually all data mining domains and have proven to be effective in BioData mining as well.

This paper describes some of the techniques that have been adopted in recent studies in human genome analysis.

Keywords: Genome wide prediction · Machine learning · Cross validation · Predictive medicine

1   Introduction

A central challenge in systems biology and medical genetics is to understand how interactions among genetic loci contribute to complex phenotypic traits and human diseases [1]. A major goal of medical genetics is to determine a set of genetic markers that, combined with some common risk factors, can be used to predict an individual's susceptibility to developing certain diseases. Genetic markers are genes or DNA sequences used to identify the presence of specific genes or gene defects. Typically the number of markers p is large and the sample size n is small: "large p small n problem". Disease phenotypes are usually genetically complex. A natural first step to tackling these formidable tasks is to construct an annotation of the genome, which is to (1) identify all functional elements in the genome, (2) group them into element classes such as coding genes, non-coding genes and regulatory modules, and (3) characterize the classes by some concrete features such as sequence patterns [3].

Common approaches in genome analysis are statistical methods such as whole-genome regression models and association testing. These methods regress phenotypes on thousands of markers concurrently. They have been improved using for instance

© Springer International Publishing Switzerland 2015
A. Geissbühler et al. (Eds.): ICOST 2015, LNCS 9102, pp. 379–384, 2015.
DOI: 10.1007/978-3-319-19312-0_39

shrinkage or regularization in Single Nucleotide Polymorphism (SNP) regression models, nevertheless they are prone to serious over-fitting problems due to the ratio between the number of markers and the available phenotypes. Use of sequencing technologies places further challenges because several million of variants per individual may need to be taken into account in predictive models [2].

In recent studies Machine Learning (ML) techniques have been applied since they are capable of dealing with the high dimensionality problem in an efficient way. By its very nature, genomics produces large, high dimensional datasets that are well suited to analysis by machine learning approaches [3]. Learning techniques are efficient in solving complex biological problems due to characteristics such as robustness, fault tolerances, adaptive learning and massively parallel analysis capabilities, and for a biological system it may be employed as tool for data-driven discovery [4].In recent studies ML techniques in genome analysis have been used for risk prediction and treatment of cancer [5,6,7], multiple sclerosis [8],Alzheimer's disease [9,10], diabetes [11] and Legionnaires' disease[12] to name a few. This paper gives an overview of machine learning techniques used in genome wide prediction (GWP).

1.1   Machine Learning for Genome Analysis

Machine learning (ML) is a branch of Artificial Intelligence (AI). The basic idea is to construct a mathematical model based on historic data and apply it to new, unseen data. A ML model learns from historic data to make predictions on new data, for instance, predict the susceptibility to certain diseases. ML techniques are divided into supervised, unsupervised and semi-supervised methods.For supervised learning algorithms, a given data set is typically divided into two parts: training and testing data sets with known class labels [13]. Supervised ML are used for classification, for instance, to classify regions in the genome into regulatory, transcribed and functional sequence regions. Ultimately we want to find a decision function f, that classifies genome loci into labels $X=\{x_1, x_2,...x_n\}$, such that $f:X \rightarrow \{E,NE\}$, predicts if a loci is for instance a enhancer, E, or not, NE. This is a binary classification problem since we have two class labels. f is called classifier. If there are more than two class labels, it is a multi-class classification problem. For instance, if we want to identify regions such as silencers and insulators in addition to enhancers and promoters. Here we focus on classification, since we want to associate DNA sequences with specific element classes. However, it should be noted that many classifiers output the probability Pr, that a region x_i with corresponding label y_i belongs to class j:

$$\Pr(x_i | y_i = j) \tag{1}$$

To find a suitable f we need to:

1. Decide on an appropriate model for f, possible models are artificial Neural Networks (aNN), naïve Bayes classifier, boosting or Support Vector Machines (SVM)
2. Find a set of training data, for instance, a set of regulatory regions that contain enhancers and promoters
3. An estimate for the classification accuracy such as a loss function

For task 1, to decide on the appropriate model, several models are trained, and the one that predicts the label of a region most accurately is chosen. Experience shows that no single machine learning scheme is appropriate to all datamining problems [14]. To decide which scheme is the most appropriate we need a means of evaluating the trained model. Since the performance on the training set is no good indicator of performance on unseen data, task 3, evaluating the model, is tricky, especially when the set of training data from task 2 is small. We need to be able to predict the performance of the model on future data and compare it to the estimated performance of the other trained models. Cross-validation is one of the most popular evaluation methods in limited-data situations.

1.1.1 Artificial Neural Networks

Artificial neural networks (ANN) can act as universal approximators of complex functions because of their capability of learning linear or nonlinear relationships between predictor variables and responses, including also all sorts of interactions between explanatory variables [2]. There are many types of ANN, but in GWP usually multilayer ANN are used. Multilayer ANNs consist of an input layer, one or more middle layers, called hidden layers and an output layer. The input layer is given for instance SNP genotype codes, pedigree and nuisance variables as input.

A multilayer ANN consists of preceptrons, the neurons, which are interconnected through weighted connections, the axons. The basic idea of a perceptron is to find a linear function f such that:

$$f(x) = w^T x + b \tag{2}$$

where $f(x) > 0$ for one class and $f(x) < 0$ for the other class, and $w = (w_1, w_2, \ldots, w_m)$ is the vector of coefficients (weights) of the function, and b is the bias. During training the weights and bias are adjusted until prediction accuracy is converging.

In recent studies, ANNs have been used to study gene-gene interactions for biomarkers [18], to model gene-environment interactions [19] and to find splice sites in human [20].

1.1.2 Naïve Bayesian Classifiers

Naïve Bayesian classifiers are a family of simple, probabilistic classifiers based on the Bayes theorem. The naïve Bayesian classifiers builds a probabilistic model of the features and predicts the classification of new, unseen examples. Naïve Bayes can use kernel density estimators, which improve performance if the normality assumption is grossly incorrect; it can also handle numeric attributes using supervised discretization [14].The Bayesian classifier has been applied in analyzing effectors in the genome to detect the causative agent of Legionnaires' disease with an accuracy of more than 90% [12]. It has been adopted for analyzing of single nucleotide polymorphism for detecting Alzheimer's disease. Single Nucleotide Polymorphisms (SNPs) are a specific class of genomic variation responsible for about 90% of human variability [6]. A high classification accuracy has been achieved for the detection of Alzheimer's disease [9].

1.1.3   Boosting

Boosting is an ensemble learning method. It is often advantageous to take the training data and derive several different training sets from it, learn a model from each, and combine them to produce an ensemble of learned models [14].If several schemes have been trained, it can be advantageous not to choose the best performing one but to combine them all. Boosting combines models that complement each other. Boosting has several characteristics. The models are of similar type such as decision trees. Boosting is iterative; each new model is build based on the performance of the previous model. New models are trained in a way that it performs well for instances that were incorrectly handled by previous models. Also, models are weighted by their confidence and are not treated equally. Boosting has been applied to GWP in chicken, swine and dairy cattle with similar or better predictive ability than Bayes A or G-BLUP [2].

1.1.4   Support Vector Machines

Support Vector Machines (SVM) create a feature space or vector space defined by a similarity matrix (kernel) and create a hyperplane, an affine decision surface, separating the examples, for instance, enhancers and promoters, and maximizes the distance from it from the closest training samples. SVMs operate by finding a hyper surface in the space of gene expression profiles, that will split the groups so that there is largest distance between the hyper surface and the nearest of the points in the groups [17].If the training data is linearly separable, then a pair (w, b) exists such that

$w^T x_i + b \geq 1$, for all $x_i \in P$ and $w^T x_i + b \leq -1$, for all $x_i \in N$

with the decision rule given by:

$$\int_{w,b} (x) = \text{sgn}(w^T x + b) \qquad (3)$$

where w is termed the weight vector and b the bias (or $- b$ is termed the threshold) [15].SVM have been primarily used for classification, but they can also be used for regression. SVM have been successfully applied for instance in predicting cancer-causing missense variants and achieved a 93% overall accuracy [6] and for analyzing gene-gene interactions by investigating SNPs for Type 2 diabetes mellitus (T2D)and achieved an accuracy of more than 70% [11].

2   Discussion

Genome sequencing remains a challenging task due to the complexity, high-dimensionality and large size of the human genome. The number of sequences available is increasing exponentially [16]. Complex diseases such as cancer are multi-factorial in nature and interactions among genetic loci, epistatic interactions, are believed to be a major contributing factor. There exist also increasingly complex interactions between genetic variants and environmental factors that may contribute to the disease risk on an individualized basis [1]. This suggests that a one variant at a time approach might not be expedient and a more holistic approach should be pursued. It is often difficult to define the exact span of a genomic region. Biologically it could be fuzzy to define exactly where a functional element starts and ends (as in the case of an enhancer), and even if the span could be formally defined (as in the case of an RNA transcript), it is usually not known prior to machine learning [3].

The class labels of neighboring genomic regions are not independent. For example, if a base is within an intron, the next base should be either within an intron or a splice site [3].Currently, there are still likely undiscovered genomic element classes given the rapid discovery of new classes (such as many non-coding RNAs (ncRNAs)) in recent years [3]. In ML terms, this means that purely supervised techniques are not suitable. Ensemble learners have often worked astoundingly well and researchers have been wondering why. For instance boosting or random forests are ensemble learning techniques that have been used in genome mining [3,5].They have several properties which make them very suitable for GWA. A model can be trained using samples that the previous model didn't classify accurately. Juxtaposing several models can thus mitigate the error produced by the previous model. Ensemble learners tend to become very complex and it is often difficult to determine which factors contributed to the result and to what extent. Simplifying ensemble learners is one focus of our research.

3   Conclusions

ML techniques have been adopted in virtually all data analysis domains. ML techniques can generate highly complex models. This is particularly advantageous when the data to be analyzed is also complex such as, for instance, eukaryotic genes. In recent years a major paradigm shift in disease treatment towards personalized medicine strategies and network pharmacology, a paradigm which provides a more global understanding of drug action in their context of biological networks and pathways, has been surfacing. ML techniques have shown to be well suited to enable these new paradigms. In this paper, some of the more popular techniques were described, but many other techniques have been used in genome analysis. For instance, ML techniques based on hidden Markov models have become a one of the most popular methods for computational gene finding.

References

1. Okser, S., Pahikkala, T., Aittokallio, T.: Genetic variants and their interactions in disease risk prediction - machine learning and network perspectives. BioData Mining 6(1), 5 (2013)
2. González-Recio, O., Rosa, G.J.M., Gianola, D.: Machine learning methods and predictive ability metrics for genome-wide prediction of complex traits. Livestock Science 166, 217–231 (2014)
3. Yip, K., Cheng, C., Gerstein, M.: Machine learning and genome annotation: a match meant to be? Genome Biology 14(5), 205 (2013)
4. Patel, M., et al.: An Introduction to Back Propagation Learning and its Application in Classification of Genome Data Sequence. In: Babu, B.V., et al. (eds.) Proceedings of the Second International Conference on Soft Computing for Problem Solving (SocProS 2012), December 28-30, 2012, pp. 609–615. Springer India (2014)

5. Vanneschi, L., et al.: A comparison of machine learning techniques for survival prediction in breast cancer. BioData Mining 4(1), 12 (2011)
6. Capriotti, E., Altman, R.B.: A new disease-specific machine learning approach for the prediction of cancer-causing missense variants. Genomics 98(4), 310–317 (2011)
7. Menden, M.P., et al.: Machine Learning Prediction of Cancer Cell Sensitivity to Drugs Based on Genomic and Chemical Properties. PLoS ONE 8(4), 1–7 (2013)
8. Guo, P., et al.: Mining gene expression data of multiple sclerosis. PloS one 9(6), e100052 (2014)
9. Granados, E.A.O., et al. Characterizing genetic interactions using a machine learning approach in Colombian patients with Alzheimer's disease. in Bioinformatics and Biomedicine (BIBM). In: 2013 IEEE International Conference on. (2013)
10. Scheubert, L., et al.: Tissue-based Alzheimer gene expression markers-comparison of multiple machine learning approaches and investigation of redundancy in small biomarker sets. BMC Bioinformatics 13(1), 266 (2012)
11. Ban, H.-J., et al.: Identification of Type 2 Diabetes-associated combination of SNPs using Support Vector Machine. BMC Genetics 11(1), 26 (2010)
12. Burstein, D., et al.: Genome-Scale Identification of Legionella pneumophila Effectors Using a Machine Learning Approach. PLoS Pathogens 5(7), 1–12 (2009)
13. Tretyakov, K.: Machine Learning Techniques in Spam Filtering, in Data Mining Problem-oriented Seminar, U.o.T. Institute of Computer Science, Editor. Estonia. p. 19 (2004)
14. Witten, I.H., Frank, E., Hall, M.A.: Data Mining, 3rd edn. Elsevier, Burlington, MA (2011)
15. Kotsiantis, S.B.: Supervised Machine Learning. Informatica 31, 19 (2007)
16. Larrañaga, P., et al.: Machine learning in bioinformatics. Briefings in Bioinformatics 7(1), 86–112 (2006)
17. Jauhari, S., Rizvi, S.A.M.: Mining Gene Expression Data Focusing Cancer Therapeutics: A Digest. Computational Biology and Bioinformatics, IEEE/ACM Transactions on 11(3), 533–547 (2014)
18. Tong, D.L., et al.: Artificial Neural Network Inference (ANNI): A Study on Gene-Gene Interaction for Biomarkers in Childhood Sarcomas. PLoS ONE 9(7), 1–13 (2014)
19. Gunther, F., Pigeot, I., Bammann, K.: Artificial neural networks modeling gene-environment interaction. BMC Genetics 13(1), 37 (2012)
20. Abo-Zahhad, M., et al.: Integrated Model of DNA Sequence Numerical Representation and Artificial Neural Network for Human Donor and Acceptor Sites Prediction. International journal of information technology and computer science 6(8), 51–57 (2014)

Author Index